# The Big Book of

# Virginia
# Ghost Stories

# The Big Book of

# Virginia
# Ghost Stories

*L. B. Taylor Jr.*

STACKPOLE
BOOKS

Published by
STACKPOLE BOOKS
5067 Ritter Road
Mechanicsburg, PA 17055
www.stackpolebooks.com

Printed in the United States of America

10  9  8  7  6  5  4  3  2  1

FIRST EDITION

**Library of Congress Cataloging-in-Publication Data**

Taylor, L. B.
 The big book of Virginia ghost stories / L.B. Taylor, Jr.—1st ed.
  p. cm.
 Includes bibliographical references (p.     ).
 ISBN-13: 978-0-8117-0583-7 (hardcover)
 ISBN-10: 0-8117-0583-8 (hardcover)
 1. Ghosts—Virginia. 2. Haunted places—Virginia. I. Title.
 BF1472.U6.B55 2010
  133.109755—dc22
                          2010007953

# Contents

## Central Virginia

## *South and Southwest Virginia*

## *Tidewater Virginia*

# Introduction

*V*irginia may well be the most haunted state in America. Why?
There are multiple reasons. To start with, Virginia was the site of
the country's first permanent English settlement, at Jamestown in
1607. The early settlers, and those that followed them, brought many
traditions with them, including age-old superstitions. They believed
in such things as evil omens, ghosts, witches, demons, and the existence of the Devil. As soon as they arrived, they were met by the native
Indians, long-time exponents of the supernatural. Later, other Europeans came, such as the Pennsylvania Dutch and the Scotch-Irish,
bringing still more legends, myths and fables, as did the slaves who
were brought over from Africa.

Paranormal experts contend that sites where trauma and tragedy
have occurred are fertile spawning grounds for ghosts and the like,
and no state has seen more bloodshed and early deaths than Virginia
over the past four hundred-plus years. There were two centuries of
constant conflict between the pioneers and the Indians. Then came
the Revolutionary War, with many battles fought on Old Dominion
soil. The American Civil War followed eighty years after this, and
much of the major fighting occurred here.

Another reason for so many hauntings, experts say, is the pre-
ponderance of old manor houses and plantations in Virginia. A great
number of these still-standing structures date to the eighteenth and
nineteenth centuries.

Among the alleged ghosts in the commonwealth are some of the
most famous names in history: George Washington, Thomas Jefferson,

Patrick Henry, William Henry Harrison, John Tyler, Woodrow Wilson, Thomas "Stonewall" Jackson, Jefferson Davis, and scores of other notables.

In short, more history has been written on these storied grounds than anywhere else in America. That alone is possible just cause for the abundant amount of psychic phenomena that is still prevalent here, from the northern tip of the Shenandoah Valley to the hills and hollows of the state's southern border, and from the mountains of the west to the Eastern Shore. Ghosts abound in Virginia!

# Northern Virginia

# Chasing George Washington's Ghost

During more than a quarter century of research on the ghosts of Virginia, I have been fortunate enough to find some form of psychic phenomena associated with many of the famous names of the commonwealth: Thomas Jefferson, James Monroe, John Tyler, George Wythe, Peyton Randolph, Patrick Henry, Stonewall Jackson, and Robert E. Lee, among others. But such data on the biggest name of all, George Washington, is relatively scarce.

There is a ghostly legend linked to his mother, Mary Ball Washington; his favorite niece, Nelly Custis; and his brother-in-law, Fielding Lewis. There is, too, a persistent rumor of a psychic vision Washington was said to have experienced during the Revolutionary War. There have been several accounts of this alleged vision, and most of them seem to stem from an article published in the *National Tribune*, a military service newspaper, that first appeared in December 1880. The publisher of that paper told of an interview he had in 1859 with one of the last surviving veterans of the Revolutionary War, a man then said to be ninety-nine years old. His name was Anthony Sherman.

Sherman claimed that he had overheard a conversation Washington had at Valley Forge during the harsh winter of 1777. The Commander in Chief was reported to have said he saw a "singularly beautiful being" in his tent after he had given orders not to be disturbed. Sherman quoted Washington as saying, "Gradually the surrounding atmosphere seemed to fill with sensations, and grew luminous. Everything about me seemed to rarify, the mysterious visitor also becoming more airy and yet more distinct to my eyes than before. I began to feel as one dying, or rather to experience the sensations which I have sometimes imagined accompany death."

Sherman said Washington then witnessed "dark manifestations inside the tent, including black clouds, lightning bolts, the light of a thousand suns . . . the thundering of the cannon, clashing of swords, and the shouts and cries of millions in mortal combat." Some have theorized that Washington was sensing the continuation of the Revolutionary War and a premonition of the Civil War and either World War I or World War II. Washington reportedly acknowledged that the vision said, "Three great perils will come upon the Republic. The most fearful for her is the third. But the whole world united shall not prevail against her." The vision then vanished, and Sherman said Washington concluded: "I started from my seat and felt that I had seen a vision wherein had been shown me the birth, the progress, and destiny of the United States."

Whether or not such an event actually happened is thus based on the thinnest conjecture—the testimony of a very old man whose name could not even be found in Revolutionary War records. There are thousands of Washington letters and documents on file, not to mention the general's voluminous diaries. In carefully researching the supposed vision, archivist John Rhodehamel concluded that "nowhere in any of this material is to be found a reference to a vision or any other mystical experience." Could it have occurred and not been recorded because of its ethereal nature? Possibly, but not probably. It is an interesting legend nonetheless.

## Protected by the Great Spirit

There also have been a number of reports of a "phantom rider" on a white horse sighted late at night galloping around Woodlawn Plantation, adjacent to Mount Vernon. Woodlawn was Washington's wedding gift to his foster daughter (Martha Washington's granddaughter), Nelly Parke Custis, upon her marriage to Lawrence Lewis, Washington's favorite nephew. Some have speculated that this is the spectral return of the general, out surveying his property.

In the Fairfax County Library there is an old newspaper clipping that quotes a security guard at Mount Vernon who couldn't explain some happenings he encountered there several years ago. Gerald Pettit said he heard footsteps coming up the stairs behind him at the mansion one night. He turned to see who or what was there and was greeted with "an icy current of air that sent a shiver down his spine." He could offer no rational explanation for the sensation. Pettit added that in his fifteen years of keeping watch over Mount Vernon he had become accustomed to strange occurrences. Among these were "door knobs turning on their own, furniture changing positions in locked rooms, and an eerie tapping on windows at night." But he never saw an apparition of Washington.

While the legends—some supernatural, some not—continue to swirl around Washington, embellished with the passing years, one intriguing and little-known anecdote carries more weight of authenticity than most others. It was related by Lawrence Lewis, the general's nephew, and was recorded in the 1830s by Samuel Kercheval in his book *History of the (Shenandoah) Valley*. It occurred during the French and Indian War, probably sometime in the 1750s. At that time Washington was an aide to British general Edward Braddock. Lewis learned of the account from Daniel Craig, then of Winchester, Virginia. Craig had become acquainted with Redhawk, a distinguished Indian warrior. In conversations with Craig, Redhawk asked who the young officer was who was mounted on a fine young horse, who rode with great rapidity from post to post during the action between Braddock and the Indians. Craig said it was Colonel Washington. Redhawk then said, "I fired eleven deliberate shots at that man, but could not touch him. I gave over any further attempt, believing he was protected by the Great Spirit, and could not be killed by a bullet." Redhawk added that his gun was never known to miss its aim before.

## The Gristmill

It is known that Washington operated a gristmill, making flour and cornmeal, on his large estate at Mount Vernon for almost three decades. The structure now standing on Dogue Run was built on the original foundation of that mill. Washington ground wheat into flour, which he loaded onto Potomac River ships from a nearby wharf. After he died in 1799, the mill gradually fell into ruin, but it was restored in the 1930s by the commonwealth. It is now operated by the Mount Vernon Ladies' Association, which oversees Washington's estate.

In a newspaper article written more than thirty years ago, Michael Malone, then the curator of the mill, was quoted as saying, "People often say Washington haunts this place, but you never know." It is known that the building was the last place Washington visited before his death. On an inspection tour in December 1799, he caught the chill that led to his demise a few days later.

"I enjoy and relish the thought of meeting a new spirit," Malone said in an interview. "If you are good to them they will talk to you." Malone noted that he had not had any personal conversations with the ghost, but admitted that several "eerie occurrences" had taken place in the mill. He said the spirit, or something, had carried a papier mâché statue of Washington up three flights of stairs in the building, leaving behind a trail of droppings from the mannequin. Malone at first suspected burglars or pranksters, but an examination revealed no damage, and, in fact, the locks on the doors were tightly in place.

Sometime later, Malone said he and other employees had discussed buying a new broom, and the next day a broom mysteriously turned up on his desk. Everyone said they hadn't bought it. "I know this mill inside and out," Malone added, "and I know there wasn't one here when I left the night before." Other manifestations included a light bulb that was inexplicably unscrewed in a locked closet, and a cord to a lamp which was frequently found unplugged by unseen hands.

Malone said stories of Washington's reappearance have been told for more than two hundred years. "On stormy days on the old Colchester-Alexandria Highway, people said they heard Washington's voice calming his horse." It was also said that the general's spirit-world horse was sometimes sighted tied to a sycamore tree in front of the old gristmill—a half century after it had died. It was as if the faithful horse was still waiting for its master to return from his inspection of the mill and head home to Mount Vernon.

## Mount Vernon Ghosts

In February 2002, James Rees, executive director of Mount Vernon, said, "There are not a lot of ghost stories related to Mount Vernon, but several of our tour guides swear they have seen ghostly images in the mansion. On a few occasions furniture seems to have moved mysteriously in the locked and secure house. We know this because the furniture comes in contact with our 'electric eye,' causing a false security alarm."

One who claimed to see such images was a former employee named Rebecca Starbridge, who said she once had a "face-to-face encounter" with George Washington one night when she was closing up the place and was checking the doors. "I saw him sitting in a chair behind the desk in his study," she recalls. "I could actually see right through him! He was busy writing something with a quill pen. It took him over a minute to notice me standing in the doorway. When he finally looked up and saw me, he motioned for me to come in. I took a couple of steps toward him, but he just faded away."

Two former resident directors at Mount Vernon had varying experiences. "I have sometimes felt that something more than myself takes care of the site," the late Charles Cecil Wall, who was at Mount Vernon for forty-eight years, once said. Most mornings at seven, Wall jogged around the courtyard and hiked the trails. He said he would "occasionally see Washington riding horseback on his daily rounds."

Neil Horstman, the other former resident director, said that in 1990, "my wife, daughter, and I had a picnic after hours on Mount Vernon's piazza to watch a full eclipse on the moon. At the moment of the full eclipse all three of us heard a loud noise. We all turned to look. The knob of the door from the dining room to the piazza was shaking and making a loud racket. The mansion was empty, locked up, and the security system was on. A week later, a guard dog on the piazza went berserk, chewed a hunk out of the dining room windowsill and gnawed the brass doorknob." Horstman added that over the years many guards have heard whispers here from "beings" who passed undetected by the alarm systems, and, at times, perfume from invisible ladies scents the air.

It is interesting to note that Mount Vernon now conducts a ghostly tour of the mansion each year during Halloween week. Does the great George Washington appear on these occasions? "Come and see for yourself," says a historical interpreter there. "One never knows what one may find."

## A Deer-killing Ghost

The following narrative is extracted and excerpted from a January 1894 issue of the *Washington Post*, in an article headlined, "Ghost of

Mount Vernon." The subhead read: "Tale of a Bloodthirsty Wraith Which Used to Kill the General's Deer, as Told by an Old Negro Mammy." The mammy was known as "Aunt Weavy." She lived at the mansion during the Civil War with a Mrs. Stewart, who was taking care of Mount Vernon for the Ladies Memorial Association.

On New Year's Eve, 1863, Aunt Weavy told her story. It concerned the old wine vault down under the hill by the deer park. It had a sinister reputation, "and not one of the stalwart Negroes on the place could be induced to take the (Potomac) river road past the fateful spot after the sun had set behind the heights above the river." Aunt Weavy said the time of the haunting occurrences dated from before the beginning of the eighteenth century, and involved a man named West Ford and "his adventure with the wine vault spectre."

She said it had been a terrible time around the big house in those days, with "sumpin what dey say done haunt dat ribber shore eben befo' the big house been built on the hill yonder. It was bout den de fust boats come up de ribber an' bring de Injuns whisky to get drunk on. It mus' a been some of dem got killed wid de devilment, but all I ebber heard—what they saw it say, it were a woman. It had been killin' deer in de park, what lately been started. It warnt no common hant. De men, day lay fer it, and de dogs, dey run fer it, but after de fust time, dey jes cow down an' wail pitiful. An' ebbey mornin' dey fine a deer down in the woods, killed stone murdered dead, an' its throat cut on one side, jes like sumpin drink all de blood out de body an' leave it lay there without takin' de trouble ter tote it off.

"West, he powerful bad drinkin' man, an' one night, when he had been crost de ribber dancin' at Oxen Hill, he come back in de skiff late at night, most toards morning. He jes' too drunk to know what he's doin', and jes as his boat run up on de shore, he see a wavering light through de trees. Fust, he thought somebody comin' down from de house wid a lantern, and then he thought, it bein' New Year's Eve, an' dat de time what de hant mos' likely ter walk.

"He took one big drink out'n his flask, an' den walk up de bank, an' dar were de door of de old wine vault standin' open, an' inside dey was shinin' a light. An' West, he look, dey come sumpin' walkin' out inter de moonlight. He say it were de most grand lookin' woman he ebber saw. West say she were dress all in white an' round her neck dey was a necklace of stones shinin' like diamonds, only dey was red an' flash like blood, wid de fire shinin' on it. An' her face was pale like she ben dead for days! An' outta de corners of her moth dey was teeth, white an' sharp, most jes like er big bat!

"An' West, he didn't know what ter do, wheter to run or stay wher he was. Den dey come a deer, one of de young ones, down along de path, an' when it see de woman in white, it jes crouch down and nebber try to move, but jest moan pitiful. An' West say de hant woman nebber walk or run, jes glided like, and when it git whar the deer were layin,' it stoop down an' sink de teeth in de deer's throat an' drink de blood!

"An' West, he lit for de house, and when de thing see him run, it sweep round ter de front of him an' he feel sumpin cold an' white, an' den he nebber know nuthin' more till de hands dey found him dar on de groun' in de mawning wif de teeth marks crost his throat. An' dey do say dat de ole wine vault was de place what were all at de bottom of it!"

## Washington's Death

Did George Washington have a premonition of his own death? Quite possibly, according to R. M. Devens, who wrote about it in his 1877 book *Our First Century*. Devens wrote that Washington was "one who was accustomed to consider the brevity of life and the uncertainty of human affairs." This was evident "from the tenor of his conduct and conversation, and from occasional passages in his correspondence." Washington, a few months prior to his death, wrote to his secretary of war, "My greatest anxiety is to have all these concerns (private affairs) in such a clear and distinct form that no reproach may attach itself to me when I have taken my departure for the land of spirits."

Washington also had been making funeral arrangements just days before the attack of illness which terminated in his death. He had written instructions for the construction of an improved tomb, and speaking of this, said to a relative, "I am of a short-lived family and cannot expect to remain very long upon the earth." Yet Washington was in excellent health right up to the days before he died, on December 14, 1799. He was sixty-seven years old.

On December 11, Washington may have perceived an omen. He wrote in his diary, "The day was blustering and rainy, and at night there was a large circle around the moon." His secretary, Tobias Lear, later said, "the general rode around his plantation for five hours on December 12 in weather very bad, rain, hail, snow falling alternately, with a cold wind." The next day a heavy snow fell, and Washington "had taken cold." Nevertheless, he went out again.

On December 14, he was bedridden with a high fever and doctors were called in. At five that afternoon, he spoke again as if he had been given a glimpse of the future. He told a doctor, "I die hard, but I am not afraid to go. My breath cannot last long." An hour later he said he felt himself going. "Let me go quietly," he said, "I cannot last long."

Then, curiously, he added an odd request which could be interpreted as a fear of being buried prematurely while still alive, a common fear at that time. He said, "Have me decently buried; and do not let my body be put into the vault in less than three days after I am dead." When his secretary acknowledged that he understood, Washington said, "'Tis well." These were the last words the Father of the Country spoke on earth. He died shortly after 10 P.M. that night.

The ancient family vault in which Washington's remains first reposed was situated under the shade of a small grove of forest trees, a short distance from the mansion and near the brow of the banks of the Potomac River. His body was later removed to a lot near the corner of a beautiful enclosure—a site selected for a tomb by Washington himself in the later years of his life.

## Washington's Tomb

There is rather a strange footnote to the George Washington-Mount Vernon saga. In 1937, during the Great Depression, Works Progress Administration writers had this to say about Mount Vernon: "In such veneration is this spot held, that on every ship of the U.S. Navy, while passing by, the flag is lowered to half mast, the bell tolled, and the crew drawn up at attention. During the whole of the Civil War, this ground was tacitly held neutral by both sides. In 1814, when the British fleet sailed up the Potomac to attack the city of Washington, so great was their respect for the dead leader of the enemy that every ship fired a salute.

"George Washington and Martha were originally buried in the old family vault on a slope overlooking the Potomac River. The old tomb was built in 1745 by Washington for his brother, Lawrence, in accordance with his will. Later, George, Martha, and his nephew, Bushrod, were buried here. Although the President had left express instructions in his will that a new brick tomb be built, even naming the site, the work was not undertaken by his heirs until 1831, shortly after an attempt had been made to steal Washington's skull from the crumbling old tomb.

"After the death of Bushrod Washington, John Augustine Washington, the elder, took over the management of Mount Vernon. Early in 1830, he discharged an employee who, in a moment of drunken rage, returned by night and broke into the old tomb, intending to steal the skull of George Washington. He was caught with a skull, but it was that of a nephew also buried in the tomb.

"After the attempted theft, John Augustine Washington set about building the new tomb which Bushrod had neglected. It was completed in 1831, and the bodies from the old tomb were removed to it. In 1837, the open outer vault was added and the two sarcophagi set in it. The last person buried in the inner vault was Jane Washington in 1855.

"The doors were then locked, and the key thrown into the Potomac River!"

# The Last Tantrum of Thomson Mason

George Mason, many historians contend, is one of the most underrated patriots of American Independence. A contemporary and friend of George Washington, he was a reluctant public servant who spent a considerable part of his life trying to avoid the spotlight of colonial politics only to be drafted into service time and again. Mason was sometimes called the "Pen of the Revolution," because he was the author of the Fairfax Resolves, the first Constitution of Virginia, and the Virginia Declaration of Rights; the latter of which, scholars say, was used as the model and inspiration for the American Bill of Rights.

Mason's Declaration of Rights declares that all men are created equal, free, and independent; that all power is derived from the people; that government is instituted for the common benefit, protection and security of the people; that no man or set of men is entitled to exclusive or separate privileges; that all men having common interests in the community should have the right to vote; and that the freedom of the press should never be restricted. Not bad foresight. Little wonder this retiring farmer was so highly respected by his legendary peers—Washington, Jefferson, Madison, Henry, etc.

A Virginia travel brochure reads: "These builders of our nation also built beautiful houses. Mount Vernon, Monticello and Stratford Hall are noted as much for their architectural beauty as for their historic associations. In this important company stands Gunston Hall." This was the house Mason had built in 1755. It is located nineteen miles south of Washington, D.C., on the Potomac River at the town of Lorton. The Virginia Landmarks Register calls Gunston Hall "one of the nation's most remarkable examples of colonial architecture." It is open to the public.

The travel brochure further points out, "There is more to a visit to Gunston Hall than the discovery of a beautiful house and gardens. It is also an introduction to the spirit of a great American patriot." How apt, for it is also apparently haunted! In a 1990 newspaper article, Mary Lee Allen, assistant director at the site, said, "The real ghosts are shadowy images left on some of the eighteenth-century Georgian mansion's walls that tell researchers where ornate carved decorations once hung."

But many, including both tour guides and visitors, contend there also are otherworldly spirits at "the Hall." Employees have reported hearing strange sounds in the house when no one is there. And tourists occasionally claim to have sighted "glimpses" of shadowy figures. These brief encounters generally have been attributed to former Mason family members who had occupied the house at one time or another.

And there is one fairly well-known psychic happening that transpired late in the nineteenth century and was experienced by George Mason's great-granddaughter, Helen, when she was just seven years old. It has been included in Margaret DuPont Lee's collection of *Virginia Ghosts* and elsewhere. Young Miss Mason was at Gunston Hall when, one evening around supper time, she peered out a window overlooking the garden and saw the apparition of her grandfather, Thomson Mason, who lived at Hollin Hall, five miles away. The sighting appeared only to Helen; when she called her mother to the window, she saw nothing.

The incident was often recounted with relish by an old servant known as Uncle Jasper, who also was just a small boy at the time, but was present when Thomson Mason died. With some paraphrasing for clarity, here, in essence, is what Uncle Jasper used to tell: "I must have been a little brat, not more than five or six years old. It was like this: Master Thomson was one of those fidgety folks, always flying into a tantrum, and he just naturally despised to shave. He wouldn't let anybody do it for him, but insisted on doing it himself. One day he put it off till tea time, and then he called for some hot water and he had Alec [a servant] hold the mirror, and he got two others to hold up some lights so he could see.

"Alec got so tired of holding the mirror that it began to wobble in spite of everything, and the master cussed at him and told him to hold it still, and then Alec made faces at him from behind the mirror and I started laughing out loud. The master, he turned around with the razor in his hand, and he was raging mad.

"And right there, he fell down in a fit. Alec dropped the mirror and it broke in a thousand pieces. Old Ike, he grabbed him quick and they laid him on the sofa. He was stone dead!"

It was at that precise moment, five miles away, that little Helen Mason saw her grandfather in the garden. When she called her mother to the window to see, she exclaimed, "What is grandpa doing out there in the garden in the wet? And he's got his neckcloth off, and his knee buckles are undone. Why, he must be shaving!"

## Terror in the Aquia Belfry

What is it about an old house or building reputed to be haunted that fascinates people? Elmwood in Essex County near Tappahannock quickly comes to mind. When newspaper accounts of supernatural activities there were published eighty years ago, hundreds of people tramped through the woods every time the moon was full to see for themselves what eerie happenings might unfold in the then-vacant mansion. Near West Point, literally thousands of curious onlookers have braved many a cold and damp night on a set of railroad tracks in order to catch a glimpse of the mysterious train light that is said to appear and then mysteriously disappear on occasion. And in Portsmouth a half century ago, so many people clustered around a small frame house after it was reported there was a resident polter-geist inside that the police had to barricade the place to protect its mortal occupants.

Aquia Church in Stafford County, about twenty miles north of Fredericksburg, is such a place. It has held generations of area young-sters spellbound with the oft-told tales of its haunted past. In fact, this venerable 260-year-old structure has to be guarded around the clock every Halloween because so many teenagers otherwise would descend upon it, as they did in years past, occasionally rendering it harm. Could it be the element of danger that is so intriguing, espe-cially in the case of Aquia Church? One must wonder about the san-ity of those who want to explore its ghostly interior to prove their manhood, so to speak, because it was on just such a venture, a long time ago, that a young man allegedly lost his life.

The church itself, according to the Virginia Landmarks Register, is a "good illustration of rural Virginia's use of ecclesiastical architecture endowed with urbanity and sophistication." The register adds that its "elegant classicism contrasts with its isolated woodland setting." Is that not a perfect setting for ethereal happenings?

Ill winds swirled about the church even before its completion. Begun in 1751, it was seriously damaged by fire on February 17, 1754—three days before construction was to be finished. The inte-rior was rebuilt over the next three years. The church preserves a unique three-tiered pulpit as well as the original Ionic reredos, west gallery, and pews—all excellent examples of colonial joinery. Three times in the history of the church, its precious silver—including an old dish, chalice, cup, and paten—have been buried for safekeeping: during the Revolutionary War, the War of 1812, and the Civil War.

The hauntings at Aquia stem from a night of horror in the church more than two hundred years ago, probably during the time of the

American Revolution. A young woman was murdered in the chapel by a highwayman or men, apparently after a violent struggle. Her body was hidden in the belfry, and as the church was not in use during this period, it was years later before her skeletal remains were found, with her golden hair still intact.

It is said, too, that the bloodstains from where the woman was slain were clearly visible for more than a century, until early in the 1900s when a new cement floor was laid. Not only was this physical evidence present, but there also has been, through the years, a continuous stream of scary psychic phenomena, so much so that reportedly, through most of the eighteenth century, even the parishioners were afraid to go into the church at night. The most prominent and persistent manifestations are said to be recreated by the victim. They include, with only slight variations, the sound of feet running up and down the stairs to the belfry, loud noises of a struggle, and the apparition of a terrified woman standing at one of the windows.

While these oft-repeated happenings are the most common, they are by no means the only ones. There is, for example, the story of the prominent socialite who spent her summers in Stafford County in the 1920s, and who became interested in the church through the spectral tales related to her by her maids. She decided to see the spirits herself, but couldn't get any of the strapping men in the area to accompany her. They all politely but resolutely backed off when they learned she was going at night. Undaunted, she recruited two "scientists"—likely early twentieth-century ghost busters—from Washington. They entered the church on a dark night, led by the determined socialite. But just after she walked through the front door, an unseen hand slapped her sharply across the face. The two men ran inside and searched everywhere, but they found nothing, and had no rational explanation for what happened. But that it did happen was evident in the fact that the mark on the lady's face remained for several days!

There is also a time-honored legend of a "whistling spirit" at Aquia who saved the lives of two Confederate soldiers during the Civil War. It has been passed down for generations. The originator was William Fitzhugh, who during a scouting mission in 1862 stopped off in the church with a comrade to rest. They had heard about the ghost there, but were too tired to care. They promptly went to sleep in the square pews.

Sometime during the night they were roused by what Fitzhugh described as "unmistakable footsteps at the rear of the church on some stone flagging." Then they heard someone or something whistling the tune, "The Campbells are Coming." Frightened out of their wits, they jumped up and struck a light, but saw nothing. Then they went to the door and looked out. A troop of Union soldiers was advancing along the road heading directly for the church. They raced to the back of the building, leaped out of a window and escaped. Fitzhugh later attributed the whistling ghost to saving his and his friend's lives.

Was it the spirit of the murdered girl? And is it her apparition that Robert Frazier and his son have seen flitting among the tombstones in the Aquia cemetery? Frazier, a former caretaker there, told two reporters about thirty years ago that he had often sighted "things" running through the graveyard. He said they appeared "blurred and funny." He added that they were white but not transparent. The sightings were all at night, and when Frazier and his son went over to see what or who it was that was darting about, the figures disappeared. "They just fade away, kinda slow like," he told the journalists. He said he couldn't tell if they were men or women because they were so blurry. But he was convinced he knew what they were. "Everybody says there's ghosts up here. Me and my son seen 'em. They're here!"

The death caused by the ghost or ghosts of Aquia Church supposedly occurred more than one hundred years ago. "Supposedly," because while the tradition has been told and retold with relish and enthusiasm enough so as to defy disbelief, there is no documented record of who the victim was or when the event took place. What is told is that in the days when everyone was afraid to approach the church at night, one young man—perhaps taunted by a dare—declared that no ghost could get the best of him. He said he would go inside, in the dark of night, and even climb to the haunted belfry. Those he made the boast to, however, were skeptical, so they gave him a hammer and a nail and told him to drive the nail into the wall, so they could tell for sure later whether or not he had lived up to his word.

Alone, he set out through the woods toward the old church. When the young man had not returned hours later, his friends became worried and went to the church to find out what had happened. They found him in the belfry—stone dead! In the darkness, he had hammered the nail into the wall through his coat. When he turned to leave, he was held fast. Evidently thinking he was in the grasp of an evil spirit, it is said he died of fright.

# The Brentsville Jail Ghosts

One of the nicer historic sites to explore these days is the Brentsville Courthouse Historic Centre, located roughly halfway between Haymarket to the west and Dumfries on the east, a few miles directly south of Manassas. Here, on an 18-acre tract, one can jog or hike over scenic trails or have a picnic. Other Brentsville attractions include the original courthouse and jail (built in 1822), a church, a cabin, a one-room schoolhouse, and a wood-framed smokehouse. Brentsville served as the Prince William County seat from 1822 to 1893. The buildings and grounds here were damaged during the Civil War, when Confederate colonel John Singleton Mosby conducted some of his most daring raids on Union troops in the area. A long period of decay followed the war when the complex was virtually abandoned. But through the fundraising efforts of concerned citizens, the courthouse buildings have been lovingly restored to their nineteenth-century splendor, and reopened to the public in 2007.

There is yet another reason for visiting. The courthouse and particularly the jail are reputed to be haunted. Site manager Robert Orrison says there are at least three tales of ghosts that make their presences known in the jail. "It's one of those buildings that gives you the creeps," he notes. "Your mind plays tricks on you sometimes, but, yeah, it's a scary place, especially when it's dark. There's no electricity." Adds a county resident who lives two miles away, "It's truly haunted. Every time I've been there, weird and creepy things happen."

A Web site for the historic center says, "Search the woods and cabin for the ghost of a once-incarcerated mad man of the Brentsville jail." Such intriguing paranormal enticements have drawn the attention of regional ghost-hunting groups. One such northern Virginia organization, DCMag, has been here a couple of times, and came away with some eerie sounds on tape recording equipment, made by suspected spirits. One angry voice thundered, "Get out! Get out of here!" Another said, "Don't turn out the lights!" Another member said he had a spool of fishing line thrown at him by something unseen. Others have glimpsed shadowy figures darting about. Interest in the ghostly reports has been so keen, officials now conduct haunted jail tours in October.

Just who these spirits are and why they return is open to speculation, but in researching the rich history of the center, a number of prime candidates pop out. Over the many years the jail was in operation, there were a number of murders and suicides. Then, in the years before the Civil War, the jail was used to incarcerate runaway slaves and even white abolitionists who protested slavery. One man, identified only as "Crawford," was jailed for stating he believed "a Negro was as good as he was." Some free blacks were also unjustly imprisoned and subsequently sold into slavery. Dangerfield Newby, a free black, tried in vain for years to free his wife and children, but they were eventually sold and sent to Louisiana. That may be the reason he joined John Brown in the infamous attack on the Harpers Ferry arsenal in 1859. Newby was the first person killed in that fighting.

In 1839, a slave was accused to setting a fire in the jail. The court record reads: "He was moved and seduced by instigation of the Devil." He was hanged. Six years later, in times when racial tensions ran high, a land owner named Gerald Mason was murdered by a slave named Katy, and she was convicted here and executed. In 1856, five slaves were brought to the jail and courthouse for the brutal slaying of their master, George E. Green. "Nelly" confessed to the crime, saying she and the others went into the house and she hit him with an ax. When the victim got up and ran outside, the five slaves pursued him with shovels, sticks, and the ax, then dragged him back into the house and set fire to it. When asked why they had killed Green, they said he was a "hard master" who would not let them go to meetings, starved them, and did not clothe them.

The trial aroused widespread interest, and a most curious petition, submitted by a medical student at the University of Virginia. If the five were to be hanged, he wanted the bodies for dissection. "Anatomy without subjects for demonstration," he wrote, "is as fruitless as geometry without diagrams." Nelly and two others were executed, but two young twins, Elias and Ellen, were pardoned by the governor because of "their youth and feeble intellect."

## The Leading Candidate?

In 1872, a sensational story broke in Prince William County—one that led to an extraordinary sequence of events, including one of Virginia's most famous trials. That trial attracted, in a circus-like atmosphere, national attention in the nineteenth century equal to that attained by O. J. Simpson's trial more than a century later. It all began when the county's commonwealth attorney, James F. Clark, considered a rising political star in the state, was accused of abducting and seducing a sixteen-year-old girl named Fannie Fewell, the daughter of a prominent Manassas citizen. She was described as "a great beauty and had a most engaging manner." Clark protested his innocence, but he nevertheless was summarily placed behind bars in the Brentsville jail to await trial. Newspapers called it a "deplorable affair," and the charges infuriated the populace. One report said, "Clark has attached to him a stain which can never be effaced."

The event also involved two prophecies, which turned out to be remarkably accurate. An armed guard was placed around Clark "to protect him from summary vengeance which he suggested might be inflicted upon him by the relations of Miss Fewell." The second prophecy was offered by a reporter for the *Alexandria Gazette*, who wrote: "Excited interest in the case is on the increase and will undoubtedly continue until the trial has been concluded and he (Clark) shall leave the county, or, what is feared by many, been buried beneath the already blood-stained sod—the victim of vengeance of a grief-crazed father or an enraged and desperate brother."

On the morning of August 30, 1872, Lucien Fewell, Fannie's brother, boarded a train in Lynchburg and arrived hours later in Brentsville with revenge in mind. Curiously, there were no guards on duty in the jail that day. Clark, inside in a cell, awaited trial, and the building was unlocked. Fewell calmly walked in the front door, asked a prisoner where Clark was being held, then marched up to his cell and opened fire with a pistol. The first two shots missed the terror-stricken victim, who then grabbed the gun when Fewell pushed it through the bars for a better shot. Fewell then pulled out a second pistol and shot Clark in the chest, killing him. He then walked out of the jail and proceeded, unhindered, up the street.

Fewell was later arrested, charged with the crime of murder, and jailed. His trial triggered a second sensation. The courthouse overflowed with viewers, and the defendant was represented by two former Confederate Civil War generals. One, Gen. Eppa Hunton, defended Fewell by saying, "When a man's wife or daughter (or sister) has been seduced, the laws of Virginia confer upon the injured party the privilege of taking the life of the seducer!"

The jury was out for just five minutes, then returned a verdict of "not guilty," which was greeted by raucous applause in the courtroom—a verdict the *New York Times* called a stunning travesty of justice.

And that is why many who have witnessed the paranormal manifestations that have been reported at the Brentsville jail believe at least some of them are caused by the ghost of James F. Clark—who never lived to have his day in court.

## The Vengeful Return of the Ghost Slaves

During the first half of the nineteenth century, the meanest man in Loudoun County, and perhaps in all of northern Virginia, was Joel Osborne. Actually, he was known as Devil Joel Osborne because there apparently was a custom in those days, in this region at least, that anyone who habitually used profane language was commonly given the sobriquet "Devil" in front of their name. Joel, more than anyone around, earned that dubious distinction.

He was a hard, embittered, and cruel man. For obvious reasons, he never married, and lived alone on a farm near the little village of Woodrow. Devil Joel's only companion was an old slave named Ben, who lived a dreadful life. He was continually mistreated by his sinister master.

It has been documented in the bulletin of the Historical Society of Loudoun County, and in the 1958 book, *Tales of Old Virginia*, by Joseph V. Nichols, just how harsh things were at the Osborne farm. There was no rest for Ben. He plowed, weeded, cultivated, and cleared the ground during the week, and on Sundays and at times when the land was too wet to work, Devil Joel made Ben dig out rocks from the stony soil and stack them up in piles that were six feet high and eight feet in diameter. It was said there were at one time at least a dozen of these piles surrounding the farmhouse.

Whenever Devil Joel had been drinking, which was often, or when he thought Ben wasn't piling rocks fast enough, he had a nasty habit of banging Ben over the head with a club. This usually knocked the slave to the ground and sometimes rendered him unconscious. Slowly, Ben would recover, stagger to his feet, and continue his arduous task. Ben's friends and even some of Devil Joel's relatives urged the poor slave to escape, but he never managed to summon enough courage to do so.

As the years passed and Devil Joel's drinking became heavier, the beatings increased. Finally, one particularly rainy day, as the two sat in a wagon husk waiting for the storm to let up, Devil Joel became enraged for no apparent reason and struck Ben a hard blow with a hoe handle, again knocking him senseless. But this time Ben did not get up. He was dead.

Curiously, Devil Joel was brought before the county justices and no charges were filed. It was determined, according to the law at that time, that if a slave owner accidentally wounded or killed one of his slaves—if there was no intent to kill—there was no crime. Devil Joel was free. At least he was free according to commonwealth law. But perhaps there is a higher authority sitting in judgment, for after that brutal act, Devil Joel became a haunted man. He could not sleep at night. He had, he said, terrifying nightmares. He seemed to be withering away. His relatives became so worried about his condition that a cousin, Joseph Osborne, temporarily moved in with him to see if he could determine what was happening.

The two men slept in the same room, with both doors bolted shut. One night Joseph was awakened at midnight. He looked up and heard Devil Joel cursing Ben. Joseph lit a candle and saw his disturbed cousin thrashing about at nothing that could be seen. Devil Joel then backed away, fell onto his bed, and begged the apparitional Ben to leave him alone. Joseph shook Joel but he was shaking violently and perspiration was running down his face. These ghostly visitations at night went on for several months, causing the frightened Devil Joel to drink more and more; one night he died in a delirium, at age fifty-five.

There is a postscript to this affair. In the days following the Civil War several ex-slaves in the area swore that on certain bright Sunday evenings, as they passed by the Osborne farm, they could see the ghostly visions of Devil Joel, sitting on a stump with a big club in his hands, and Ben, nearby, stacking rocks in a neat pile.

## The Ghosts of the Hanged Slaves

To understand one of the other prevalent ghostly legends of Loudoun County, this one in Leesburg, one must go back more than 250 years to when the county was formed, in 1757. At that time there was a major fear throughout Virginia that the increasing slave population would try to rebel against their white masters and fight for their freedom. Consequently, many slaves were treated very harshly. Runaways were severely whipped or beaten. They were rarely killed for trying to escape, however, because they were of substantial monetary value.

African American criminals were treated even worse. For an assault, especially on a white person, or a murder, the penalty was most often death by hanging, either after a trial in which there inevitably was little or no hope for the defendant, or by lynching without even the semblance of a trial. And sometimes the body would be desecrated and displayed in public as a graphic example of what would happen to any potential perpetrators.

Such was the case on July 28, 1768, when a slave named Mercer was brought to the Loudoun County Courthouse to be tried for murder. Following is an excerpt from the actual transcript of that trial:

> The said Mercer, being led to the Bar and publicly arraigned and asked whether of the Offence for which he stood charged, he was Guilty thereof or not Guilty, says that he is guilty of the murder aforesaid of which he is charged.
>
> Therefore, it is considered by the court that the said Mercer for his Offence be hanged by the Neck until he be dead, and that the Sheriff on Friday the twelfth day of August next drag the said Mercer to the Gallows and there hang him pursuant to the aforesaid judgment and then sever his head from his body and place the same on a pole near the said Gallows, and also set up his four Quarters, Vis-à-vis one at Thomson Mason, Esq, his Mill, another at the forks of the Road at John Griffiths, one other at the place where the Ox road leaves Alexandria Road below Goose creek, and the last at the Fork of the Roads at Moss' and Sorrells.

Apparently, however, the powers that be may have had second thoughts and considered the post-hanging treatment to be excessive, for there is a handwritten note on a court document which states, "This sentence was mitigated as thinking it might prove too extreme, and his head only to be severed and set on a pole near the gallows." Mercer was hanged, and his head was placed on a pole for all to see, to act as a deterrent to others who may have been contemplating mayhem.

There are many today who believe the mutilated slave returns in ghost form at the site of the old courthouse, either seeking his severed head, justice, or both. Currently, guides who conduct haunted tours in Leesburg each Halloween stop in front of the courthouse and tell viewers the present structure, built in 1894, replaced an earlier building, which in turn was erected over the original edifice dating to the mid-eighteenth century. The guides then say, "Little remains of this first county courthouse, except, perhaps, there lingers the spirit of one who was tried, sentenced, and hanged here by the royal court back in the 1700s." The guides' prepared script goes on: "As you can imagine, today many people say that Mercer's spirit still haunts the courthouse grounds. Several members of the court staff tell of hearing strange sounds, and some people even report seeing a phantom face staring out the courthouse windows."

"That's true," says Alice Alkire, administrative assistant to Judge Thomas Horne. "We do hear sounds. We first noticed it about ten years ago. Everyone in the courthouse has experienced it at one time or another. I never dreamed I would be saying this. I don't believe in ghosts, but there is a definite presence." Alice says voices are heard whispering in the courtroom and in the judge's offices. "We hear papers being moved around and voices, but whenever we go to check it out, there is no one there." There are other manifestations: the sounds of someone working the keyboard of a word processor, toilets flushing when no one is the restroom, books and papers being shuffled, mysterious footsteps on the stairs, doors opening and shutting on their own.

"It almost always occurs at dusk or at night," Alice adds. "No one wants to work late in the building. The main courtroom has a balcony. One night a young law clerk was working up there and heard a noise under the balcony. She said it sounded like a 'whoosh.' She thought at first another clerk was playing a trick on her, but he wasn't in the building. She was alone. When she realized this, she raced outside. Sometimes when I come in to work on the weekend I bring my two dogs with me, a Brittany and a yellow Lab. They won't go in the building. They freeze. Their ears go back against their necks and their tails tuck between their legs."

Alice says the phenomena come in waves. Things will be quiet for two or three months, and then a rash of inexplicable happenings occur. "If I could relate it to a specific case, I would, but so much has happened here over the years," she says. "They used to hang people from large trees in the jailyard near here."

Could it be those victims who return? Or could it be, as many believe, the ghost of Mercer, still seeking vengeance for the dismemberment of his body more than two hundred years ago? Whatever the identity of the spirits, this is one stop on the October ghost tours in Leesburg where the building really is haunted.

## The Ironhorse Devil

That the dread of superstitious fear could drive Virginia slaves to embrace the most absurd, preposterous beliefs is patently evident in a passage in James L. Smith's 1881 autobiography. Smith was born into slavery in Northumberland County, near Heathville, and was so profoundly depressed by his hopeless condition that he tried to kill himself. Later, he "got religion," and with two others successfully escaped to the north before the Civil War. The following episode, excerpted, took place during the escape, and dramatically portrays Smith's unshakable, deep-rooted terror of the supernatural. It is reprinted here from the online edition of his book through the courtesy of the University of North Carolina at Chapel Hill.

"Griffin Muse, Zip's wife, and myself started for Smith's Plantation, about two miles from Heathville, where Zip was secreted. When we arrived where Zip and Lorenzo were just starting, it was nearly 11 o'clock; they had waited for me till they thought I was not coming. Two minutes more and I would have been left behind. When we came to the river, we stood on the beach and embraced, kissed, and bade each other farewell. The scene between Zip and his wife at parting was distressing to behold. Oh! How the sobbing of his wife resounded in the depths of his heart; we could not take her with us for the boat was too small.

"We took a small canoe and crossed the river till we came to a plantation owned by a man named Travis. He had a large sail boat that we desired to capture, but we did not know how we should accomplish it, as they took a great deal of pains generally to haul her up, lock her up, and put the sails and oars in the barn. As it was on the Sabbath day, the young folks had been sailing about the river, and instead of securing her as they usually did, they left her anchored in the stream with the sails and oars all in the boat. This was very fortunate for us, for the house was very near to the shore, besides they had very savage dogs there. So all we had to do was to run our canoe along side the boat and get on board.

"As soon as we got ready and the sails set, the wind began to rise, and all that night we had all the wind we could carry sail to. By the next morning we were a great distance from home. We sailed all day and night Monday and until Tuesday night about nine o'clock, when we landed at Frenchtown, Maryland. Then we took our bundles and started on foot. We went into the woods and laid down on the ground and slept for an hour or so, then we started for New Castle.

"I found that I could not keep up with my companions, for they could walk much faster than myself and hence got far ahead, and then would have to wait for me; I being lame, was not able to keep up with them. At last, Zip said to me, "We shall have to leave you, for the enemies are after us, and if we wait for you we shall all be taken; so it would be better for one to be taken than all three.'

"So after he advised me what course to take, they started, and in a few minutes left me out of sight. When I had lost sight of them I sat down by the roadside and wept, prayed, and wished myself back where I started. I thought it was all over for me forever. Then a voice spoke to me, 'not to make a fool of myself, you have got so far from home (about 250 miles), keep on towards freedom, and if you are taken, let it be heading towards freedom.' I then took fresh courage and pressed my way onward towards the north with anxious heart.

"It was then two or three o'clock Wednesday morning. I came to the portion of the road that had been cut through a very high hill, called the 'deep cut,' which was on a curve. When I got about mid-way of this curve I heard a rumbling sound that seemed to me like thunder. It was very dark and I was afraid that we were to have a storm; but this rumbling kept on and did not cease as thunder does, until at last the hair on my head began to rise. I thought the world was coming to an end!

"I flew around and asked myself, 'what is this?' At last, it came so near to me it seemed as if I could feel the earth shake from under me, till, finally, the engine came around the curve. I got sight of the fire and smoke. Said I, 'It's the devil, it's the devil!' It was the first (train) engine I had ever seen or heard of. I did not know there was anything of its kind in the world, and being in the night made it seem a great deal worse than it was. I thought my last days had come. I shook from head to foot as the monster came rushing on towards me.

"The bank was very steep near where I was standing. A voice says to me, 'fly up the bank.' I made a desperate effort, and by the aid of the bushes and trees which I grasped. I reached the top of the bank where there was a fence. I rolled over the fence and fell to the ground, and the last words I remember saying were that 'the devil is about to burn me up, farewell, farewell!' After uttering these words, I fainted.

"I do not know how long I lay there, but when I recovered, the devil had gone. Oh! How my heart did throb. After I had gathered strength enough, I got up and sat there thinking what to do. I made up my mind that I would not lose any more time; hence I crawled down the bank and started on with trembling steps, expecting every moment that the monster would be coming back to look for me.

"Thus, between hope and doubt, I continued on foot till at last the day dawned and the sun had begun to rise. When the sun had risen as high as the tops of the trees, the monster all at once was coming back to meet me. I said to myself, 'it is no use to run. I had just as well stand and make the best of it,' thinking I would make the best bargain that I could with his majesty.

"Onward he came, with smoke and fire flying, and as he drew near me, I exclaimed to myself, 'why! What a monster's head he has on him! Oh!' said I, 'look at his rushes (teeth), I am a goner!' I looked again, saying to myself, "look at the wagons he has tied to him.' Thinks I, they are all the wagons that he carries souls to hell with.

"I looked through the windows to see if I could see any black people that he was carrying, but I did not see one—nothing but white people. Then I thought it was not black people that he was after but only the whites, and I did not care how many of them he took. He went by me like a flash. I expected every moment that he would stop and bid me come aboard, but he did not, so I thought that he was going so fast he could not stop. He was soon out of sight, and I, for the first time, took a long breath."

After recovering from his paralyzing fright, James L. Smith moved on northward and eventually gained his freedom. His graphic description of seeing a passenger train for the first time, and mistakenly believing it was the devil incarnate, is indicative of the enforced ignorance in which so many of the slaves were entrapped.

## Apparitions Aplenty in Old Alexandria

There may well be more ghosts per square mile in old Alexandria, across the Potomac River from Washington, than in any other town or city in Virginia. Here are a few examples.

A poltergeist named John Dixon is said to haunt the Michael Swope House at 210 Prince Street more than 230 years after he was reportedly erroneously executed for being a colonial spy during America's war for independence. Many have felt his "presence" when they were alone in the house. A few have seen him in Revolutionary-era clothes. And neighbors have told of hearing him playing the piano when no one was home.

There is also an account of an English lady who was inspecting the house in the 1930s with the intention of buying it. She was shown everything from the darkened root cellar to the rooms on the first and second floors. She liked what she had seen. But then, as she was ascending the stairs to the third-floor master bedroom, where Dixon had slept, "a force" stopped her dead in her tracks and refused to let her through. "I'd love to own this house, but something is preventing it," she later said. "I'm very psychic, and I can tell you that there definitely is a ghost here—one that, for one reason or another, does not like me." The reason, some think, is that she was British and Dixon was still harboring a grudge more than two centuries old.

### The Tragedy Atop Red Hill

There is a house called the Anchorage atop what was once Red Hill and is now known as Braddock Hill in northeast Alexandria. There lived, in the late eighteenth century, a reclusive couple, a sea captain and his lady. When he was at home they were rarely seen in public, and, human nature being what it is, rumors sprouted. Some even thought they were witch and warlock. It seemed difficult for anyone to believe that they were simply a couple deeply in love who cherished their solitude.

Whenever the captain sailed, usually for voyages to faraway places, which lasted several months, his wife would toil endlessly in her garden. Then, as time neared for his return, she would watch daily from the top of Red Hill for his ship to sail into harbor. On one mission, however, the captain was struck with a severe illness and had to stay over in Europe for a lengthy recovery. Another officer brought his ship home, and when the lady saw the ship dock but did not see her husband disembark, she assumed the worst. When she saw someone from the ship approach the hill, coming toward her, she feared he would tell her the captain had died. Grief-stricken, she went into her beloved garden and shot herself before the messenger arrived.

In the 1920s, a woman then living on the hill saw a woman she didn't know. She was tall and slender, had dark hair and "large lustrous eyes," and wore a cloak thrown carelessly over one shoulder. She called to the woman and invited her into her house. The figure vanished! Startled, she related the incident to a friend, another woman who had lived in the area all her life. When she described what she had seen, her friend smiled and said, "You saw the ghost of the sea captain's wife."

### The House that Isn't There

It has been described as the largest and most beautiful mansion ever erected in Alexandria. At one time it occupied the entire 1100 block of Oronoco Street. Built in 1785, its traditions were deeply rooted in the soil of Virginia. Writes Betty Smoot, who owned the mansion in the mid-nineteenth century, "The grounds included a whole square block and were enclosed with an ancient brick wall ten feet in height." The remains of an old garden flanked the Colonial-period house and there were airy rooms on either side, with impressive wings and various outbuildings. It was called Colross.

Tragedy shrouded the estate. It is documented that Thomson Mason, son of the colonial patriot George Mason, won Colross in a game of cards. He is the one who built the high brick wall. It is known that a notorious bounty jumper by the name of Downey and at least two Civil War deserters were shot in front of the wall. This probably explains the legends of the ghost of a soldier who haunts the wall. But he is not the principal spirit, or rather spirits, of Colross.

In the 1850s, Mason lived at the estate with his wife and their two young children, William and Ann. One spring day, as they romped in the yard, a terrible storm whipped up suddenly. William took shelter in an old chicken coop. Gale-force wind gusts toppled the creaky old building and killed him instantly. The house was in mourning for weeks, and none took it harder than young Ann. She walked about in a constant daze and seemed totally oblivious to reality. Soon after, she drowned in a bathtub. Both children were interred on the grounds in a small locked vault. The Masons, emotionally destroyed by the twin tragedies, moved away from Colross.

From that time on, new residents of the house, including Mrs. Smoot, often reported hearing the distinct sounds of children playing on the grounds when no children were in the house or nearby. They heard giggling, singing, and talking sometimes on an almost daily basis. Their cheerful presence was so strong, in fact, that successive owners at Colross had great difficulty in retaining servants. Many past residents and servants also told of seeing the apparitions of a young boy and girl. And while these sightings recurred over a period of thirty to forty years, the children, always dressed in pre-Civil War clothing, never grew older!

There was one other psychic oddity here that was never satisfactorily explained. The door of the vault where the children were buried was sealed with a large iron lock. Strangely, though it was exposed to the harsh elements of the weather for more than seventy-five years, the lock never rusted. Even more unbelievable was the fact that the lock, to which there was only a single key that never left the house, would never stay locked more than three days in a row. Mrs. Smoot, among others, could not explain this peculiar phenomenon. "Father would lock it himself," she once said, "and open it would come. Never was the lock broken."

Was it the mischievous spirits of young William and Ann who regularly broke the iron bonds so they could play on the grounds where they once enjoyed such happiness? We may never know, for early in the twentieth century Colross was moved to a site in New Jersey. The vault, with its mysterious lock, was destroyed and the bodies of the two children were reburied at a neighboring cemetery. There were no further reports of gleeful activity from unseen youngsters at the new location. William and Ann, children of the Old South, apparently had no desire to venture north.

## The Stamp Collector From the Beyond

Some years ago, a stamp collector in Killeen, Texas, successfully bid on the "mystery lot" at a major auction house. It was a trunk full of stamps on album pages, small collections, loose stamps, covers, packet material, plate blocks, and other items. The purchaser spent months going through the trunk, sorting and cataloging his stamps, and had so many left over he decided to sell them as a dealer. He placed ads in stamp newspapers offering three hundred stamps for one dollar.

One day he received a letter from a lady who lived in the North Ridge section of Alexandria. "You sent a package of stamps to my father," she wrote. "He was a stamp collector, but he passed away two years ago. Are you just now getting around to filling an order that he may have placed with you before his death?" The man who bought the trunk was thoroughly puzzled by the letter. He couldn't remember sending any packet to Alexandria. But he had all orders on file, and he went through his lists, but he could not find the gentleman the lady had mentioned, nor anyone else from Alexandria. So he wrote her back telling her it couldn't be an old order, because he had only been in business a short time, and he had no record of any order from her father. He couldn't explain what had happened, but he did tell her about the trunk and how he acquired it.

Shortly after that, he got a call from the lady. She asked him to describe the trunk he had bought. He did. "That was my father's trunk," she exclaimed. "And that was the auction house to which we consigned the stamps after his death." So the man suggested that maybe the lady's father had left a slip of paper with his name and address in the trunk and it somehow got mixed up with his sales orders. The lady agreed that it might be a logical explanation. But the man knew otherwise. He knew that nothing like that had happened. He himself had been a brigade commander in the Army, and he had gained a reputation for his organization and neatness.

In passing along this incident to a newspaper reporter, however, he offered his own explanation. "The lady's father was an accumulator," he said. "And a little thing like death was not going to stop him."

## The Vanishing Pitt Street Ghost

The following account is extracted from the July 20, 1885, issue of the *Alexandria Gazette*.

"A year or two ago several individuals, at different times, were scared out of a seven years growth by catching glimpses, at night, of a somber clad tall figure, supposed to be of the feminine persuasion, whose way it was to glide noiselessly along the pavement in front of St. Paul's Church, or to suddenly emerge from either of the alleys on that thoroughfare and stand in front of some related pedestrian until each separate hair on the latter's cranium assumed a perpendicular position.

"From whence it came or whither it went—Hades, the abode of the blessed, gehenna or sheol—none were able to tell. The spook, or whatever it may have been, rendered many credulous persons nervous, and caused others to go out of their way on more than one occasion rather than risk a sight of the supposed spirit by walking to their homes over the dreaded square.

"All sorts of suggestions intended to clear up the mystery were advanced, the generally received theory being that the apparition was nothing more than a harmless colored woman, slightly demented, who was accustomed to leave her home in the witching hour of night and walk around the neighborhood.

"The sensation, however, like all mundane things, died out, until last Saturday night, when it was once more revived by the 'ghost' making its appearance to Mr. James Wood, who was on his way home at the time. Mr. Wood lives on the north side of Wolfe, between Pitt and St. Asaph Streets. It was twelve midnight, that lonely hour when the grave yards yawn, and lunar's gibbous form had just sunk behind the western hills, when this gentleman, with a box of fried oysters under each arm, started from the Opera House restaurant for his home.

"He had arrived at the southwest corner of Prince and Pitt Streets, intending to pass over the square opposite St. Paul's Church, when directly in front of him there suddenly appeared the irrepressible figure he oft had heard of—not in sable habiliments, however, but snowy white. Mr. W. claims to be no believer in ghosts, hobgoblins, fairies or spirits, so he determined to catch up with and carefully survey whoever or whatever it was that glided—not walked—so stealthly before him.

"Accordingly, he accelerated his gait to the utmost to overtake the specter, but despite his every exertion, he could get no nearer than five feet of the apparition. He smoked up vigorously on a cigar he had in his mouth, for the purpose of shedding as much light on the scene as possible, when, in the twinkling of an eye, the spook vanished as suddenly as a ring of smoke or a burst soap bubble.

"At this denouement, our hero, sultry as the weather was, felt a cold chill meandering down the spinal column which soon eventuated in a tremor throughout the frame, and concluding that he had had enough of that adventure, became panic stricken and beat a lively retreat back to the restaurant he had previously left, arriving at which he rushed up to the proprietor in such a disturbed state of mind that the latter imagined him to be in a bellicose humor and prepared himself to act upon the defensive.

"Mr. Wood, however, soon explained himself by giving a thrilling account of his adventure, which he closed by informing some of the bystanders that they would have to accompany him to his home, as he was completely unnerved. A 'committee' kindly volunteered for that purpose, and the course of half an hour, Mr. W. was safe within his own domicile.

"His disbelief in visitants from the unseen world is not so strong now as formerly."

## The Multiple Haunts of Woodlawn

It is perhaps the least known among the great plantations of Virginia. It also may be the most haunted. This is Woodlawn.

The land and manor house were wedding gifts from George Washington to his foster daughter (Martha Washington's granddaughter) Nellie Parke Custis, upon her marriage to Maj. Lawrence Lewis, Washington's favorite nephew. The generous gift included two thousand acres adjacent to Mt. Vernon. The location was well chosen. It commands a breathtaking view of the surrounding countryside, including the Potomac River and Maryland on the other side. Washington called it "a most beautiful site for a gentleman's seat." Unfortunately, the first president died before construction on the house began. When completed in 1805, it consisted of a large central block with north and south wings connected to it.

Designed for lavish entertaining, Woodlawn in time acquired a reputation throughout the region for outstanding hospitality. Many elegant parties on a grand scale were held here, and leading dignitaries of the day were feted. But the plantation has known more than its share of sadness as well. Of the Lewises' eight children, only three survived. Most died in infancy at the house.

In the nineteenth century, after Woodlawn was passed along to other owners, it suffered greatly from neglect. In 1896, it was severely damaged by a hurricane, and for the next six years was left abandoned, battered and desolate. Two eccentric brothers moved in at the turn of the century, along with their aged mother and sixty-seven cats! They helped restore the great mansion to its former glory. Today, Woodlawn is lovingly maintained by the National Trust for Historic Preservation.

There are two things that are different about the spirits which apparently haunt Woodlawn. The actual manifestations of psychic phenomena, which are commonly witnessed there, are not necessarily out of the ordinary. They run the gamut: footsteps; thumpings on floors and walls; furniture moving about in rooms, seemingly on its own; doors locking and unlocking with no one around; candles extinguishing themselves; glimpses of gauzy figures which seem to vanish before one's eyes; objects disappearing and reappearing without rational cause or explanation; sudden rushes of cold air in specific areas or rooms; inexplicable shadowy images appearing on photos taken in the house; apparitions of "see-through" colonial-clad men and women; and mysterious taps on shoulders by unseen fingers, among others.

What is different about the phenomena at Woodlawn is that strange things seem to surface in virtually every nook and cranny of the place. Generally, psychic encounters are limited to a specific area of a house—the attic, the basement, a stairway, or a particular room. Here, however, things happen everywhere: the Lafayette bedroom, the boys' bedroom, the master bedroom, hallways, the center hall, the attic, the gift shop, the north wing, the south wing, what have you!

The second unusual aspect of Woodlawn is the great number of people who experience sightings and sensings of the presences. Past residents, tourists, and staff members alike all have been involved, and over a long period of time. Normally, spectral beings are felt only by one family, or even a single member of a family. Rarely is the phenomena so widely shared.

What are some of these experiences? Fortunately, many of them have been reported on and chronicled. Author Judy McElhaney wrote a booklet called *Ghost Stories of Woodlawn Plantation*. Area newspaper reporters have a field day covering spooky accounts every Halloween, and there are numerous other magazine articles and book excerpts about the hauntings. Here are a few selected examples:

- Experts believe when a mortal being comes in contact with a visitor from the spirit world, there is a very real sense of a chilly, sometimes icy-cold sensation. If contact is made, a cold dampness is felt. Many people have either fainted of felt faint when this happened. Woodlawn employees have felt such rushes of cold air in the master bedroom. One woman, securing the room for the night, turned out a small lamp and started for the door, only to hear a distinct click behind her. She wheeled around to see the lamp lit again. No one else was there. As she hurriedly headed for the door she felt a rush of frigid air pass her. This happened in the middle of summer when the house was not air-conditioned.

- Author McElhaney states that many people have reported sighting "smoky figures" and "circles of billowing light" dance and seemingly float down the halls and staircase in the south wing. Also, patches of "gray light" and "circles of grayish matter" have shown up in photos taken in this area. No one has found a reason for this.

- A guest staying in a south wing bedroom in 1978 said she was awakened long after midnight by an eerie feeling that she was not alone. She opened her eyes in the dark and saw, at the foot of her bed, "a smoky glowing figure of what appeared to be a man." He was wearing a mask or veil and said nothing. He just stared at her. After several minutes, he faded away. The woman could not sleep the rest of the night.

    Two years later, another guest in the same room said she was awakened and saw "something luminous, perhaps ectoplasm, hovering about four or five feet off the ground." This "pulsating mass" moved about for several minutes and then "slowly disappeared in the night." Other guests have told of similar occurrences. One saw the forms of two men neatly dressed in "suits of long ago." She was mesmerized by the figures until they evaporated.

- Residents of Woodlawn between 1905 and 1925 often told of hearing phantom footsteps in the house, unusual in the sense that they sounded like someone with a peg or wooden leg thumping up and down stairs at night. John Mason lived at the mansion in the middle of the nineteenth century. He had a wooden leg. Also, the original owner, Lawrence Lewis, suffered badly from arthritis and gout, and is believed to have used either a crutch or a cane.

- Multiple manifestations have unfolded in the Lafayette bedroom. Blown-out candles relight themselves. Oriental rugs have been turned over when the room was empty. Chairs have rearranged themselves, and items have disappeared from the closet. In the early 1930s, a woman living at Woodlawn said she took her infant daughter into the Lafayette bedroom one evening and placed her in her crib. The baby was only a few weeks old. Shortly thereafter, the woman heard the baby screaming and ran to the room. She found the child out of the crib and lying on top of a tall dresser across the room! There was no one else in the house. This mystery was never solved, but the woman and her family abruptly moved out of the house.

- Author McElhaney shares a story told to her by a former employee about an encounter on the south wing's back stairs years ago. As the woman went up the stairs, she sensed someone or something there. "It was," she said, "as if you feel someone is looking at you. I looked up to see who was there and saw what I can only describe as an aura. It's hard to explain. There was some density to it." The woman lurched back in surprise, but then fought her fright and climbed the stairs. "The sense of someone was still there," she recalls. "It was that of an impish youngster, most like a girl, six or seven years old. I'd gone through her!"

- It is widely believed, among parapsychologists, that animals have a greater sensitivity for the supernatural than humans. Cats and dogs in particular seem to be able to see and hear things that mortals cannot. At Woodlawn, the Center Hall is feared by the house pets, which sense an invisible ghost or ghosts unseen by anyone else. Cats especially have shown a strong dislike for the hall. They avoid it and become terribly frightened and agitated when carried through the area. And they have to be carried. They won't walk through the room on their own.

    Case in point: In 1987, a cat named Samantha ruled in the house. Each evening the person responsible for closing the property after the tourists had departed had the chore of making sure Samantha was either put outside or brought over to the southwest room. A former employee told what happened one night when she reached the center hall with the cat. "Samantha would start to hiss and get angry. Just as we would get near the main hall staircase, her head would jerk towards the staircase as if she were looking at something I couldn't see.

She would always struggle to get out of my arms and would flee to the southwest room by herself.

"Well, on this particular night I was determined not to let her get the best of me. I decided to hold her tighter than usual. I was walking through the main hall and immediately her ears pulled back and she started hissing a terrible fit, her head looking straight towards the spot on the main hall staircase. She was so angry or scared by something that she struggled ferociously to escape. Her strength was super powerful. She ripped into my hand and got one of her claws in so deep I couldn't hold her anymore. I let her fly out of my arms, and where she went I never knew nor cared. To this day I still wonder what it was that Samantha sensed on that staircase."

It is known that years ago a past resident had a German shepherd at Woodlawn as a house pet. He guarded the place with a fierce determination. Did Samantha and her fellow felines sense this dog? Or do they see the spectral images of their ancestral cousins? Whatever is there, it is very real to Woodlawn's pets.

• According to legend, says Brian Goldstein, who has written extensively about Woodlawn, "homes built atop wells are inevitably haunted. This is because wells forge deep into the earth to connect with streams, and, for metaphysical, symbolic and mythical reasons, running water has long been associated with the spirit realm." This may help explain why there is so much psychic activity at Woodlawn. There is an old well here, in the gift shop. It was built into the floor of the connecting hallway between the main block of the house and the south wing, which housed the kitchen. It has been called the "Well of Souls."

Goldstein says a well "allows spirits a means to travel up from the water," and into a house. This is one reason, he adds, that in most historic homes wells are found outside or in separate structures. "When a well is open," he adds, "spirits can freely pass between the water and the house. When the well is closed, however, spirits supposedly become confused, disoriented, and occasionally angry and violent." This frustration causes them to materialize and search throughout the building for an alternative means of returning to their world. Goldstein says more than half of the reported sightings of ghosts at Woodlawn have occurred when the well lid has been closed. Also, there have been numerous instances when the lid had been shut at night, only to be found open the next day.

This covers only a portion of the plethora of unearthly activities that continue to occur at historic Woodlawn Plantation, which is open to the public. Says Goldstein: "The most compelling evidence for ghosts is their appearances and sightings, and of these, Woodlawn has many."

## The Spectral Return of John Brown

Harpers Ferry, thirty miles north of Winchester, today is in West Virginia, but until 1863 it was part of Virginia's Jefferson County. It is one of the most scenic and unusual towns in America. It may also be one of the most haunted. It was here, in 1859, that abolitionist John Brown staged his infamous raid on the federal arsenal, and was later hanged for his efforts.

In describing the natural beauty of Harpers Ferry, Thomas Jefferson, as he so often did, may well have said it best: "The passage of the Potomac [River] through the Blue Ridge [mountains] is, perhaps, one of the most stupendous scenes in nature. You stand on a very high point of land; on your right comes up the Shenandoah [River], having ranged along the foot of a mountain a hundred miles to seek a vent. On your left approaches the Potomac, in quest of a passage also; in the moment of their junction, they rush together against the mountain, rend it asunder, and pass off to the sea. This scene is worth a voyage across the Atlantic."

In his classic book *History of the Valley*, written in the 1830s, author Samuel Kercheval wrote: "It is scarcely necessary to inform the reader that this [Harpers Ferry] is the location of the United States armory, and in the several shops are generally employed about 300 first-rate mechanics, engaged in the manufacture of arms for the purpose of war. There are annually made about six or seven thousand muskets, two or three thousand rifles, besides an immense number of swords, pistols and other side arms."

It is somewhat ironic, amidst all this scenic splendor and colorful history, that the town probably is best known for the notoriety of being the site where a madman went amok prior to the Civil War, resulting in a number of murders and hangings, and maybe even providing the cause for some ghostly presences who have lingered here over the decades.

His name was John Brown.

Above all else, Brown was a true enigma. He was a hero to many, a devil incarnate to some, loved, hated, and especially feared. Ralph Waldo Emerson once called him "a new saint." A Kansas minister who knew him well described him as "impressed with the idea that God had raised him up on purpose to break the jaws of the wicked." Brown himself once declared, "I am an instrument in the hands of Providence! God told me what to do." What Brown did was create chaos virtually everywhere he went. A hardened abolitionist who deplored slavery, he was a deeply religious man who used violence as a key tool to force his beliefs on others.

In 1859, Brown concocted a diabolical plan which he felt would eventually free the slaves throughout the South. He would lead a group of his faithful followers, heavily armed, into Harpers Ferry and storm the federal arsenal. Once he had established his authority, slaves would rise up from the farms and plantations of the Shenandoah Valley, race to the armory, arm themselves into a veritable army, and rise up in rebellion.

And so it was on Sunday, October 16, 1859, that Brown and his motley crew of fifteen white recruits, including his sons and four black recruits, loaded a wagon full of arms—nearly 400 rifles and pistols and 950 iron-tipped pikes—and headed toward Harpers Ferry. There, under the cloak of a cold, wet darkness, the raiding party surprised the few defenders of the arsenal. They commandeered several buildings, traded gunshots with a few townspeople, and took a number of hostages. Brown set up headquarters in a brick fire engine house and waited for the slaves to come to him seeking their freedom.

Instead, he was met by a federal force of marines commanded by none other than Col. Robert E. Lee. The troops stormed the buildings and quickly overpowered Brown's men. Brown, however, held out in the fortified firehouse. One of the hostages later reported that "Brown was the coolest and firmest man I ever saw. With one son dead by his side and another shot through, he felt the pulse of his dying son with one hand and held his rifle with the other, and commanded his men with the utmost composure, encouraging them to sell their lives as dearly as they could."

The marines soon overran the firehouse and captured Brown, who had been wounded in the fighting. He was turned over to Virginia authorities and tried for treason against the state, and conspiracy to incite insurrection. But Brown, in a sense, won his day in court. That is, as the country watched, he used the courthouse as a platform to denounce the cruelties of slavery, and in so doing stirred the national conscience. Some historians believe this was one of the most important incident-causes which helped lead to the Civil War. Brown was convicted of his crimes, nevertheless, and was hanged at age fifty-eight, on December 2, 1859, at nearby Charles Town.

There is a curious footnote to the hanging. It is told by Shirley Dougherty, author of *A Ghostly Tour of Harpers Ferry*, although this particular event does not appear in her book. According to the legend Shirley tells on her weekend ghost tours, when they took Brown's body down from the gallows, those present were frightened by his eyes. They were said to shine with an eerie luster, as if they could still see. In fact, Shirley says the doctors examined him three different times after declaring him dead, and the eyes continued to almost glow. Finally, candle wax was poured over them.

Brown's body was then carted to Harpers Ferry, where his wife was waiting to take it back to Elba, New York. It is said that when they prepared the corpse for interment the candle wax was removed from its eyes—and the eyes continued to appear incredibly lifelike!

If ever there was reason for a ghost to return to the site of its mortal death, certainly John Brown had one. And perhaps he did reappear among the streets of Harpers Ferry. While there have been no reported reappearances of Brown's apparition in the firehouse, the armory, or anywhere else for that matter, a strange and curious thing happened some years ago. A man closely resembling Brown appeared in the town, the likeness so startling that people's heads would turn when he passed. It was told that a few visitors asked the stranger to pose for pictures with them.

When the pictures were developed, however, the John Brown look-alike was mysteriously missing in the prints!

## The Demise of Dangerfield Newby

Aside from this rather odd occurrence, the only other ghostly phenomenon tied to the John Brown raid centers around a man named Dangerfield Newby—a former slave who had tried to buy the freedom of his wife and seven children, then still on a farm near Warrenton, Virginia. Newby had raised the money but when he confronted the slave owner, he had been rebuffed. Incensed, he joined Brown's group, hoping this might lead to his family's freedom.

But during the sometimes fierce street fighting that ensued that grim October in Harpers Ferry, Newby, in baggy trousers and an old slouch hat, was killed at the arsenal gate on Monday, October 17, 1859. There is some confusion as to just how he was killed. One writer said he was shot through the neck by a bullet; another said he was slain with a six-inch pike. In either case, the wound left a gaping hole in his neck, and the townspeople were so upset at the raiders that his body was left in the street where he fell for more than twenty-four hours.

Then, gruesomely, it was dragged to a nearby alley and dumped in a spot where hogs roamed. Author Joseph Barry was a witness to what happened next. He wrote, "A hog came up, rooted around the spot where the body lay, and at first appeared to be unconscious that anything extraordinary was in its way. After a while, the hog paused and looked attentively at the body, then sniffed around it and put its snout to the dead man's face. Suddenly, the brute was apparently seized with a panic, and with bristles erect and drooping tail, it scampered away, as if for dear life. This display of sensibility did not, however, deter others of the same species from crowding around the corpse and almost literally devouring it.

"This writer [Barry], saw all this with his own eyes, and at the risk of further criticism, he will remark that none of the good people of Harpers Ferry appeared to be at all squeamish about the quality of flavor of their pork that winter."

Ever since that time this spot, between High and Potomac Streets, has been known as Hog Alley. And, according to a newspaper report years ago, visitors have told of periodically seeing a man wandering about there—a man wearing baggy trousers and an old slouch hat, a man with a deep, ugly scar across his throat. The chilling vision is seen but a few brief seconds, and then vaporizes.

## The Haunted Houses of Robert E. Lee

If there was, or is, a ghost of Robert E. Lee—and certainly there would be plenty of just causes for one, grieving over his lost or starving troops—one might suspect his spirit would reappear somewhere in his beloved Virginia, perhaps at the Wilderness, Cold Harbor, Seven Pines, or Petersburg. Or perhaps his presence would be expected at the Lee Mansion in Arlington, or possibly even out of state, say at Gettysburg.

But such is not the case at any of these sites. Nevertheless, it is interesting to note that there are recurring reports, documented and witnessed by many, of strong psychic phenomena at two historic Old Dominion houses in which Lee lived, one as an infant and toddler, and the other as a young boy and teenager. And at least at one of these locations, some believe it is the spirit of a very youthful and exuberant Robert who is heard and occasionally sighted romping around.

Lee was born at Stratford Hall Plantation, in Westmoreland County, on January 19, 1807, the third son of "Light Horse" Harry Lee. Stratford Hall has been described as one of the great houses of American history. A brochure points out: "Its magnificent setting on a high bluff above the Potomac River and its bold architectural style set it apart from any other colonial house." As one Lee biographer wrote: "No picture of the mansion gives any adequate ideas of its chateau-like massiveness. Fashioned of brick made on the site, and timber cut from virgin forests, its fortress-like walls are two and a half feet thick."

And yet, as imposing as the mansion and its surrounding 1,600-acre estate are, an even more impressive distinction arises from the prominence of the family that resided there for so many years. Indeed, the Lees of Virginia certainly were one of the—if not *the*—most renowned families in the country. Richard Henry Lee, for instance, made the motion for independence in the Continental Congress. Light Horse Harry Lee was a hero of the Revolutionary War and a favorite of George Washington.

At Stratford today, however, tour hostesses are mostly reluctant to mention the presence of any form of psychic phenomena. They prefer to dwell on the rich history and superb architecture and setting of the house and grounds, and well they should. The plantation's grandeur is more than enough in itself to warrant visits and revisits. Stratford Hall has been faithfully restored to its original elegance and contains many fine pieces of period furniture, family portraits, and other items of Lee memorabilia.

As with so many worthy old estates, there is ample justification for ghostly encounters here, for along with its integrity and elegance, the great house and some of the family members have had their share of tragic events. Late in his life, Light Horse Harry Lee and some of his friends were brutally beaten by an angry mob in Baltimore. They were stuck with penknives and had hot wax poured into their eyes. Lee had part of his nose cut off and was permanently disfigured. Would not one speculate that his spirit might return to his ancestral home, scene of much happier days? As we shall see, maybe it did.

There is the case of Henry Lee, Robert's older half brother, who got his wife's sister "in the family way." That unfortunate incident, plus the tragic death of their young daughter, undoubtedly contributed to the fact that Henry's wife, Ann, eventually became addicted to a powerful drug, and Henry earned the dubious sobriquet of "Black Horse Harry."

Mrs. Walker Allard, who has worked at Stratford Hall for more than forty years as a historical interpreter and custodian of historic buildings, says the only fragmentary account she ever came across concerning psychic energy was the reported sighting of a ghostly figure at a desk in the great house. "Yes," she says, "that happened some time ago. There was a young maid who said she did see a man's figure at the desk." The woman opened a door to the library to go in the room to clean it. She went in and came right out again. Her supervisor asked her what happened and she told her she "didn't want to disturb the gentleman in there." When they reentered the library no one was there. Could it have been Light Horse Harry? The maid said the figure seemed to be checking over some papers. "She became very frightened and ran from the house," Mrs. Allard says. "But like I say, she was very young and probably very impressionable. I think just about every old house has a ghost if someone wants to see a ghost."

Stratford Hall, it appears, after conversations with a number of both current and retired employees, is no exception to this theory. There have been, in fact, numerous accounts of psychic activity. Margie McGrath, a former hostess, was taking a couple through the house one day. As she stopped to answer questions near the end of the tour, she felt "a sharp tug" at her hoop under her full, period-costume skirt. "I kept talking, but I brushed my hand to the area where I felt the pull, and my skirt wasn't hiked or out of place or anything, and no one else was in the room," she recalls. "Then I felt the tug again. Something or someone had pulled on my skirt."

Mrs. McGrath says that on another occasion a few years ago she escorted a psychic on a tour. "When we passed through the great hall on the second floor, she stopped and said, 'Oh, I have so many good impressions,' and then she said she could see the room full of Lees, and that there was dancing and music and entertainment. At the end of the tour she came to me and said that the Lees were pleased with how the house was being taken care of. And then she told me she had seen more of the family playing croquet on the lawn as she had approached the main house. I was fascinated. I don't laugh at any of this."

Jo Ann Boyer, a former chief hostess at the mansion, now retired, also has heard some strange stories and had a chilling confrontation of her own. "I have heard that the gentleman who the maid said she saw in the library that day has also appeared in one of the outbuildings," she says. "He has been seen with a ledger in his hands. Those who saw him say he was dressed in black with a ruffled shirt and white stockings, much like the clothing worn in the eighteenth century."

Mrs. Boyer says her personal encounter occurred on a dismal, dark winter afternoon. "It was late in the day when I took a group through the house," she recalls. "Toward the end of the tour we were in the far upper west end, and I had my back to the door and the people were facing me. Suddenly, I saw a woman and a child in the room in colonial period costume. The woman had on a gray cape and the child a red cape, and their hoods were up. I just thought to myself, who was that child with Mrs. McGrath, who was another hostess on duty with me that day. She had remained downstairs when I went on the tour. She had grandchildren who occasionally come to the house, and I just assumed it was her. But I couldn't figure out why she was upstairs, and why did they have hoods on?

"So when the tour was over, I went downstairs and asked Mrs. McGrath, and she looked at me like I was crazy or something. She said she hadn't left the room downstairs, and no one was with her. At first I thought she was joking, but when she realized that I was serious, she lifted her hand and covered her mouth, and said that I had finally seen 'them.' I had seen Ann Lee, the distraught and broken-hearted wife of Black Horse Harry Lee, and their little daughter, Margaret, who had died in the house at age two after falling down the stairs. People have heard the woman calling the little girl, and the sound of a child running and then both of them laughing, as if they were playing together. We had talked about it, but it never dawned on me when I saw them that day, that it was Ann and Margaret Lee." Mrs. Boyer says little Margaret Lee died in 1820.

At least two Stratford Hall security officers have experienced various forms of psychic manifestations in recent years. They voluntarily recounted the events, but asked to remain anonymous. "A lot of things happen, sometimes in the great house, and often in the southwest dependency building," one of them says. "We have heard all kinds of noises at night, but never found any physical reason for them. What kind of noises? I mean racket. Loud racket at times." Both of the officers have reported the sounds of heavy furniture being moved about, but investigations revealed nothing out of place. Both have heard distinct footsteps on the second floor of the house when it is closed to the public and no one is in it. Both say they have heard the sound of "stiff clothing," possibly rustling petticoats and skirts, rubbing against chair and tables.

"It's like a cloak, or a coat, or a stiff skirt, or something like that," one says. "But how can you hear something and you don't see anything? That's what I can't explain. How can you hear furniture being moved around, yet you don't see it? I have no idea." One officer reports he has heard fiddle music on occasion and once heard a harp being played. "I've heard doors slamming at two or three in the morning, but I could never find any cause for it," he says. "Now, I know in an old house there are going to be a lot of sounds anyway. Floors creak. The house settles. But I'm talking about noises that aren't like settling sounds. I was in the dependency one night when I heard something that sounded like a cinder block hitting the cabinet right behind me.

"And I'll tell you something else," the officer continued. "I was sitting in a chair one night when something got hold of my sleeve and lifted it up. Lifted my arm straight up! How do you explain that? Another time I was reading a book one night when I put it down to make my rounds. When I came back, the book was gone. No one else was on the grounds. I was alone. Did this scare me? At first, maybe it did. But I got used to it. Whatever it is, or was, it didn't cause me any harm. It didn't bother me. But it did frighten some others. We had one man who started to work one night—his first night on the job—and he quit after just one hour. He wouldn't even talk about what happened to him." Another time, one of the officers said he met a psychic from Hanover County who had just been through the house. "He seemed all shook up, so I asked him what was the problem, and he told me, 'you won't believe it, but there are ghosts in that house.' I asked him how many and he said five!"

Of all the phenomena the two officers have been exposed to, perhaps the most interesting was the sighting of a young boy, about four years old. Both have seen the apparition, on separate occasions. "I saw him late one afternoon," one says. "He was standing by the fence on the road some distance from the gate. He was wearing dark purple britches and a light-colored purple shirt, kind of like what they wore in colonial days. As I drove past him in my truck, he came out into the middle of the road, and then he motioned toward the cows in the pasture, as if he wanted them to come to him.

"Well, I thought he might be lost so I stopped the truck down the road apiece and got out to ask him where his parents were. Now I could see in all directions for at least a quarter of a mile or so, but that boy had disappeared. He just vanished. I looked all around, but I never found him. I believe he was a spirit. If he wasn't, where did he go?"

The other officer saw the same young boy at least twice. Once he sighted him in the old slave quarters. The second time, he saw him in the dependency building. He walked across the room as if he had lost something and was looking for it. "He appeared to be white all over," the officer says. "He was a little boy as near as I could tell. I believed he was either a ghost or an angel. I called the other officer and asked him what I should do, and he said not to worry, that whatever it was I was seeing wouldn't hurt me. And then he disappeared."

Who was this mystery child? Here, historically, there is at least a clue. Phillip Ludwell Lee was the son of Thomas Lee, the founder of Stratford Hall. And he had a son also named Phillip. According to family tradition, this boy fell down the stairs in the great house one day in 1779 and died. He was to have been the heir to the estate. He was four years old at the time of his death.

And, finally, there is the testimony of J. R. "Butch" Myers, who lives in Richmond. Myers is a craftsperson who had been at the mansion over a weekend in June 1989, demonstrating his skills with leather. He travels around the country recreating how eighteenth-century shoes were made. Myers had a frightening experience that drove him from the dependency building just south of the main house. Here is his account of what happened:

"We had just completed the show Saturday evening and a few of my fellow craftspeople had gathered in the dependency where I was to spend the night alone, just to talk over the day's activities and compare notes. The session broke up around 12:30 A.M. I had lit six candles in stands, as there was no electricity in the building. As I was getting ready to turn in, I had sort of an uncanny feeling. I can't quite describe it. But then I saw a couple of sawhorses and a heavy sheet of plywood in the corner of the room, and it struck me that this would make a good bed for the night, so I unrolled by bedroll on top of it.

"As I kicked my shoes off, I heard the approaching footsteps of the security guard making his rounds. I grabbed a cigarette and started toward the door to chat with him for a few minutes. It was a particularly hot evening, with the temperatures in the nineties during the day, and it hadn't cooled off much that night. I took about two steps toward the door when a sudden downdraft of freezing cold air hit me, taking my breath away. I mean it was icy cold! It was like walking into a cold storage locker. I got goose bumps all over. And just as this happened, there was a thunderous noise in the chimney. It sounded like the whole building was going to collapse. I didn't find this out until later, but the chimney was sealed top to bottom. There was no way anything alive could be in it.

"If this wasn't scary enough—and believe me, it was—I turned around just in time to see the candles go out. And they just didn't go out at once, as if blown out by a downshaft of air. They went out one at a time, in sequence, as if someone was snuffing them out. So I said to myself, 'okay, who's playing funny?' Now, I have some relatives in the area, some cousins, and they had told me about how Stratford Hall was haunted, and all that. So I figured maybe one of them was playing a little joke on me. But I was sober as a judge, and I didn't see anybody in the room except myself. How could anyone have done that with the candles?

"I got to the door and told the security guard what had happened. He didn't seem particularly surprised. He just said, 'Oh, you've just met our friend.' He asked me if I had seen anyone, and I had to say no. In a little while he walked on off to complete his rounds and I went back inside the room and relit the candles. Now you can believe this or not, I don't care. But the icy coldness in the room hit me again, and the racket kicked up in the chimney, which really scared me now, because the guard had told me about it being sealed. There was no breeze or wind at all in the room, but someone or something very methodically extinguished each candle again, in reverse order this time. And I knew now, for a fact, that no one else was in the room, at least no one living. I was by myself.

"But there definitely was something there, a presence or whatever you want to call it. And that was enough for me. I said, 'Listen, you can have the room. Just let me get my pillow and blanket, and I'll get out of here.' And I did. I got out of there as quick as I could and I went over to the dependency on the other side of the mansion, where the guard was, and I told him I was spending the night with him! The next morning I went back to the room and everything was just as I had left it. It was cool inside but the air wasn't freezing as it had been the night before. I gathered up my stuff and left.

"I went back to Stratford in the summer of 1991 for another craft show, but I didn't stay in the dependency. No sir! I walked around to it one evening, and in front of the big house there was a nice gentle breeze blowing. But when I got to the front of the building everything was deathly still. Nothing was stirring. It was an eerie feeling. I put my hand on the doorknob and it was like clutching an icicle. That's as far as I got. I wouldn't go back into that room. There was something in there that didn't want me inside. The guards told me it wouldn't hurt me, but that's easy for them to say. They didn't feel what I felt in that room. I'm not saying definitely that it was something evil, but I didn't want to stick around to find out for sure.

"It had made its point with me. I'm not psychic or anything, but I definitely believe there is something to ghosts and spirits, and there's a lot we don't understand about all that yet. But I can say for sure that I am certain there is something strange at Stratford Hall. There was something in that room. And one experience with whatever it was, or is, was enough for me!"

## Lee's Other House

Young Robert E. Lee moved from Stratford Hall when he was just three-and-a-half years old, after his father more or less "lost" the great estate through a series of bad investments that eventually landed him in debtors' prison. Soon afterward, the family settled in a still-standing house at 607 Oronoco Street in Alexandria, built in 1795 by John Potts. In the late 1790s George Washington often visited here.

Although Lee's father was no longer present—he was convalescing on the island of Barbados and died before he could return home—Robert enjoyed much happiness here. So much so, in fact, that it is recorded that after his surrender at Appomattox in 1865, Lee rode his horse, Traveler, to Alexandria, and leaped over the garden wall to see if the snowballs were in bloom the way he remembered them from his childhood.

It also is well documented that this house, like Stratford Hall, often has been the site of strange psychic phenomena, although the occurrences surfaced long after Lee himself died in 1870. Those who have witnessed and written about these encounters agree that the spirits present are, as one author put it, "some of the friendliest ghosts you'll ever want to meet." Another writer added, "no one complains that the old Robert E. Lee mansion in Alexandria is haunted, because its haunts are among the most delightful and inventive ever to be recorded."

Most of the manifestations apparently took place in the early 1960s, before the house was acquired by the Lee-Jackson Foundation of Charlottesville. At the time the property was owned by an investment banker named Henry Koch and his wife. They had a seven-year-old son, William. Things began popping the day they moved in, June 10, 1962. The couple reported hearing sounds of small footsteps running and childish laughter upstairs. They assumed it was William but later learned, to their amazement, that he had not been near the area where the sounds were coming from.

The laughter and patter of "little feet" continued in the weeks that followed, sometimes several times a day. Mrs. Koch was quoted as saying, "It sounded as if it were coming from a child about four years old. The laughter was at about the level of our knees." Sometimes the invisible giggler would seem to follow the Kochs as they walked through the house, especially in the front hall and up and down the stairway.

Mrs. Koch told Susy Smith, author of the book *Prominent American Ghosts*, that the sounds were always "cheery." The laughter went on frequently for about six months and then trailed off. That the Kochs weren't "hearing things" was supported one day when a milkman asked them if they had heard "the little Lees." Mrs. Koch told him that they had, and he smiled and said, "Well, if you don't bother them, they won't bother you."

Another example of psychic phenomena sometimes flowed through the house on Oronoco Street in the form of musical strains from "some kind of stringed instrument." Once, Mr. Koch hosted a meeting at his house, and the men were serenaded by soft melodies floating down from upstairs. Koch assumed it was his teenage daughter playing her guitar, but he later learned that she had left her instrument at school. No one else was in the house at the time.

Mrs. Koch, too, encountered her share of inexplicable incidents. On one occasion, she had misplaced her cigarette lighter and searched the house for it. As she walked from the living room to the dining room, the lighter mysteriously came flying from "somewhere" and landed on the floor at her feet. She immediately thought it might be her young son playing a trick, but he was found in another part of the house. At other times an invisible finger would ring the front doorbell, but there was never anyone there.

Curiously, two family friends visiting the house for the first time asked, without prompting, if it was haunted. Author Smith, herself psychically sensitive, said she "got prickly sensations along my spine," followed by goose bumps, when she stood in the back part of the downstairs hall under the landing. Another writer added that while she didn't see the apparitions of laughing children, she "certainly felt their presence."

And then there was the phantom black dog. It was frequently sighted romping across the garden, and was described as a "little black dog with a long body and a long tail." Over a considerable period of time a number of people claimed they saw such a dog in the yard and garden, both of which were walled off. Yet, oddly, the Koch's two dogs, often outside when the spectral hound was seen, never acknowledged its presence in any way. It has been speculated that the little black dog may have been the pet of the giggling child or children.

Consider this: a few years ago Alexandria city archeologist Keith Barr was conducting an archeological dig in the garden area of the yard. One morning he arrived at the work site to find dog prints in the dig area, a pit several feet deep. The yard, he pointed out, was tightly and highly fenced. There was no way for a dog to get inside. But what really chilled Barr was the fact that there were no animal prints of any kind leading to the dig!

Perhaps the strangest happening of all reported at the Lee house took place one Sunday when a retired admiral and his wife, neighbors of the Kochs, came over for a visit. As they sat talking, the woman suddenly appeared to be in the midst of a swirling snowstorm! The others stared at her in wonderment. The scary scene went on for several minutes when she finally asked what on earth was happening. It was not an apparitional effect. There were real, "big fat" flakes falling on the astonished woman from about a foot above her head. Someone suggested it might be dust, but the woman shook her head firmly. "No," she said, "because I am all wet!" A quick inspection determined that there was nothing leaking from the ceiling, and it was neither snowing nor raining outside. Understandably, the shaken woman and her husband got up to leave, and the snowfall started all over again, descending upon her as she walked to the door. Once she left, it stopped.

No rational explanation was ever found, nor was it ever discovered who might be the otherworldly source for the childish giggles, the sound of little feet, or the appearances of the small black dog. Some have surmised it might be the spectral antics of a prankish young Robert E. Lee, although he was not known to have had a dog as a boy growing up in Alexandria. Others have mused that it could have been another one of the Lee children, perhaps the child who had been killed falling down stairs at about the age of four. But he never lived in this house.

There has been more or less general agreement that whoever or whatever was the cause for such occurrences was a happy spirit or spirits, content and comfortable in such historic surroundings.

## The Sad Spirits of the Weems-Botts Museum

Dumfries, Virginia, lies just off heavily traveled Interstate 95, about halfway between Alexandria and Fredericksburg. In the first half of the eighteenth century, this town was a thriving seaport that rivaled Philadelphia and Boston, but when the harbor dried up and ships could no longer reach the site to load and unload their cargos, and the tobacco trade declined, Dumfries virtually became a ghost town.

Today, the town's leading attraction is a little-known museum known as Weems-Botts, named after two prominent but equally obscure citizens who lived there more than two hundred years ago.

Reverend Mason Weems once preached at historic Pohick Church, a few miles north of Dumfries, but had such a tough time making ends meet on his paltry salary that he moved to the town and decided to become a writer. In the old wooden frame structure that now houses the museum, Weems wrote an eighty-page biography of George Washington that became, at the time, a bestseller. In it, Weems created some colorful but questionable legends about Washington that have endured for centuries: that Washington cut down a cherry tree and when confronted by this father, said that he did it, for he could not tell a lie; and that as a youth he once threw a silver dollar three hundred feet across the Rappahannock River. Although generations of children were thrilled by such tales, historians say they never happened. Weems had made them up.

He went on to write similar biographies of such notable men as Francis Marion, the legendary "Swamp Fox" of the American Revolution; Benjamin Franklin; and William Penn. These works have been described as so entertaining as to make their historical inaccuracies somewhat pardonable. Weems sold his house in Dumfries in 1802 to a celebrated defense attorney named Benjamin Botts, who was on the legal team that successfully defended Aaron Burr in his historic treason trial. Botts used the place as his law office. Botts perished in the infamous Richmond theater fire on December 2, 1811.

Thus there are two possible candidates for the hauntings at the Weems-Botts Museum: Weems, whose spirit likely would return in defense of the harsh criticism of his writings; and Botts, due to his untimely, traumatic death. Yet neither appears to be the case. Rather, the ghostly manifestations that have been experienced here may be attributable to a family who resided in the house decades later.

Little is known of the history of the building from the time of Botts's death until 1869. It was then purchased by Richard Merchant as a private residence. He added a room or two, and in time had two daughters, Violet and Mamie. The youngest, Mamie, was epileptic and subject to violent fits or seizures. In that era epilepsy was believed to be a disease of madness, or worse, a possession by evil spirits. Consequently, the Merchants kept young Mamie locked in an upstairs bedroom. It was to be her lifelong prison.

Richard Merchant died in 1905, and Mamie, mercifully, passed away a few months later. Violet, meanwhile, moved away from Dumfries and fell in love. But when her mother asked her to come back home and take care of her, Violet dutifully complied, even though it broke her heart to do so. It was a hard life. The two women struggled to make ends meet. The house was small and cramped. There was no indoor plumbing. Water was brought in from a pump in the yard and food was cooked on an old-fashioned woodstove.

Mrs. Merchant died in 1954. She was ninety-eight years old. Violet stayed in the house, alone, distraught, and reclusive. Neighbors would later say they could see Violet through the home's windows at night, wandering about and weeping silently. Rarely did anyone venture into this house of extreme sadness, and Violet never allowed anyone upstairs to the bedroom where her long-dead sister had been incarcerated. She told children the room was haunted. They believed her. Violet finally left the house in 1967, and died in a nursing home a year later.

For the next seven years the abandoned house fell into a sorry state of disrepair. It was slated to be demolished, but realizing its historical value, the people of Dumfries saved it. Extensive renovations began in 1974. It was during that effort, museum curator Katherine Fullerton and historical interpreter Debbie Ward say, when the hauntings began.

"There was a doorway between two of the rooms upstairs," says Debbie. "During the restoration, this was walled off and a large book-shelf was erected. As soon as this was done, the books started flying off the shelves by themselves. And I don't mean they just fell to the floor, they were flung halfway across the room! Somebody didn't like that passageway being closed off. Later, the bookshelf was taken out and the doorway reopened, and nothing happened after that."

The upstairs bedroom where Mamie was confined is where most of the strange happenings occur. Katherine says museum workers and volunteers have heard mysterious footsteps, and the sounds of laughter, crying, and terrible screams in that room when no one was in it. "When we go up to see who is causing it, no one is there," she says. "We have had many visitors tell us they suddenly become over-whelmed with a sense of depression and unhappiness when they entered Mamie's room. They tell us this without knowing the history of that room, because we don't openly talk about the ghosts here unless someone asks us. We also have had visitors who were para-normally sensitive, and they have told us they felt pressure when they entered, and a strong feeling of discomfort."

"I can tell you this," Katherine adds. "There is a closet door that won't stay shut. We have closed it and closed it, and every time we reenter the room it is open. I check the rooms each day when I come into the museum. One morning I went upstairs in Mamie's room and there was a deep depression on the bed. It definitely appeared that someone had sat down on a side of the bed. If it had been a mortal person the bed would have collapsed because it only has a straw mattress, which is supported by a thin piece of cracked plywood. I asked if anyone had been in the room that morning, and no one had."

Katherine and Debbie say the most frightening occurrence involved the visit of a group of Boy Scouts. When they went upstairs to view Mamie's room, the scout leader, an adult, seemed to be mesmerized. He was staring into a corner, his face flush and his eyes watered. He appeared to be confused and distressed. Concerned, a tour guide asked him if he was all right. He stammered, "She wants to know where her rocking chair is." "What?" the guide asked. He then told her that as he approached the room he saw the vision of a young woman sitting in a rocking chair in the corner. His description of the apparition perfectly matched that of Mamie Merchant. Later, a call was made to a relative of the Merchants, and the museum curator was told that, indeed, Mamie used to have a rocking chair in her room, and she loved to sit and rock.

"This house is always very cold even in the summer," Katherine says. "I think Mamie and Violet were very sad here. They both led sad lives." Some believe it is their spirits who occasionally return to make their presence known. In recent years, officials at the museum have relaxed their feelings about including ghosts in the tour commentary. In fact, each Halloween daring visitors are invited to camp out overnight in the building.

There have been many who have taken the challenge, but very few who remain the whole night through. Most abruptly leave soon after the midnight hour.

A block away from the museum is a park. A century and a half ago, the Henderson House sat here. It was used as a temporary hospital during the Civil War. Wounded Union soldiers were brought here and some were laid out on the grounds of what is now Merchant Park, where army medics evaluated their wounds. Sadly, many of these brave young men died on the lawn. Dumfries residents say there have been occasional sightings of apparitional soldiers walking through the park at night.

According to museum workers, a young girl visited the Weems-Botts house in 1997, saw a postcard of a Civil War soldier, and told her mother, "This is exactly what he looked like." She explained that she had seen such a man in uniform walking in the park. Museum workers checked. There were no known reenactments scheduled that day.

## A Village Full of Spectral Visions

A pleasant air of romantic intrigue seems to envelop the quaint town of Occoquan, which lies just off Interstate 95 near Dale City, a few miles south of Alexandria. Occoquan is an Indian word meaning "at the end of the water," and it is believed that the Dogue Indians chose this site for their home centuries ago because the nearby Potomac River offered plentiful fish and ease of travel. Early settlers liked it for the same reasons and a tobacco warehouse was built here as early as 1736. Over the next few years there was a mini-industrial boom in this area, which included the erection of an iron furnace, a forge, two sawmills, and one of the nation's first gristmills.

By 1828, Occoquan boasted one of the first cotton mills in Virginia, and within a few years had added several mercantile stores and various mechanics. Farmers and traders came from as far away as the Blue Ridge Mountains. Even after silt filled the river and large vessels could no longer reach the mills, Occoquan still seemed to thrive, in part due to its convenient location along major travel routes, and partly because of the warmth and charm of its residents and merchants, a charm that survives to this day.

Today, the town is a shopper's paradise, with a rich assortment of more than 120 shops, boutiques, artists' cooperatives, restaurants, and distinctive inns. There still are a number of old houses and buildings here that have survived the ravages of time and nature. Also surviving, and quite active today, are a host of ghosts from Occoquan's past—so many, in fact, that it almost seems there is a haunt of one kind or another in just about every other building. "Each spirit," reads a local brochure, "is authenticated by local legend and town gossip. We invite you to enjoy these stories."

Ed and Valerie Miller, owners and operators of Miller's Lighthouse, a shop of nautical gifts and DVDs, tell of the mischievous spectral man who likes to "play tricks" at times. "I never really believed in ghosts until these things started happening, but now I do," Ed says.

What things? "Oh, we've had things missing, all of a sudden turn up right under our noses. I can't explain how they got there or who put them there. They weren't there five minutes ago when I looked, and suddenly they're there! Sometimes the spirit plays around with the videotapes. We were making some copies one day when there was a sudden burst of music, and Valerie stomped her feet and told 'it' to stop fooling around. Just at that precise instant every music box in the store began to play. It was pretty eerie.

"The other thing it does," Ed continued, "is with the dolls. We have some Amish dolls. They're about two feet high. Every once in a while, when we place two of them together, like a boy and a girl, the ghost flings them apart, just throws them out on the floor or across the room. They really fly." Valerie adds that sometimes they find sooty footprints leading around their shop when they open it in the morning. The prints are generally found in the part of the building that originally was a coal bin when the structure was built, about 1888. Other times they find locked display cases opened and in disarray. Nothing is missing, but it appears "someone" had been having a good time.

A couple of doors down from Miller's Lighthouse is an unusual shop called Ebashae, which sells American fine crafts such as functional pottery, jewelry, wind chimes, and watercolors. Both here and in the adjacent Undertaking Artists' Co-op, persistent mysterious footsteps have been heard over the years, though the source has never been found. "We've had other things happen, too," says Annette Riley, store manager. "We've had pottery fall off the shelf when there were no trains or trucks going by and absolutely no wind or anything.

"This used to be a funeral home and they had a bad flood here once and it smashed through the storefront and some of the coffins were washed down into the river. Maybe that adds to the atmosphere of the place. We did have a young man who worked for us a few years ago and it was his grandfather who was the undertaker. He said he heard footsteps going up the stairs one night and he went up to look and saw a man in dress trousers and a long coat. He was certain that it was his long-dead grandfather. Maybe he comes back to check on things."

A little further down Mill Street is the Country Shop, which features quilting supplies, calico, smocking, and handicrafts. According to a publication of the Occoquan Merchants' Association, the spirit of an elderly woman keeps "an eye on things" here today. From a preferred seat in a corner, she allegedly checks out the customers at the antique counter, and also monitors the outside scene through "her" window. "This lady," notes the pamphlet, "has a reputation for shooing the children off her pavement, and she can still be seen shaking a finger at passersby."

"Yes, that fits the pattern," confirms Susan Lehto, manager of the Country Shop. Apparently, the woman has stood such guard for generations. "We think it is a lady who lived here years ago. There was such a person who would run to the door with a broom and chase children on roller skates away from the sidewalk. A lot of people who have lived in town for a long time have told us about her," Susan adds. "Some years ago there was a convention of psychics here and several of them came into the store. Every one of them said they definitely felt a strong presence."

Down the block, at Waterfront Antiques, owner Sandy Higham recalls one eventful winter afternoon when she heard the "clatter of footsteps" on the stairs to the front door before the door opened. This was strange, because she was standing in front of the shop and there was no one inside. She went in and searched and saw no one, but found a single rose lying on the staircase. She has never discovered an explanation for that or for repeated occurrences of merchandise being moved about by unseen hands, or the appearance of more flowers.

A candle that lighted itself has been the only sign of the supernatural at the Serendipity Gift Shop at 307 Mill Street. There, the owner opened up one winter morning to find a freshly lighted candle on her front counter. She asked all the workers if they had lit the candle, but no one had been in the shop since the evening before.

Perhaps the most prolific hauntings in town occur at the historic Occuquan Inn, at 301 Mill Street. There have been, for example, numerous sightings of the apparition of a tall Indian with long black hair and a dignified face. He has been seen in the smoke from a drafty chimney, inside the restaurant, and in the mirror in the upstairs "necessary." Yet when startled viewers turn around, the image disappears.

Chuck Miller and Theresa Owen run "Down Under" at the Inn, a pub-like tavern in the bottom of the building. Chuck says he has not seen the Indian, but when he was first asked to comment on psychic phenomena he said, "I've got stories you won't believe." Chuck and Theresa say they have a gentleman ghost with a puckish sense of humor. "He likes to play all kinds of games," Chuck says. "Sometimes we find the door of the ladies' bathroom locked from the inside. We unlock it and 'he' locks it again and again. Customers coming out of the men's room tell us something keeps turning on the water faucets as they leave. Other times the ghost plays around with things, like our cash register. He likes to take the quarters and dimes and stack them all up in neat rows. I can't explain how it happens, but it does."

Occasionally, Chuck and Theresa both have felt "his" presence. "We'll be sitting in the bar late at night when everyone has gone home, and we'll feel a freezing cold spell. It makes all the hair stand up on your body," Chuck notes. "He seems to linger a while and then he moves on and the chill is over." Chuck thinks it may be the spirit of a gentleman who lived upstairs long ago in a part of the building that is more than a hundred years old. "The ghost is not mean, but every once in a while it seems like he picks on a certain customer. One evening we had a group of gentlemen at the tavern, and one of them was playing a game. There was one piece missing from the game and the man was looking around for it. All of a sudden the piece came flying across the room right at him, like somebody had thrown it at him. He wasn't hurt, but it sure unnerved him."

And so it goes in this picturesque little village. No one knows for sure just when and where one or another of the multiple spirits of Occoquan will flair up, but there does appear to be a whole flock of them here, and they seem to thoroughly enjoy themselves.

# The Haunted Rail Car

In 1907 a book was published titled *Jack Thorne, Newspaper Correspondent and Story Teller.* It was a collection of Thorne's articles over the years, one of which included a true ghost account headlined "Egypt's Ghost." Egypt was the name of a Pullman sleeper rail car that ran between Union Station in Washington, D.C., and northern Virginia. The article is presented here, excerpted from the online edition courtesy of the University of North Carolina at Chapel Hill.

The narrator Thorne interviewed was a Pullman porter who was not identified.

"One evening in the autumn of 1889 I was ordered to take a load of passengers in car Egypt, an old 'sleeper' which for many years had only been used mainly for special service. But scarcity of cars had necessitated the pressing of this car in as an extra. One entire section—section thirteen—was empty. As I went on my rounds, making beds, I prepared number thirteen for a chance get-on along the road, but we passed the principal stations without a call for a bed in any car in the train.

"Late at night is the time when he, the porter, weary and exhausted from the irksome labor of bed making, falls into a wakeful slumber. I stretched myself out upon the lounge that I might enjoy this restless sleep when instantly there came a long and vigorous ring of the bell. I arose and scanned the indicator. The arrow pointed to thirteen, the vacant section. As indicators often register wrong, I walked up and down the aisle to see if there might not be a head protruding from between the curtains of some berth, but saw none. Passengers often make mistakes and go into the wrong berths. I looked in section thirteen. It was empty. I returned to the smoking room and stretched out again. The train stopped and this aroused me a second time.

"I arose and started forward to learn the cause of the stop, and just as I turned into the aisle, I saw a woman in her night robe right in front of section thirteen. Her back was towards me, and she was bent over as though in search of something upon the floor. I hastened toward her, sure she was a passenger from the car ahead, having lost her bearings, but before I could get into speaking distance of her she disappeared around the corner. The car next to mine was in charge of Sammy Boldes. Entering his car, I found him sitting at the end of the aisle blacking shoes.

"'Sam,' said I, 'why do you allow your passengers to go blundering around to find themselves going to bed in another car?' 'What passengers?' he asked. 'There are no women in my car,' I said, 'yet one was standing in the aisle just now and she came this way. Didn't you see her?' 'No, there are only two women in this car and they are both asleep there in section two. Where did the woman go? I guess you've been dreaming,' said Sam. 'You'd better go back and get to blacking up.'

"I returned to my car, searched it from end to end in every nook and corner of unoccupied space before settling down to shoe polishing. The train started up. My mind had become so perturbed over this now apparently mysterious episode that sleep had entirely forsaken me. I sat down by the window and began to meditate upon the possible truthfulness of Sam's assertion that I had been dreaming. It seemed now that I had.

"'I rang, porter,' said a soft voice, and turning my head quickly, I beheld the woman in the night robe standing in the door of the smoking room. She was running her fingers nervously through her black hair, which hung loosely down her back, and was staring over my head out the window. A damp, sickening odor filled the room, and the pale face and hollow eyes of my visitor made it seem that I was in a tomb in the presence of a resurrected corpse!

"'What can I do for you, Madame?' I stammered, attempting to rise. She fixed her gaze upon me and the look of horror in her hollow eyes riveted me to the spot. With a voice that sounded like someone far away in the dead of night, she said, 'My husband is dead. They told me he had gone on ahead of us, but he had not. He was asleep in section thirteen when the crash came. Come, help me search.' Beckoning eagerly to me to follow her, she disappeared. I arose to comply, but my limbs refused to support me, and I fell in a swoon upon the floor.

"When I came to myself, I lay upon a cot in a large, plain, white, high ceiling room. I was in a hospital. A nurse said I had been brought there two weeks ago, raving with brain fever. A few months afterward, not having fully recovered from the effects of that terrible illness, I sat waiting my turn in a barbershop, among a few other railroad men. One was Sammy Boldes. He said, 'When a man's fever is so high that he sees ghosts, his place is at home in his bed. When we got back there I answered to the summons of the frightened brakeman, you were raising Sam Henry about a woman in section 13.'

"'What car did he have?' asked a man in the barber chair. 'Old car Egypt,' said Sam. 'And the woman was no fancy," I persisted. 'I saw her!' The man in the chair spoke up again. 'There's something wrong about that old car. I've never seen anything while in her, but I heard some mighty queer noises, so much so that I left her one night while laying over and went to town to sleep.'

"Porter Cumming, a veteran in the service, sitting beside me, raised his eyes from his paper and listened intently to the conversation concerning the old car, but said nothing. 'There's a kind of sickening feeling that I can't explain which came over me when I had that old car,' said the man in the chair. 'I felt it mostly when trying to sleep in the smoking room, and to tell the truth, gentlemen, I believe it's haunted!'

"As I left the barbershop and started toward home, porter Cumming joined me. 'Your talk this morning about old car Egypt recalled to my mind a very thrilling experience of mine in connection with its history,' said he. 'That car is haunted, and I know it! But I have said but little about it to anyone for fear of being ridiculed and looked upon as loony. I see that you have been ill and it was brain fever.' 'But I was perfectly rational as regards the woman,' I said, 'regardless of the state of my mind afterwards.' 'What did you see?' he asked. I related my experience as minutely as I could remember it.

"Porter Cumming then said, 'In the spring of 1885, I was running regularly to Washington. One morning as I went to the office to report, I was told that I, with three other men, had been selected to make a special trip to Los Angeles with a bridal party. That party was to leave that evening, proceeding from the church to the train. It consisted of the bridal pair, the family physician, four lady friends, and a man and maid servant. At our disposal, we had two cars, a hotel and observation car and a sleeper, which of course was car Egypt. We were to go direct to Los Angeles and remain there about three weeks, from thence we were to journey southward into Mexico and make our way homeward by way of New Orleans.

"'It was indeed,' porter Cumming continued, 'a first-class party of rich and cultured people. The bride, a tall and handsome brunette, was the life of the party, enslaving us all by her vivacity and sweetness of disposition. She entered into everything that meant for making the trip one of pleasure and recreation.

"'One evening, just eight weeks after leaving, we pulled out of New Orleans, homeward bound. All other trains had been ordered to give up the right of way and we thundered up the road at a rate of fifty miles an hour. A few miles south of Birmingham, Alabama, a freight train, having sidetracked, had failed to throw the switch, and our train rushed into the siding and was wrecked, killing the engineer, severely scalding the fireman, and crushing the bridegroom and the manservant beyond recognition.

"'These two slept opposite the bride, who, with others of the party, escaped with slight bruises. Old car Egypt, in which they all slept, seemed to have gotten the fullest force of the blow. It was a pitiful and awful sight to see that young woman, the bride, pulling her hair in the agony of her grief as she followed us about in our search for the missing men, and when the truth was revealed to her, she went completely mad then and there.

"'She would wail softly, "Oh, Frank, don't sleep in that berth [thirteen]. I'm superstitious. Come, Frank, it's time to get up. I wonder how long it will be before we get home. I'm tired of this wearisome journey." And then she would burst into hysterical laughing and weeping. I will never forget that scene as long as I live. About six months after that I met the lady's maid and she told me that her mistress never recovered, but died a raving maniac in a private asylum in less than two months after reaching home. The two rail cars were completely overhauled and made more inviting inside and out.

"'One night at least a year afterwards, car Egypt was assigned to me for a trip. Sitting down at the window to enjoy a smoke after my passengers had retired, I could hear that wretched woman's wails and sobs just as plainly as I heard her on that night. I was so frightened that I started to go board the car ahead of me, but just as I got into the aisle, I saw just what you saw in front of section thirteen. It was that very woman with her head bent forward precisely as you described her. I turned about, went back and stood in the door until the train reached Washington. And you bet life, I was too sick to go out when the time came for me to come back.

"'That woman's ghost will follow that car as long as it exists, and the only way to lay it is to burn car Egypt!'"

## Psychic Energy at Arlington National

If ever a place was destined to be haunted, one would think it well could be Arlington National Cemetery in northern Virginia. Here is the site of the magnificent Arlington House, built by the step-grandson of

George Washington, and later the home of Robert E. Lee before the mansion was confiscated from the Lee family during the Civil War.

Here are the gravesites of John and Robert Kennedy.

Here are the tombs of the unknown soldiers of World Wars I and II and the Korean War.

Here lies buried U.S. president William Howard Taft; astronauts Gus Grissom and Roger Chaffee, who perished in the terrible spacecraft fire in 1967; Robert Todd Lincoln, the son of Abraham Lincoln; and Union general Philip Sheridan.

Here also lie the bodies of nearly fifty thousand other heroic veterans who served in the Revolutionary War, the War of 1812, the Indian campaigns, the Spanish American War, World Wars I and II, the Korean War, and Vietnam. South of the Lee mansion a massive granite sarcophagus surmounts a vault containing the remains of more than two thousand "unknowns" of the Civil War, recovered from the battlefields of Bull Run and the route to the Rappahannock.

And here is the mast of the USS *Maine*, which by act of Congress in 1910 was removed from the wreck of the ship after it was raised from Havana harbor. The mast was brought to Arlington to honor those who lost their lives in that historic disaster.

History seems to ebb and flow from every direction at this sacred site. At the mansion itself, in 1831, Mary Ann Randolph Custis married a young lieutenant named Robert Edward Lee. The grave of Pierre Charles L'Enfant, the architect of Washington, lies in front of the mansion overlooking the city that he planned.

The Confederate monument, erected in 1914, is a bronze and granite structure surmounted by the figure of a woman crowned with olive leaves, her face turned towards the south. A laurel wreath in her outstretched left hand symbolizes the crowning of the South's fallen sons; her right hand rests on a plowshare on which there is a pruning hook. Carved around the top of the memorial is the verse from Isaiah: "They shall beat their swords into plowshares and their spears into pruning hooks."

Amidst the graves of such a multitude, many tragically struck down in the primes of their lives in the service of their country, one might naturally suspect their ghosts could run rampant here, especially since most spirits are believed to be the disembodied entities of persons killed traumatically. Certainly, many if not most of those buried here would thus qualify. But such is not the case. There are, curiously, only a few reports of psychic phenomena.

Here is the Memorial Amphitheatre, a large open auditorium of white marble, designed by Carrere and Hastings after the theater of Dionysus at Athens, Greece, and the Roman theater at Orange, France. It seats several thousand. It is here, each year on Memorial Day, that the sitting President of the United States carries a wreath to place at the base of the first Tomb of the Unknown Soldier from World War I, which was dedicated in 1931. The identity of the soldier buried here is "known but to God."

There is a long-standing and intriguing tradition about this tomb. It is said that one of the soldiers who went to Europe to fight in that war was a young man with blond hair from the Midwest. It is also said that when he was a boy, yellow butterflies would accompany him wherever he went, flying about his head. The young man was killed in action. After the tomb was dedicated at Arlington, visitors often commented about the yellow butterflies that flitted around the memorial each summer.

One might assume, too, that if anyone here had just cause to return in spectral form it might well be John Fitzgerald Kennedy, killed by an assassin's bullets in 1963. But there is only one instance of inexplicable phenomena associated with the Kennedys here, involving not the late president, but his brother, Robert. It was reported by authors Brad Steiger and Sherry Handen in their 1990 book, *Hollywood and the Supernatural,* published by St. Martin's Press. They wrote that at the conclusion of the funeral services for the slain senator, in June 1968, "mourner Bobby Darin felt compelled to remain at the grave. The popular singer was a great fan of the Kennedys and was overcome with grief at Bobby's premature death. At 12:45 P.M., Darin was suddenly enveloped by a brilliant light, which formed a ball of energy that passed right through him. Darin felt an emotional cleansing that profoundly altered his life. He was convinced Kennedy's spirit was reaching out to him."

Over the years, many psychics have visited Arlington National Cemetery and reported sensing strong swirls of paranormal activity. According to Joseph Frank's book *Sacred Sites: A Guidebook to Sacred*

*Centers,* psychics have told of a "powerful energy vortex" on the grassy hill between the Tomb of the Unknown Soldier and the Nurses' Memorial. "The strongest spot is an open area on the southeast slope of the hill, between the evergreen trees and the tombstones . . . The ethereal energy is said to recharge one spiritually and physically."

# The Haunted Stone House

Of all the sites across Manassas National Battlefield Park in northern Virginia, certainly one of the most haunted is an old structure known as the Stone House. Here, of course, two great battles of the Civil War were fought at Bull Run. This house is one of only two original buildings still on the grounds. It is believed to have been built in 1828, and it served as a tavern at the crossroads for the cattlemen and wagon teamsters coming down the Warrenton Pike from the west with supplies for Alexandria and Washington.

According to a National Park Service brochure, the Stone House, even in its heyday, was "never a fancy hotel noted for fine food. The place sold hard liquor to hard men. Its success was short-lived, however, as railroads in the 1850s replaced wagons as the principal means of transportation. As the turnpike era ended, the house and its owners seemed to slip into obscurity. But it was not to be. Twice, the determined armies of a divided nation would clash on the fields near Bull Run. Both times, Stone House would be brought into the mainstream of battle, its significance marked in blood. In this house and others like it, many soldiers' dreams of heroism and valor were forgotten in the nightmare of pain and agony experienced within its walls."

Nearly twenty thousand men fell during the Second Battle of Manassas. Surgeons worked around the clock, but haste and neglect were unavoidable. Many suffered for days on the field without any attention. The utter horror of this situation was graphically recorded in official war documents. Consider the following testimony of Dr. J. M. Homiston, surgeon of the Brooklyn regiment captured at Bull Run. He said that when he "solicited permission to remain in the field and to attend to wounded men, some of whom were in a helpless and painful condition, and suffering for water," he was brutally refused. Homiston described the sufferings of the wounded as "inconceivably horrible, with bad food, no covering and no water. They were lying upon the floor as thickly as they could be laid. There was not a particle of light in the house to enable us to move among them." Homiston added that the dead lay upon the field unburied for several days after the battle.

Even more revolting was the reported desecration of the bodies. One man, searching for his dead brother, said, "We found no head in the grave, and no bones of any kind—nothing but the clothes and portions of the flesh." Mrs. Pierce Butler, who lived nearby, said that she had seen the rebels boiling portions of the bodies of the dead in order to obtain their bones as relics. She also saw "drumsticks" made of Yankee shinbones, and a human skull that one of the New Orleans artillery had, which, he said, he was going to send home and have mounted, and which he intended to drink a brandy punch out of one day.

Is it any wonder then, that Jim Burgess, curator of the national battlefield park, after saying a number of soldiers undoubtedly died in the Stone House, added, "it has every right to be haunted." Burgess related that the haunting aura about the house was first documented in the book *Four Brothers in Blue,* by Robert Goldthwaite Carter. A chapter in the book is devoted to the author's visit to the battlefield in the early 1900s. During his visit he stayed at the Stone House as a guest of the owner, Henry Ayres.

Carter wrote, "We remained here all night. This house is frequently referred to in *The Surreys of Eagle's Nest,* by John Esten Cooke as 'The Old Stone House of Manassas,' and again as 'The Haunted House' . . . Mr. Starbuck lived in the house since the war, and Mr. Pridmore after him. Mr. Ayres' daughter stated that Starbuck put a curse on the house and on Pridmore's family. Certain it is that out of the Pridmore family six or more died in quick succession, and she thinks the house rightfully bears the name of the 'Haunted House.'"

Burgess admits that several curious incidents in recent years lend support to Miss Ayres' claims. One was reported in the 1970s. "A park ranger and a volunteer were closing up the house one day," recounts Burgess. "It was after 5 P.M., late in the season, and it was getting dark. The normal procedure is to bolt the doors from the inside, set the alarm, and then go out by way of the basement. This they did, but as they were about to exit, they both heard distinct footsteps in the room above. The steps went from the big tavern room into the hallway and then into a smaller room. Thinking they somehow must have missed a lingering visitor, they both went back upstairs to look. Now, there are virtually no places to hide. There are no closets for example. They looked everywhere but found no one. At that point they got very nervous and left the place abruptly."

More recently, according to Burgess, a seasonal park ranger was on duty alone in the house on a slow summer afternoon. This employee began to nod off to sleep while reading a book as he sat just inside the front door. Suddenly, "someone or something" knocked his glasses off and he was jarred wide awake. He checked all around the house but soon discovered he was still alone.

A few years ago, when the Stone House had period furnishings, Park Service administrative officer Jane Becker, a camera bug, went to take some photos of the interior rooms after the house had closed to the public for the day. She was alone. She used a 35mm camera. When the color photos were developed, all came out well except one picture that totally puzzled her. On this single print was a large, "fuzzy white blotch" that ran across the center of the photo from top to bottom. Part of the blotch was thick, like a dense cloud, obliterating the furniture beyond it. Yet part of the wispy material was partially transparent. Becker looked at her negatives. All were fine, except this one.

She consulted photographic experts. No one could explain the phenomenon. There was, everyone agreed, no rational cause for the apparitional appearance. She keeps a copy of the photo on her desk. She has labeled it "The Stone House Ghost."

Burgess says another curious incident occurred in November 1994. "A ranger was conducting a tour of the area near the Stone House for a group of about fifteen people. At about 10:45 A.M., as the ranger was explaining the capture of a Union battery, he was interrupted by a disturbance behind him. He turned to look, but saw only leaves swirling up a short distance behind him. He didn't think much about it and continued on with his talk. Later, when the tour was over, some members of the group approached him and asked if he believed in ghosts. When he asked them why, they said they not only saw the leaves being 'kicked up' to his rear, but it also appeared that the grass was being depressed as if some unseen presence was walking swiftly across the field. Considering the lack of any wind that day," Burgess adds, "a supernatural explanation seemed to be the only other possibility."

## The Vanishing House!

In January 1986, I received the following letter from Kathleen Luisa, who then lived in Falls Church, Virginia.

"I have traveled down Route 29 through Manassas and on westward many, many times. I love the battlefields and the Stone House has been a favorite landmark for me at the intersection of 29 and Sudley Road. Many times as I waited for the traffic light there, I gazed at the house and wondered about its stories if it could talk.

"One night in 1986, I suggested we all go for a drive out to the battlefield to see if we could see Halley's Comet. My mom, her mother and father, and I got in the car and set out. As we approached the intersection I was looking in the darkness for my landmark, the Stone House, so I could make the turn onto Sudley Road and into the little parking area. I drove right through the intersection.

"There was no house!

"Puzzled, I turned around and went back. We got back to the intersection and sat at the light looking aghast at the empty lot where the Stone House should have stood. The rise of land was empty except that the well or cistern that stands in front and the fences were still there. We were very upset, figuring some land development scheme had led to its being torn down, or maybe there was some move by the Park Service to relocate it. As we drove by looking at this, I do not remember seeing any foundation walls, hole in the ground, or signs of rubble. Just an empty lot and the well. Finally, we left, shaking our heads sadly.

"Imagine my utter shock when, two weeks later, we drove down 29 during the day, dreading the spot where my 'old friend' used to stand—and the house was there! We sat at the light staring with our mouths open. I immediately asked my mom and grandparents to verify that they really had seen a vacant lot that night. They all swore they had. I know we were not at the wrong location. I know the area too well for that."

In November 1997, I got another letter, this one from Beverly Kish of Merrifield, Virginia.

"I experienced a ghostly encounter of sorts in January 1997, but I didn't know about it until I read about the lady who said she drove by the location of the Stone House and the house had disappeared.

"The same thing happened to me!

"I was living in Manassas at the time and wanted to take a drive one night. It was clear with a moon out. It wasn't pitch dark. I was alone. Having lived in the area twenty years, I know exactly where the Stone House is. In fact, I took a tour there a couple of years ago, yet on this night it was gone! I even turned the car around and said to myself, 'that's funny, I'm at the right intersection,' and all I saw was a patch of grass with the glow of the moon on it where the house had been.

"And you can't miss this house. It's close to the road. So I can personally vouch for what the other woman saw—or rather, for what she didn't see."

## The Ghost of the Airline Pilot

The following singular experience was published anonymously on the Internet in May 2007.

"I was a long haul trucker for many years," the narrator says. "In December 2004, I had a delivery at Winchester, Virginia. I was delayed and didn't get unloaded until after 2 A.M. I left Winchester heading east on Highway 7. Around 2:30, I came to the intersection of 7 and Route 601, near Bluemont, about halfway between Berryville and Leesburg. I pulled in at a closed gas station to check my map. There was virtually no traffic going by at that hour. It was a cold, moonless night.

"While I was sitting there, someone knocked on my door, startling me. I jumped, and turned off my interior light so I could see outside, then I rolled down my window. A man was standing there. He was wearing an airline flight uniform. He had four stripes on his shoulder epaulets, indicating he was a captain. He didn't have on a jacket, and it was a very chilly morning. He climbed up on the side of the cab. He smelled like he had bathed in kerosene. When he got close to my face, I cold see that his cap had a TWA insignia on it.

"'Could you give me a lift?' he asked in a raspy voice. I was really taken off guard. It was odd. Here I was, in a dark, rural area on a freezing night, being asked by an airline pilot wearing only a short-sleeved shirt, for a ride. I asked him where he was headed. 'I am with TWA,' he said. 'I have to get to Dulles Airport to work a flight. Please give me a ride. I'll pay you.' 'Well, how about I give you a ride to the next open store where you can call a taxi?' I managed to say. 'Okay, thank you,' he mumbled. Then he added, 'he said we could descend.' I didn't know what he was talking about, but I didn't want the guy to freeze out there. 'Go around and hop in,' I said.

"He climbed down and shuffled around the front of the truck. When he passed the first headlight, I was struck by the fact that he seemed to have long sideburns, like Elvis. Then, he suddenly and totally vanished! I don't mean he faded away. He just ceased to exist! I jumped down out of the truck and looked all around with a flash-light, even under the truck. He was gone! As I continued on down the road, I remembered something curious. TWA had gone out of busi-ness over two years ago. What was going on? I was totally perplexed and shaken by the experience.

"When I got home I did some online research. What I found turned my beliefs upside down. I've always thought that ghost sto-ries were hokum, but with what I learned, I'm no longer sure. It turns out that on December 1, 1974, a Boeing 727—flight 514—descended prematurely through a low cloud deck and slammed into a rocky out-cropping on Mt. Weather, Virginia. The aircraft disintegrated, with all ninety-two people on board killed! The flight had originated in Columbus, Ohio, and was supposed to land at Washington National Airport. It was diverted to Dulles because high winds had closed National.

"According to cockpit voice and flight data recordings, the crew mistakenly believed that air traffic controllers had cleared them to descend to 1,800 feet. This error, combined with strong wind down-drafts, caused the plane to hit the mountain at 1,670 feet. At the last second, they apparently broke out of the overcast only to see the rock- and snow-covered mountain looming on their windscreen. The cap-tain's last words to his co-pilot were, 'Get some power on!' seconds before the recording abruptly ceased.

"The site of impact was less than a mile south of where I encoun-tered whoever or whatever it was that I saw almost exactly thirty years later. I don't want to definitively say it was a ghost, but the fact remains that there was someone who appeared to be an airplane pilot, with a very dated hairstyle, wearing a uniform of a defunct airline. I am no longer a trucker, but this has troubled me ever since it happened."

# The Shenandoah Valley

# The Phantom Master of Abram's Delight

Abraham Hollingsworth must have been quite a character. A Quaker, he came to Winchester early in the eighteenth century and found a beautiful site occupied by Shawnee Indians on rich land beside a good spring. He was so impressed he acquired hundreds of acres there and called the area "a delight to behold." He then moved his family to Virginia from Cecil County, Maryland.

Although Abraham never lived in the impressive stone house that is now the historic showpiece of Winchester, his ghost has been a familiar haunt there for the past two hundred-plus years. The house is called Abram's Delight and today is open to the public as a museum, restored and furnished in the style of the period by the Winchester-Frederick County Historical Society. The Virginia Landmarks Register notes that the house was built in 1754 by Abraham's son, Isaac, and calls it "an austere dwelling." Built of native limestone, with walls two-and-a-half feet thick, the house has three stories if one counts the basement, which today includes a gift shop. The house fell into disrepair during the Civil War when Winchester changed hands between the Union and Confederate forces a number of times. Much of the land's timber was lost, livestock was appropriated, and the farm was left untended.

Just how long old Abraham Hollingsworth has roamed through the hallways and out the side door to the garden is not exactly known, although there have been reports of his haunting presence dating back generations. And, in fact, he may be joined by one or more other spirits. Marguerite DuPont Lee, in her 1930 book *Virginia Ghosts,* told of one of Abraham's female descendants who often played the piano in the house and sang hymns. Miss Hollingsworth said there were times when a woman's voice, "a voice from another sphere of existence," joined in as she sang. At other times residents of Abram's Delight told of hearing laughter and music, "as though a party of young people were making merry." These sounds were always heard when there was no one else in the place.

Throughout the years the most prominent specter at Abram's Delight has been Abraham himself. He has been seen, heard, and felt in the house for generations. Historical interpreters who lead visitors on tours say a large number of tourists and employees have seen his apparition both inside the building and outside in the garden.

The most common manifestation is Abraham's appearance at the top of the stairs on the third floor. He descends the stairs and goes out a side door leading to the garden. He walks across the lawn and vanishes. Author Lee wrote, "So familiar is this apparition that work-men, seeing the ghost, would lean on their shovels and watch for its reappearing. They were never disappointed." Indeed, the interpreters say the vision is still seen, and has been witnessed by laborers who eat lunch in the garden. One tour guide told of a school group that was touring the house one day. They later assembled in the garden. One boy said he had seen a ghost—a tall man dressed in black wearing a broad-brimmed Quaker hat, standing behind a bush.

It appears that Abraham remains in the house to keep an eye on it, to see that it is being kept up properly. And when he doesn't like something or someone, he lets people know he is not pleased. A good example of this occurred a few years ago when a ceremonial signing was to take place in the house. The mayor and board of supervisors came to Abram's Delight to participate. The signing was to take place in a third-floor room, but when the officials tried to enter, the door wouldn't open. Hard as they tried, it wouldn't budge. Workmen were summoned. It took four men to wedge the door open. Inside, they found that a heavy file cabinet had been shoved up against the door. Since no one had been in the room, the question remains: how did this happen and who did it? Employees said it was Abraham express-ing his displeasure at the intrusion.

Virginia Milner, who serves as manager, has experienced more psychic happenings in the house than anyone else. She lived here for seven years. "I am not a believer in ghosts," she says, "but I have to say there have been a lot of things that have occurred here that I cannot explain." Most of them seem to take place on the third floor. "We've had a number of people here who have said they felt definite presences on this floor," Virginia said. "This happens most often in the hallway. I have heard noises when I was alone there. One time I heard something crash in the attic. I went up and searched, but I couldn't find any cause for the sound. I always kept all the doors closed on that floor in the winter to prevent the heat from escaping. The doors were latched shut, yet I often found them open, and I hadn't opened them and no one else was there."

Virginia also recalls one time when a person, possibly a Hollingsworth descendent, died and was lying in repose in a casket on the third floor. When employees came in one morning they found all the rugs had been "balled up in the hall." How this happened has never been satisfactorily explained. And there have been other strange incidents. Virginia was particularly upset when she found a valuable vase lying on its side on a chest one day. "It could easily have fallen to the floor and been broken," she says. But when she questioned employees no one knew anything about it. Another time, she found one of the Hollingsworth's Quaker hats on the floor. No mortal had touched it. Tour guides say they often come into the room where the hat is placed on a dresser and find it has moved from where it should be. "We also have a lovely old piano in the house," Virginia adds. "Sometimes you can hear it being played when no one is there."

Although Virginia says she has never seen a ghost in the house and doesn't believe in them, she admits she can't explain why her pet dog, a schnauzer, was so upset at Abram's Delight. "He would never go upstairs to the third floor," she says. "Once a grandchild of mine picked him up and took him upstairs. He wiggled loose and raced down the stairs and then just stared upward like he could see something no one else could." Virginia also tells of a curious happening that transpired early in the twentieth century. At that time a young man, a Mr. Graham, worked here when it still was a farm. He used to say that when he went out to bring the cows in, a ghost would appear and "wave them away."

There are many questions left unanswered at this quaint old stone house. Is the ghost actually Abraham Hollingsworth? If so, why does he reappear since he never lived at his "Delight"? And why does whatever presence or presences that exist here seemingly express his or her occasional displeasure by rearranging furniture, blocking doors, moving a hat, and walking from the third-floor landing down the stairs, out the side door and into the garden? Is Abraham letting today's living mortals know that he is still in charge of the house that bears his name? Most of the people who work here believe this is so.

# A Spectral Reconciliation

The following is an unusually well-documented account of one of the strangest and most compelling cases of rare psychic phenomena in America on record. It began in the middle of the eighteenth century, a time when many Europeans came to the United States to escape religious persecution. Once here, however, it did not necessarily mean that they had reached satisfaction. Consequently some sects, in disagreement with mainstream churches, splintered off on their own. One of the most unusual of these was a group of German mystics who became known as Dunkards. They settled in a tiny colony called Ephrata, in Pennsylvania.

They lived chiefly upon roots and vegetables, and the single men and women resided in separate quarters. They allowed marriages but considered celibacy a virtue. They led lives of great industry, frugality, and purity and were nonviolent. But even as austere as these practices were, there still were some who were not happy with life at Ephrata. They sought even greater isolation for "the quiet life of esoteric meditation." Thus, these few dissenters sought to settle as far away from civilization as possible. These members migrated south to the remote regions of the Shenandoah Valley in Virginia. Here, they were labeled as recluses and hermits. And here they formed mystical brotherhoods.

They are not to be confused with the great movement of Germans into the valley to farm. This was more a small renegade band of what most described as religious fanatics. Author Klaus Wust, in a 1964 article in the *Virginia Magazine of History and Biography*, wrote: "The valley was still largely a wilderness when the first German mystics sought refuge there to be as far away from all worldly temptation as possible." One of their beliefs, he added, was that the end of world was near, and they wanted absolute isolation to prepare for it.

One of the most charismatic members of the sect at Ephrata was a man named Christopher Beeler. When he was evicted from that community for adultery in 1740, he moved south with his children and built a home near the present town of Berryville. His first wife died a short time later in Pennsylvania. Beeler's second wife, after bearing three children, contracted an illness on the farm in Virginia and died in 1758. He then married for a third time, to woman named Elizabeth, and took her to Berryville.

It was there that the ghostly manifestations began on the night of January 10, 1761. They continued almost every night thereafter for a period of about four weeks. Most of the apparitional appearances were made by Beeler's dead second wife, but on the last night, his first wife, also deceased, materialized as well. That was when they commanded the Beeler family to return to Ephrata and "have a session with the spirits at the twelfth hour of the night." It was then that Elizabeth Beeler told in detail of the ghost visitations, which were subsequently printed in a thirty-nine-page pamphlet in 1761. Following are excerpts from her narrative:

"I, Elizabeth Beeler, in the year 1760, married Christopher Beeler. I am his third helpmate. In this connection an incident occurred of which, since rumors of it have been spread already about the country, I want to render a comprehensive account for the contemplation of posterity. And if there be someone who doubts the truth of the matter and thinks it is an old wives' tale, he ought to go to the trouble of pursuing the matter with the many eyewitnesses. For herein I call upon the testimony of my husband's children, our neighbors, people in Winchester, and many inhabitants of Ephrata where the affair was settled at last.

"On the 10th of January, this 1761st year, in the morning while I was still lying in bed but awake, I suddenly was overcome by a slumber. Then I felt as if my husband was beating me hard which saddened me very much, and I implored him to let me be and promised to move out of the house. When I was about to leave, it seemed to me that the door opened and an old woman came in. I had a good look at her and felt assured within myself that it was my husband's late last wife in which belief others, whom I described her appearance to, supported me afterwards.

"She stepped in front of my husband's sideboard, opened it, and placed so much gold and silver in it as she could hold in one hand; locked it again, placed the key on the table and came toward me. There was a chair nearby on which she put me down. The bruises on my arm where she had touched me while setting me down were visible for several days. Thereupon she said do not go away, but stay here with my husband. 'I am an old woman. I do not like it, and shall go away again. You are the third and rightful wife, and because you are good to my children, I shall reveal everything to you, for you will not be here much longer. Go to the kitchen in the twelfth hour, where you shall find my money behind the pewter sideboard.'

"While she was speaking, the horses passed the window on their way to the pond with such noise that I awoke whereupon the spirit made off. I was convinced that had I not been interrupted, she might have told me everything clearly then and there what she tried to reveal afterward in confused language at different times.

"My husband arrived and wondered about my sleeping unusually long. I revealed the whole affair to him and at the twelfth hour of the day, after having removed everybody else from the house and locked the same, we both went into the kitchen to the indicated spot. My husband pulled the sideboard from the wall and with a stick, I scraped up an old rag that was well held together by means of pins. To our surprise we found a Virginia five pound note in it. When we examined the bill, we discovered that it had not been issued till four weeks after the death of the said woman which made us suspicious of the whole affair. She had died in March and the subsequent month of April was the date printed on the bill. With it was a piece of silver as flat as a button beaten with the hilt of a sword.

"We spent the following day in a state of amazement and did not know what to make of this thing. But it was to be only the beginning of a strange comedy played hereafter for four weeks about which I shall now give a true account as it happened. The next night, toward daybreak, I fell again into a slumber. The ghost soon made herself known again and spoke: 'Go behind the stove to the sideboard in the twelfth hour. There you shall find something for Hanna [a daughter]. When we emptied the sideboard the following day, we found some cambric [a fine white linen fabric] and money hidden in a skein of hemp.

"Otherwise, this incidence affected my human body so severely that I thought I might lose my life. All of a sudden I vomited half a pint of blood and this still went on for 24 hours. Since we did not know what might happen the following night, my husband took it upon himself to guard me, and he sat at my feet. Once midnight had passed and the sun began to approach our horizon, the ghost appeared and spoke: 'Go with me. There are 30 pieces of silver and gold buried at a certain spot. You shall give these to Samuel [a son], when he will be 18 years old. I shall show them to you.'

"I refused to go and I did not want to go. She tore my left shirt sleeve out of the seam at the shoulder as if it has been severed, and threw it on the floor at my husband's feet. He saw it lie in front of him and thought it was the ghost and when he kicked it with his foot it moved by itself. Then he called for his son to bring in a light. Now both of them took up the guard, my stepson at my head, my husband at my feet. But before they realized it, the ghost was there. The air in the room stirred as if moved by a gentle breeze. The light began to quiver as if it would go out. All of a sudden she [the ghost] reached from under my stepson, seized the sleeve of my other arm on which I was lying, tore it out, too, and threw it into my stepson's lap.

"As I continue to relate this, I must ask the esteemed reader to imagine how it felt being treated so roughly. When my husband saw this he said to me, 'There is nothing else we can do. You must go along lest the ghost kills you. We shall go with you and risk our lives as well.' We had deep snow and since we did not know whither the ghost would lead us, we put enough clothes on. I took a shovel and knife for digging. No sooner were we ready than the ghost appeared. She walked ahead of us.

"I could see her distinctly as a shadow on the snow. She led us into the milk house. We moved some wood out of the way and I began to scratch on the ground and uncovered a board under which stood a small calabash [gourd]. I picked it up and noticed a little hole on its top that had been stoppered with a chunk of salt. But I was ordered to keep it intact and thus did not open it, but put it aside, sealed as it was.

"Now I began to get accustomed to this business because it went on all night and at times into a good part of the day. She returned the following night and I was spellbound by her as if I were dead. Then she spoke—through me! It was somewhat indistinctly, but in a manner that everybody could hear and understand: 'Go to the sideboard behind the stove where you shall find three yards of cambric and 30 shillings of money for my daughter, Hanna.'

"When I came to, I wrote it all down for my memory's sake which had been weakened very much by the procedure. The latter we found already. Thereupon we searched once more through the said sideboard and opening up the hemp we found another skein that contained both cloth and money. After we had discovered this much, curiosity drove us to check also the calabash. Upon opening it we found nothing of the 30 pieces of money save six copper pence so new as if they had just left the mint. With them was a brass ring. The children of the deceased woman said that she had owned a golden one just like it.

"The affair was getting familiar to me at long last, and the neighbors knew all that happened at our place. Hardly a night passed during which she did not make herself known, but she would never appear without first dulling my senses through slumber. My husband, having most reason to hush up the affair had there been fraud involved, since much of it concerned him personally, finally exhausted his patience. He tried by every means to prevent me from slumbering in order to bar the ghost's access to me. Yet all his efforts were futile because before he was aware of it, I passed out as if dead and all persons present heard me speak, not in my usual manner, but imperfectly, crudely, and somewhat indistinctly. Yet everyone could understand it.

"I want to tell of another strange happening which will show clearly to everyone that the ghost uncovered unknown things. Once, the ghost wandered into a house with me in which money and sundry household items were lying around such as cloth, linen, etc. There were also people dividing it all up among themselves. However, the ghost flew amidst the things in the shape of a dove and exclaimed: 'Oh, injustice! Injustice!' Thereupon, when I came to, I recounted this just while the deceased woman's daughters were with my husband. One of them turned pale and spoke: 'Now I shall not conceal it any longer. These things did happen in our house at one time because we did distribute secretly many things our late mother had left us unbeknownst to our stepfather.'

## Poltergeist Activity

"At last," Elizabeth Beeler writes, "she (the ghost) was no longer afraid to make herself known during daytime. Once, she seized the ribbon with which my husband had tied his hair, pulled it off the hair, and threw it on the floor. Knocking sounds and all kinds of things flung to the floor now were nothing new to us anymore. Once, she took the tea service and cast it into the middle of the room. Strange it was only that everything broke except what the deceased woman had used for serving her husband when she was living. Another time, the books, one by one, came flying off the shelves onto the floor.

"One day I put on a shirt and other clothing and sat down on a chair. It was not to the ghost's liking. She wanted me to go away. My husband, who was watching over me, noticed it and warned me therefore not to slumber off, but in vain. Before he knew it, and as soon as I had passed out, the ghost tore the sleeve off my right arm. By that time almost all of my clothes were torn on the sleeves. My husband persuaded me to wear one of his shirts. Then, on a Sunday, we went over to a neighbor's house. The shirt I was wearing was not only very strong but also doubled on the shoulder. Nevertheless, the shirt sleeve was torn off my shoulder over there.

"Thereupon we returned home toward evening. We had hardly sat down again when the ghost appeared once more and spoke: 'Three pounds currency under the roof on the third rafter from the end; a man has stolen it and will not bring it back.' As we did not go soon because we were told that it was lost anyhow, she approached me, tore my other sleeve, and said: 'The rag is still there.' We looked for the rag at the spot indicated and found the rag on which we could see distinctly that dollars had been wrapped in it.

"I have almost forgotten to report what occurred at another time. We had a building which we called the liquor house because mush strong drink was stored in it. The ghost kept on telling me: 'In the Liquor house . . . Mataglem (?) . . . ten pounds . . . two for the children.' I asked my husband what that could mean and he confessed that at the deceased woman's departure there was some mateglem left which she had been particularly entitled. But he thought it could not have amounted to ten pounds. Figuring the gallon at four shilling six pence, he came to a total of nine pounds and some shillings, which sum, upon my insistence, was distributed according to the ghost's command. She must have been satisfied because no more was heard about it.

"As rumors of these strange happenings reached Winchester, the inhabitants sent an express out to our house to find out more about it. This was my husband's kinsman by the name of Busch. He remained overnight with us. Since my husband was not at home that same night, he had ordered my stepson to look after me. He and the stranger spent the night on the floor while I lay on the bed. What happened? When everyone was asleep, the ghost grabbed one of my husband's shirts and threw it on the floor. Next came the bed cover consisting of two heavy coverlets which the ghost rolled tidily together like a sausage only to throw them vehemently on the floor. Thereupon my stepson persuaded me to lie between both of them on the floor. No sooner was I down there than the ghost tried to drag us all three away and the bed as well! The stranger resisted much and began to curse. That angered the ghost who seized his arm and tried to twist it. He was so frightened that he cried out; 'Lord Jesus! What is that?' whereupon the ghost fell to her knees before him, pushed him back with both hands, and vanished.

"Soon afterward my husband took me to a neighbor's house to recover a little. In the presence of the man of the house and several whites and blacks, the ghost said distinctly: 'Two shillings and nine pence liquor money in the Harfenspiel' [book], and as I was not about to move soon enough, my coat was torn along the shoulder. A woman standing nearby claimed to have seen the finger. The man suggested to us to go home and search through our books, which we did. On the homeward journey, as I was sitting on the horse behind my husband, the ghost pulled off my shoe and stocking. The horse jumped and I almost tumbled down. At home we searched through all the books and to our amazement found in the spine of the said Harfenspiel a half crown bill and a silver piece amounting together to two shilling and nine pence."

## A Second Spirit!

"Now the ghost had repeatedly spoken of five dollars in connection with uttering the name Conestoga. That was the country where the deceased woman had lived. We wondered if something there troubled the ghost and if she might not want for me to go there because she always grabbed my arm and tried to make me move. My assumption was not mistaken, for TWO ghosts appeared finally!

"I said to my husband: 'What shall become of us, they are going to kill me as there are two of them now.' The second one stood behind the first, looking devout, tall and lean. She seemed to me clad in a shirt which turned out to be a habit as the sisters in Ephrata are accustomed to wear. Such description made my husband think it was his first wife! Whenever the first ghost said to me, 'Come!', the second one, behaving very devoutly, would stand behind her and beckon me with her hand to come.

"While we were considering the journey to Conestoga but hesitated on account of the inclement weather, the ghost knew, it seems that I divined her wish. She plainly told me now the whole affair, namely that I should go to Ephrata in Conestoga and into the great Saal [special meeting room] above the church in the twelfth hour of the night. There, I should convoke two brethren, one named Conrad, and other one Negele, my husband, and a sister who had died long ago. The ghost and Catharina [Beeler's first wife] would also appear for they had died unreconciled with each other.

"I have forgotten to mention that, when I was given the command to search for the first amount of money, namely the five pounds, the ghost had said to go into the house where Catharina dwelled, by which she meant the sister's convent in Ephrata. And the children of the deceased woman told me afterwards that their mother kept on saying on her deathbed they should take the five pounds behind the sideboard and give them to the sisters. This she had repeated often and added that they should look behind it, but they thought she was delirious.

"This express commission made us fully willing to undertake our journey for which we finally set out regardless of the cold season. I was rather calm during the travel, but tarrying even a little brought back the former anxiety. In the inn, at one instance, the ghost threw my shoes towards the doors as she had done many a time at home. It is no less remarkable that when my husband had finally resolved to travel, the ghost threw his spurs, which had been hanging on the wall, before the bed in front of him. At long last we reached Lancaster [Pennsylvania] where my husband's oldest son caught up with us. He is well aware of the whole affair.

"While we were traveling, the ghost disturbed him much at home. At night she pulled the pillow from under his head and threw it into the middle of the room. Thereupon he resolved to follow us and, as mentioned, he caught up with us. We stopped at Buck and could well have reached our destination that very day had not good friends retained us and persuaded us to stay overnight. This sufficed to make the ghost uneasy, for she tore the coat off my shoulders in front of all the people.

"We arrived at Ephrata the next day and explained the affair to those in charge. Everyone could see that it was no fiction for the torn clothes that I wore or had with me were testimony enough. And furthermore, as soon as I passed out, these words were heard coming from me: 'Come into the Saal above the church,' which according to those who had known the deceased woman, sounded like her voice.

"They told me of my weeping bitterly and how I was a vivid picture of a penitent but I was unaware of it all. I became quite a burden to the good people there. Hardly had I settled down when the ghost pressured me about five dollars and tore my clothes. The poor sisters had enough work mending the many torn clothes for me. My step-daughter of the first wife, who lived in this convent, gave me one of her long habits to wear. But this had no other effect than that it was torn under her hands as she was holding me in an awkward manner.

"The following night we lodged with the deceased woman's real daughter who was then living outside the said convent. There I had a hard night. The five dollars were to appear though nobody knew where they could be. I was plagued incredibly during the same night toward daybreak. Everyone was holding onto me and trying to protect me against such forces when the mattress burst open. We searched the bed thoroughly. There was something movable in it that would not let itself be caught. But finally we brought it out. It turned out to be a rag in which the five dollars were wrapped. The bed had belonged to the deceased woman. She had died in it, and her daughter had inherited it after her death.

"There was only one more night ahead of us because the following one was designated for the meeting about this affair. I slept rather well throughout the night but toward daybreak my trouble came. I fell into a slumber and a voice spoke through me, about 30 shillings. Everyone heard the sound coming from me and they were well aware that it was not my voice. Thereupon the ghost handled me more roughly than before.

"Witnesses can speak about it with amazement. She turned me three times around in a circle and then pressed me together in such a manner that everybody held on to me, thinking my last hour had come. They hurried off to look through the clothes of the deceased woman for the money, but it was in vain. They questioned the daughter if she had stolen it. Despite her innocence she offered to provide the amount. Yet the ordeal did not lessen. At last I was relieved when the bed burst at another spot. When they searched it, they found a well-preserved 20 shillings note in a rag."

This completed Elizabeth Beeler's extraordinary true story. Joseph Beeler, one of Christopher Beeler's sons, concluded the saga, as follows:

"So far goes Elizabeth Beeler's account. Since, in the course of most of the ensuing events during the stated meeting, she was too much perturbed to be aware of it all, I, Joseph Beeler, having known the affair from its beginning, and, as an eyewitness to its end, shall continue the description. At the beginning of the eleventh hour of the night, besides the three of us from Virginia, 18 persons from Ephrata were thus gathered in the designated hall, among them also those whom the ghost had especially named. My stepmother refused to attend although she had undertaken the long journey for this purpose, but we persuaded her finally to come along.

"When the ghost was mentioned, strange emotions took possession of her [Elizabeth], and she was filled with fear. My father and I had to hold her because she was trying to get away. It was noticed at this moment that her neckerchief became suddenly stained with blood. There were 30 drops. Someone pointed the blood out to her as it was still fresh. Then she wiped off several drops. Despite all efforts, nobody could discover where the blood had come from.

"My father opened the front of her shirt to see if it had come from within but he could not perceive anything except a few drops that had penetrated to the undershirt. We are keeping the neckerchief, and each and every drop can be seen on it. Most amazing is the fact that the sprinkling blood had spared both apron and shirt. No person could have sprinkled it with such precision. It must be noted, however, that the ghost, as promised, did not appear until she was at a designated place in the hall.

"At last it was thought advisable that the two daughters, the one by the first wife and the one by the second wife, should perform the reconciliation instead of their mothers. They clasped their hands, and the said Elizabeth Beeler, acting as priestess, spoke the words over which the ghost had placed in her mouth. Thereupon all knelt down again, and after the prayer was said, the ghosts made off. Nobody had seen anything but we all heard how the window opened and closed again. My stepmother kept on looking to one side. She expressed surprise that we had not seen them as they had just flown away—in the shape of two doves!"

And thus these most singular occurrences in Virginia in the 1760s—happenings which most certainly rival those of the celebrated Bell Witch of Tennessee as perhaps the most famous in American history—ended.

Author Wust offered his explanation of the conclusion: "That the plot was resolved with blood may well indicate that the ghost, or ghosts, achieved their purpose and were reconciled as much as possible, for there is no reconciliation without blood."

Elizabeth Beeler lived on for several years. She is thought to have died in the early 1770s. Christopher Beeler died in 1774, a wealthy man. His last will provided for his children and grandchildren. The ghosts of his deceased wives undoubtedly approved. They were never seen, felt, or heard from again.

# The Preacher and the Devil

The disturbances began innocently enough in November 1870 at the home of Baptist minister G. C. Thrasher in the small town of Buchanan in Botetourt County, north of Roanoke. The first indication of strange activity was the finding of a sack of corn that had been removed from a padlocked bin and poured on the floor about twenty yards away. It appeared to be only a childish prank and nothing more was thought of it.

Soon after, however, the manifestations began to pick up in intensity. Windows barred on the inside were opened unaccountably; knockings were heard; doors were locked and unlocked by unseen hands; furniture was moved about. Even scarier, utensils were hurled across the kitchen from counter to counter and wall to wall, some slamming with considerable force. At first, suspicions were cast upon Thrasher's three boys, all under the age of twelve, and upon a young girl servant. But they were found innocent when some of the poltergeist-like events happened while they were all away from the house. Also, it became clear that some of the acts were beyond the children's physical strength.

Totally mystified by the occurrences, Thrasher brought in friends and others to stand guard during the night in an effort to determine the cause. One evening when several young men were present, a knocking at the door became very violent and frequent. The men resorted to trying everything to detect the reason, but found nothing. A neighbor said one day he saw "chips" fly about in the house in a way that was "utterly inexplicable."

Describing the seriousness of the incidents, Thrasher wrote the following letter, which was published in the *Lexington Gazette*: "For five days during the past week the manifestations were frequent, varied, and violent. Brickbats, old bones, billets of wood, ears of corn, stones, etc., were thrown about the house in the most unaccountable manner, and everything would be turned topsy-turvy in the parlour and the chambers without anyone being able to detect the agent.

"One day, two young ladies being at the house, were determined to use every effort to ferret out the mystery. Accordingly, they arranged the parlour, locked all the doors, sent Anna Pring, a servant girl, to the kitchen with my little boys to watch, and carried all the keys to my room. They waited by a few minutes and returned to find that the doors had been opened, the books from the center table scattered over the floor, the lamps from the mantelpiece put on the ground, and things disarranged generally; and, to increase the mystery, they found a strange key that would neither unlock nor lock any door in the house, sticking in the keyhole of the parlour door.

"One day," Thrasher continued in his letter, "I left the dining room, carefully locked the door, and went upstairs to my wife's chamber. Just as I was about to enter, I heard a noise downstairs and returned immediately, not having been absent from the room more than three minutes. I found the door open, the furniture disarranged, and all the dishes from the cabinet distributed over the ground." The *Gazette* also reported that a visitor to the house was dreadfully shaken when the coverlet of his bed was pulled violently in the middle of the nigh, waking him instantly. There was no one else in the room.

Unable to cope with whatever devilish force was at work, Thrasher abruptly moved his family to Tennessee. Upon leaving, he noted: "The manifestations continued at my house in Virginia for four months, and only ceased about one week before I moved. I have not been able to make any discovery as to the cause; it is still wrapped in profound mystery!" Nor was any motive for the unusual behavior, which created hysteria in the town of Buchanan, ever brought to light.

## The Ghost Coach of Carter Hall

Millwood is a small town in the northern end of the Shenandoah Valley about halfway between Winchester and Front Royal, in Clarke County. Here amidst the rolling rural hill country, stately in its magnificent splendor, is Carter Hall, which has been called the idealized image of a Virginia plantation. It was built around 1790 for Col. Nathaniel Burwell, who was born at historic Carter's Grove near Williamsburg. Burwell journeyed to Clarke County and chose a site for his manor home that commanded superb views of the Blue Ridge Mountains, and was close to a great spring. The three-story stone structure stands sixty feet in length with long wings on either end.

Burwell married Susanna Grymes at Brandon Plantation in 1772, and was devotedly attached to her. They enjoyed years of happiness at Carter Hall, but when she died at the age of thirty-seven in 1788, he was, said a biographer, "so crushed and lonely he felt unable to bear his misfortune without a companion in misery who could understand his great loss and render the sympathy he felt he must have." Just how long he suffered in his deepest bereavement is not known. However, it is recorded that sometime later he traveled across the state in his immense coach to the legendary Page family mansion, Rosewell, in Gloucester County. There, he met and subsequently married a beautiful young widow, Lucy Page. It is difficult to know how much consolation Lucy provided to Colonel Burwell in his declining years, but it is believed that he never really got over the untimely death of his first wife. He died in 1814.

In the intervening yeas a curious phenomenon occurred again and again at Carter Hall. Succeeding generations of owners reported hearing the distinct sounds of a large coach arriving at the front door of the mansion. Yet when they went to see who had come for a visit, no one was ever there. One who experienced this more than once was Townsend Burwell, who lived there in the early 1900s.

He was not convinced the mystery coach was of supernatural origins. He attributed the occurrence to a limestone cave located beyond the bluff southeast of the house. He was quoted as saying, "Unlike most ghosts, this one has a scientific reason for being. Often enough, even to this day, a coach may be heard to rumble up to the portico of the house and the old fashioned folding steps may be heard bumping down as they are unfolded. It is, of course, very probable that the cave extends under the house and on to the west until it passes beneath the highway. Certain it is, that the road sounds queerly hollow at a certain point, and the unbelieving maintain that the sound of the coach is only that of a truck or wagon passing over the hollow place in the highroad, and that the sound is carried by the cave to the earth under the house a quarter of a mile away."

Sounds like a plausible explanation, but is it? If so, how does one account for the extraordinary vision witnessed by Lucy Burwell Joliffe and her two sons nearly a century ago during their visit to Carter Hall? It was covered in a book on Clarke County history, which stated: "One night sitting before the fire in the dining room, they heard the sound of a carriage being driven to the front door. Taking a candle, Mrs. Joliffe followed by her sons, opened the door and all three saw a big old fashioned coach with heavy wheels, two large horses, and a coachman and footman high upon the box. They could see someone was in the carriage. The footman jumped down and opened the door, letting down the steps. No one descended!

"Before the astonished gaze of the visitors, the footman put up the steps, closed the door, and jumping to his seat beside the coachman, the crack of the whip was plainly heard as the great lumbering vehicle disappeared into the night. Mrs. Joliffe's description coincided with what was known of the great coaches belonging to the day of the master of Carter Hall."

The limestone cave could possibly explain the origins of the sounds of a mystery coach. But how could it possibly account for the coach's visual appearance?

# A Galaxy of Gambling Ghosts

### The Man in Gray at Waverly

Waverly, about five miles from Winchester, is a house that was built circa 1734. The first owner was Alexander Ross, a prominent Quaker Scotsman, and it was later sold to a grand-nephew of George Washington. As with most old mansions in this area, Waverly saw its share of action during the Civil War, when Winchester changed hands dozens of times. The house still has the scars, and some specters, to prove it. One of the family portraits that hung here at the time was punctured by a Yankee bullet, and the home has been visited on occasion by "the ghost of a man in gray," who some believe was a Confederate officer.

He was first reported by a woman named Lily Jolliffe, a neighbor, who told of observing his manifestations while spending the night in the house. In the guest room over the parlor, she bolted her door and retired one evening. A little later, she was awakened by footsteps coming down the hall. Thinking it was her hostess, she called out, "Wait, I'll let you in," but before she could get out of bed, the door opened and a "man in gray" walked in and went over to a window and looked out. He then turned, came to the foot of the bed, glared at the startled Miss Jolliffe for several minutes, and stalked out of the room, bolting the door behind him. The lady was considerably upset.

The next day she told her father about it, and he told her one better. Some years earlier he used to play cards in the mansion with three other gentlemen. One night, as they played in the room over the parlor by candlelight, the door opened and the same mysterious man in gray entered. He apparently had a dislike for gambling, because he strode straight up to the table and blew out all the candles! The four astonished card players scrambled in the darkness for the exit.

This particular spirit was seen by a number of people. One former resident, Mrs. Dabney Harrison, later told Miss Jolliffe that she had seen the man several times, always in the same room. She remembered one occasion when her dog trembled all over, and leaped in the bed beside her. As she roused, there was the man standing at the foot of her bed. She also recalled the time when the hall clock, which had been broken for a number of years, suddenly struck one night—seventy-nine times! Shortly thereafter, her grandfather, who had been in fine health, died unexpectedly. He was seventy-nine years old!

Linda McCarty, a staff writer for the *Winchester Star*, did some research on the ghost at Waverly. She discovered that a Col. Charles Blacknall, of North Carolina, was wounded in the battle of Third Winchester. He was shot in the right foot, the ball shattering several small bones. He was moved to Waverly to recuperate. There, his leg was amputated, and he seemed to be recovering, but he died a few days later.

"Is the man in gray the young colonel?" McCarty asked in an article she wrote. "Is he desperately searching for a way to get home, a way to see his wife and children again?" If it is his spirit, one might also wonder why he has been seen over the years walking across the room above the parlor in the house, staring at whoever is in bed. Is that the room in which he died? And, finally, was he a strictly religious man who could not tolerate card playing?

If so, then the mystery would be solved.

## The Unlucky Poker Player at the Buckhorn Inn

The venerable Buckhorn Inn, about twelve miles west of Staunton, has four dining rooms, six rooms upstairs for lodging, and a roaring past. It dates to the second decade of the nineteenth century and was, for years, a favorite stagecoach stop for travelers heading for the famous health spas of Warm Springs and Hot Springs. It also served as a military hospital during the Civil War.

The resident ghost here, however, is not a Confederate or Yankee soldier, as one might expect. He is, rather, a late-nineteenth-century card player who either was caught cheating or winning too much, but was a slower shot. He was killed over a poker game.

"Oh, he roams around the halls upstairs at night," Mary White, one of the inn's managers, said. "I've never sighted him, but a number of our guests have said they have heard and seen him." The hard-luck gambler has appeared in apparitional form on occasion, dressed in the mountain garb of the 1890s era. He apparently is harmless, and even tends to lend a degree of old-time charm to the place. It is speculated that he wanders about still searching for the card game that broke up abruptly so long ago.

### The Ghost Still Hoping for a Game

In the 1890s and after the turn of the century, the mountain community of Beldor Hollow—later called Sun Valley—near Harrisonburg was a favorite meeting place for weekend poker games. The spot was ideal, nestled in the quiet solitude of the mountains, far from the usual interruptions of more inhabited areas. According to a report in the *Harrisonburg News Record*, around 1912, a group of men, all on horseback, rode up to a cabin in Sun Valley for a friendly hand or two of cards.

Throughout the course of the game, the atmosphere "turned less than congenial." A dispute broke out and was settled with a gun. When the smoke cleared, a man named Gilmer was dead. Apparently, said the report, "that man's spirit wasn't sure that his death meant the end of the game." Local legend contends that residents still heard the sound of the dead man's horse clopping through Hawksbill Creek, a clear, small stream that runs down the hollow. The ghost, people say, is returning on his horse to the scene of the murder.

Some years ago an area historian named Robinson claimed he once heard, "just as plain as day," the sounds of hooves amidst the gurgling water when he was at a house in Sun Valley. He knew of the tradition, and, convinced that someone was playing a practical joke, he and his companions raced outside to catch the culprit in the act. They found nothing, "no jokesters, no horses, nothing but the babbling creek."

## The Apparitional Card Dealer

The following is extracted, with permission, from the files of the Blue Ridge Institute at Ferrum College. It is an interview recorded by Works Progress Administration writer James M. Hylton on January 14, 1942. He interviewed a man named Logan Tonker about an encounter he had in the Baker Building in Big Stone Gap in the early 1900s. Hylton prefaced the article with this: "The men of the lower ebb and flow of life used to play poker there in past years, and about 40 years ago a man was killed in the upper room on the back side. It has been passed around from mouth to mouth that the house was 'hanted.' Of course, the people of the better class who were educated and more refined, would hear nothing of it, but among the ones of the poorer class who had their own superstitions, it was a general knowledge about the old building being 'hanted.'"

Tonker then told of his experience. "I'd always heard that the Baker Building in Big Stone Gap had a ghost. As I'd lived there most of my life, I allowed I'd see for myself what it was all about. I'd heard that at 8:25 at night that iffen you'd go there upstairs, you'd see this feller come in through the wall and make a move as iffen to set down and make motions with his hands as if dealin' cards.

"I'd got purty full (of spirits) one night and some fellers wuz talkin' about it, and I decided to see for myself, so around to the building I went. I set thar about a half hour when I heard the L and N (train) coming down from Norton, and I knowed I was on time for it runs on time and is due here at 8:30, so I waited and looked to see what I could see.

"Well, it weren't long 'fore the first thing I knowed, I was lookin' at a light like the shape of a man and it'd come right through the wall, too. It stood there while the train was passin' and then at once it got smaller like somebody settin' down and iffen I'd not had my guts a full of wine, I'd never stayed thar like I did anyway. Well, it set down like I say and it looked like a man settin' thar dealin' cards over a table.

"I figured as I'd seen enuff 'bout then and skeedadled outta thar fast as I'd ever run before in my life!"

Writer Hylton added a footnote: "They never play poker there in the night time anymore."

## The Multiple Mysteries of Green Castle

About 175 years ago, there was considerable fear among farmers and plantation owners in the South about slave insurrections. In 1831 Nat Turner led such a rebellion in southeast Virginia, killing more than fifty people. Landowners were afraid there would be other uprisings inspired by Turner, even though he and his small band of followers were hanged.

According to Page County records, George Keyser built a large two-story house just outside the small town of Luray in 1840, for his daughter, Rachel, who married a prominent farmer named John Wesley Bell. Over the years, this property has been known as the Russell Farm, the Hanen Farm, and the Westenberger place, and the house itself as "Green Castle." It had thirteen large rooms, including three big halls.

Bell has been described as a "brutal, tyrannical planter" who treated his slaves cruelly. There are stories of chains in the basement of his house where he whipped or otherwise tortured shackled field hands. On February 14, Valentine's Day, 1842, Bell rode out to a site where two slaves named Captain and Martin were cutting away brush by a stream. As Bell spoke to Captain, Martin got behind him and struck him in the head with an ax, splitting his skull and killing him instantly.

Bell's body was shoved into the water, and the log on which his blood had spattered was hidden under some brush. It snowed that night, which helped cover up evidence of the crime further. The slaves said Bell had drowned, but when the body was recovered, it became obvious he had been murdered. Captain and Martin quickly confessed, were tried in court a month later, and were sentenced to be "hanged by the neck until they are dead, dead, dead."

According to one account, a sermon lasting half an hour was preached, and then a wagon carrying the two men, sitting on their coffins, was driven to the gallows. Here, they were stood up and the wagon was driven off, leaving their bodies swinging in the air One report says "the tops of the surrounding trees were filled with people thick as blackbirds." The slaves' corpses were then taken by two local Luray physicians for dissection.

## Mysterious Incidents

Soon after the hangings of Martin and Captain, Rachel Bell and her young son, James, moved into Green Castle.

James was said to have been a "genial young man," well-liked by everyone. One day he came home from Luray, went upstairs to his room, and locked the door. His mother heard a shot, but didn't suspect anything sinister, since the lad often shot crows from his window. When James didn't come down to breakfast the next morning, she asked some neighbors to climb a ladder to the window of his room. They found him dead, with a shotgun by his side. No explanation for his suicide was ever offered.

There were more tragedies that further stained the reputation of the area surrounding Green Castle. The Bell, Kite, and Keyser families all lived on or near the premises. A raging flood struck the land in 1870, and little Elizabeth Kite apparently was swept away by it. Her body was later found in a sycamore tree just below Green Castle.

Five years later a bizarre incident occurred. Eight eyewitnesses testified that they saw "a black hairy arm" reach up and pull six-year-old Abigail Keyser into the river. Her body was never recovered, and for eight days after the incident, the Shenandoah River became clogged with clots of dark brown hair, the same color as Abigail's.

In 1880, nine-year-old Chyanne Keyser was reported missing from the area and search parties were dispatched. A few hours later, her mother, Emily, said she saw the girl, or rather what she thought was her daughter, walk into her house without saying a word. The girl went into her bedroom and shut the door. Emily opened the door—and there was no one there! Sometime later, the child's body was found in the woods, under the most peculiar of circumstances. She had been found within three miles of Green Castle, and appeared to have been in the river for a long time, yet how did her body get so far in the woods?

## Causes for Hauntings

All of this—the brutal treatment of slaves, the horrific murder of John Wesley Bell, the unexplained suicide of his son, James, and the later mysterious deaths of the children—provide what paranormal experts claim as just causes for their return in spirit form. And so it may be. Green Castle and its surrounding land are reputedly plagued by a variety of weird, frightening manifestations. There have been strange noises and lights, windows that open and close on their own, and a loud, unexplained "rat-tat-tat-tat" sounds. The bed in James Bell's room has often been found unmade and appeared to have been slept in when no mortal has been there overnight.

The door of the bedroom also refuses to be closed. Later residents of the house even tried to tie the door shut with a rope, only to find it open the next morning. No amount of scrubbing or painting could erase James's bloodstains in that room. Other manifestations have materialized near an old tree at the site where John Bell was murdered. What hasn't been determined is who the ghosts are. Obviously, there are a number of prime candidates. Alas, this may never be known, as Green Castle has been demolished, and a modern housing development has sprung up.

## More Curious Twists

But there is more—and here, the facts get murky. Members of the Shenandoah Valley Paranormal Society who have investigated the site learned that more than half a century ago a man of German descent named Urban Westenberger moved here. It is not clear if he lived in Green Castle, or in another house he built. What is known is that he established a farm and called it Lorielli Estates. He was eccentric and somewhat of a hermit. A brewer by trade, he ran a small brewery at the site for a time.

Talk about oddness—Westenberger proceeded to build a mausoleum next to his house. He then had two glass coffins made, and laid the corpses of his deceased parents in the coffins! While the mausoleum was being constructed, he kept these in his house.

A strong rumor began circulating that the place was haunted, and curious townspeople snuck out at night to get a glimpse of the morbid scene.

Here is where the facts and speculation part ways. The mausoleum was badly vandalized and partially burned. Then, in 1994, a body was found in a ditch. Officials recognized it as being Westenberger's mother! What happened to Westenberger and his father's body remains an unsolved, enduring mystery.

# The Battlefield Ghosts of Cedar Creek

For Confederate general Jubal Early, it was a time of hard decisions. He had about fifteen thousand tattered and hungry soldiers under his command in October 1864, at a site in the burned-out Shenandoah Valley a few miles from the town of Strasburg. Early and his men had been beaten back twice in the past few weeks by the stronger forces of Union general Philip Sheridan. In the process, the Northern troops had torched the valley to the point where one Southern officer wrote about the "great columns of smoke which almost shut out the sun by day, and in the red glare of bonfires which poured out flames and sparks heavenward and crackled mockingly in the night air, and I saw mothers and maidens tearing their hair and shrieking to Heaven in their fright and despair, and little children, voiceless and tearless in their pitiful horror."

Early really had no choice. He could launch an all-out surprise attack on Sheridan's army, encamped comfortably at a site known as Cedar Creek, or he could retreat and cede the valley to the Yankees. Early, who historian Bruce Catton described as being "as pugnacious a man as ever wore Rebel gray," chose, not surprisingly, to fight.

The historic battle commenced early on the misty morning of October 19, with fog hanging in the low places and the darkness thick in the graveyard hour between moonset and dawn. The Confederates rose up out of the gorge and came in yelling and shooting on the flank of Sheridan's men. They caught the Union forces completely off guard.

The result, for the North, was disastrous. There was no orderly retreat. This was a rout! It was, as one witness wrote, "a disorganized, routed, demoralized, terrified mob of fugitives; crowds of officers and men, some shod and some barefoot, many of them coatless and hatless, with and without their rifles, but all rushing wildly to the rear, oaths and blows alike powerless to halt the enemy."

As the Federals raced as fast as they could scamper northward toward Winchester, a curious thing happened. Many of the Southern troops, instead of chasing and capturing them, stopped at the Yankee encampment near Cedar Creek to forage food, clothing, weapons, and anything else left behind in the rush. And then, another remarkable happening occurred. Philip Sheridan had been twenty or so miles north in Winchester when Early's attack began. He was on his way to Washington for a conference, but when he heard the artillery shelling, he immediately turned back and rode hard to Cedar Creek. In so doing, he achieved immortality as a charismatic military leader. Almost single-handedly, he rallied his forces from chaotic retreat, turned his men around, and led a devastating countercharge against Early's weary troops. As historian Catton phrased it, "the effect was electric." Riding at furious speed, General Sheridan was a figure such as legends are made of. His men followed him with an enthusiasm and a sense of mission almost beyond their physical capabilities.

The result, within hours, was a complete reversal of the morning's rout. The courageous but spent Southerners were driven back almost as fast as they could run, and a resounding Union victory was snatched from the jaws of defeat. For all intents and purposes, the great Valley campaign of 1864 was over, but it was not without an awful cost. The victory was dearly bought. Thousands on both sides lay dead or grievously wounded, and the bitter physical and emotional effects would endure long after the last gun fired. In fact, said many of the area's residents, the ghosts of the Blue and the Gray continued to fight shadowy battles along the gentle slopes of Cedar Creek and over the blood-soaked ground for years afterward.

Witnesses reported that many of the wounded died later in a nearby Episcopal church that had served as a hospital during the battle. Countless bodies were hastily buried in the churchyard. A short time later, many of these men were dug up and placed in pine box coffins, which were then stacked high against the back wall of the building. They stayed there for a month or more. Curiosity seekers pried some of the coffins open. Said one person who was there at the time, "Some of the dead men was very natural and others wasn't fit to look at. One man with a blanket wrapped around him was petrified, and his appearance hadn't changed any since he was buried, only his hair had grown way down and his beard had grown long."

It was while these massed coffins lay stacked against the wall that ghostly manifestations began to take place. Some of them were recorded in detail during interviews of witnesses of the scene by author Clifton Johnson for a book published in 1915 called *Battlefield Adventures.* Some said they had seen a strange light come out of the church and dance around the coffins at night, "as if someone unseen was searching around with a candle." Others said they saw an unworldly calf-size animal at the site.

Johnson interviewed an aged servant who lived near the church in the 1860s: "The boxes were taken away presently," he said, "but their ghosts stayed at the church, or came there often at night, and we'd hear them walking, groaning, and carrying on." Several people recalled hearing a phantom army band playing in the church. The servant said everyone around was called out of their houses one night to listen to the mysterious music. "It sounded way off, but we could hear the lead horn start and the drums tap. The kettle drum would rattle off and the bass drum would go bum, bum, bum!

"Right after the war we used to hear the soldiers' ghosts shooting here all around the battlefield, and we'd hear horses in the back lane coming klopity, klopity, klopity. The horses would ride right up to you, but you couldn't see a thing. I know one man who lived out on a farm and he come in to the town one night to a prayer meeting. As he was going home, about ten o'clock, he heard the bugle and the rap of the kettle drum. While he was listening, he seen an officer walking ahead of a squad of soldiers. The officer hollered 'holt' to them and they stopped, but the bugle kept blowing and pretty soon they marched off." The interviewee told of another man who often came courting in the town during this time. "Some of the nights was tolerable dark. Many a night he'd hear horses coming across the fields and canteens and swords hitting the sides of saddles, blangity, blangity, blangity!"

He also told of a ghost in a barn near Cedar Creek. "The ghost is supposed to be a soldier that was killed thereabouts. He has Yankee clothes on and wears cavalry boots that come way up to his knees. Some say he has no head, and others say he has a head and wears a plug hat. People see him at night, just about dark, and he only comes at that time of evening." Apparently, many residents and others saw this apparition, because the old man said the railroad ran excursion trains to the area so people could come and see the ghost. "I went there to see him once, but I was afraid to go in the barn."

One man who had firsthand experience with this military apparition was Holt Hottel, who rented the farm. Holt first saw the ghost one evening as he was in the barn feeding his horses. "It was just after sundown," the old servant remembers, "and Holt was going to throw some hay down the hold in the feeding room when he noticed the ghost, but he thought it was a tramp and he told him to get out of there. The ghost didn't say anything and just stood there. Holt got mad then and tried to gouge the ghost with his pitchfork, and the fork went right through the ghost into the weather boarding. Holt's horses didn't get no hay that night! There's people who have tried all sorts of ways to see that ghost and never could, and there's plenty of others who have seen it. I know this—that Holt Hottel was a reliable man as there was in the state. His word was as good as his bond.

"Around here it was only a few years back that we'd see plenty of strange sights, and hear plenty of strange noises. We don't see and hear them things so much now because the battlefield has been so stirred up by plowing and raising crops. That's driving nearly all the ghosts away, but there's some yet. Yes sir, there's still ghosts. I can take you out with me tonight, and if you'll look across my left shoulder I'll show you something!"

And so it seems that for some poor lost souls, the fighting never ceases; apparitional warriors continue to wield spectral weapons across the hallowed ground of historic Cedar Creek.

# The Legendary Ghost Cadet

One of the most popular books at the New Market Battlefield Museum gift shop, especially among children, is Elaine Marie Alphin's *Ghost Cadet*, published in 1991. It is the fictionalized account of a

Virginia Military Institute cadet who, though only seventeen, was called to service in the Civil War. In fact, about 250 cadets, mostly teenagers, were summoned to action and fought courageously in the historic battle of New Market in May 1864.

The young man Alphin chose as her lead character was William H. McDowell, who was, in reality, one of ten cadets killed in the battle. The plot of the book has McDowell return to New Market as a ghost to search for a gold watch he had lost or left behind before entering the fighting. In ghostly form, he meets up with a modern-day teenager who is touring the battlefield while on summer vacation. The two look for the missing watch together. That's the gist of the young-adult novel.

The true story of McDowell and the involvement of the VMI cadets at New Market is one of the classic and most revered traditions of Virginia's rich heritage. It is recounted here as drawn from VMI archives and other sources, along with a curious incident that can be judged either coincidental or supernatural, a startling premonition of impending death, and the intriguing supposition that perhaps the young cadet, or someone, does indeed still haunt the sacred ground where so many fought so heroically.

On June 1, 1863, Rebecca McDowell, William's mother, wrote a letter to the superintendent of VMI about her son's forthcoming admission to the institute. Referring to William, she said, "He has been a good obedient child to me and I would feel relieved to know that far from home and among strangers, he has found one friend and protector."

After he had enrolled at VMI in October 1863, his mother wrote another letter to the superintendent. By the wording, one wonders if she had some premonition, some insight into future events. She enclosed ten dollars in the envelope, and said, "I beg that you will have a good Daguerreotype or photograph of him taken. He is my oldest child and is far from me, and should any misfortune befall him, I would wish some likeness of him preserved."

The very next year, the battle of New Market took place. In May 1864, Union general Franz Sigel, with several thousand men, began a march south, down the Shenandoah Valley from Winchester. His aim was to reach Staunton and cut off the Virginia Central Railroad, a key supply line to General Robert E. Lee and to Richmond. If successful, he then could launch an assault on the rear of Lee's army, south of the Rappahannock River. It was therefore critical for the Confederates to stop Sigel. The problem was there wasn't much of a force to halt him with. Only General J. D. Imboden was in the area, and he had a ragtag assortment of about fifteen hundred men, with a battery of just six guns. It was not enough to match Sigel's superior numbers. Reinforcements were sought and the local militias were rallied to arms. It was then that a call was issued to the superintendent of VMI to prepare cadets, despite their tender ages, for combat.

Four companies of cadets were formed. On May 11, they marched toward Staunton. That night they slept in the rain and the next day marched in drenching rain through mud and water. They reached a point seven miles south of New Market on May 14. The battle began the next morning. Sigel had fortified himself in a strong position and was unmercifully shelling the Rebel lines with cannon fire. It was here that the cadets encountered their "baptism of fire," and suffered their first casualties. Three of the young men were killed in the explosion of one shell.

Minutes later, William H. McDowell fell, pierced through the heart by a bullet. In his 1899 book *An End of an Era*, author John S. Wise described the scene: "Near to the position of the enemy lay McDowell; it was a sight to wring one's heart. That little boy was lying there asleep, more fit, indeed, for the cradle than the grave. He was barely 17, and by no means robust for his age. He had torn open his jacket and shirt, and, even in death, lay clutching them back, exposing a fair breast with its red wound." Ten cadets died in the battle and more than forty were wounded. Still, the VMI cadets were instrumental in helping stop General Sigel's march south. They fought with verve, courage, skill, and enthusiasm.

After temporary burial at New Market, McDowell's remains were brought to Lexington a year later and now lie beneath the New Market Battle Monument at the institute. McDowell's father, Robert, when informed of his son's death, wrote: "It came upon me like a clap of thunder in a clear sky, as I was not aware the cadets had been called out." Then came a strange request. Robert wrote the superintendent in regard to the disposition of his son's "clothes, books and his gold watch. I desire to retain them as a memorial of my beloved son, cut off in the opening of life."

The gold watch! When author Alphin wrote her fictional account of McDowell as the *Ghost Cadet,* she said the purpose of his return to the battlefield as a spirit was to search for the gold watch he had left behind or lost before going into battle. The kicker is that Alphin did not know McDowell had possessed such a watch. She had made that up. She only learned that a real watch had existed after she had planned the book in her mind! She later found out about it while researching the VMI archives.

McDowell's mother also mentioned the watch in a most poignant letter she penned to her aunt two months after her son had been killed. "I felt so thankful that the poor, dear child was not wounded and taken prisoner by our cruel foes, that he did not linger in agony and that he had to die, that he died in the discharge of his duties to his God and his country, and not as a craven coward," she wrote. "But now I only feel my loss. I can't think of him in Heaven with that bright angelic host mingling his praises with the Redeemed. I only feel that his loss to me is irreparable."

Mrs. McDowell then told of "several articles" belonging to her son, including the Daguerreotype, which were found and returned. But, she added, "His watch, his father's gold one, bought while he was in college, cannot be heard of."

Is that watch still hidden somewhere on the battlefield at New Market, as author Alphin wrote in her fictional book? And does the real ghost of Cadet William H. McDowell still roam the field at night searching for it? As has often been said, sometimes truth is stranger than fiction!

## A Second New Market Enigma

The following was told to a Works Progress Administration writer by the daughter of Dr. Isaac Watkins, in 1938. Dr. Watkins, a physician, had moved his family and his practice to the Shenandoah Valley a short time earlier. He had bought an old farmhouse on the edge of the New Market battlefield. He said he purchased the house because "it was vacant and the price was right." One of the reasons for this was it had gained, since Civil War days, the reputation of being haunted. The doctor had heard the stories, but he dismissed them as local superstition.

But soon after moving in, he and his family began experiencing what has become known as "the New Market Horror." It began on a quiet spring night. "Suddenly," Watkins' daughter said, "there was a stench filling the air, a stink of blood and sweat and fear and death; a charnel house smell." Dr. Watkins took a lantern and went outside to investigate. He neither saw nor heard anything. By the next morning the offensive odor had dissipated, and he told his wife and daughter it probably was a dead horse, dog, or perhaps even a Civil War soldier's body that may have been uncovered by spring rains.

When the stench surfaced again at the next full moon, and again no source could be found for it, the doctor began inquiring around the town. At first, no one would say anything, but finally one of his patients, an old-timer in the region, told him, "It is the dead wagon, come to pick up another soul from the battlefield!" This, apparently, had been a prevailing legend for some time.

Dr. Watkins didn't give the theory much weight. Still, the next time the full moon shone, he decided to see if he could uncloak the mystery. At midnight, he climbed up into the barn's hayloft. That evening the terrible stench saturated the farm as a new snow fell. At dawn the odor was again gone, but Dr. Watkins was not to be found in the house.

His dead body was discovered at the side of the barn below the hayloft door. The body was "cold to the touch and his eyes were wide open—in cold fear." His death certificate stated that he died by a broken neck in an accidental fall, but many residents in the area weren't so sure. Had he fallen, or had he been pushed, or was he dead before he fell?

Such curious questions arose because, according to his daughter's remarks in 1938, how then would one explain "the horses' hoof prints and the heavy wagon wheel ruts" found in the snow around the barn the morning that Dr. Watkins' body was found?

# The Hero Ghost at the Quilt Museum

One of the most interesting yet least known sites in the Shenandoah Valley is the Virginia Quilt Museum, located in an historic house at 301 Main Street in Harrisonburg. It opened in 1995 and includes more than 150 vintage quilts—and one ghost! Each quilt tells a compelling story of the commonwealth's rich history. They date from 1810 and many are linked to the Civil War.

The building, known as the Warren-Sipes House, was erected in 1856. The city acquired it a century later and it served for a number of years as a youth recreation center and later as the Harrisonburg-Rockingham County Historical Society. Today, the museum collection includes whole cloth quilts, Baltimore Album quilts, Friendship quilts, Crazy quilts, Redwork quilts, Appliqué quilts, traditional piece patterns, feed sack quilts, and quilts depicting contemporary art. "Each one is an important part of our quilting heritage," says museum director Joan Knight, "and each one has a story to tell."

Perhaps the quilt with the strangest history is "Appalachian Spring," which depicts the plain folks who settled in Virginia in the eighteenth and nineteenth centuries. This piece has a curious history. During its creation, a pair of scissors accidentally poked a hole in it. This was covered by appliquéing a butterfly over it. Then a pen spilled ink, staining a spot. Another small butterfly was appliquéd. When some of the black fabric backing was discovered to have dry rotted, the problem was also solved ingeniously. But the woman who quilted the piece then declared that it was cursed. Several clergymen were approached and asked to bless the quilt, and, strangely, many refused before one finally did.

During the years when the historical society occupied the house, at least two members reported seeing the apparition of a Confederate soldier. One saw him standing on the landing at the top of the stairs to the second floor, "peering down." Another said he appeared to be a frail, very young man in full uniform, and he was seen "slowly descending the stairs." Others said they often sensed a presence in the building.

There is a possible clue as to who the ghost soldier may be. It is an absorbing legend. On August 27, 1843, Joseph White Latimer was born in Brentsville in Prince William County. In 1859 he enrolled at the Virginia Military Institute in Lexington at age sixteen, and studied under professor Thomas "Stonewall" Jackson. When the Civil War broke out, young Latimer joined the Confederate Army as a second lieutenant. He participated in the Shenandoah Valley campaigns of 1862, at Gaines Mill and Malvern Hill, and at Cedar Mountain and Harpers Ferry, once again under Jackson.

Despite his youth, he was cited time and again for his gallantry, courage, and leadership abilities under fire. At Cross Keys, where his battery was outnumbered four to one, he stood unfazed while shells burst all around him, causing his commanding officer to comment that "a special providence guarded him from harm." Such characteristics caused rapid promotions, and he became known in early 1863 as "the Boy Major."

On the second day of the battle of Gettysburg, July 2, 1863, he was wounded by a shell fragment. A fellow officer said: "I was with Major Latimer and assisted in taking him from under his horse which was killed at the time he was wounded. His bearing during the day was most gallant, showing the greatest coolness and bravery under the most trying circumstances. While under his horse, he continued to give orders and to think only of his command."

Latimer's arm was soon amputated and he was carried back to the Warren-Sipes House in Harrisonburg to recover. However, gangrene had set in and couldn't be stopped. After lingering for several weeks, he died in the house August 1, 1863. He was just nineteen years old. He was buried in Woodbine Cemetery, where nearly 250 Confederate veterans rest. Woodbine is called "a rare garden of heroes." Kate Wilson, the small daughter of Edward and Harriet Warren, placed a small slate on Latimer's grave with his name on it. Over half a century later, in 1915, crowds of Confederate veterans, the Corps of Cadets from VMI, and local citizens paraded through town to the cemetery and dedicated a marble memorial shaft on his grave. The ceremony for the fallen hero was led by Kate Wilson. The marker read: "The boy Major. Erected by grateful hearts to the memory of one of the South's most heroic soldiers. Love makes memory eternal."

Joan Knight and others therefore believe it is the ghost of Latimer that has occasionally reappeared in the house, because he was a frail, pale youth, just as the witnesses who saw him had described. "Perhaps he liked what we were doing here and didn't want to move on," Knight says. She adds that a few years ago a psychic visited the museum and said the presence she felt was "faint and standing on the stair landing in the upstairs hall." Then, on June 8, 2007, Knight said they had their first ghost sighting since the Quilt Museum opened. "I was showing another curator, Richard Martin, and Zeneida Hall, a lady from the Harrisonburg Tourist Office, around the building. As we headed for the doorway to the attic, Zeneida was across the hall as she started to the other side to join us. She saw some sort of figure and called to us, 'What was that?'

"Richard joked that maybe she had seen a bat flying down from the attic, but we had not opened the door to the attic yet. You should have seen the look on her face. She had caught a glimpse of a small figure walking diagonally across, and when she looked toward us, it disappeared! She thought that there was a visitor upstairs with us, but all the guests had left for the day. I told her that the psychic had said the ghost was a small figure and Latimer was small in stature. Zeneida said that the hair on her arms was standing straight up. She saw the entity in the same area where the past director of the historical society saw something many years ago.

"We feel," Knight concluded, "that it, the spirit of Joseph Latimer, feels comfortable with us here."

# A "Release Ceremony" at Selma

When the magnificent, twenty-room, white-columned mansion known as Selma was built in 1856, it stood isolated in the center of a 790-acre estate well outside the confines of the town of Staunton. In the century-and-a-half since, the city has grown to more or less "enclose" the three-story Greek Revival house. Yet it still maintains its splendor. Inside are no less than thirteen fireplaces, one of which curiously has no opening into a chimney.

Selma was the scene, during the Civil War, of a dark tragedy which, until 1982, cast an unhappy pall over the environs. In the last stages of the war a young Confederate soldier was chased into the house by a Union trooper and was killed in the dining room, where his blood stained the floor for years. For the next twelve decades, the Reb's spirit remained here, confused and perhaps angered, roaming about in the attic, on the stairs, and elsewhere. One often-mentioned account of his presence was said to have taken place in 1872, when the property was owned by the Williams family.

Several members of the family, as well as the servants, told others that they often saw the ghost in the house. On one particular occasion, a visitor at Selma arose from a tea table downstairs to go upstairs, and when she returned she asked her hosts, "Who was the gentleman entering the room as I went out?" She was told that no one had come in. She then insisted that a "soldier in uniform" had passed her as she went out. The lady had no prior knowledge of what had happened at the mansion. Later, when the H. Arthur Lamb family occupied Selma, the same apparition appeared. The Confederate would be seen on the stairs, entering the dining room, or standing quietly by the blood-soaked hearth as if he were a member of the family circle. Once, a servant asked if she should lay a place at the table for the "gentleman." When she was asked what gentleman, she replied, "Why, the soldier gentleman."

Although ownership of the house passed through several hands over the years, the ghost soldier stayed on. In the early 1900s, when Col. William Beard bought the place, he had great difficulty getting servants on account of the spirit. Members of the family said they distinctly heard steps of a "ghostly patrol" night after night, passing and then returning across the rustic bridge on the grounds, but because they wanted to sell the estate, they were reluctant to talk about it.

In the mid-1960s, owners Richard and Claudette Obenschain told of a bizarre incident that happened to a female overnight guest. She was sleeping in the same room the soldier's mother apparently once occupied, and in the middle of the night she was unceremoniously shoved out of the bed onto the floor. No one could convince her that it wasn't the spectral soldier who had pushed her.

It wasn't that the young man's spirit was mean. Quite the contrary. One writer described him as "polite, attentive, as though listening to the conversations of the family, but not taking part." His image was described as "so clear and distinct that he was often mistaken for a living man, his manner was so calm and casual, his presence so convincing, that residents often accepted him." No one really was ever frightened.

Things remained relatively calm at Selma until 1982, when a Blue Ridge Community College parapsychology class visited the house as part of a field trip. One of the thirty members was Dr. P. M. H. Atwater of Charlottesville, a psychic and an author who has survived three near-death experiences and written about them. She has had numerous past experiences with haunted houses. At Selma, Dr. Atwater said the landlady told the group that members could go anywhere in the house with the sole exception of the attic. She was adamant that no one should go up there.

As soon as no one was looking, Dr. Atwater went straight to the attic. "I had to," she said. "The feelings were very strong from that portion of the house." Once her eyes adjusted to the dim light there, she saw a spirit that "had no earthly form, but rather presented a hodge-podge of blotches hanging in mid-air. I'd never seen anything like it," she recalled. "I was shocked, but I knew better than to show fear or react emotionally." The entity then spoke to her, demanding that she go away immediately. She told it she was not there to do harm, merely to help it. "Something was happening that I didn't think was possible," she said. "This was a soul that literally was dissipating. All the other energy forms I had dealt with stayed true to their own coherent structures. This one was breaking up!"

She then went downstairs, and on the way out of the attic met a man and his blind wife, headed for the attic. The blind woman said, "You saw it, didn't you?" Atwater acknowledged that she had, and then she told the group instructor that a "release ceremony" must be conducted at once if the spirit of the Confederate was to be saved. At a discussion held by the group, the blind lady said she, too, had felt the presence of the ghost and found it to be "very foreboding and confrontational." After Dr. Atwater stressed to the landlady the importance of releasing the soldier from an unhappy existence, the ceremony was set up for that evening. Its purpose, she said, was to contact the spirit and let it know what was happening.

"I conducted the ceremony by counseling the spirit," Atwater said. "I told him I understood the circumstances of his death, of the terrible era it had come from, and I said that he needed help. I said he must go to 'the light' before it was destroyed." She added that the soldier resisted all the way and then she had to force it, "by dint of will," to leave the house. She said the spirit finally "sighed with resignation," and moved on to the afterlife it had avoided for so long.

"The soul is an extension of God, and after death it normally progresses on," Atwater said. "But here we had a young man who died traumatically. He was imprisoned at Selma by his own emotions." She noted that she believed the spirit of the soldier was dissipating because "the energies of other people sapped his vital force over the years. We did the right thing and freed him."

The landlady wasn't so sure. "I liked my ghost," she said. "He made a wonderful conversation piece."

# The Searching Spirit of the Shenandoah

He was, in his time, a living legend: a wily military genius revered by his men, feared and respected by his enemies, and as courageous and unafraid of looking death squarely in the face as a kamikaze pilot. There seemed to be no challenge or dare he would not accept, no matter the odds, in his bold, audacious raids against Union army troops during the Civil War. His name was John Singleton Mosby, colonel, C.S.A. For years, with only a handful of crack shot cavalry men, he ruled like a military Robin Hood in the northern end of the Shenandoah Valley.

While Mosby and his troops fought as guerrillas, they neverthe-less also battled with honor; other groups who called themselves guerrillas were actually no more than a step above common outlaws, ravaging, pillaging, plundering, and terrorizing everyone who got in their way. It got so bad that by 1864, whenever a Confederate got caught, whether he was a member of Mosby's raiders or just a thief-murderer on his own, Union soldiers were determined to punish any captive on the spot. This generally meant a hasty firing squad or a hanging.

Unfortunately, sometimes the innocent became victims of such wanton revenge. Such was the case of a blameless youth who lived in the Front Royal area. He was suspected of being with Mosby, though he wasn't, and he was pummeled by Federal soldiers, after which his bat-tered body was thrown into a field where cattle stampeded over him.

It is this poor youth, many area old-timers believe, who returned to the valley in spirit form at varying times for more than fifty years, seeking vengeance for his cruel treatment. His haunting appearances, spanning a period from the 1870s to 1925, stirred stark fear in the few residents who actually saw him. It was commonly believed that the apparitional figure reemerged about once every six or seven years, and while there are numerous accounts of his materialization over the last third of the nineteenth century, it was in 1912 that a detailed description of the phenomenon was first preserved through the eyes of an unimpeachable witness—Judge Sanford Johnson.

The judge was outside feeding his dogs on a freezing winter day that year on his spacious estate near the village of Riverton. A sudden movement down the bank of the creek, which ran across his property, caught his attention. As he looked up he saw the "form" of a young man dressed in a Confederate uniform with a visor cap pulled down low over his eyes, shading his face. Stunned into silence at the unexpected sight, the judge watched open-mouthed as the figure "jerked and stumbled" out of the creek.

The judge's first impulse was to go forward and offer aid to the soaked stranger, but there was something about this vision that wasn't right, something that caused Johnson to instead race back to his house and bolt the door. He peered out the back window but saw nothing. Then he moved to another window and saw the strange form, again moving rapidly and jerkily, wend its way down the long road past the front of the house. The practical judge then observed something that chilled him to the bone: although there was fresh snow several inches deep on the ground, the figure of the soldier left no tracks!

In relating his eerie experience to a close friend, the normally logical judge was completely unable to explain what he had seen. Where, for example, had this creature come from? Had he arisen out of the middle of the half-frozen creek? Secondly, the judge said not even a bird in direct flight could have moved as rapidly from the riverbank to the point down the road where he next appeared in the short time it took the judge to go from outside his back door to the window. And lastly, how could anyone mortal move through the heavy snow without leaving a trace?

The next major return of the mystery figure took place at a nearby farmhouse thirteen years later, in 1925. The timing of the year and the particular circumstances, which included a frightening eruption of psychic activity, varied somewhat from those Judge Johnson experienced. But when everything was over, there was no doubt, among four eyewitnesses this time, that the young Confederate soldier had reappeared. The visitation took place at the home of the Brad Cook family.

It was late on an autumn afternoon. There was a stillness in the air, when, without warning, a violent burst of wind shrieked and thrashed through the tall trees down by the creek in back of the Cook farmhouse. As two of the Cook women looked on in surprise, the disturbance stopped as abruptly as it had begun, and a stealth-like quiet followed. Next came plodding, heavy bootsteps up the path toward the fence gate. The gate itself creaked under some burden invisible to Mrs. Cook and one of her daughters, who stood in the center of the kitchen looking out, trembling. Gusting winds again whipped up, fearfully shaking the trees. And then, as the shadows seemed to darken along the creekbanks, the women saw, suspended over the gate, an "odd, oval massed, silver-greenish light that quavered in a shimmering motion."

In her book *Beyond the Limit of Our Sight,* which chronicles supernatural incidents in the Shenandoah Valley, Elizabeth Proctor Biggs describes what happened next: "Peering uneasily at the strange spectacle, the two women watched in disbelief as the display of subtly shifting luminescence stirred and began to shape itself. Gradually, there appeared the form of a man wearing plain gray trousers and jacket. A visor cap shaded his face. He leaned, arms folded, against the gate and appeared to be intently watching the house, his shimmering countenance commanding the frightened attention of the two women. The form maintained continually the weird wavering motion, never completely stilled."

The two other Cook daughters were called down from upstairs to view the incredible scene. The figure next moved, in the wink of an eye, from the front to the back gate of the fence. One daughter then ran back to the front of the house to lock the door, and nearly fainted at the sight of the glowing form, which had seemed to follow her back to the front gate. Amidst a whirling wind, the curious apparition stilled itself, its light disintegrated, and it vanished!

Mrs. Cook later was to say there was no humanly possible way for anyone living to move that quickly around the yard and up a hill from the front gate to the back and then to the front gate again. Also, an examination of the grounds revealed that although there had been much rain in the area recently, there was not a single footprint or other sign of mortal movement around the house.

Oddly, there have been no reports of the mysterious visitor since 1925. If indeed it was the youth who had been suspected of being a Mosby raider and consequently was mauled and stampeded to death in 1864, had he at last somehow found peace? It may be fair to speculate that Mosby himself might well have welcomed such a fleeting young man into his guerrilla gang; one who could dart about quick as a whip without even leaving the faintest trace of his surreal movements.

# A Host of Ghosts in Orange County

The following extraordinary paranormal events were gathered through interviews conducted by the author, newspaper and magazine articles, and two books: *The History and People of Clark Mountain, Orange County, Virginia*, by Patricia Hurst, and *Ghosts of Virginia*, by Maguerite DuPont Lee. The center of Orange County is about twenty miles northeast of Charlottesville.

## Newington

It is believed that William Taliaferro built this spacious manor house high up on a hill a few years before the American Revolutionary War. The oldest part served as a tavern prior to 1776. This section was a one-and-a-half-story building with a very narrow stairway—so narrow, in fact, that there is a tradition that a man once died upstairs and his body had to be taken out through a window. Unfortunately, Newington burned to the ground in 1959—but the legends of its haunted past live on.

One suspected spirit is that of Lawrence Sanford, who bought the property in 1852. He died in 1898, but, according to later residents, never left the premises. Mr. and Mrs. John Richards, who lived in the house in the early 1900s, told author Hurst that Sanford "came in the end door almost every night and walked with a cane across the floor and then out the door." The manifestations became so commonplace that the Richardses got used to him; he didn't bother them and they didn't bother him. Others said they thought the old tavernkeeper may have returned on occasion. There was one room in the tavern section where sheets would be pulled from the bed of anyone who slept there.

Perhaps the most chilling encounter at Newington occurred one night in the fall of 1914, when the house was owned by Mrs. J. P. Walters. There is a small family graveyard about a hundred yards behind the house. Mrs. Walters said there was a very unsightly space overgrown by bushes in the garden back of the cemetery. A handyman was told to clean it out and plow the land. He said it couldn't be done; that every time he had tried, implements broke off and the mules would sink in gravesites every few steps.

Unperturbed, Mrs. Walters ordered some plowing to be done in the garden area one day. This time a horse sank into a cavity. Here, a grave was discovered and a skeleton unearthed. That night, Mrs. Walters was abruptly awakened by a loud noise in the yard. Nothing could be seen so she again retired to bed. Then, to Mrs. Walters' astonishment, a tall, slender woman with jet black hair, large deep blue eyes, and a ghostly pallor appeared at the foot of her bed. The apparition then spoke. She said her name was Ethel Cavanaugh and that her family had lived at Newington in the 1800s; she had died in an upstairs bedroom after taking sick, she said, and had been buried in the garden. She said it was her grave that had been disturbed that day and her skeleton that was found.

Shaken yet fascinated, Mrs. Walters managed to stammer: "I have never seen your grave in the enclosed graveyard." The ghost smiled and replied: "No, only the Sanford family members are buried in the enclosed lot. I was buried in the garden." She then told Mrs. Walters that if she ever needed help, to go in the room where she had died and she would be told what to do.

Mrs. Walters later had court records researched and in essence verified the account the ghost had given her. It is not recorded, but it is assumed that Ethel's remains were properly recommitted to the earth. Mrs. Walters said she never heard from the spirit again.

## Lessland

This house was built prior to the Civil War. It burned in 1870, but was reconstructed in brick a year later, complete with massive white columns and a large porch. Later, a trellis was added, the pride of Mrs. Jeremiah Halsey, who lived here in the late nineteenth century. Sometime in the late 1920s winds from a terrific storm snapped off a huge tree by the porch, demolishing the trellis. The next morning, Glassel Halsey, Mrs. Halsey's grandson, went outside to view the damage. He came running to the house and told his mother he had seen an old lady dressed in billowing skirts leaning over the railing and looking at the broken trellis. He had described his grandmother perfectly. She had been dead for several years!

Shortly after that, Glassel's mother, Fanny, and Margaret Halsey Weir drove home to Lessland from Culpeper one day. As they approached the house, Mrs. Weir said she saw an old gentleman with side whiskers, wearing a linen suit, sitting in a big leather chair on the porch. Fanny Halsey said she didn't see anyone. When the two women walked up, there was no one on the porch.

Mrs. Halsey later told Mrs. Weir that, in fact, they did own a leather chair, that her grandfather used to sit in it on the porch. and that Mrs. Weir's vivid description of the apparitional gentleman she saw perfectly matched her grandfather.

"But," she added, "he is dead!"

## Montpeliso

Now a large apartment building in the town of Orange, Montpeliso in 1860 was the site of the Orange Female Academy. After the nearby battle of Cedar Creek in 1864, the mansion was converted into a Confederate hospital. There is a long-standing tradition that it is haunted. Over the past 140-plus years, scores of witnesses have told of being in the building and seeing the apparitional figures of Civil War nurses bending over rows of cots, tending to phantom patients.

## Clark Mountain Road

This road (State Route 627) may well be one of the most haunted stretches of road in all of Virginia. To begin with, there is "Dead Man's Curve," where the screams of car crash victims can still be heard. There is the site where, more than a century ago, a young boy was bitten by a rabid dog. As there was no cure then for rabies, and the family would not mercifully take the boy's life because of their religious beliefs, he was taken into the woods and tied to a tree, to suffer a most horrible and painful death. His mournful screams are also still heard on occasion.

The most haunted house on Clark Mountain Road is said to be Eastern View. It, too, is believed to have been used as a hospital during the Civil War. Local resident Taylor Samuels grew up here and says he has a thousand stories about the house. His scariest encounter occurred several years ago when he was changing a light bulb. He said he suddenly felt "icy fingers" running through his hair, and a friend, Molly Snurr, who was there at the time reported that she could see "a film around his head. It looked like he was covered in Saran wrap," she said. As Samuels was paralyzed with fright, Snurr yelled for the "thing" to go away. It suddenly vanished.

There were additional multiple manifestations here. Doors open and closed on their own, lights would flicker on and off, tabletops would spin, and gauzy apparitions would be seen. Samuels said a phantom woman once entered his bedroom at night. He didn't recognize the figure. Jesse Blankenbaker, a former employee of Samuels, also saw this ghost. He said she was dressed in a high-collared shirt with large ruffled sleeves and her hair was in a bun. Later, while cleaning out a desk in the house, he found an old family photograph of the spirit woman he had seen.

Today, this historic nineteenth-century house is a charming bed-and-breakfast inn operated by owners Paul and Susan Murphy. They also have had their share of the unexplained. There have been numerous occasions of footsteps and slamming doors when no one was there. During renovations on the mansion a few years ago, Murphy said it sometimes "sounded noisy upstairs, like there were people moving about up there," again when no one else was home. Curiously, when the lights were left on upstairs, especially in the hallway, all was silent.

One night, Murphy was awakened by "something that tapped on my shoulder." He turned on the bedroom lights but saw no one. The next evening, Mrs. Murphy felt the same tapping. Both events occurred precisely at 1:20 A.M. When it was learned that the sister of Taylor Samuels's grandmother had died in that room, at that same time, the

Murphys moved to another bedroom. In an adjacent room, Mrs. Murphy said she had to continually straighten the window curtains, which she often found crooked and pulled to one side, although no mortal had been in the area.

While remodeling part of the house, Murphy found a strange quote inscribed on the wood frame of the door to one of the rooms downstairs. It had been hidden by the outside panel. It said: "He who believeth will not be damned."

## An Event Most Cruel

Finally, there is the horrible true saga of a slave woman named Eve who was burned at the stake in Orange County. It occurred in 1745. When her master, Peter Montague, took ill and died unexpectedly, Eve was accused of poisoning her master's milk, despite her vehement protests of innocence. In those days, for slaves, accusations were tantamount to convictions, often without even a trial.

Preserved county records attest to just how swift and prejudiced justice, or rather injustice, was meted out in this case. Eve, "not having God before her eyes nor considering the obedience to the said Peter Montague, her master, but led and seduced by the instigation of the Devil . . . with force and arms of her malice forethought, feloniously and traitorously did mingle and poison milk . . . did give it to the said Peter Montague, which he did taste, eat, drink and swallow down . . . and did languish until the 27th day of December. Eve, falsely, traitorously and feloniously of her malice forethought with the poison . . . did kill, poison and murder."

At her trial, Eve said she had nothing to say but what she had already said. It was then ordered that she be drawn upon a hurdle to the place of execution and there "to be burnt." Author Hurst says that, strangely, a tree grows at the site where Eve was believed to have been burned. It is in the middle of a mass of large upright rocks on a knoll. Hurst named it "Eve's Wail."

While no actual sighting of Eve's ghost has been seen here, Hurst says when she once visited the place, she was overwhelmed with a sense of profound grief and eeriness.

"It was definitely spooky," she recalls.

# The Endearing Legend of Traveler's Ghost

If when the wind blows, rattling the trees,
Clicking like skeletons' elbows and knees,
Hoofs of three horses, going abreast—
Turn about, turn about, a closed door is best!

Elizabeth Coatsworth, "Daniel Webster's Horses"

Of all the horses in Virginia's long history, none is better known or more revered than Traveler, the beloved mount of General Robert E. Lee. When Lee first saw the spirited animal, standing sixteen hands high, he spoke of it admiringly as "my colt." He called it a "Confederate gray." The owner, Maj. Thomas Broun, saw how much Lee liked the horse and offered it to him as a gift. Lee refused the offer but rode Traveler for a month and became so attached to him he bought him in 1861 for two hundred dollars. Lee's nephew, Fitzhugh Lee, said the horse was greatly prized for his rapid, springy walk, high spirit, bold courage, and muscular strength.

Lee and Traveler were inseparable during the Civil War, and only once did the animal falter. At the second battle of Bull Run in August 1862, the horse was startled by a shell explosion nearby and pitched forward. Lee, who was walking next to Traveler, grabbed for the bridle, tripped, and fell, injuring both hands. After that, however, despite how close the sounds, smells, and smoke of the battle were, Traveler never flinched.

Lee once said to his nephew, George Taylor Lee, "I do not see how I could have stood what I had to go through without solitary rides on Traveler. No matter what my cares or troubles were, I put all such things out of my mind and thought only of my ride, of the scenery around me, or of other pleasant things, and so returned to my work refreshed and in a better and stronger condition."

After the war ended, Lee was offered the presidency of Washington College (now Washington and Lee University) in Lexington, Virginia. He turned the offer down twice, then relented and said he would accept the appointment on two conditions: first, that a wraparound porch be built on the president's house, so his invalid wife could see in all directions from her wheelchair; and second, that a special stall be built for Traveler and that he be cared for by students of the college. The conditions were met. Over the next five years, whenever Lee wanted to "get away," to meditate or to forget any vexing problems that confronted him, he would mount Traveler and ride across the rolling countryside. The man and the horse were inseparable.

In 1870, Lee suffered a stroke in the dining room of his home in Lexington. His bed in an upstairs room was dismantled, brought down, and set up in the dining room to make him as comfortable as possible. He lingered for three days before passing on. It had rained hard the whole time Lee lay dying, but stopped almost the minute he died. Then some strange things happened. There was no suitable coffin for the general. During the three days' downpour, city streets had flooded, and the coffins in the undertaker's building washed away. Men were dispatched to find a suitable resting place for Lee, and a coffin was finally found some distance away, on the banks of a creekbed.

There was another problem. Lee didn't fit in the coffin. It was an inch or two too short. There had been instances in such cases where the body's legs were broken so it would fit, but this was not seriously considered. After much thought it was decided—against the wishes of some of the general's former officers—to bury Lee without his boots. The officers felt this was a sacrilege and some of them refused to attend the funeral.

Fitzhugh Lee wrote: "Traveler, who had borne the great leader in so many battles, led by two old soldiers, slowly walking riderless behind the hearse, covered with sable trappings of mourning, was a tender and touching sight."

Traveler survived his master by two years, although it was obvious to observers that the horse greatly missed Lee. Then, in the summer of 1872, while grazing on the college campus, the horse stepped on a rusty nail, tetanus developed, and Traveler died in the barn near the president's house. A feather bed was placed under him by college students. His skeleton is preserved in the Lee Museum in Lexington.

A short time after this, Mrs. Lee and others began hearing some inexplicable noises at Traveler's empty stall adjacent to the house. It sounded like a horse snorting and scratching with its hooves at the stall doors, which were closed. Mrs. Lee believed it was the spirit of Traveler trying to get into his stall. And so, a sacred tradition began. Mrs. Lee ordered that the stall doors be opened and never again closed, so the ghost horse could enter. This done, the mysterious sounds stopped.

Students at the college helped make sure the doors remained open, and saw that fresh oats were always placed in Traveler's trough. Only once in the past 140 years has Mrs. Lee's order been violated. One college president shut the doors. The students nearly revolted. The president was unceremoniously told to keep the doors open or leave the premises himself! To this day, as one walks up the gentle slope on Washington Street to the president's house, the doors to Traveler's stall can still be seen—wide open.

# A Contract with the Devil

In 1904, C. A. Bryce published an autobiographical book called *Ups and Downs of a Country Doctor*. It chronicled the life of a rural doctor in the Shenandoah Valley late in the nineteenth century. One chapter, here excerpted, is titled "A Visitor from the Other World."

"Most sensible men do foolish things at times and I plead guilty to having been a party to a very foolish contract in my earlier years of rustic practice. I had been through the revelations of the dissecting room, and had tricks upon me in which the dead bodies would mysteriously raise a warning and threatening hand at me as I worked alone in the dead house in the wee small hours. In the hospital I had seen the awful and sudden taking off of my fellow men—until I felt that nothing could unnerve me. But what I subsequently experienced was enough to make me careful not to go out of my way to hunt up trouble ever thereafter.

"I had a patient, a colored woman, dying of consumption, who lived about a quarter of a mile from the main county road in a little clearing in the pines. The road ran through a dense forest for a mile or two with no habitation in sight or call, and about midway of this forest, the little detour to this poor patient's house or hut struck off and within an equal distance beyond tapped the elbowing road again.

"It was the month of March and as the days grew longer, this poor creature's breath became shorter. [The doctor is speaking of Becky, the wife of a man named Peter Adams.] Poor Peter supplied her with every-thing in his reach to tempt the appetite and improve her strength. Her entire diet consisted of corn bread, hog meat, and buttermilk.

"But before her demise, the poor woman expressed much grati-tude for my efforts to ease her pain and prolong her life, and regretted that there was no way in which I could possibly hope to receive any compensation for my services. I told her that she was welcome to all I had done for her, and I would make one request of her if she would agree to it, and it could not possibly do any harm if nothing ever came of it. It was that, after her death, she would come back and unmistak-ably satisfy me that it was possible for a spirit to return to earth.

"To my surprise, she received it very reasonably and became a willing party to the contract, agreeing to reveal herself to me within six months after her death if such a thing was possible. Soon after her demise I kept a sharp eye open for revelations, especially when pass-ing along that neighborhood after dark, but seeing nothing I soon for-got all about the matter.

"One very rainy day in the early fall I was sent for to see the wife of a man living a mile or two above the point of which I have written. [After this visit, the doctor was invited to spend the night here, but the woman had died and there was much sadness, so he decided to leave.] Night was coming on, it was raining straight from the heavens, and a ten mile ride lay ahead of me to reach my house. The storm was far preferable to remaining another half hour in that house. I had not rid-den 15 minutes before the darkness was so great that I could not see my hand in three inches of my face. The darkness was so intense that I made no attempt to see or guide my faithful horse, Prince.

"Noble beast! How could I forget your companionship over the lonely road, day and night, through the burning heat of midsummer and the blinding snowstorms of winter, you who have safely carried me over icy road, pole bridge, ditch and fence, in darkest night and amid the storm's awful roar, in forest when the lurid lighting has riven the tall oak into splinters at our very feet—you and I have trembled together, but we have never turned back when duty called us.

"My reins were dropped over the pommel of my saddle and I with-drew myself from the outside world and settled into a semi-sleepy reverie while the rain poured in torrents over my rubber suit and kept time to the regular slash, slash, of my good steed's footsteps in the mud. All at once my horse stopped so suddenly as to almost unseat me, and gave a snort of unusual alarm. In a moment I was thoroughly aroused and trying to solve the problem of his terror. It was useless to try to see anything, for I could not see the faintest outlines of my frightened horse.

"At first, I thought it might have been a drunken man in the road, or a horse or some disabled animal, and I knew if such were the case, he would soon investigate it and pass along by or over it, for he would go anywhere I urged him. This time he refused to move and responded to all of my urging with increased snorts of real alarm and trembled so violently that the bottles in my saddlebags rattled like marbles.

"Up to this time I had not felt the slightest alarm or nervousness, nor could I discern anything natural or supernatural, but it gradually came to my mind that I was in all probability somewhere in the neighborhood of Peter Adams' late residence. And while I am, or was, not a bit superstitious or cowardly, my legs began to quake and my tongue plastered itself up to the roof of my mouth! So there were the two of us in rather an unsettled condition. There I sat upon the back of a badly frightened horse that no power on earth could move out of his tracks, and I positively could not move or speak. But with all of my nervousness I could not see anything, not even by the aid of a very vivid imagination. At last, I realized that if I did not do or say something to break the spell, I would stay there forever and become petrified or turned into a pillar of salt which undoubtedly would be melted down before morning under the torrents then falling.

"Reaching out, I could feel my horse's ears pointing straight ahead of him and I knew that he was looking at something certainly not prostrate on the ground. I drew a revolver, slid off my horse, and, stepping in front of him, fired a shot, and involuntarily said, 'I am satisfied now.' My horse immediately followed me without further alarm. I felt around and broke a few twigs and bunched them up on the ground that I might identify the spot in the morning. Then I remounted and rode home without further adventure or mishap.

"The next day I found my bundle of twigs and branches exactly in the mouth of the bridle path leading from Peter Adams' house into the main road. A reference to my notebook reminded me that poor Becky, his wife, had been dead exactly six months that night.

"I do not know positively what frightened horse and rider that night, but I have never solicited any interviews with the departed since; for I am informed by my stable boy that 'hosses kin certainly see ghostes.'"

# Grandma Moses Sees a Ghost

She was, for decades in the twentieth century, the most popular and revered folk artist in America. Self-taught, a widow, and the mother of ten children, she didn't start her career until the age of seventy. Yet she lived to be 101 years old (1860–1961) and produced more than a thousand paintings, which today sell at prices in the tens and hundreds of thousands of dollars. She portrayed happy bucolic scenes and pictures of history. In some works, figures are dressed in eighteenth-century country costumes. She worked from memory, picturing a way of life she knew intimately. The people in many of her paintings are actively engaged in farm tasks; the landscapes are shown in panoramic sweeps.

Her name was Anna Mary Robertson, but she was known worldwide as simply "Grandma Moses."

Although she was born and lived most of her life in New York, it is a little-known fact that she spent twenty years in the Staunton, Virginia, area as a young woman. It was here that she had a true ghost sighting. She described it best in her 1952 autobiography, along with a scary practical joke she once played.

"After we took the Dudley place," she wrote, "we hired a colored man, Andy Stewart. He was freed when he was about three years old, but he would take on the master's name, because he didn't have any of his own. The nine years he worked for us, he was Andy Moses. He helped with all the farm work, plowing and haying, things like that.

"One day we sat down in the kitchen talking, and we got tired and kind of halfway started for bed. Andy had not got home yet, and Mattie [a friend], says, 'Do you see that wagon coming? That's Andy. Oh, I just would love to scare the blue beans out of him.' 'All right,' I said. 'What shall we do?' Mattie said, 'let's make up a scarecrow to put up in the wagon shed.'

"So we ran down to the wash room underneath. There was a lot of dirty clothes on the basin, such as table cloths, sheets and overalls and shirts. We stuffed the overalls full of the soiled clothes, then we stuffed the shirt, then tacked them together, stuffed a pillow slip to make a head, tacked it on the shirt, and ran right down with it to the wagon shed, carrying a sheet and a table cloth. Up over the shed was a big wheel. Mattie climbed up on that and dragged the sheet over, so it would flap with the breeze when the door was opened.

"Then we hung the made-up man underneath it and hitched it to the post of the door. Oh, we had it all planned. Poor Andy! After we had it done, we heeled it back because we could hear the horse and buggy coming. We went underneath the brickwork and stood there and listened for Andy. We could hear him singing to himself till he got to the wagon shed. Then all was quiet. He unhitched his horse and put it in the stable, then he went back to push his buggy into the shed. As he opened the door, the post that the door was hitched to dropped, and down came the 'dead man,' and it hopped right at him. He said it jumped right at him.

"We heard him coming towards the house, and we heeled towards our rooms. Mattie went into her room and stuffed the pillowcase into her mouth, and I buried my face in the pillow in my room. We had hardly settled till we heard Andy come to his room. 'Oh, Mr. Moses, oh, Mr. Moses, come here quick,' he stammered, 'there is a dead man!' Thomas [her husband] and Charlie started to come and see what the trouble was. And then Thomas thought, and called, 'You girls been up to anything?' 'No, we were sound asleep.'

"So they went trotting down the back stairs, down to see the dead man. Thomas thought there was a rat somewhere, he didn't know where, but the minute he saw it, he knew. Andy didn't speak to us the next day. Mattie told him, 'Well you mustn't be out so late at night."

Grandma Moses continued, recounting her real ghostly encounter: "They always laugh about me, but I saw a spirit at the Dudley place. I don't know if it was so, but I think so anyway. There was a long flight of stairs going up to the chambers. There, we had three large sleeping rooms, and I had the largest room for myself. Loyd [her son] was about a year old. I used to have him take his nap about four o'clock. That evening I had taken Loyd up to take his nap. I had lain him down on the bed and lain down with him myself. I thought I would stay there until Thomas came in. I didn't drop off to sleep, but I was there, very quiet, with my eyes closed.

"All at once I looked out in the room, and there stood a man, and he stood right where I had a little round table, and as I looked at him, the table seemed to be a square stand with a big book on it, and he was turning the pages of the book. He was quite an old man, his hair was gray, something like how father used to wear it. He had on spectacles and a black frock coat. His nose was long and was humped in toward his lip. I said, 'How did you come in here, where did you get that book, and where are my flowers that were on the table?'

"I looked him over good. I could almost draw a picture of him now. He was standing there where the stove should be, and pretty soon I heard something downstairs and he commenced to fade. I expect it was Thomas coming, and when he came into the house, my man had all vanished. I said to Thomas, 'I have seen a ghost!' He says, 'Oh, you have been dreaming,' and I said, 'No, I had not been dreaming. I had not shut my eyes.'

"But my ghost was gone. I described it to Thomas and he laughed at me till the next day when our neighbor, Mr. Keister, came in, and we told him about it. He said, 'That was the old captain who had built this house.'" Grandma Moses had described him perfectly.

"For a long time I could not get it out of my mind," she said.

## Scary Scenes at Stonewall Cottage

I am indebted to attorney Joseph B. Yount III, of Waynesboro, who in 1979 wrote a paper about his family and its associated history with Stonewall Cottage in Rockingham County, near Harrisonburg. He graciously shared a copy of it with me. The paper is titled, "Ghosts and Frights at Stonewall Cottage." Yount says, "All of these events happened before I was born. I have done my best to recount them exactly as they were often told me by my late father, Joseph Bryon Yount Jr. I have tried to be as accurate as possible. The various stories about the cottage and its haunts have been a part of my family folklore all my life. Truth is stranger than fiction, they say, and I have no reason to believe that any of this is untrue."

Some downright scary things have happened over the years at Stonewall Cottage and a few of these remain inexplicable and are linked with the supernatural, while others have been caused by quite natural and rational, if unusual means. Yet the effect has been much the same—spine-tingling chills.

Take the case of the reburial of Uncle Joseph Dovel, for example. It seems that in 1938, several family graves were to be moved from land at the cottage to lots in Woodbine Cemetery in Harrisonburg. Among those to be moved was that of Capt. Joseph Dovel, a Confederate Army soldier who died in 1863 at age twenty-three. The undertaker hired a crew of African-American laborers to exhume the bodies. They found Captain Dovel buried in a cast-iron, bullet-shaped coffin with a glass window over his face. The hinged coffin was held shut by two large bolts.

"Aunt Bettie Post and my father were present when the iron casket was raised," Yount says. "The men dusted off the window and there was the captain, looking as if he were merely asleep. He was laid out in his uniform with a crimson sash for decoration. Aunt Bettie asked the undertaker if he would open the casket for a moment, to enable her to see her uncle in full regalia. The men unscrewed the screws and lifted the top. As soon as he air hit inside, there was a mild, soundless implosion. The body disintegrated instantly into dust before everyone's eyes." Yount adds that some of the men ran off in all directions, and Aunt Bettie rushed back to the house. This ghostly excitement is not paranormal, Yount says, but must have been equally hair-raising.

Yount's father was the sole witness to another frightening, though not quite paranormal, incident. This one occurred in 1934, when Aunt Laura died sitting up in her chair one night. She had apparently suffered a fatal attack during the evening before coming upstairs to bed, and her body was not discovered until the next morning. Aunt Laura had left instructions that she wanted to be buried in a shroud. "The undertaker had prepared the body in the coffin and placed it, as was the custom, in the front parlor," Yount recalls. "The house was dark, and the shutters were closed in the front, seldom-used rooms. My father went around to the rear where the family and friends were gathered. After a while, Aunt Sallie asked him to go over to the parlor to get her something from behind the organ. He had to pass through several rooms and the hall to get to the parlor.

"My father always said he wasn't afraid of anyone living, but didn't like to fool with the dead. Nervously, he entered the parlor and glanced down at Aunt Laura. Her eyes were closed, her form lying stiffly in the coffin. He walked over to the organ. Suddenly, he heard a loud snap, sounding something like a rat trap going off. He looked around and saw Aunt Laura—sitting bolt upright, her eyes open and apparently staring at him.

"He was so much in shock that it took what seemed an hour for him to recover and leave the parlor. He called out the front door to the undertaker, who came immediately. What had happened? Because of the delay in discovering the body, staying as it was in a sitting position all night long, rigor mortis had set in. The undertaker had braced her mouth shut with a brace under her chin, obscured by the high collar of the shroud. My father somehow jarred it loose as he walked across the creaky wooden floor. The brace slipped, throwing the head ajar. My mother remembered well how white and pale he looked when he returned to the cottage kitchen."

Yount says one of the unexplained psychic manifestations concerned an old lady who always sat by the fireplace smoking a clay pipe. "After her death, others in the house could still hear her knocking out her pipe against the fireplace after everyone else had gone to bed for the night. This was verified by my father and his sisters. They all said without question that the lady knocking out her pipe was Martha Cowan (1806–1895)."

Under a heading called "Restless Spirits that Wander," Yount wrote: "I now come to what I believe to be the true ghost story of Stonewall Cottage. It happened in 1902. It was witnessed by my father, who was five at the time, his first cousin, Addie Yount Wood, who was 15, and my grandfather, Joseph B. Yount. Addie was a favorite niece, and well remembers the excitement caused by the incident.

"The cottage in 1902 was the home of Mary Dovel Stephens, 72, and her two daughters, Laura, 40, and Sallie, 32. They were well-to-do, but it was very burdensome work for the three women to operate the big farm with often undependable hired labor. One late summer day in 1902, Mary, at dinner, remarked to her daughters that there was some important business she needed to tend to at once. They thought she intended to change her will. After dinner, Mary laid down to rest on a fainting couch and without warning, died instantly of an apparent heart attack. She was buried in the family cemetery south of the house near the orchard. A week or so after the funeral, Sallie and Laura asked their brother-in-law, Joseph B. Yount, to come to the cottage for several days to help them with business affairs in connection with the settlement of the estate. He brought his five year old son, my father, along with him.

"The first night of their visit, Joe and his son went to bed in the front upstairs bedroom, a room in which an old rocking chair was located. Sallie and Laura were supposedly asleep in the upstairs bedrooms to the rear of the house. Shortly after they went to bed, Joe and his son heard the distinct sound of the front door being opened and the tread of footsteps lightly ascending the main stairs. Suddenly, the door to their bedroom blew open and the rocking chair began to rock as if some ghostly figure was sitting in it. Grandfather attributed these strange happenings to the wind, arose from bed, and closed the door. He said his son fell asleep. When they awoke, the bedroom door was open again, with no indication that it had been opened by anyone else in the house.

"Grandfather said nothing, not wanting to alarm the recently bereaved sisters-in-law. The next night, perhaps out of caution, he pulled a side chair against the inside of the bedroom door to insure that the wind could not blow it open. He and his son were nearly asleep when, again, they heard the front door open and close, the sound of footsteps ascending the stairs, and then, to their amazement, the bedroom door was pushed open, as if by some invisible force, sliding the side chair back against the wall, and then the rocking chair began to rock.

"This was too much for my grandfather. He abruptly arose, hurriedly dressed, took my father by the hand, and walked to the rear of the house, where Sallie and Laura were supposed to be sleeping. To his surprise, he found them both awake, each with a frightened look. The expression on his face caused them to say, 'Well, you have heard it, too! It has happened every night since mother was buried. We thought we were losing our minds. If it continues we will have to move away from here.'

"The next day, my grandfather took Sallie and Laura to see their minister and told him of the apparent poltergeist. That night at the cottage, he and another preacher joined the two ladies, and my grandfather and father, for prayers. The ministers said appropriate words from the Bible and led the group in prayer. My father described the words as some verse about restless or troubled spirits who wander.

"The prayers and readings were enough to summon the spirits, and the mysterious footsteps were soon heard. Further prayers were said, and one of the ministers exhorted the spirit, 'in the name of God, what do you want?' There was no response, so the minister said, 'in the name of God, be at rest!' The prayers and exhortations were effective. Never again during the remaining 36 years of family occupancy did the restless spirit wander the halls of Stonewall Cottage.

"My father always professed to believe that it had been the ghost of Mary Dovel Stephens, who had died before attending to her important business and who could not rest. All I can promise the readers of this account is that I have not exaggerated it one iota. I have written it as it was told to me by one who was there."

## The Haunted Highland Inn

For years the rumors swirled around the historic Highland Inn located in Monterey, Virginia. It was said that a high-ranking German official visited here in the early 1930s, seeking information about the strategic military tactics used by generals Robert E. Lee and Stonewall Jackson in the Shenandoah Valley during the American Civil War. There was strong speculation that the mysterious German was none other than Erwin Rommel, the legendary "Desert Fox" of World War II fame. Whoever he was, he smoked a specific, peculiar brand of pipe tobacco—one that tourists continued to smell for years afterward, leading to the belief that Rommel's ghost returned to the site long after his death.

Current inn owner Gregg Morse, however, says while the rumor had some founding in fact, the suspected spirit is not that of Field Marshal Rommel. There is no documented evidence that he ever traveled to the United States. More likely it was Col. Friedrich von Boetticher, who was known to have visited Civil War battle sites during the 1930s with Virginia historian and author Douglas Southall Freeman.

Morse says that while the Rommel tradition cannot be supported, there are other extraordinary incidents that have occurred here that hint of the possibilities of murder, suicide, arson, and even elements of the supernatural.

The Highland Inn, formerly known as the Monterey Hotel, was built in 1904 and is considered to be the premier architectural landmark in Monterey, the seat of Highland County, which the local chamber of commerce calls "The Switzerland of America." It was erected to serve hordes of visitors who came to Highland County in the early 1900s seeking a healthful mountain climate in which to spend the summer season at one of the commonwealth's famed mineral springs.

It quickly became a mecca for the social elite. Guests included Henry Ford, Thomas Edison, Harvey Firestone, and composer John Phillip Sousa. Then, changes in transportation and lifestyles eventually led to the demise of nearly all of Virginia's original mountain resorts and spas. The Highland Inn is one of the few exceptions that survived.

Aside from the phantom German who allegedly still returns occasionally to have his peaceful pipe smoke, there may well be other spirits residing at the inn. Morse says guests sometimes tell him of hearing a child running on the front balcony at odd hours of the night. This is thought to be the ghost of Janet Patterson, daughter of the second owner of the hotel. She died at the age of eleven in May 1912. H. B. Wood, then publisher of the *Highland Recorder* newspaper, served as a pallbearer at her funeral and wrote: "Janet was a bright and interesting little girl. She will be remembered by all." Some feel she returns because she so loved her home here.

The third owners of the inn were the Carwells, and their short tenure was marred by tragedy, mystery, and scandal. In fact, notes Morse, some surviving relatives still avoid talking about the terrible series of events that played out from 1919 to 1921. J. Edgar Carwell and his wife, Amanda (Mandy), purchased the hotel in September 1919, along with Charley Pullin, Mandy's brother. It was soon rumored that the new owners were having a hard time financially.

Then, suddenly, on Thursday, January 22, 1920, just four months after the purchase, a fire was discovered in a third-story storage area. A general alarm was sounded, most of the local citizens rushed to the scene, and the blaze was extinguished, resulting in water and smoke damage. The origin of the fire, says Morse, was a mystery and arson was suspected.

Then, inexplicably, four days later on January 26, 1920, Mandy Carwell died at about 2:30 in the morning, supposedly from suffering ptomaine poisoning after eating a can of sweet potatoes. The town was shocked, and her death caused much speculation. Had these twin tragedies resulted from an attempt to collect fire and life insurance claims? The circumstances were very suspicious. Morse wonders. "She had dinner at about nine in the evening," he says, "and died six hours later. Generally, when a person has ptomaine poisoning, they don't get sick until several hours after they have eaten—but Mandy Carwell expressed severe sickness at the dinner! That leads me to believe that the poison may have been administered hours earlier."

On top of all this strangeness, townspeople were shocked again when Edgar Carwell abruptly closed the hotel, and kept it closed for several months. It was said he used insurance funds to pay his quarterly mortgage installments. Then, on March 26, 1921, a year and two months after his wife's untimely death, Carwell himself flatly disappeared. As Morse notes, "mass searches and calls to distant relatives turned up no hints of his whereabouts." Talk of suicide and foul play ran rampant in the community. Oddly, during his absence, Charley Pullin reopened the hotel.

Eight months later, on December 9, 1921, a headline in the *Highland Recorder* read: "Skeleton of J. E. Carwell Found on Mountain." Two boys out biking discovered his remains on Jack Mountain. It appeared he had not been robbed because he was still wearing a ring and a watch, but a roll of money he always carried was not found. He had been shot in the back of the head. A jury of inquest was adjourned due to lack of evidence, and it was contended that he had taken his own life. But as Morse and others have pointed out, it would have been extremely difficult, if not impossible, for him to have shot himself in the back of his head. "It remains one of the unsolved mysteries of Monterey," Morse says.

Many inn staff members, past and present, believe the spirit of Mandy Carwell still is active at the site she so loved in life. There are numerous unexplained manifestations to support such a theory. Most of the activity seems to center in the kitchen area. Morse says craftsmen doing restoration work in the 1980s reported seeing "a period dressed woman seemingly walking on air in the kitchen." She disappeared at the ceiling! They later learned that the spot where she vanished was where an old stairwell had stood.

"Sometimes pots and pans go flying about on their own," Morse says. "Usually, a staff person will just holler, 'cut that out, Mandy!' In 2003, a punch bowl shattered in place when no one was near it. Now let me explain. The bowl did not fall. It was sitting on top of a shelf and suddenly went to pieces right there. And there wasn't any extreme heat or cold to cause it. We bought another bowl, and a week later it, too, shattered in place!" Punch bowls are no longer kept in the kitchen. Other times, when staffers are in the kitchen all alone and they open a door to the refrigerator or a cabinet, they get a strong feeling that someone unseen is peering over their shoulder, seeing what they are getting. They are convinced it is Mandy, keeping an eye on her old hotel.

Gregg and Deborah Morse invite those interested in ghosts to come and sit a spell at the Highland Inn. Who knows what may develop? But they warn in advance, the kitchen is off-limits to guests.

# The House of Four Ghosts

In and around Lexington, it has been known for decades simply as "Jack's House." That's because the last owner was Jack Roberson, a colorful character who seemed to be friends with just about everyone in town. He died in 2002, but the legends of this decaying, spooky-looking house on Jefferson Street live on. A towering oak tree in front almost conceals the entrance. Overgrown shrubs hide the front porch from view, and creeping vines snake upward on all sides. The house looks haunted. And, say old-timers, it is.

Deed documents say the house was built in 1790. For generations it has been known as the Vanderslice-Roberson House. It is a popular stop on the Lexington ghost tour, and was covered by Anne McCorkle Knox in her 1981 book *The Gentle Ghosts*. Jack Roberson told rare visitors that the house was made of blue poplar, wood that covers an underpinning of huge bricks of unusual shapes, some as big as loaves of bread, some as big as pillows. According to Roberson, who had intimate knowledge of the town's history, the Lexington Methodist Church was founded in the living room in the early 1800s.

The Methodist reverend Vanderslice moved into the house in 1837, and it became a religious center. Notable visitors included President Andrew Jackson and Civil War heroes Robert E. Lee, Stonewall Jackson, and J. E. B. Stuart. Knox writes that "inside the house the shadowed sunlight reveals the mellow patina of old, wax-rubbed furniture and gleams on brass and handsome ornaments collected in the Shenandoah Valley" by Roberson.

Tour guides tell of at least four different ghosts believed to haunt the site. Not much is known about the origins of two of them. One apparently is a young man who occasionally, especially on dark, moonless nights, stomps up onto the porch and knocks four times on the front door. No one knows who he might have been or why he wants to enter. There have been, too, the sightings inside the house of a young woman who walks down the stairs from the upper floor. The tradition is that she is still there searching for a "lost lover" of bygone days.

More is known of the third ghost. It is the apparition of a "little old lady" who for some reason creates a noisy ruckus when she appears. She also comes down the stairs, dragging heavy chains! The sounds, witnessed by many residents and guests over the years, are quite unmistakable. In an interview thirty years ago, Roberson said the old lady has been seen and the clanking chains heard ever since the middle of the nineteenth century. He noted that "Mrs. Lewis, who was married in this house sixty-five years ago, and who was the great-granddaughter of the Reverend Vanderslice, said the ghost in chains had traveled the house day and night and that everyone had seen and heard it."

It is the fourth phantom that has been sighted the most. Tour guides describe her as a "lady in red," a beautiful young woman who many have seen sitting by a window, brushing her long, gleaming hair. She is believed to have been the wife of the reverend. The legend is that she was much younger than her husband and often flirted with, and may have even entertained, some of the young students at Washington College.

Accordingly, the jealous reverend would lock her in an upstairs room whenever he went out of the house. It is at the window in this room in which she most often appears. When Roberson was asked if he lived in the house alone, he sometimes replied, "No, I live with

Mrs. Vanderslice." He added that one evening a guest told him he saw the apparition of a young woman standing in a doorway. Nonchalantly, Roberson replied, "Oh, that's just the reverend's wife."

Roberson himself helped perpetuate the haunting rumors that have surrounded the house for decades. On some nights the melodic sounds of a sixteenth–century organ could be heard by those passing by. It was Roberson at the organ, but those who experienced the sensation were convinced that the ghosts inside were acting up again.

## Poltergeists in the Pottery

A few miles north of Charlottesville, on Route 29, is the small town of Ruckersville. Turn west, and one passes through scenic mountain vistas on the way to Harrisonburg. Here, at the summit of Swift Run Gap, is a granite monument flanked by historical markers. It is a site made famous three centuries ago by an adventure-loving band of prosperous Virginia settlers known as "the Knights of the Golden Horseshoe."

Writers from the Works Progress Administration during the Great Depression had this to say about what happened in 1716: "Here is a junction with the Skyline Drive. Through this gap Indians guided Governor Alexander Spotswood and his merry gentlemen. Hoping to find a new pass westward, they started from Germanna (west of Fredericksburg) on August 29, well provisioned, especially with liquors of several kinds. At the slightest provocation, they drank to the health of the king.

"They traveled westward by easy stages, amusing themselves shooting deer, bear, turkeys and snakes, and making the expedition a pleasure trip. The party reached the top of the Blue Ridge in September, drank a special toast to the king and to Governor Spotswood, and named a peak for each. Riding into the Shenandoah Valley, they ceremoniously claimed the land west of the mountains for the king, then returned home. A short time later, Spotswood presented each member of the group with a jeweled miniature horseshoe of gold, thus they became known as the Knights of the Golden Horseshoe."

In time, a trail was cut through the area allowing passage across the mountains to the great valley of Virginia. George Washington's diary notes that he crossed here in 1784. Swift Run Gap was a strategic point during the Civil War. Additionally, since Spotswood's time, the gap has fostered a reputation for being haunted. John W. Wayland made reference to spectral entities here in his 1957 book *Twenty-five chapters on the Shenandoah Valley*. He said: "Around the region today, sound rather than silence prevails, but perchance in some quiet midnight hour a dreamer may sense a ghostly presence and hear a muffled hoof beat upon a stony path."

The road to the gap leads past the hamlet of Standardsville and on to another spooky site—Blue Ridge Pottery. The main structure at this complex dates to 1827, when it was used as a stagecoach inn that served travelers on the route through the mountains in the nineteenth century. The pottery studio's Web site says: "Over the years the building has been used for many purposes and has a history of being haunted . . . Many say there have been at least seven murders here, including the results of a gunfight on the stairs in the early 1800s, and reports of a landlady who killed tenants for their goods."

The pottery studio was founded in the late 1980s by master potter Alun Ward. Owing to the firm's reputation for turning out beautiful crafts, people flock here from all over the world. The Wards sell everything they make. Some visitors, however, come to investigate the alleged ghosts. While Ward himself refuses today to talk about the paranormal activity, others will talk about it. A Greene County Historical Society member said she once had an overwhelming feeling that someone was with her when she was upstairs in the shop when there was no mortal being around. She said she was freezing in the heat of a sultry summer day. This occurred in the area where a card player was said to have been shot dead long ago.

"There are a lot of things that happen here that I can't explain," Ward reluctantly admits. "If you had asked me about the ghosts here a few years ago, I would have told you about them, but not now. They're not happy when you talk about them. Still, stories do abound here. A lot of people have seen things. This building stood vacant for several years before I bought it. No one wanted it because of its reputation. I couldn't even get anyone locally to come out and cut the grass. It's hard enough to get artists to come and work here as it is, without the rumors of the hauntings."

Henry Galt, a staff writer for the *Greene County Record*, the local weekly newspaper, said, "I was told there was a bloodstain at the bottom of the stairs that can't be removed. I've also heard that the main building is haunted and no one will go there at night." Henry added: "I have a friend whose sister once worked there. She told him she once saw a piece of pottery rise up off a shelf, sail through the air, and land, unharmed, on a nearby table. She quit on the spot. There also is supposed to be a little girl ghost who roams about. Sometimes she breaks one of the plates and then tries to wipe up the pieces and hide them. Her tiny handprints are seen."

The newspaper ran an article on the paranormal activity at the pottery a few years ago. Ward was quoted as saying, "These ghosts are pranksters. I talk to them and it seems to calm them. It's hard to know what to believe, what's lore, what's been built up over the years, and what's truth. I really believe we have spirits here. We hear unexplained noises very regularly." Ward adds that once his daughter, Heather, was running the studio when he was out of town. He called her. "There were no customers in the store," he recalls, "and I could hear sounds, like ghosts moving furniture around upstairs." Heather won't work alone there anymore. Of another daughter, Mindy, Ward says, "One time she was sitting at the top of the steps with a friend when one of the ghosts, believed to be a Confederate soldier, turned the lights on and off six times." It should be noted that the building served as a hospital during the Civil War.

Ward was further quoted about noises and incidents that seem concentrated at the top of the stairs and in a room on the right. "Spectral activity on the stairs might be explained by a gunfight that took place there back in the days when this was an inn. There is a legend about a group of men from the valley who were taking their cattle to market in Richmond. Apparently, they were paid in gold coins at the market and they stopped off at the inn for the night. They were gambling and one guy won quite a bit of money. Then, as he went upstairs, a man he had beaten at cards pulled a gun and shot him. He fell down the stairs, and his blood still won't come out of the floor. The stains show right through layers of paint."

Ward also tells the tradition of a Civil War soldier and a pot of gold. "We've heard a lot about the gold being buried on the property," he says. "A soldier had it and he didn't want to bring it to the front with him. He apparently was killed, but there is a rumor that he wrote a letter to his wife telling her where the gold was hidden. She never received the letter, however, so perhaps the ghost is still searching for it. People want to come here with metal detectors, but I don't want that.

"I think the spirits should be left in peace."

# The Telepathic Cat

The following poignant narrative is excerpted and recounted, with permission, from Elizabeth Proctor Biggs' 1978 book *Beyond the Limit of Our Sight*. For privacy protection reasons, Mrs. Biggs did not include names of the persons involved, or the specific location, although she concentrated much of her work on the northern end of the Shenandoah Valley. The true story is told by a young woman who lived with an elderly aunt in a small, isolated cottage near the edge of some woods on the outskirts of a village in the 1920s. It covers the fascinating subjects of telepathy and animal communications.

The aunt, an animal lover, had found a starving stray cat in a roadside ditch, half dead with pneumonia, some time before the young woman had moved in with her. She named the cat, whose age was undetermined, Grace, short for Gracious. Through loving care, Grace was slowly nursed back to health, and she paid her rescuer back in many ways.

The cat was described as special, "possessing a degree of intelligence that permitted it to mental stimulation." The young lady said, "I have witnessed on countless occasions, the frantic search for a thimble, a change purse, a particular book, and a myriad of other lost objects, successfully terminated following a closed, silent session between my aunt and the cat. Grace would move in a selected direction and sit there until the area was searched. Only rarely in this way did she fail to reveal the lost item; and perhaps what appeared to be her failure was actually our own to interpret accurately.

"Grace could be predictive also. Translation to human perception of this quality was rather more difficult for her than the simple act of unearthing lost articles. Our region was once grievously surprised by a fully matured tornado. Brief but deadly, it had come spiraling and exploding in fiendish uproar in mid-afternoon. All day, the cat had hidden stubbornly in the dark earth cellar of the cottage. Puzzled, my aunt had repeatedly called the cat up out of the cellar without success. Finally, she ordered me to collect the other house cats, and with them join her down in the basement immediately.

"Surprised and thoroughly frightened by her tone, I had done instantly as I was told. In rapid order, our household of a number one cat, two minor felines and two women collected in a dark corner of the cellar under the cottage. Only minutes later, the tornado tore part of the roof off the house and ripped away the small porch, tossing it over the trees like a matchbox. In the cottage, plaster fell, furniture was dislodged, crockery broken, and two front windows shattered. But we were safe, because Grace had somehow communicated a sense of approaching danger to my aunt, who acted without question upon the warning.

"I accepted from my aunt the teaching that all these forms of life could communicate on what she termed an "inner level" if the mind was seriously put to that purpose. She said that if a person really understood that life in all forms actually sprang from one source, contact could be made in that source among all levels. When I asked her once if she worked magic on animals she healed, she replied with a counter-question: 'Can you accept the palpable fact that animals instinctively or intuitively communicate with one another?' Of course I could and did. 'Well, then,' she suggested, 'just examine the idea that this communication takes place in every living thing, only on varying levels of development. I have found that it is possible under certain conditions for one level of consciousness to intelligently respond to stimulation from a different kind.'"

One day, years later, both women anxiously observed a sudden deterioration in Grace's response and habits. "My aunt had watched her cat, dismayed that at long last the life of her friend was preparing to vacate the body. Each morning was expected to be the last for the frail animal. She slept much, crept about too weak to walk properly, drank endless water, and was fed at intervals with an eye dropper. At night she would be wrapped in an old comforter and put beside her owner for sleep and for the consolation of companionship in the dwindling hours. Aunt herself was advancing in age (she was eighty-five), and made frequent reluctant reference to the prospective transition that ever more closely approached them—herself and her creature.

"Last evening, when my aunt had started up the short stairway to bed, the old cat followed, pushing herself forward up the steps as if her hind legs were defaulting. In pity and distress, my aunt had scooped her up in her arms for the remainder of the climb. Before settling for sleep, I had looked in on the woman and the cat, and found the two lying close in a pathetic attitude of mutual protectiveness. From the dim hall light, I saw my aunt's eyes gleaming with tears, the old chin trembling weakly, as she stroked the dull fur and bony body of the cat. 'I think she'll be gone for sure by morning,' she said. Aunt had then left the bed and went to the kitchen to mix a few drops of brandy with a spoonful of warm milk. This she had brought back to the bed and fed to Grace with the eye dropper.

"Presently, the cat got to her feet and moved to sit facing her friend. All of life's energy seemed to accumulate back of her eyes and out to the eyes of my aunt. They remained for a full minute involved in the eyes of one another. I stood watching this strange transmittance. And this is what it was, transmission of some cognition between them. It was a pattern familiar to me in my aunt's treatment of animals. When necessary, the two communicated clearly in this way."

The next morning the niece awakened late. "Immediately, I assumed that Grace had finally died in the night and my aunt, distracted by sadness, had overlooked calling me. I opened the door to my aunt's room and looked toward the bed. The cat was pressed motionless against my aunt's back. The room seemed very cold despite the June morning. She lay with her back to the door, the cat's face half hidden. Grace did not move at all and from where I stood, uncertain and uneasy, she looked to be stiff in death. We had expected the cat's death for nearly two weeks. This was no surprise.

"Then fear had suddenly taken flight and relief moved in as I watched Grace slowly stretch her long legs, get to her feet, and turn to face me. She yawned hugely, healthy pink gums showing, bright eyes openly wide, and silver fur glimmering. Muscular and strong, she sprang from the bed and walked over to the door to rub against my legs in greeting. I stared at the cat in disbelief. I viewed afresh the amazing overnight transformation of the animal. From emaciation and lassitude, dullness of coat and filminess of eye—to miraculously restored vigor, health and beauty!

"How heedlessly I had rushed to the bed to awaken my aunt to the wonderful recovery of Grace. I placed my hand on her shoulder to shake her awake, and snatched it back at once. Aunt was the cold of marble! Looking into her face, I saw at once she was long dead.

"My aunt believed that the forms of lower levels of consciousness did quite often, out of love or urgency, strive by strange, ambiguous means, to project acquired information to higher forms of awareness. Messages are often misread. Grace was conveying, 'It was not my call.' She had assumed the guise of death to alert her friend.

"My attention was reclaimed by the cat that morning, and speared by the fixed stare that might have been saying to me: 'Well, in the only way given, I did try to tell you. I did try to show you both.'"

# Paranormal Vignettes of the Shenandoah Valley

Here is a sampling of short ghost legends with unusual twists from this historic region.

## Help from the Beyond

One of the most intriguing folklore tales from the mountainous area bordering the Shenandoah Valley, told and retold for generations, occurred sometime in the late nineteenth century and involved an old country doctor named Anderson. One night in the middle of winter, with a mantle of snow cloaking the ground, the doctor heard a pounding at his door just after midnight. He opened the door and saw a shivering, frail young girl about twelve or thirteen years old, dressed in a blue coat with a white muff. He had never seen her before.

With frosty tears in her eyes, she told him her mother was deathly ill and needed immediate medical attention. When he asked her who her mother was, she said, "Mrs. Ballard," who lived in the "old Hostler place." It was about three miles away. The girl then said she thought her mother had an advanced case of pneumonia and that she lived alone. There was no one else to help her. Could the doctor come at once?

Dr. Anderson said he would, but before he could get dressed, the girl darted out of the house and disappeared in the darkness. He bundled up, saddled his horse, and rode off. He saw no sign of the girl on his way, nor did he see any footprints in the fresh snow. Strange, he thought. There was a faint glow of a lamp when he reached the cabin, and he found a woman, alone, lying on a bed. She had a high fever. He built a fire in the fireplace, heated some water, and gave her some medicine.

The woman responded quickly to the treatment. Then she asked how did he know to come to her aid. He told her that her daughter had come to summon him. The woman looked surprised, then said, "but I have no daughter. She died three years ago!" Dr. Anderson then described the girl to her, saying she was about twelve or thirteen, had on a blue coat and a white muff. The woman gasped. She said that her daughter had such a coat and muff. They were hanging in the closet.

He looked and found them. When he felt the coat and muff they were still warm and damp from perspiration!

### The Feathered Mourners

It was a real-life scene straight out of Alfred Hitchcock's classic movie, *The Birds*. Scott Hamilton Suter recounted the incident in his book *Shenandoah Valley Folklore*. Early in the twentieth century, near the village of Singers Glen in Rockingham County, there lived a very mean old man, so mean that his favorite pastime was to sit on his front porch and shoot every bird that alighted on the fence that separated his yard from the road. For years he killed hundreds of birds.

The man eventually died. On the day of his funeral his casket was to be carried down the road toward the cemetery. As the pallbearers approached the dead man's house, they stopped for a moment and stared in disbelief at an unusual sight. They all plainly saw that the fence in front of the house was lined, wing to wing, with scores of birds, so densely that no space could be seen between any of them.

## The Cat that Purred from the Beyond

In the first half of the twentieth century, near a small town west of Strasburg, Virginia, there lived an eccentric woman affectionately known as "Miss Effie." A spinster, she lived in a tiny frame house accompanied only by an old gray cat unimaginatively named Tom. She took the feline everywhere, even to church services on Sunday mornings. This caused some consternation, especially to the local preacher, because when Miss Effie stroked Tom in her lap, the cat would purr loudly enough to disrupt the concentration of members during silent prayer. Efforts to persuade Miss Effie to leave Tom at home proved futile. She countered that certain men in the congregation snored louder than her cherished pet purred.

Finally, at the ripe old age of eighteen, Tom passed away. This spurred a round of spirited speculation among the townspeople. They wondered whether the grief-stricken Miss Effie would attend the church service the following Sunday. Consequently, the church was packed. Everyone sneaked glances toward where Miss Effie was seated. Then there were gasps. It appeared that she was stroking something invisible on her lap. The woman, they thought, had gone mad. Could she possibly think Tom was still alive? There was a stir of murmurs among the pews.

After a rousing sermon, the preacher called for a moment of silent prayer. It was then that everyone craned their necks, opened their eyes, and stared, with open mouths, toward Miss Effie. As she continued to stroke, the distinct and unmistakable sound of a cat purring was heard throughout the building. It was so loud, some said, that the church windows rattled!

## The 'Meanest Man' Meets His Match

The following account was found in a collection of papers on Shenandoah Valley folklore compiled by historian Elmer L. Smith, a former professor at James Madison University in Harrisonburg. It was titled "The Mysterious Death of Drummer Jake."

"A short time before the Revolutionary War, there lived in the valley a character known as Tambour Jockel, or 'Drummer Jake.' He was a quarrelsome, heavily drinking, bullying person who was disliked by his neighbors. After a particularly violent argument with another man, also of low reputation, they agreed to a fight to settle the matter. However, before the date of the fight occurred, the other man died and was buried in a little church cemetery.

"On the day the fight was to have taken place, Drummer became very intoxicated and declared that he was going to the cemetery to fight his enemy. People tried to persuade him not to do anything in the graveyard, but that night he went there anyhow to call upon the dead to come forth and battle him. In the dark of night people heard Drummer scream for help in piercing cries, but those hearing him were too frightened to go to his aid.

"The next morning he was found dead, lying nearly naked in the churchyard, his clothing ripped to shreds. The ground seemed torn up in places and some of the bushes were broken in what appeared to have been a violent struggle."

## The Floating Coffin

In the fall of 1942, George and Loretta Keene were driving west through the Shenandoah Valley, heading toward West Virginia to see their friends, Clarence and Betty Morgan. They were bringing a new bicycle for the Morgans' daughter, Victoria. At precisely 6:50 P.M., when it was quite dark, they rounded a curve in the road and George suddenly slammed on the brakes. There, directly in front of them only a few feet away, was a small, glowing coffin floating in midair, in the center of the road. And inside, it appeared to be the ashen-faced body of little Victoria Morgan! The Keenes were stunned. They confirmed to each other that they both had seen the same thing.

As the couple sped away, they tried to make sense out of what they had envisioned. Was it a mirage? Was it a hallucination? But both had seen it. How do you explain that?

Two hours later, when they arrived at the Morgans' house, they noticed there were a number of cars in front of it. When they went inside they were shocked to see little Victoria lying lifeless in a coffin in the parlor. It was identical to the coffin the Keenes had seen in the roadway. They were told Victoria had been riding a bicycle in the street when she was struck by a passing car. She died instantly.

The time of the accident? It was precisely ten minutes to seven that evening!

## Repentance from the Spirit World

In the late 1800s, when spiritualism was in full swing in America, one of the best–known, most-gifted psychics was a woman named Belle Cross, who had a cottage in the foothills of the Blue Ridge Mountains. One winter she invited a clergyman named Arnold and his wife to spend some time with her there, because the Episcopal Church Arnold presided in had closed its doors.

One evening, when Miss Cross entered her bedroom, she was overwhelmed by the strong smell of stale liquor. This was strange, because no one in the house drank. Then, before the woman's eyes, the figure of a man suddenly appeared. Startled, the psychic asked, "What does this mean?" The apparition pointed down the stairs, toward Mrs. Arnold's bedroom, and in a creaky voice said, "I belong to her." He then evaporated.

The next morning Miss Cross asked Mrs. Arnold if she had ever known anyone who drank liquor to excess. Mrs. Arnold expressed shock at the question, then said her first husband had been a heavy drinker and had died long ago after a life of excessive wine. When Miss Cross told her of the ghostly visit she had experienced, Mrs. Arnold said if "he" should return, she would like a word with him.

Miss Cross picked up a pencil, and it seemed as if a spirit entity was controlling her hand. In deep pencil marks that nearly cut through the paper, it was written: "Forgive! Forgive! Forgive!" A few minutes later, the pencil began moving again, once more as if it was being guided in Miss Cross's hand by something unseen. This time the writing was much lighter and more delicate. The message spelled out was, "My dear child, God is love. Love can bring no evil to its object. What you thought was evil was but given you to strengthen you spiritually. I am with you often. I love you still."

Mrs. Arnold immediately recognized the handwriting. It was her dead mother's! To prove it she got a sample of her mother's writing and compared it. The scripts were identical.

Incredibly, the specter of Mrs. Arnold's first husband appeared to her a week later, asking her forgiveness. She agreed, and asked the spirit if he could help her and her present husband. Soon after that, Reverend Arnold was offered a new job in a country parish.

## The Phantom Mourner

Mac Rutherford, creator of the "Ghosts of Winchester" tours, tells of a curious paranormal occurrence that happens periodically at historic Mount Hebron Cemetery in that city. Here, General George S. Patton, of the 22nd Virginia, grandfather of the famous hero general of World War II of the same name, was mortally wounded in the Civil War during the third battle of Winchester. His brother, Waller Tazewell Patton, died at Gettysburg, and both are buried in the same tomb in the Confederate section at Mount Hebron.

"What people claim to see," Rutherford says, "is a man in full military coat and cap, who seems to be regarding the Patton brothers' tomb with respectful reverence. He often appears to tilt his head to look at those approaching the gravesite, but when you get to the tomb, he's not there!"

# Central Virginia

# The Graffiti House Ghosts

Historians agree that it was, by far, the largest cavalry battle of the American Civil War. It involved more than seventeen thousand horsemen under the leadership of legendary Confederate major general J. E. B. Stuart and Union major general Alfred Pleasonton. The action occurred, purely by chance, at a little crossroads junction called Brandy Station, five miles northeast of Culpeper.

The date was June 9, 1863, less than a month before Gettysburg. Suspecting a large buildup of Southern forces, Pleasonton moved his men at 4 A.M. across the Rappahannock River. Shielded by mist and fog, they surprised one of Stuart's brigades, which promptly withdrew and regrouped with others at a site known as Fleetwood Hill. Here, the oncoming 12th Virginia Cavalry crashed head-long into the Federal horsemen in what has been described as "a classic cavalry fight."

Renowned Civil War historian and author Bruce Catton wrote of the battle: "It was a wild, confused action in which cavalry charged cavalry with sabers swinging, dust clouds rising so thickly that it was hard to tell friend from enemy, and the rule was to cut hard at the nearest face and ride on fast . . . There were charge and counter charge all up and down the Fleetwood Hill slopes, Confederate troops riding through a battery of Yankee horse artillery and cutting down the gunners, and the air was full of dust and the thunder of pounding hoofs and the clang of steel and the sickening sound of head-long columns crashing bodily into one another."

An even more graphic narrative was recorded by one of the participants, Pennsylvanian William F. Moyer. He wrote: "The field presented a scene of grand and thrilling interest. A whole brigade of cavalry, in columns of regiments, was moving steadily forward to the attack on our side, while the enemy's cavalry in new formation stood in glittering lines awaiting the assault, and his artillery, stationed on every hill, with rapid flash and continuous roar belched forth a con-centrated fire on our advancing columns.

"Still, with undaunted firmness, the brigade moved forward—first at a walk, then quickening their pace to a trot; and then, as the space between the battle fronts rapidly shortened, the gallop was taken, and when scarce 50 paces intervened, the order to charge rang along our front. In an instant a thousand glittering sabers flashed in the sunlight, and from a thousand brave and confident spirits arose a shout of defi-ance which, caught up by rank after rank, formed one vast, strong, full-volumed battle-cry, and every trooper, rising in his stirrups, leaned forward to meet the shock, and dashed head-long upon the foe.

"First came the dead, heavy crash of the meeting columns, and next the clash of saber, the rattle of pistol and carbine, mingled with frenzied imprecations; wild shrieks that followed the death blow; the demand to surrender and the appeal for mercy—forming the horrid din of battle."

Finally, after hours of such hand-to-hand combat, the Federal forces withdrew, yet most historians consider the Battle of Brandy Station, more or less, a draw. Northern forces lost 868 men, while the Southerners lost 515.

A number of the wounded and dying soldiers were taken into a two-story frame house nearby that had been transformed into a temporary hospital. It had been built only three years before the war broke out, and had been used earlier when casualties from the first battle of Man-assas were brought here.

Today, this building is called "the Graffiti House," because many of the soldiers treated here scrawled their names, comments, messages, and drawings on the second floor. The earliest such inscription is from April 1863, following a Confederate victory nearby. It was obviously written by a Southern soldier, who penned: "Yanks caught hell!"

The house and its historic graffiti have been lovingly preserved by the Brandy Station Foundation, a dedicated group of volunteers who annually offer tours of the house and the battlefield, as well as inform-ative lectures each month from March through October. The Web site www.brandystationfoundation.com says: "Entering the second floor of Graffiti House gives you the same exhilarating feeling as examining ancient hieroglyphs in a lost cave. Generations of wallpaper have been peeled back to reveal handwritten notes, drawings and patriotic messages written by soldiers on both sides of the Civil War.

"If the effect is dramatic on visitors, imagine what it was like for the young man who discovered it in 1993. His grandfather had sent him on an errand to salvage some wood paneling from the dilapidated, vacant house in advance of its demolition. Beneath the paneling he discovered the first of the soldiers' chronicles, which now are the main attraction here. Visitors can go room to room reading and contemplating the inscriptions."

## Visions of Victims

Sites where so much tragedy and trauma took place, and where so many young men died prematurely, represent prime grounds for hauntings, paranormal experts say. Apparently, this theory rings true at the Graffiti House. One Web site states, "Over the past few years we have had a dozen or more strange events that have occurred, and other visitors have told us of stories that go back 50 to 60 years."

"Oh, there have been plenty of incidents that have kept people wondering here," says Della Edrington, who is in charge of the volunteer work schedules. "There is no paid staff. It is all volunteers, and I would say about twenty percent of them have reported experiencing things unusual." She adds that almost all the incidents seem to happen upstairs, and about ninety percent of them involve one room. "We call it 'the ghost room.'"

The manifestations include a wide range of activity: footsteps upstairs when no one is up there, or the appearance of a phantom face peering out of an upstairs window. One no-nonsense volunteer opened the house one morning and was greeted by someone who shouted "hello." He yelled back, and then searched the entire house. He found himself alone.

"Once, we had scheduled two volunteers for work, but we didn't know one of them had died from a sudden heart attack," Edrington says. "He was only 39, and we didn't have time to reschedule another worker. So the dead man's partner went into the house by himself. Just as he was closing the house for the day, he heard a large framed picture fall off the wall upstairs and there was a loud shattering of glass. He raced up, and there was nothing out of place. He said it must have been his dead co-worker's way of letting him know about the ghosts."

One report that has been passed down concerned two young girls who were living in the house in the 1930s. They decorated a Christmas tree in an upstairs room and when they finished they said the decorative balls began to swirl on their own in a counter clockwise movement. They there was no wind, and, of course, no air conditioning or central heating at the time.

Edrington noted that during a Christmas party a few years ago, a young female volunteer went upstairs and entered the ghost room. She said she saw a mist, or cloud-like thing forming in a chair, which slowly began to take the shape of a man. Stunned, she said a blessing, and the form evaporated before her eyes.

Such unexplained incidents caught the attention of an area ghost hunting group, the Virginia Paranormal Institute, and the group was invited by the foundation to set up an investigation of the house in the fall of 2007. They were accompanied by Edrington and Donnie Johnston, a columnist for the *Fredericksburg Free Lance Star*. They weren't disappointed.

In the ghost room upstairs, sophisticated energy-measuring instruments went wild, racing off the charts. One member, Jackie Hicks, a self-described "sensitive," then sat in the chair where the misty form of a man had appeared some years before. She began asking the spirits to manifest themselves. Newspaperman Johnston quoted her as saying she felt something putting pressure on her wrist. "I feel it," she said. "It is moving up to my hand. It is like someone is squeezing my hand." Instruments recorded abnormal energy near her hand. Finally, Hicks, feeling herself drained, got up from the chair.

Edrington then sat down but although she says she sensed something was present, she didn't feel any squeeze. "I suppose the spirits here are just used to me," she noted.

The capper came from what happened to Johnston, who was also shooting film for a planned documentary. One of the paranormal group members spoke out in the darkness: "If you are here, make your presence known to us; touch one of us in some way." Johnston recalls, "there is absolute stillness and quiet, and I am smiling, thinking that this is all a lot of superstitious rot.

"Then, suddenly, I feel something touch my back, between my shoulder blades, just below my neck. It begins almost as a muscular twitching and I instinctively reach around to try and scratch the spot. Before I can get my hand up, however, the twitching sensation becomes more pronounced and now it is without question a tapping from without. Now I am smiling no more. Now the hair is standing up on the back of my neck. Now I have a strange feeling that someone or something is there in that four-inch space between my back and the 150-year-old interior wall.

"Then I hear a gentle thump on that wall, and I slowly turn to find that the large picture frame behind me is moving! It is the frame that is tapping me on the back. But how can it be moving? There is no breeze, no heater stirring air on this cold moonless night. And there is no freight train rumbling down the adjoining railroad tracks that might make the wall vibrate. But even a freight train wouldn't push a large picture frame four inches out from a stationary wall. What is doing it? You tell me, brother!"

Johnston concluded his write-up by asking, "Are there ghosts in the Graffiti House? As for me, well, I don't know what to believe. That night when I went home, I slept with the lights on."

## The Insolent Hostess of Castle Hill

A funny thing happened to British colonel Banastre Tarleton at historic Castle Hill just outside of Charlottesville during the early morning hours of June 4, 1781. He and his troops got waylaid, in a friendly sort of way, by genial host Dr. Thomas Walker. And had not the good doctor detained the colonel and his men for as long as he did, the course of U.S. history may have been very different; some historians have surmised that America might have remained under English rule for generations longer than it did.

Nearly 230 years after this curious yet crucial episode occurred, it almost mystically remains little more than an obscure historical footnote. Equally perplexing is the fact that the hero of this underplayed drama, Jack Jouett, remains virtually unknown. Yet, in terms of the importance of his contributions to the liberation of his nation,

Jouett, experts agree, should rank as high on the scale as Paul Revere, if not higher!

Jouett, through nearly superhuman effort, plus a welcome and necessary helping hand from Dr. Walker, saved the fledgling country's key legislators, including Thomas Jefferson, from virtually certain capture by Tarleton's forces. Here's how the story unfolded: On the evening of June 3, 1781, Jouett, a happy-go-lucky giant of a man at six foot four, and a captain in the Virginia militia, happened to be supping at Cuckoo Tavern in Louisa. He saw a large group of British cavalrymen outside, moving through the area. It was Tarleton, with a contingent of 180 dragoons and 70 mounted infantrymen.

The fast-thinking Jouett quickly analyzed the seriousness of the moment. British general George Cornwallis had launched a spirited attack across Virginia, and about forty key members of the commonwealth's legislature had strategically retreated from the colonial capital in Richmond to the more remote Albemarle County, where they met at Jefferson's home, Monticello. Jouett realized that Tarleton was sweeping stealthily toward Charlottesville in a surprise move to capture the Virginians. In addition to Jefferson, Patrick Henry, Richard Henry Lee, Thomas Nelson, Benjamin Harrison, and many other noteworthy leaders were among the intended prey.

At about 10 P.M., after the troops had passed by, Jouett slipped onto his steed and headed due west to warn his fellow countrymen. As Tarleton took the main road, Jouett, aided by a full moon, struck out along an old Indian trail that had not been used for years. It was a rough and dangerous ride through forests, thick patches of thistles, and hanging wild grapevines. Jouett was to carry facial scars caused by the boughs of trees for the rest of his life. Nevertheless, he rode so hard for about forty miles that his horse gave out near Castle Hill. He told Dr. Walker of the perilous situation and was given a fresh mount in the pre-dawn blackness. He continued on to warn the legislators at Monticello.

A short time later, near daybreak, Tarleton and his men arrived at Castle Hill, stopped to rest, and demanded food. Dr. Walker and his wife obliged them. First, they plied the officers with rounds of well-spiked mint juleps, all the while telling the kitchen help to delay breakfast preparations as long as possible. The ploy worked. Tarleton became irate at the stalling tactics and stalked into the kitchen demanding the cause. A cook told him, "De soldiers dun eat up two breakfuses as fast as I kin cook 'em." By the time the colonel was able to remount his troops, Jouett had reached Monticello, and Jefferson and most of the legislators were able to escape. It was a brilliant and heroic effort that helped shorten the war and secure the independence of the colonies. Yet curiously, it is, in the estimation of many historians, an event that has never been given due credit.

Stately Castle Hill not only figures prominently as a fascinating vignette in Virginia heritage, but also, through the centuries, has been host to a series of psychic manifestations. Strangely, they do not involve Jouett, Tarleton, or Dr. Walker. Rather, they center on the fussy and selective spirit of a woman who was an early resident in the mansion and has lingered on to see that no further unwelcome intruders overindulge in the house's longtime reputation for outstanding hospitality.

The oldest portion of this two-part house was built by Dr. Walker in 1764, in the colonial Virginia frame tradition. Some of the intellectual giants of that era were close friends of Walker, and often were guests at Castle Hill. It is recorded that Jefferson played his fiddle there on occasion, and that a youthful James Madison danced to the lively music. The estate was later owned by William Cabell Rives, a U.S. senator and a Confederate congressman. Years afterward, Castle Hill descended to Rives' granddaughter, Amelie, a distinguished novelist of her time. When her novel *The Quick and the Dead* was published in the late 1880s, Amelie, only twenty-five years old, became famous overnight.

Amelie Rives married Prince Pierre Troubetzkoy, a Russian artist of international renown. During their long tenure at Castle Hill, it became a showplace for the Charlottesville-area gentry, complete with a magnificent garden shaped like an hourglass, and a front lawn the size of a golf fairway, lined by immense boxwoods. It was during these years, including the early decades of the twentieth century, that the hauntings first surfaced.

The manifestations took many forms. Guests told the Troubetzkoys that they heard footsteps ascending and descending the stairs late at night, or heavy pieces of furniture being shoved around after midnight. Some said they heard voices, but found no one causing them. A number of visitors, including the prince, told of smelling the distinct scent of roses, particularly on the stairways, when there were no fresh flowers in the house. Amelie did not wear such perfume. Shaken servants came to the princess several times to tell her they had seen an apparition of her grandfather.

A former housekeeper, "Mrs. Brown," said she was standing at the entrance to the study one day when someone grabbed her keys. She turned around but no one was there. She lived in a cottage on the estate and said that there were times when "something" would grab her ankle if she slept on the bed without covers. She was asked if she thought these incidents were caused by a ghost. "I don't know how else you would explain them," she replied. In more recent years, overnight guests have reported hearing the sounds of a lively party going on downstairs. They heard doors opening and shutting, chairs being pushed back against the drawing room walls, glasses clinking, and music playing. No source for the apparent merrymaking was ever discovered.

While such unexplained phenomena were spread throughout the house, there was one particularly persistent feminine spirit who seemed to confine her lively appearances to a certain ground-floor room in the back of the house, known as the "pink bedroom." Her exact identification has never been fully determined, although Amelie Rives, taking into account the descriptions given her by several of her guests, once said she believed the ghost to be her aunt, Amelie Louis Sigourney, who drowned with her husband and three children when the ship they were on sank in 1870.

One who encountered her was writer Julian Green, who didn't believe in such things as spirits. However, after spending a night in the pink bedroom, he abruptly left Castle Hill early the next morning with scarcely a word of explanation to his hosts. Another who experienced a meeting with the strange lady was a gentleman from the University of Virginia who was to spend a weekend in the house. When he appeared Sunday morning, though, he was pale and obviously uncomfortable. Without saying why, he, too, left in a rush. It wasn't until a month later that the Troubetzkoys found out the reason for his hasty departure. A friend told Amelie that the man said he had been awakened in the middle of the night by a "charming looking woman dressed in the fashion of long ago, and carrying a tiny fan." He was understandably unnerved at the sight. The woman told him, over and over, "You must please go. You must go away. You must not stay here!" The warning was more than enough. The gentleman said he would never again stay in that house. Later, when asked about specifics of the incident, he would mumble incoherently, wave his arms anxiously, and steadfastly refuse to discuss it further.

Nor were these two the only ones to share the inhospitality of the apparitional hostess. At least three other people, including one woman, declared they not only were asked to leave the place, they were, in their words, literally "pushed out of the house" by an entity not wanting them to stay there. Yet, apparently, this ghost was selective in who she chose to drive out. Many visitors slept peacefully in the pink bedroom without a disturbance. The legend is that this room once belonged to the lady ghost and she, and only she, determined who may occupy it in peace. All others were given specifically strong psychic messages, which they unfailingly obeyed.

It must be admitted that it was a novel way to get rid of guests who overstayed their welcome.

# The Sad Return of Sarah Henry

"I know not what course others may take, but as for me, give me liberty or give me death!" Those, of course, were the famous words of Patrick Henry, whose great oration on March 23, 1775, helped launch a war that won American independence. Today, practically every school child in the U.S. can recite lines from that stirring speech. Yet very few people, then or now, were aware that the feisty Henry was heartsick the day he spoke, from a deep, still-burning, personal tragedy. Only recently had his first wife, Sarah, died following a long, terrible illness that emotionally drained the entire family, and which haunted them, both literally and figuratively, long afterwards.

This all occurred during the seven years Henry lived at Scotchtown, a sprawling estate in upper Hanover County, a few miles west of Ashland. The house is believed to have been built in 1719. The Virginia Landmarks Register calls it "probably the largest one-story colonial home in the commonwealth." It is more than eighty feet long and nearly forty feet deep. Eight additional rooms are in the full-height basement and there is an enormous attic in which parties and balls were held. Patrick Henry bought the place in 1771 for $18,000.

Here were open fields, woods, and a river providing a vast playground for Patrick and Sarah's six children. It was time for Henry to establish himself as a country squire with an imposing home. One biographer wrote: "Henry might have enjoyed the amenities of life on a large plantation with a number of slaves, while continuing his legal and political activities, but fate intervened." The author was referring to the distressing and traumatic illness of Sarah Henry that was to darken the great speaker's days at the mansion.

There are reports that her sickness began about the time of the birth of her sixth child, in 1771. She apparently suffered from a protracted mental illness. The son of a doctor who treated her penned: "At Scotchtown, Henry had to encounter many mental and physical afflictions. Whilst his towering and masterful spirit was arousing a nation to arms, his soul was bowed down and bleeding under the heaviest sorrows and personal distresses. His beloved companion had lost her reason, and could only be restrained from self destruction by a strait-dress" [a forerunner to the straitjacket].

Sarah was confined, for how long is uncertain, to two dungeon-like rooms in the cold basement of the house and watched after by servants. When Henry was home from his frequent travels, he would visit his wife by descending a secret staircase off the back hall. In those ill-informed days, people with mental illnesses were often considered to be demon-possessed. As time wore on, with Sarah imprisoned, fear spread through the plantation. Many servants were afraid to go into the house. When the tormented woman died, she was buried in an unmarked grave, as was the custom in the eighteenth century for the burial of "crazy" people.

Although crushed with grief, Henry somehow was able to put the finishing touches on his famous speech at St. Johns Church in Richmond. For the next two or three years he was away much of the time, and in 1777, he sold Scotchtown and moved to the newly renovated Governor's Mansion in Williamsburg. The great house in Hanover County went through a number of owners over the next 180 years and eventually was abandoned. It was for a time even occupied by squatters who quartered goats in the basement and raised chickens in one of the first-floor rooms.

In June 1958, the Association for the Preservation of Virginia Antiquities bought Scotchtown, then in a sad state of repair, and began the mansion's restoration. This has been accomplished with dignity and integrity, and today the house is open to the public. It also is haunted.

There are, conceivably, multiple spirits here, but certainly the most prominent one, as attested to by many who have claimed to have seen and heard her, is Sarah Henry. "It is a very spooky place," says Ron Steele, former Scotchtown director. "It can get very scary inside, especially at night when the wind is blowing. You hear all kinds of noises."

Steele and his wife, Alice, would check on the house during the off-season, and he says there were occasions when both he and the local police were reluctant to go into the house at night. "We had motion alarm systems inside, and someone had to be at least four feet tall to set them off," Steele recalls. "They went off many times, and when the police arrived they wanted me to go in first. We never found any source for the alarms."

Alice had a terrifying experience of her own one night. "We had a bad storm and the lights in the main house went out. I went out with a flashlight to turn them on. You have to open a door to the secret stairway to the cellar. I turned the key but the door wouldn't open. It was as if someone were on the other side holding it. Finally, when I got in, the flashlight went dead, even though I had put fresh batteries in it. I got a feeling that someone was standing right behind me in the dark. I could feel the hair on the back of my neck standing up. I just knew Sarah's spirit was there. There definitely was a presence."

The Steeles said that pieces of furniture seemed to get moved around inexplicably at times. Once, when the house was closed, they discovered a tea caddy had been moved from the center of a table and placed on a chair seat and the top of the teapot had been removed. "It appeared like someone was having a little tea party," Alice says. Several times in a downstairs bedroom, a cradle that belonged to the Henry family was found out of place. "Sometimes we went into that room in the dark and banged our shins on the cradle, because it had been moved from its place beside the bed to the middle of the room," Alice says. "Yet we were the only ones with keys to the house. How could this happen? Maybe Sarah puts it back to where it was 230 years ago."

"Patrick Henry's great-great-great-granddaughter was reluctant to talk about it, but she became convinced the house was haunted," says Ron. "She would never come here at night. She pulled into the yard one night and saw a candle lit in the house. It suddenly disappeared. At that instant, she saw a 'fleeting image,' which looked like someone holding a candle." No one was in the house at the time. Ron adds that several witnesses have heard what sounded like chains being dragged across the floor in the attic, when no mortal is there.

Alan Ward, a former official at Scotchtown, says he was in the basement area by himself one evening when he felt "something there" in one of the rooms. "I didn't see anything," he remembers, "I just had the feeling that there was a very real sensation of a presence." He later learned that was the room in which Sarah had been restrained, and later died. "I'm not the kind of person who believes in ghosts," he says, "but there definitely was something there."

John Taylor of Ashland told a *New York Times* reporter forty years ago that when he and his brother were boys, they remembered seeing the "ghost of a lady at dusk, passing from the basement to the slave quarters." He said they tried to catch her, but she evaporated. Mary Adams says she experienced all sorts of psychic phenomena when she lived at Scotchtown in the 1930s. "We were scared at first," she recalls, "but we got used to it. There were a lot of unnatural sounds, especially screams.

"Once, I guess there were about eight or ten of us children in the house playing. All of a sudden we saw this figure. It looked like a woman with a long, flowing gown. She was all in white. We just stared at her. We were transfixed. Somehow we knew it wasn't a real live person. The only thing we could imagine was that it was a ghost. It was right scary, I can tell you that. We must have watched it for a half minute or more, and then it just disappeared. We bolted out of there and ran to our folks, but, of course, by the time they investigated, the room was empty. But even after I moved from there I would always get the feeling whenever I went back to visit that the ghost lady was there. I think she still is today."

"Was it Sarah Henry? I really don't know. It could well have been."

# Does a Ghost Guard the Beale Treasure?

The ghost of Thomas Jefferson Beale, if there is one, must either be crying in complete, total, absolute frustration, or laughing so hard his sides ache. Beale is the Virginia gentleman, or hooligan (and there are strong arguments for either term), who is said to have buried a legendary horde of gold, silver, and precious gems somewhere near the town of Bedford, west of Lynchburg. The cache allegedly included nearly three thousand pounds of gold, more than five thousand pounds of silver and hundreds of thousands of dollars worth of jewels. According to the tradition, Beale and his associates buried the treasure in iron pots in the ground, leaving behind a complex code system which, once broken, would reveal the precise location of their loot.

But nearly two hundred years later, a burning question remains unanswered: was any treasure buried at all, or did Beale pull off one of the greatest hoaxes in history? If he did, his spirit must be rolling in laughter at the thousands of people who have searched in vain, some squandering their own life savings in the process, for the pots of gold. But if he really did hide a fortune, then he must weep ghostly tears because no one has been able to find even a single coin!

Over the years, the Beale treasure has become bigger than life. It has been the subject of countless newspaper and magazine articles, books, and television documentaries—to the point where it rivals some of the top unsolved mysteries of all time, such as the fabled Lost Dutchman mine in Arizona, and the eternal search for Bigfoot. It certainly qualifies as Virginia's most enduring and alluring enigma.

Thomas J. Beale is believed to have been born around 1792. Some writers have described him as a well-educated gentleman, evidently of good family, and with popular manners. Others have said he was a black sheep, a gunslinging genius who was constantly bailed out of scrapes by his more respectable brothers. Beale claimed, however, that he and thirty individuals "of good character" were seeking adventure when they headed westward on a two-year expedition hunting buffaloes and grizzly bears in 1817.

It is still a puzzle as to exactly where this curious troop of Virginians wound up in the west. Some have said New Mexico, some Arizona, and some south-central Colorado. There is no consensus, but most researchers feel Beale and the others were somewhere in the vicinity of Santa Fe, New Mexico, when they discovered gold in a small ravine. They mined it for several months and then the pile grew so large they became apprehensive, so the men designated Beale to lead a small contingent back with the gold to bury it in Bedford County, in a remote spot between the mountains.

And so, in November 1819, Beale arrived back home, supposedly with two wagonloads of gold and silver nuggets. In the Goose Creek area, he followed a narrow and seldom-used trail leading into a gap in the foothills of the Blue Ridge Mountains, within sight of the Peaks of Otter. As snow fell, the party dug a large square pit six feet deep, lined it with flat stones, placed the pots full of gold and silver on the stones, and covered everything up with dirt, rocks, and forest debris. Beale then went back two thousand miles to the mining site. Later, he repeated his long trek east with another load of the precious metals. This was buried at or near the original site in November 1821.

Beale next devised an elaborate system of incredibly complex codes, which, when broken, would reveal where the treasure had been buried. They covered three sheets of paper with a long series of numerals. Cipher number one tells how to find the hidden pots. Cipher number two describes the contents of the treasure vault, and the third one lists the names of the thirty men who were to divide the contents equally.

The codes were carefully placed in a metal strongbox fastened with a hard lock. The nine men who had buried the ore agreed to leave the box with Robert Morris, innkeeper at the old Washington Hotel in Lynchburg, a man they all knew and trusted. They stayed at the hotel for a few days, then left again for the west to continue their mining.

Morris never saw Beale or any of the other men again. The mystery was beginning. Two months after the adventurers had left Virginia, Morris did get a curious letter from Beale, posted from St. Louis, then a small hunting and trading post on the western frontier. It said the papers in the strongbox would be meaningless without the proper decoding keys. These keys, Beale said, were in a sealed envelope that had been given to a friend in St. Louis, with instructions to mail it to Morris in June 1832—ten years later—if by then the band of thirty men had not returned themselves to claim the money.

Morris hid the box under some clutter in an old shed adjacent to the hotel. The ten years passed, and not only had no one from Beale's party come back, but there was no letter from St. Louis. Also, incredibly, Morris had forgotten about the box. It was not until 1845, twenty-three years later, that Morris stumbled upon the strongbox while searching for a harness in the shed. He had the lock broken and opened it. Inside were some old receipts, a couple of letters, and three sheets of numbers. One of the letters, from Beale, told the details of their western expedition, how they found the gold, and in general terms, where they had buried it.

Morris tried to decipher the codes, but as thousands of others have since then, found them too difficult. Again, inexplicably, he set the box aside. Seventeen years later, a year before he died, Morris, by then reasonably sure that no one was going to return, handed the box and its contents over to James Ward, a trusted family friend. Driven more by curiosity than greed, Ward worked day and night on the perplexing codes. Purely by accident, he discovered that the second code was keyed to words in the U.S. Declaration of Independence.

Laboriously, he deciphered it. It read: "I have deposited in the county of Bedford, about four miles from Buford's Inn, in an excavation or vault six feet below the surface of the ground, the following articles belonging to the parties whose names are given in number three [the third coded sheet] herewith. The first deposit was ten hundred and fourteen pounds of gold and thirty-eight hundred pounds of silver. This was deposited November 1819. The second deposit was made December 1821, and consisted of nineteen hundred and seven pounds of gold and twelve hundred and eighty eight pounds of silver. Also jewels in St. Louis. The above is packed securely in iron pots with iron covers. The vault is lined with stones and the vessels lie on solid rock and are covered with other stones. Paper number one describes the exact location of the vault, so no difficulty will be had in finding it."

Ward then worked feverously on the two remaining unbroken codes, till his determination and his family fortune ran out. Finally, in 1885, he gave up and published "The Beale Papers," which included copies of everything that had been found in the box, as well as the deciphered code number two, and an account of his own efforts to break the other two. He also issued a warning, which has turned out to be excellent advice that has rarely, if ever, been heeded. He said, "devote only such time as can be spared in the task, and if you can spare no time, let the matter alone."

The Beale Papers spread across Virginia like wildfire, and from that time on, for well over a century, vast hordes of fortune seekers have descended on rural Bedford County to search for the lost gold and silver. Armies of cryptographers, computer programmers, historians, professional treasure hunters, and just plain common folks have tried to decipher the codes, running the numbers through thousands of books, documents, and other papers that were published before 1822. And thousands of tons of Bedford dirt have been dug and re-dug all across the county. Even with all the tools of modern technology—the most advanced computers, the most sophisticated metal detectors, and the powerful arms of backhoes and the blades of bulldozers—nothing, not even a minute nugget, has been found. Ironically, small fortunes have been lost in the search.

Millions of words have been written about the Beale treasure, thousands of maps have been drawn up, and countless teams of experts have been formed, but all efforts have been in vain. The rich cache, if it exists, remains as safe in the ground today as it did the day Beale and his friends buried it. There are many who believe the treasure is one of the most elaborate and cruel hoaxes ever devised. But for everyone who doubts its existence, there are ten who will not let go of the dream of a lifetime. The hunt goes on. Each spring and summer new or renewed hope blossoms and yet more people descend on Bedford to try their hand, as others work incessantly into the wee hours of the mornings at home trying to break the maddening codes.

Is the treasure real? Will the codes ever be denuded and the grand prize found?

To longtime Bedford residents, such questions seem almost academic today. Many of them are convinced that the ghost of Thomas

Jefferson Beale hangs close in the vacant valleys between the mountains somewhere out in the vicinity of Buford's Inn, either laughing or crying, as a haunting reminder of the foibles and frustrations of his fellow man in the eternal quest for fame and fortune.

# The Unhappy Bride of Tuckahoe

Tuckahoe is considered by architectural historians to be the finest existing early-nineteenth-century plantation in America. It sits, undisturbed, on a bluff overlooking the James River about fifteen miles west of Richmond in Goochland County. For generations writers have outdone themselves heaping superlatives on the house and grounds. Said one: "Not only is this mansion priceless because of its completeness, but it contains some of the most important architectural ideas of the early Georgian period."

The name Tuckahoe stems from the Indian word, "Tockawaugh," which was an edible root found in the area, one that tasted like a potato. The oldest portion of the house, the north wing, was built for Thomas Randolph, perhaps as early as 1712. It is of unusual design. There are two major wings, each twenty-five feet deep and forty feet long, connected by a great hall twenty-four feet wide, giving Tuckahoe the shape of the letter H. It is believed to have been modeled after the Virginia capitol building in Williamsburg, which was built (in an H shape) in 1699.

Thomas Randolph died in 1729, willing his estate to his only son, William, who was a burgess in Goochland. He died in 1745, leaving the property and 1,200 pounds sterling to his two daughters. It was at that time that Peter Jefferson came to the plantation as an overseer and guardian. He brought along his young son, Thomas, who spent seven of his first nine years at Tuckahoe, attending classes with the Randolph children in the tiny schoolhouse on the grounds.

As with many of the great manor homes in Virginia, Tuckahoe has its share of ghostly legends, some of which have been experienced by highly credible witnesses, and are fairly well documented. There is, for example, the legend of an itinerant peddler, a colonial-era traveling salesman who sold everything from primitive cosmetics and miracle healing substances to trimmings and dress goods. He allegedly arrived at Tuckahoe one day to vend his wares, but instead got into a fierce altercation with a member of the household and was murdered. He is said to reappear at times in the southeast chamber, seeking retribution.

There also is "a little gray lady" at the site. Some believe such ladies in gray were servants or slaves, as they wore gray uniforms. In a book titled *Historical Gardens of Virginia*, published in 1923, there is a reference to a "dainty little Gray Lady," who, when the midnight hour has come, "steps gently out from a cupboard in the 'Burnt Room' to mingle with the mortals for awhile." A second mention of this particular spectral entity is attributed to Mrs. Richard Allen, whose husband bought Tuckahoe in 1850. She and a friend were standing in the dining room one day when both of them distinctly saw "the figure of a small woman in gray enter through the hall door and pass out the little entry door leading to the outer kitchen."

A *Richmond Times Dispatch* article written in 1935 described a time when Mrs. Allen was sitting in the upstairs hall, unpacking a box. The only other person around was a maid who was washing windows. Mrs. Allen heard someone call her first name, Jennie. She looked up, saw no one, and continued to work. Then the call was repeated, in "loud and anxious tones." The mystery voice bellowed, "Jennie! Jennie!" This aroused her to her feet and she hurried into the room where the maid was, to see if something was wrong. She found the servant quietly washing a window. Just then, a loud crash startled them both. They raced back into the room where Mrs. Allen had been, and found that a large portion of the ceiling had fallen and completely demolished the very chair upon which she had been sitting!

Some years earlier a traveling man who had spent the evening in the same room said he had been awakened in the middle of the night by a rocking chair swaying violently back and forth. He got up, lit a lamp, and saw the chair rocking, but there was no one in it. No window was open so no draft could have set the chair in motion. He went back to sleep only to be reawakened by the same manifestation. This was enough for him. He hastily dressed and vacated the house, telling a perplexed servant that nothing on earth would induce him to stay in the room again.

There is an earlier tradition, too, about an unusual dream of a "frag-ile wraith." It was experienced by Thomas Mann Randolph III, great-grandson of the builder of the house. After the death of his wife, he dreamed one evening that a young lady opened a closet door in his bedroom and brought him a glass of water. The next day he spoke of the apparition and said the face was so clear that if he ever saw it again he would recognize it. Accordingly, years later, he met the woman he had dreamed of in New Jersey. He proposed to her, married her, and brought her back to the mansion.

Since moving into Tuckahoe many years ago, current owners Tad and Sue Thomson say they have either heard of, or personally experi-enced, a few strange things at the house. "The most memorable one," says Sue, "was the time in the middle of the night when I woke up and heard the vague hum of voices downstairs, along with a tinkling sound, like glasses or a chandelier. It was like a party was going on. I roused Tad and asked if he heard it, and he said he did. Tad went down to look but he didn't find anything.

"There have been a couple of other things," Sue adds. "Once I saw someone or something in white at the little schoolhouse building. The door was open and I thought it was Tad, but it wasn't, and I never learned who it was. Other times I feel like I hear a baby crying in another part of the house, when I know all my children are accounted for. On another occasion, some friends were leaving Tuckahoe early one morning when they happened to look toward the house. They said they saw a figure in white near the garden. They said it was sort of hovering above the ground."

By far the best-known spirit at Tuckahoe is the "distressed bride with flowing hair," who, dressed in a wedding veil and satin gown, wrings her hands as she rushes along the "Ghost Walk," a charming pathway down a turfed alley lined with giant boxwoods. It was named for this spectral presence, seen by many for more than two hundred years. The belief is that she is running away from a husband three times her age whom she was being forced to marry.

One account, in a faded newspaper clip published decades ago, tells of "a sad little ghost whose tragedy is a matter of family record." She had been married when very young and much against her wishes. Shortly afterwards, she died, presumably of a broken heart, and lies in the family burial ground on the estate. The facts in this case were set down in an absorbing monograph on the plantation by Jessie Ball Thompson Krusen in 1975. She wrote that sometime in the early 1730s, one of the Randolph daughters, Mary, breaking with her family's desires, married her uncle's overseer when she was still a teenager. His name was Isham and he apparently was not well-liked by the landed gentry of the day.

Mrs. Krusen said that the "unfortunate Mary" was later brought home and forced to marry the much older Mr. James Keith. Thus she speculates that it is Mary's pitiable figure that is seen wringing her hands as she flees her elderly husband along the Ghost Walk.

## The Lost Treasure of Whichello

Mr. and Mrs. J. Donald DeVilbiss were gracious hosts who took obvious pride in showing their historic house at 9602 River Road on the outskirts of Richmond. In the parlor to the right as one enters the house on the main floor is a large fireplace; there is, in fact, one in every room. Just to the right of this is a room in which legends persist. One is that of the skeletal remains of a former owner, which allegedly are buried seven feet beneath the hearth. The other is that treasure is hidden either somewhere in the structure or on its grounds.

The house is the famous Whichello. The land on which it sits is believed to have been owned at one time by the Randolphs of nearby Tuckahoe. It was built in 1827 at a cost of $2,000. From its earliest days, the house was used as a tavern for those traveling between Richmond and Charlottesville or Lynchburg. In the early 1840s, the place was sold to an Englishman of questionable character named W. Richard Whichello. As owner and operator of the tavern, he is said to have accumulated wealth, which, according to one report, "was not come by in manner befitting a Christian gentleman." He was described as being miserly and cruel to his slaves. It was rumored that he ran games of chance, including cockfighting, that were not always honest and above board

Whichello's reputation was noted by A. H. Moncure, who was quoted in a 1935 article in the *Richmond Times Dispatch*. At that time, well advanced in years, he had this to say: "One night about dusk in the year 1850, a cattle drover from the valley region to the west arrived at the tavern with a herd which he bedded in the corrals near the inn, and there he slept overnight. The next day he continued into Richmond and sold his cattle, returning later to again spend the night at the tavern.

"After dinner that night, Whichello invited his guest to accompany him to a barroom a short distance away. There, the two men drank heavily and then became engrossed in a poker game. The result was Whichello went home with all the man's money. In the morning, attendants found the innkeeper on the floor of his bedroom. He had been brutally murdered, his head beaten in with an axe. The drover was gone and so, it was thought, was the money. No trace was ever found of him, and no other solution for Whichello's death has ever been set forth."

It was said that the man's sudden death caused a curious problem for what few friends he had. Where should they bury him? They were afraid that if his body was interred in a cemetery that the slaves he had so harshly mistreated might dig up his remains and treat them to varied indignities in retaliation.

Moncure tells what happened: "The friends secretly dug a hole alongside the east chimney of the old tavern. Then, from this hole they tunneled to beneath the great brick chimney and shoved the coffin into the tunnel until it rested under the stack. That is Whichello's tomb, and from that fact arose many of the reports of the ghost of the old owner returning to guard the treasure which his killer may not have found, and which, to this day, is believed buried around the building."

The rumors of the hidden cache of treasure have persisted, and there have been a number of fruitless searches for it through the years. At some point the fireplace containing Whichello's remains was dug into and the wall adjacent to it was ripped apart.

One of the most intriguing incidents was recalled by Mrs. Joseph Crenshaw, who ran a tea shop in the house in the 1930s. "Many attempts have been made to find the reputed treasure," she stated, "and some tall tales are told, such as the one an old Negro told me. 'Uncle John' came to me one day and said he had a device which could locate all kinds of metal, and he wanted to try it out. He dug in what is now the kitchen, but found nothing. He assured me that no less than three times he had struck the very box which enclosed the wealth, only to have the 'spirit trove' vanish. 'You really saw it, Uncle John?' I asked. 'I sure did, deed I did.'" Mrs. Crenshaw said he told her that "Each time he saw it, it sank further out of sight, and the holes filled with water."

Mrs. Crenshaw began to feel that the house was haunted. Visitors to the tea room complained of eerie feelings. The sensation became so strong that some left their refreshments on the table and rushed out of the house. Then there was the mysterious clicking noise that wouldn't go away. Mrs. Crenshaw said it sounded like an invisible telegraph key, and it seemed to follow her throughout the house.

"I became interested in the legends," she said, "and began to wonder what did cause so many strange incidents." She consulted a psychic who told her that there was, indeed, treasure in the house and that it was hidden in the east chimney. "You may be sure," she added, "that I eyed that fireplace and chimney many times, but I never did have faith enough to go ahead and tear up the property.

"The news about the ghost soon spread and I received several requests from those interested in that sort of phenomena, to hold a meeting in the house. All of these, I granted. The first group came out and we were sitting around a table in the tea room. The lights were on and there was a fire in the fireplace. One of the guests began to speak of a 'little girl' ghost visitor. She said the apparition gave a flower to one of the women, then she was gone. The woman who got the flower said the description of the little girl precisely fitted her niece."

Mrs. Crenshaw continued: "Next, the medium, if that is what she is called, turned to me and said an old Negro mammy was beside me. She described her and told how her head kerchief was tied in a peculiar way. It appeared to be my mother's old mammy who had taken care of me as a child. The medium said how glad the spirit seemed to have me know that she was with me again.

"At last, I asked this woman if she had noticed a queer feeling upon entering my tea room, and she said, 'Why yes, as soon as I arrived. Didn't you see me stop at the door?' I replied that I had noticed her delay in entering, and then she said, 'That was because there was a man standing just behind you. He was dressed in old hunting clothes and seemed to live here.' This was my first actual contact with Richard Whichello's ghost! Since then, several others have told me of seeing this apparition."

At another séance held in the house, Mrs. Crenshaw said a letter in spirit writing materialized. It said: "My treasure is not in the house, but in the yard. You should look in the backyard about 100 feet away from the house and marked by a little fence, and it is about five feet under the earth." The writing, scrawled in a wild scribble, was signed with the initials "W. R. W."

The DeVilbisses did not encounter any forms of psychic activity in their more than thirty years in the house. Mr. DeVilbiss did note that he once heard strange noises in the east chimney, but upon investigation found a nest of flying squirrels. So one may well ask, has the ghost of Richard Whichello given up in his quest for being avenged? Or is he finally satisfied that his ill-gotten treasure is safe at last from those who so desperately have sought to find it? Or will he yet be heard and seen again, should some future tenant or owner begin the search anew?

The words of Mrs. Crenshaw, uttered three-quarters of a century ago, may well be the most prophetic: "There's something supernatural about that place," she said, "and many are the people who have confirmed my opinion."

# A Convention of Ghosts

The following narrative is extracted and excerpted from the May 1851 issue of the *Southern Literary Messenger*, a nineteenth-century magazine of high quality once edited by Edgar Allan Poe. It was written anonymously by a man who told of a singular encounter he had one night in Richmond, where he saw and heard a whole assembly of ghosts reenacting scenes that occurred in real life more than twenty years earlier.

"Some two weeks since, I was quietly walking down Broad Street at a somewhat late hour of night when my attention was arrested by the unusual appearance of lights, though faint ones, in the old African Church. As I drew nearer, there seemed to be a large group of persons entering the front door of the building, and I could not but conclude that some matter of special interest had called the citizens together. The hour was past midnight—the last gas lamp had been extinguished as the moon showed her waning disk over Church Hill, and the most slumberous stillness reigned around.

"I walked up to the main entrance with some little curiosity, not at all lessened by the silence that seemed to pervade the building itself. There was neither sound of human voices nor of human footsteps within. By this time, my desire to solve the mystery became eager and I at once entered. The church was but dimly lighted by a few flickering candles, and the faces of the company were strange to me. But I thought I had never seen such intellectual looking men before. Pallid they seemed, and venerable, like a convocation of the heroes that have been carved out of Carrara marble. Yet fleshly withal, etherealize. And they moved about, though noiselessly.

"I ventured to ask one of them the nature and object of the meeting, but he made no recognition of me whatever, as if wholly unaware of my presence. I therefore seated myself and awaited the action of the assembly. For some minutes nothing occurred from which I could divine the why and wherefore of so mysterious a gathering, but then a tall and impressive figure advanced towards the pulpit, whose majestic countenance was familiar to me. Many years had flown since I had seen it, but the features were the same, except that they seemed glorified by some wondrous transfiguration. One look satisfied me that the person was none other than the shade of a former illustrious Chief Justice of the United States [John Marshall, who died in 1835].

"Upon this, I began to examine a little more curiously into the faces of the rest of the company. Here and there I recognized others that I had seen in days past. I marveled more and more as I came to the conclusion—that the body in whose august and ghostly presence I was seated—could be none other than the Virginia Convention of 1829–30!

"Yet for what purpose had these canonized men burst the cerements of the tomb and revisited the scene of their former labors? Why had they come together by the 'glimpses of the moon' to hold their ghostly counsel? It did not escape my attention, held as I was in agitated suspense by the novel scene before me, that none of those members of the old convention who yet survive—were among the figures present! Each individual was a goblin. The assembly was of course smaller than it had been aforetime, yet more than a quorum were in attendance.

"By and by, I began to perceive that disquietude rested upon their spirits, for the expression of their countenances was very sorrowful. At last, the convention was called to order by the sepulchral voice of a phantom-like chairman, and there he rose to address them—a figure of most extraordinary appearance. It was tall and thin, and its face was sad to a degree beyond even that of its lachrymose colleagues. But there flashed from beneath the brows, an eye so glittering, yet so sub-duing, that the beholder was by turns fascinated and overpowered by its influence.

"An indescribable feeling of terror crept over me as this figure arose. There was something, too, in the tones of the speaker's voice that exerted a powerful charm. At one time shrill almost to a painful extent, then suddenly relapsing into a strain of unearthly sweetness, it ran the whole gamut of articulate music, with an ease and brilliancy that I never heard from mortal lips. The effect was such as we might fancy from an orator combining the better elements of Whitfield and Patrick Henry!

"'Mr. President,' said he, 'it is a grievance of no ordinary character that can call from the tomb, spirits that have long enjoyed in repose. But sir, the evil times upon which our good old Commonwealth has fallen, have surely enough of alarm in them to vex the shades of the departed. It is not therefore remarkable that we are here to confer together in our ghostly perturbation. How, indeed, sir, could we lie quietly in our graves while such scenes are enacting in the halls of our former triumphs, while the iconoclasts are shattering the idols of our former veneration?

"'How have we waited, Mr. President, before coming together to enter our unhappy protest against the doings of these microscopic [and current] Constitution-makers, for the action of our colleagues who are yet among the living! You and I, and all of us, might have lain undisturbed, indeed, if the excellent members of this [the current] convention, who yet walk the earth, had lifted up their voices against the nefarious projects of our degenerate successors. But sir, they sit supinely while they should cry aloud and spare not, and we come together now to speak our minds as by a necessity that we cannot withstand.'"

The voice heard by the narrator then goes on to blast the living members of the current convention, saying, "what sins of omission and commission are there of which these men have not been guilty?" He accuses them of malfeasance and larceny, and the reckless destruction of the progressive legislation enacted by the 1829–30 convention. He adds, "the injuries they have inflicted on our hapless memories, whereby we stalk abroad at midnight and cannot rest." The diatribe went on for some time.

In summary, the narrator, the man who experienced this haunted scene, says, "a lethargic influence seemed to pervade the atmosphere. I fell into a state of coma. How long I slept, I know not. It could not have been very long, for when I awaked, it was yet dark. But the assembly had vanished into thin air, and left behind no trace of their singular meeting. Slowly, I walked to my home, pondering much on the ghostly oration I had heard."

## The Non-Ghost that Became a Corpse

Talk about a practical joke that backfired—this must be the ultimate case. In his 1942 book *Home to the Cockade City*, author M. Clifford Harrison tells of a most extraordinary unintentional murder that occurred in Petersburg late in the nineteenth century. It had been told to him by his grandfather. It seems, at that time, there was a shoemaker who had gained the reputation among the townspeople as being totally fearless. It was said that he had never been scared in his life.

Apparently, some young men, with mischievous intentions, decided to put the cobbler's courage to the test. They set up a coffin in an abandoned house and one of them laid down in it. The shoemaker was then told that the house was haunted, and that a person had recently died there, but because of the threat of ghosts, no one would "sit up with the dead." It was the custom then for someone, or a group, to sit up all night in the parlor with a deceased person. The man accepted the challenge.

He took some tools of his trade with him so he could repair some shoes during the nocturnal vigil. As Harrison wrote: "An open coffin stood in the middle of a bleak room. Outside, the wind wailed. Eerie creaks and groans sounded through the house. The shoemaker unceremoniously drew up a chair and went to work."

At about midnight, the "corpse" began to rise until it was sitting up in the coffin. Instead of being frightened out of his wits, the shoemaker looked at the scary figure and commanded, "Lie down!" The "body" laid down. An hour or so later, the same thing occurred. The body rose again. This time the cobbler shouted, "Lie down and stay down, and I'm not going to tell you again!" The order was once more obeyed.

At about 2 A.M., the body arose a third time. The shoemaker, without a word, took his hammer and cracked the skull of the corpse's head! As Harrison concluded: "This time the practical joker in the coffin, whose friends had powdered him up to make him look cadaverous—was a corpse sure enough."

# A Night in a Haunted House

The following is one of the most intensely frightening narratives I have found in more than thirty years of ghost research in Virginia, one that has all the elements of terror and stark fear caused by superstitious beliefs in the supernatural. It was written anonymously by a young man who dared to spend a night alone in an old house suspected of being haunted, and was published in the June 1855 issue of the *Southern Literary Messenger*.

"Within a stone's throw of the Richmond and Petersburg railroad line, not more than half a mile from the James River, stand the blackened and roofless walls of an old brick building. Passersby have been struck by the lone and desolate appearance of the house, and it long has had the reputation of being haunted. Indeed, its situation alone might well raise evil surmises in the minds of a superstitious turn. No other house stood near it; no pale or hedge enclosed it; no tree or shrub or flower grew in its vicinity; nothing but the bare and sterile earth, over which a few consumptive cows and lean, broken-down horses, turned out to die, wandered about in quest of such subsistence as the place afforded.

"Its unsheltered site exposed it to every wind that blows sweeping across the river, which raved and roared about the old mansion in such a way as to put timorous misgivings into the heart of any chance tenant who happened to occupy it. It was built by a man of wealth and standing in the days of our grandfathers. Why he selected so singular a location I have been unable to learn. Whether the strange sights and sounds that gave the house its evil reputation made it unpleasant to him, or whatever else was the cause, it is certain he abandoned it.

"After his departure, the place fell from time to time to various tenants who were attracted by the low rate of rent. None, however, remained long, for it was remarked that misfortune seemed to brood over the house; that sickness and death were alarmingly frequent within its walls; and that its stately halls and paneled chambers were haunted by preternatural visitants or not, they certainly were singularly often the scenes of the heaviest afflictions that human life is heir to.

"It is now many years since I paid the old house a visit. My curiosity was excited by the current tales in regard to it; for I always had rather a taste for superstitious marvels. I found it a large and stately building, finished in the old aristocratic style of Virginia. At the time of my visit it had been but a few weeks abandoned, and several pieces of furniture of small value were still left in some of the rooms. In one of the principal chambers here, I observed an old black walnut cupboard, which may have been used as a wardrobe, a stick-backed chair without the top board, and a black hair sofa. On seeing the old sofa, the thought occurred to me that as the weather was warm and no covering required, it might be made a tolerable couch for the night, if I had courage enough to despise the popular stories about the place, and defy the powers of evil that were supposed to hold their revels there.

"The thought, I confess, was a little startling, but I was vain enough, at 19, to think such idle superstitions as shook the souls of the weak and credulous were far below that serene region in which my thoughts were accustomed to soar. In short, I resolved to pass the night in the haunted house, and thus put to proof my courage. Accordingly, I returned to Richmond, and after nightfall, having wrapped up a candle in a newspaper, and put a book and matchbox in one coat pocket, and a loaded pistol in the other, set forth without communicating my purpose to anyone. It may raise a smile to think I should arm myself against ghosts with a pocket pistol, but I felt my courage could somehow be firmer, and less liable to surprise by any sudden assault if I had such a staunch and trusty supporter at hand in case of need.

"It was a clear, moonlight night in midsummer, and the walk was not unpleasant. The lonely old building looked particularly grim by moonlight, and I felt an uneasy misgiving as I approached it. But I had gone too far to think of retreating. An old white horse, that in the moon's uncertain light, had a pale and ghostly appearance, stood a few rods from the front porch. He seemed, I thought, to be worn out with years of privation and evidently was not destined to much longer sojourn in this world of sorrow.

"The front door was open, just as I had left it that morning. I paused on the threshold an instant, and then, bracing my nerves with a long, deep breath, entered and stood a few feet within the hall. All seemed deserted and still as a churchyard at midnight. The moon, shining through the casements, showed me the staircase leading to the room I had elected to stay in, and I commenced ascending. Every step resounded through the great empty house with a prolonged reverberation that was almost appalling. I lost no time in lighting the candle, and then looked carefully round to see that no lurking thing of evil lay hidden in any of the recesses. All was empty and still and no enemy near. I then reclined upon the sofa, propping up my head on a cushion. Finally, I drew the book from my pocket, and, resolving to give my imagination the least possible leisure for idle vagaries, tried to immerse all my thoughts in reading.

"Several times I almost started at what seemed the sound of human footsteps in the adjoining apartment. I listened attentively, and thought the noises, though strangely loud for such a cause, were produced by the multitude of rats with which the old house abounded. They scampered about in every direction, squeaking and gibbering in such a way as to deepen the vague feeling of terror which, in spite of all my philosophy, I found was fast creeping over me.

"Suddenly, there issued from the next room the most demonic yell I had ever heard, which made me bound quite up from the sofa. Again, the frightful sound arose; but accompanied this time with certain sputtering noises and lengthened wailing cadences, which I had heard too often to find a difficulty in recognizing. 'They are only cats, after all," I mentally exclaimed, 'but bless my soul! How much like devils in conflict their voices sound.' Taking the candle from its stick, I advanced to the next room, though with some trepidation; for old tales of the alliance of cats with the infernal powers officiously forced themselves upon my memory at the instant. On entering the room, immediately two of these animals, one grey and white, the other as black as a demon, rushed out of the opposite door and down the staircase.

"Returning to my room, I readjusted the candle and lay down again. It was now nearly one o'clock. I extinguished the candle and tried to compose myself to sleep. How long I slept I cannot tell, but probably only a short time, when I was waked by a heavy pressure on my chest. The moonlight was sufficient to show me the cause of the disturbance. The large black cat I had chased out of the adjoining room had returned, and, seated on my breast, was gazing intently into my face with great glassy eyes. I gave him a smart blow with my clenched hand, on which he bounded away and disappeared. I then rose and bolted the door; after which I returned to the sofa and lay down again.

"The next thing I knew, a sound burst upon the silence and re-echoed through the house. It seemed a hollow, maniac laughter, choked and throttled by sudden strangulation. A second time it resounded from the next room, and a moment after appeared to float upon the air within the building. All my philosophy vanished in an instant, for such unearthly sounds could scarcely be imagined to proceed from a thing of this world.

"I lay trembling with terror, and covered with a cold sweat, but what was my horror when, a few minutes after, the hideous sounds were heard in the very room I occupied! Starting half erect from the sofa, I saw by the light of the setting moon, which now shone broadly at the western window, what seemed an enormous spectral head, with horns and great glaring eyes, peering from above the old cupboard in the corner. With a suppressed shriek, I fell back upon the sofa on which the phantom spread its wings, and, gliding out of the nearest window, again sent forth a peal of fiendish laughter, as if in derision.

"It was an owl, the great horned owl of Virginia!

"I was now too much agitated to sleep again. These repeated alarms had disordered my imagination so far that it had become a prey to all sorts of fancies; and the reason which by daylight derided superstitious tales, failed me at my utmost need. It is true, nothing had occurred during the night which might not be easily explained on natural principles. Cats and owls are apt to haunt deserted buildings, especially when peopled with rats as this house was. But still, the concurrence of so many startling incidents was extraordinary; and might have been designed by some preternatural power to punish that proud conceit of my own reason which had led me into the present undertaking. It is surprising what an effect thoughts of this kind, which came thronging into my brain, had upon my excited imagination.

"In this state, I remained a considerable time, my mind tossed to and fro, in the contest between fear and reason, and my disturbed fancy, incessantly conjured up fresh sources of alarm. The question of returning to Richmond was suggested. But the moon was now set, and a cloud which had for some time been gathering, had overcast the sky and rendered the night intensely dark. I thought I should probably be unable to find my way back to the city before daylight.

"The house had now become comparatively quiet. The rats no longer ranged about with the same restless energy, or fought with the same fury as before. Except an occasional squeak, or a slight scrambling noise, they were now silent and still. The darkness, it seemed, was too thick and impenetrable to allow even them, imps of the night as they were, to roam about with freedom. The pattering of the rain which had begun to fall was almost the only sound audible. I was beginning to feel the soothing influence of this continued quiet, and my imaginations were gradually assuming a less excited cast.

"But an indistinct noise of what sounded like irregular tottering footsteps at length reached my ear. I listened with a beating heart and an undefined dread, fearing the sounds were the precursor of something terrible. Nor did my apprehension deceive me. A noise as of violent struggling ensued, followed by a dreadful groan which seemed to roll upon my ear out of the pithy darkness in which my room was shrouded. And such a groan, so long, deep and agonizing, surely never fell on mortal ears before. It was such as might have come from one of the lost spirits of Dante's Inferno—so much of hopeless convulsive anguish seemed poured out in the sound.

"Then followed a heavy stamping and struggling, as of hoofs on the floor, and again and again those awful groans resounded through the house. At length, the sounds grew fainter, appearing to come far and farther away from the depths below, as if the condemned spirit my terrified imagination supposed it to be, had been seized by his jailor demon, and borne struggling downward to the dark prison from which he had escaped.

"All this time I lay half-mad with terror. Indeed, I think I must have been for a time in high delirium; for I lost all distinct consciousness of my situation, and fancied myself begirt by such horrible phantoms, as only an insane imagination could have presented. Devils grinned in my face and yelled blasphemies in my ear; sheeted ghosts glided by gazing at me with their dead, rayless eyes; and cold clammy corpses laid their lifeless faces against mine, and sought to fold me in their embraces. How my reason escaped an utter wreck I can scarcely conceive; but surely no one ever approached nearer the gulf of raving madness without falling into it. Then, I did!

"At last, I began to recover consciousness and I found that the day was perceptibly dawning. My courage in some degree revived; and I ventured to hope I might after all survive that dreadful night. Still, my limbs were twitching convulsively with nervous excitement, and I feared to move, or look around, lest some frightful specter should blast my view. I remained therefore lying on the sofa, trembling and anxious, till it grew light enough to distinguish surrounding objects clearly. I then summoned courage to look around my room, almost expecting some strange and terrible sight would meet my glance. Everything, however, appeared just as I had left it when the candle was extinguished the night before.

"At length, I rose and opened the door, glancing fearfully into the next room as I passed through the passage. But nothing was to be seen that could help to explain the mystery. I then descended the stairs, and reaching the front door, was about to sally forth, too glad to escape from such a pandemonium; when I was startled and shocked to find the old white horse of the night before, lying dead on the porch steps, with his head and forefeet resting on the flooring of the porch, which in some places was smeared with blood and foam. I gazed at him a moment with a feeling of pity, not unmoved with terror, and then, forcing my way with some difficulty, I hurried from the fatal house.

"My mind was still so much disturbed by the deep agitations it had recently suffered, that for a time I never thought of connecting the frightful sounds of the previous night with the death of the poor old horse. But while walking across Mayo's Bridge on my way to the city, the truth flashed upon me at once. He had been seized with one of those painful disorders, perhaps intestinal worms gnawing his vitals and causing intolerable anguish. In his distress, he remembered having seen me enter the haunted house; and with the instinct which drives domestic animals to seek relief from men, he endeavored to make his way up the porch staircase he had seen me ascend. But his strength had failed, and he sunk on the steps, and the dreadful sounds which had driven me almost to madness, were the groans and convulsions of his dying agony. How I came to think the noise proceeded from my own room, I cannot well explain. Perhaps terror, combined with the startling loudness of the reverberation through the old empty house in the dead of night may have suffered to produce the illusion.

"I returned to the city, not a little humbled and crestfallen, and reached my place of abode before the family had risen. The night's adventures, I kept a secret from everyone; for I had no mind to encounter the ridicule which my ambitious design and ignoble failures merited; but they taught me a lesson that I have never since ventured to play the hero, or indulged the conceit of a mission to attack and exterminate popular superstitions.

"If the reader is disposed to sneer at the timidity displayed under the circumstances I have recounted, permit me to suggest that he can scarcely anticipate how he would himself act in a like situation, unless his strength of nerve has been fairly proved by some similar trial. In ordinary conjunctures my courage, I flatter myself, may compare with that of other men. But the imagination, when fully roused, is an agent of fearful power; and my own experience recommends it as a safe and wise maxim, never to subject it, without necessity, to dangerous experiments, in which it may escape beyond the control of the judgment, and lay reason prostrate in the dust!"

# The Ghost Carpenter of Cocatamoth

The small headline in the Sunday, September 27, 1874, *Richmond Enquirer* said cryptically: "The Henrico Ghost: A Spectre Carpenter Running His Saw." The brief article beneath it described an extraordinary mystery that has remained unsolved for more than 130 years. It occurred at the old Cocatamoth estate about three miles below Richmond on the long-extinct Osborne Turnpike. The house was an old-fashioned two-story framed building which, in that day, commanded a scenic view of the James River. It bore a splendid reputation and was the scene of many hospitable gatherings.

All of that changed abruptly shortly after J. W. Southard, a gentleman of good standing, moved into the house with his family on September 23, 1874. On that night "commenced manifestations upon the premises which are beyond the ken of any man, and which, to say the least, are passing strange." Southard, who slept on the ground floor, was rudely awakened that evening by a noise of what he described as "the drawing of lines on the underside of the floor of his chamber with some blunt instrument." This was followed by the unmistakable sounds of sawing and blows of a hammer and other noises similar to those made in using various carpenters' tools.

Southard got up and investigated, but could find no source for the disturbance. The next night he heard the same sounds, but again could find nothing. In fact, as soon as he got out of bed, the noise stopped. He walked around the house and then stood outside in the dark for some time, but heard only the natural sounds of nightfall. Maddeningly, as soon as he returned to bed, the phantom carpenter began banging away again, and continued until about two in the morning.

When the sawing and hammering commenced once more on Friday, the third successive night, Southard decided he had had enough and was going to get to the bottom of things once and for all. By this time, his wife, terrified, said she was leaving to visit relatives in the country until things cleared up. Working like a man possessed, Southard tore up the floorboards of his chamber, but there was nothing there. He then loaded his double-barreled shotgun, took extra shells, and grabbed a knife and a lantern. He went outside, placed the knife in his teeth, pirate style, and crawled as far under the house as he could go. He then fired both barrels in the direction where the noises seemed to be coming from.

Satisfied that he had done all he could, and if the noises were being made by any mortal being, he had silenced the source for good, he retired to bed. No sooner had he turned down the lamp and pulled up his covers when the hammering and sawing began anew and continued through the night. Curiously, it was noted that Southard had two fearless dogs that slept under the house. Not once during all the commotion did they stir, except when he blasted the shotgun.

Southard was described in the article as an "ex-Confederate soldier, and a man who is afraid of nothing, and not the person to make a statement of this character unless it was true." In fact, he offered to take anyone to his place that doubted his experience with the ghost, and said he was determined to solve the mystery if possible.

There is no record of what happened after that, or if he ever did find out the cause of the manifestations, or whether the incessant nocturnal work of a persistent spirit carpenter eventually drove him and his family from the house.

## The Spirit that Saved a Soldier's Life

The following narrative, here excerpted, was written by Civil War veteran J. L. Marye, and published in the October 13, 1897 issue of the *Alexandria Gazette*. It was titled "The Ghost of the Battlefield."

"On that eventful afternoon of the 2nd of May, 1863, when Stonewall Jackson hurled his corps upon the right flank of the federal army at Chancellorsville, our battery was attached to the division of A. P. Hill. We proceeded along the plank road for several miles, throwing a few shells now and then at the flying enemy. We then turned off from the road and entered the forest and soon found ourselves in that wild and weird section of country known as 'The Wilderness.'

"Night coming on and the battle and pursuits having receded almost out of hearing of us, we began to look around for a suitable place to make camp. We had been passing the dead and wounded lying upon the ground, as we rapidly followed up the battle, and coming upon one of those small openings that occur here and there in that section, we parked our guns and bivouacked for the night.

"I was sergeant of guard that night and was to go on duty at midnight. The corporal had the first half of the night and came to waken me at 12 o'clock. We had three sentinels, one of whom was over the guns that were parked near the skirts of a dense wood. I was sitting in the guard tent trying to read an old newspaper I had picked up on the battlefield, by the dim light of a lantern, and had not noted that the time was one o'clock, when I heard the sentinel call sharply, 'Sergeant of the guard, post number one!'

"He repeated the call several times rapidly, as I ran towards his post. I found the man with his drawn saber in his hand, pale and seemingly agitated. He said that while walking up and down on his beat as he approached the woods, an 'object' resembling a woman clad in white had come out on the edge of the field and beckoned to him, and that it had happened twice before he called out for me. The scene around was lonely and wild enough in all conscience to arouse the superstition of most anyone, but this man I knew was one of our staunchest soldiers and I confess I felt somewhat puzzled. I remained talking with him awhile, telling him that he was no doubt mistaken, through instructing him to keep a sharp lookout, and turned to walk back to the guard tent, when my steps were arrested by the sentinel shouting out, 'Look, sergeant, there it is again!'

"Running back to him, I distinctly saw on the edge of the woods, what appeared to be a woman, as well as I could discern in the moonlight, frantically waving her hands and beckoning to us. Seizing the saber out of the sentinel's hand, I ran towards the woods with all the speed I could, the sentinel calling after me, 'for the Lord's sake,' not to go. As I neared the woods, the woman in white vanished along what I found to be a narrow path. I followed on the run and had gone about 100 yards when I pitched head foremost over something lying right across the path. Picking myself up and stooping over to see what it was that had tripped me up, I discovered a dead federal soldier. I felt on his face. It was cold and he had evidently been dead some time. I could see in the moonlight that the blood had run down and made a dark spot in the sand, and his musket was lying by his side.

"I then walked on a little farther and discovered another, a live one this time, and an officer. He seemed badly wounded, his blouse was open and his shirt front was all bloody. He heard my steps and begged piteously for water. 'I will bring you water,' I said, and hastening back to camp, I awoke the relief, ordered them to get a litter, and catching a canteen of water, returned to the wounded officer and soon had him comfortable in the guard tent.

"Arousing our surgeon, he dressed the wound and staunched the blood and informed me that had the officer laid on the field another hour he would have died from loss of blood. We sent him back to the hospital at break of day and I learned afterward that he was duly exchanged. I reported to the captain what had occurred on my watch. He ordered me to send out a detail to bury the dead soldier in the woods, but paid little attention to my account of the woman in white, saying that the battle had turned all kinds of animals loose in the woods, and probably this was a white horse.

"The sentinel and I did not agree with him, however, and to this day all I know is that the appearance of this specter, or whatever it was, certainly saved that officer's life!"

## Ghosts of the Crater

It was, arguably, one of the most daring and ingenious tactics in military history. The only problem was that, unlike the legendary Trojan Horse of ancient Grecian times, this clever plan backfired! The idea was terrific, but the execution of the plan left much to be desired. We are talking about the historic Battle of the Crater, just outside Petersburg, that took place on July 30, 1864.

By midsummer of 1864, the armies of Union general Ulysses S. Grant and Confederate general Robert E. Lee had settled into deep-trenched, highly fortified lines facing each other in a prolonged stalemate. Neither side could move without suffering unbearable casualties.

In mid-June, Lt. Col. Henry Pleasants, commanding the 48th Pennsylvania Infantry of the Union IX Corps, came up with a novel proposal that possibly could break the deadlock and lead to a victory for the North. Pleasants had been a mining engineer in civilian life, and had a number of former coal miners under him. He suggested that a tunnel be dug beneath and beyond the Confederate lines and then eight thousand pounds of gunpowder be exploded. This would not only kill a great number of Southern soldiers, but it also would cause a large breach in the Rebel line that could pave the way for a Yankee frontal assault.

When the plan was submitted to Grant and other generals, they doubted it would have any major effect, and although they didn't kill the idea, they didn't support it either.

Colonel Pleasants thus had to scrounge for materials himself. To shore up the tunnel with timbers as it was being dug, an old bridge was dismantled. To remove the dirt, handmade sledges were made from cracker boxes. Ventilation shafts were driven into the earth as the project proceeded.

Toward the end of July the tunnel stretched more than five hundred feet and was fifty feet deep. Finally, Grant gave the okay, and the mine was filled with 320 kegs of gunpowder.

On the morning of July 30, Pleasants lit the fuse, but it burned out before detonation. Courageous soldiers crawled deep inside and relit the fuse. At 4:44 A.M., the charges exploded in a massive, horrific shower of earth, men, and guns. It created a crater 170 feet long, 70 feet wide, and 30 feet deep. It is estimated that roughly three hundred Confederate soldiers were instantly killed in the blast.

The battle plan called for a division of African American troops to charge to the site, rim the crater, and then move forward. They would be followed by two other divisions. It was then that a crucial decision was made that doomed the project. The black troops, who had been thoroughly trained for the mission, were held back and another division was chosen to lead the assault. The problem was, these men had not been trained, so when they charged, instead of ringing the perimeter of the crater, they jumped down inside it, thinking it to be an ideal rifle pit.

Instead, it became their instant tomb. The Confederates, recovering quickly from the stunning shock of the explosion, raced to the edges of the crater and began firing down at the hapless Yankees, in what one officer later described as a "human turkey shoot." Because of the incompetence of the Northern commanders in switching divisions at the last moment, causing confusion and chaos, the overall attack failed miserably. The Confederates reported losses of 1,032 men in the battle; Union losses were estimated at 5,300! Grant was to later say, "It was the saddest affair I have witnessed in this war." After the fighting was over, both sides returned to their trenches, and the siege of Petersburg went on for several more months.

Today, the Crater is a major tourist attraction, visited annually by tens of thousands of Civil War enthusiasts. Psychic experts contend that such sites of disasters, causing the tragic and traumatic deaths of so many well before their time, often provide a reasonable cause for the return of victims in spirit form. And such may well be the case at the Crater, for over the years there have been numerous reports of unexplained activity here.

One father-son team of Civil War reenactors said they feel "presences" every time they approach the Crater. "It really moves me," the father told a newspaper reporter. "People were slaughtered here. There are many reasons for dead soldiers to be rolling around in their graves." (Many of those who lost their lives in the battle are buried in nearby cemeteries.) There was one account of "a uniform" strolling near the site—devoid of a body! Joggers in the area during early-morning hours say they have seen Civil War soldiers emerge from the fog, then vanish. A park ranger once followed such an entity into a nearby abandoned storage shed. She said whoever or whatever it was flatly disappeared.

Consider, too, the grisly experience of Ashleigh Moody, a part-time reenactor. In the 1960s, he says, "they were building a new road that leads through the park, and had moved some of the ground near the crater. I was out one morning early, looking for bullets that might have been unearthed, and I noticed that a shoe was sticking up out of the mud." He cleared some of the dirt away and found a foot attached to a leg. He called the park rangers, and they dug out a body, complete with its rotten uniform and some Union buttons, but the head of the unfortunate soldier was never found. "Maybe he was blown up by the crater explosion and now his ghost haunts the scene," Moody says.

Beth Brown of Richmond, author of *Haunted Battlefields*, told a reporter that she heard so many tales of strange things seen and heard by reenactors, neighbors of the park, and motorists driving by at night, that she was certain "something odd was going on." During a research visit to the area, she said she uncovered nothing conclusive, but "I felt that the eerie sensations I experienced there were clues that something unseen was present."

Perhaps the most compelling account of ghostly activity occurred on a humid summer night in 1978, when Jimmy Blankenship and some of his fellow National Park Service rangers sat on the grass next to the Crater with the stated purpose of "picking up something, anything, paranormal." It was around midnight, he recalls, when they all heard distinct whispers coming up from the bottom of the pit. "We jumped up and split," he admitted. "We had no idea of what the voices said, and we didn't really care. We just wanted to get the hell out of there! It was a really creepy experience.

"I am convinced that there are ghosts out there," Blankenship concluded. "On that battlefield, young people died dramatic deaths before it was their time. And there are just too many stories about them. There must be some truth to it."

## The Woman who Married a Ghost!

The following extraordinary case is recounted from the book *Ghost Dogs of the South*, by Randy Russell and Janet Barnett, with the express permission of the publisher, John F. Blair of Winston-Salem, North Carolina.

The account involves a woman named Elizabeth MacLeod, daughter of Roderick MacLeod of New York. During the 1920s, when Elizabeth was sixteen years old, she was sent on a tour of her ancestral home, Dunvegan Castle, on the Isle of Skye in Scotland. Family legends dating to the thirteenth century covered the full spectrum of Scottish lore and included "royal battles, personal tragedies, murders most foul, and, above all, great loves."

One day while there, Elizabeth encountered an old woman in a black dress and a blue bonnet as she walked near the castle. The young girl greeted her pleasantly, but the woman walked on by without looking at her or saying a word. When Elizabeth mentioned the incident that evening, she was told it was the "widow witch of Skye, one of the haunts of the area. She had birthed seven sons by seven

men in her life," each with a different last name. The first six had married and raised families of their own, but the seventh son had not
found a wife in Scotland, so the old woman had sailed to America
with him to find a bride. No one knew the last name of this son.

That night, as the MacLeod hounds were baying outside the castle, Elizabeth was startled awake to find a tall man sitting on the edge
of her bed. She was terribly frightened, but when he smiled at her,
the fear faded. She said he was handsome and his eyes were bright,
but she could not recall their color. He gently took her hand in his,
smiled again, and then just vanished without saying a word. She got
out of bed and searched, but found no trace of him. Strange, she
thought.

Then she looked down and found a pair of embroidered gloves of
intricate design in blue thread, with white cuffs, on the edge of the
bed where the man sat. They were monogrammed, but she could not
make out the initials. When she awoke the next morning, the gloves
were gone. Before she had time to mention the visit, her relatives gave
her a little black puppy to take back to America with her. She named
him Pepper.

Back in New York, Elizabeth, a pretty young lady blossoming into
womanhood, was courted by a steady stream of suitors. Pepper liked
none of them, but Elizabeth fell in love with a charming young man
from Virginia named Kenneth Warren. When he finished his study of
law, they were married and settled in an apartment in the city. Sometime later, news of the death of Kenneth's mother arrived, and the
couple decided to move to her house in Dinwiddie County, south of
Richmond. Kenneth said it was a large house, but in need of repair.
It was, Russell and Barnett write, "a three story mansion done
entirely in brick and stone," in a remote wooded area far from the
nearest neighbor. The huge estate included several hundred acres
and the house reminded Elizabeth of Dunvegan Castle. She fell in
love with it at first sight.

And so, while Kenneth commuted to practice law in nearby Petersburg, she supervised the renovations and worked in the garden. The
couple was very happy. Only one thing seemed to bother Elizabeth.
Pepper was acting very strange. He never left her side, refused to go
out alone, and acted as if Kenneth didn't even exist. He wouldn't come

when her husband called him, wouldn't take food from him, and hid under the furniture whenever he was home.

One of Elizabeth's pet projects was to trim away the dense leafy vines that covered the entire back wall of the house. Periodically, she would chop away at the growth as best she could. Then one day, after they had been at home for four years, she decided it was time to get rid of the vines once and for all. When Kenneth came home one evening and found his wife hacking at them, he expressed a strong desire that she not remove the vines, but she was determined.

A day or so later, as she was cutting again, Elizabeth saw "something poking out at her from the vines." It looked like the bone of a crooked white finger! As she pulled away more of the foliage, she suddenly stopped and screamed. There, before her, was an entire human skeleton standing against the house! It appeared as if someone had been buried standing up against the wall, and "vines laced in and out of the openings of a human skull." Elizabeth ran into the house, and when Kenneth arrived she told him of the skeleton. "Whose bones are they?" she asked. "Has there been a murder?" She could see, from the expression on Kenneth's face, that he knew about the gruesome discovery.

"The bones," he said, "are mine!"

With that, "Kenneth disappeared. He went through the door without opening it. Or perhaps he evaporated in thin air before her eyes." She fainted dead away. When she recovered, only Pepper was at her side. She then locked the front door and went upstairs to her bedroom. And there, on the bed, lay a pair of lambskin gloves with white cuffs! Pepper grabbed one of the gloves and shook it viciously. Elizabeth picked up the other one and recognized the initials on it as being those of her husband's.

The next day, when Elizabeth asked some neighbors about Kenneth's mother, she was told, to her astonishment, that no one had lived in the house for over a hundred years. Later, she learned that no one in Petersburg had ever heard of a young lawyer named Warren. She told the local sheriff about the skeleton and upon examination it was determined to have been "several generations old." If a crime indeed had been committed, no one living could have been involved. The remains were buried in an unmarked grave in the public cemetery, and Elizabeth moved back to New York. It is not known if she ever married again.

But as Russell and Barnett concluded, "If dogs could talk, Pepper would have told Elizabeth that no one real was ever there for four years of marriage."

# The Psychic Wonders of Haw Branch

In recent years the spirits have seemed to settle down somewhat at historic Haw Branch Plantation in Amelia County, thirty-five miles south of Richmond. This is noteworthy because for generations there had been a plethora of psychic manifestations here. They included: phantom footsteps in the night; the unexplained sound of heavy falling objects; the spectral appearance of a woman's figure; frightening, full-throated screams that occurred on specific dates at six-month intervals; and a most puzzling portrait that mysteriously transformed from a black-and-white charcoal rendering to full color.

Col. Thomas Tabb and his wife, Rebecca, were the first owners of Haw Branch, built in 1748. The estate grew to 2,700 acres by 1798. The name is derived from a small stream on the property, the banks of which were lined with hawthorn trees. The large white mansion house is considered a splendid example of Georgian-Federal plantation architecture. For much of its history the house was connected with the prominent Tabb and Mason families, active in state and national affairs, and friends with many celebrated citizens such as John Randolph of Roanoke, a frequent visitor.

In 1965, William Cary McConnaughey and his wife, Gibson, bought the house and 120 surrounding acres, and began its renovation with loving care. "I was nine years old when I first saw Haw Branch," Gibson says. "My grandmother brought me out to visit because the home had been in our family from the time the plantation was established until Reconstruction days following the Civil War. The place was in dreadful condition. It had been unoccupied for years, windows were out, and cows were wandering through the English basement. The exterior hadn't been painted since 1929."

Three months after moving in, the McConnaugheys and their children began experiencing a series of strange and singular events. "I'm not a believer in ghosts myself," Gibson says, "but I have to say I can't explain some of the things that have happened here." In the late-night hours of November 23, 1965, for example, the entire family was awakened by a woman's bloodcurdling screams that seemed to come from somewhere upstairs. Cary and Gibson raced upstairs while their two dogs stood shaking with terror. But no source for the sound was found.

Precisely six months later, on May 23, 1966, the woman's screams were heard again resounding throughout the house. Inspections turned up nothing. This strange phenomenon happened twice more at six-month intervals. Then, on May 23, 1968, instead of the shrieks, the family heard heavy footsteps walking across the yard and an eerie, screeching wail outside the house. The children said they saw a giant bird with a wingspan of at least six feet in the moonlight. Such screeches were heard several other times and always on the dates of May 23 and November 23. "We never learned anything about the significance of those dates," Gibson says.

This puzzle was only one of Haw Branch's many mysteries. The family had been in the house only a few months when they all heard a loud thud outside that shook the whole building. "It sounded as though a very heavy solid object such as a safe had fallen from a great height and landed on some bricks," Gibson recalls. "We rushed outside, but there was nothing there." This particular manifestation was repeated a number of times.

There have also been some ghost sightings. Just past midnight one summer evening in 1967, Gibson went into the dark kitchen to get a glass of milk. In the light shining from the open refrigerator, she caught a glimpse of something in the hall. "I could plainly see the silhouette of a slim girl in a floor-length dress with a full skirt," Gibson remembers. "I could distinguish no features, but she was not transparent. I saw her for perhaps ten seconds and in the next instant, she was gone. There was no gradual fading away; she simply disappeared from one instant to the next."

Gibson later learned that earlier residents at Haw Branch had seen the same apparition. One relative said that Gibson's great-grandmother had told of seeing the "lady in white," and had once even been awakened from a deep sleep by a touch from the spirit. On other occasions, the McConnaugheys have heard footsteps descending from the second floor to the first. There have also been unexplained strange odors. Several times the strong scent of oranges was sensed in the library when there was no fresh fruit in the house. The attar of roses has also been smelled when no flowers were around.

Curious noises seemed to center in the attic. At one time or another all members of the family reported hearing what sounded like furniture being dragged across the attic floor late at night. Yet when they searched, the dust-covered furniture was unmoved. Sometimes a rocking chair was heard rocking in the room, but the chair was broken and no one could sit in it. Once, a humming sound was heard in the basement. It sounded like an old English folk tune. Incidentally, there is a sealed room in the cellar, a chamber completely closed off by brick and masonry. The housecats seem fascinated by it.

Gibson says there has been a lot of interest in the psychic phenomena, and a number of people, including ghost hunters, came to visit. It got too much for the couple, and the house is no longer open to the public. Before then, however, several writers came. One was a young woman who was doing a magazine article on haunted houses. She said she was a skeptic. "We let her spend the night in one of the upstairs bedrooms," Gibson says with a smile. "Sometime during the night, she told me, she was awakened by the sound of footsteps approaching her bed. Just then our cat, Fink, shot out of the bedroom. Now fully awake, the woman heard the footsteps come right up to the edge of her bed. She sat up and the sounds ceased. When she turned on the light there was only emptiness in the room. She said the experience made her a believer."

But of all the many and varied psychic manifestations that have surfaced at Haw Branch, the most intriguing involves a portrait. It is a large pastel rendering of a young woman named Florence Wright. She was a distant relative and little was known of her except that her parents lived in Massachusetts and that Florence died before the painting was completed, although she was only in her twenties.

After two decades in storage, the painting was given to the McConnaugheys by a cousin, who told them it was a color piece. This bewildered Gibson because, in her words, "when the picture was uncrated and the massive gilt frame and glass were painstakingly dusted, the portrait appeared to be a charcoal rather than a pastel. No color was evident; everything was a dirty white, gray, or black."

There was no signature of the artist to be found, and the back of the frame was tightly sealed. Gibson left it that way and hung the picture over the library fireplace.

A few months later, Cary McConnaughey was sitting in the library reading a newspaper when he looked up and noticed that the rose in the portrait seemed to have taken on a pink tinge. The girl's black hair also was beginning to lighten, and her grayish skin was turning flesh-colored. These changes continued gradually over the next year until the portrait miraculously transformed into pastel brilliance. Says Gibson: "A partially opened rose in the painting began to take on a definite pink cast, when previously it had been grayish-white. Other changes went on for several months. Some people connected with the art departments of neighboring Virginia colleges saw the portrait from the time of its arrival, and confirmed the changes in its coloring, but could offer no logical explanation."

A psychic expert came to investigate. He reported that Florence Wright's spirit was tied to the portrait because she died before it was finished, and that she had the power to remove the color from it when she was dissatisfied with where it was placed. She apparently liked Haw Branch. "Who can say his theory isn't correct?" Gibson asked. Today, the girl's clear blue eyes look rather sadly out beneath her curly reddish-brown hair, and her pink and white complexion looks as if she were still alive. The green and beige upholstery on the gnome-carved gilt chair she sits in is a deeper shade of the carved jade jar on the table near her. The rose that was first seen to change color slightly is now a clear, soft pink.

In 1971, Gibson wrote: "Much about the portrait still remains a mystery. How did the young girl die? Did the pink rosebud in the crystal vase foretell her early death, or was it added symbolically after she died? Who was the artist, and why did the pastel portrait's coloring change without human assistance? There is a slight lead on the artist's name. When the painting first arrived, the owner had told me that it was painted by a famous American artist and signed by him, although she couldn't remember his name."

About a year later, some of the answers were found, in a most curious fashion. One summer evening in 1972, one of Gibson's daughters and a friend of hers were sitting on the floor in the library beneath the portrait. They moved over to the sofa, and seconds later the supports of the picture's heavy frame pulled loose. The painting slowly slid down the wall until the bottom of the frame reached the mantel shelf where it crushed a row of porcelain antiques, tipped forward slightly, slipped over the edge of the mantel, and fell to the wide pine floorboards. As the girls sat, transfixed, glass shattered all across the floor. The portrait fell face-down on the exact spot where the girls had been sitting only moments before!

"Although the painting itself was undamaged, the big wooden frame was broken," Gibson said. "Lifting it up, we found underneath, where what had been the tightly sealed backing of the frame, a brass plate that gave the girl's full name, her birth date, and the date of her death. Though we searched carefully for the artist's signature, it could not be found. The next day the frame was repaired, the portrait placed back in it, and the glass replaced.

"It was late in the day when we arrived back at Haw Branch. The sun was red and low in the sky. As my husband and I lifted the picture from the back of the station wagon, I happened to tilt my end of the frame slightly upward. Suddenly, as though a red neon sign had been lit, the name 'J. Wells Champney' appeared. It had been signed in pencil on the apron of the dark mahogany table in the picture. Only under a certain angle of light could it be seen."

The McConnaugheys later learned that the girl's parents had commissioned Champney to paint the portrait. Before it could be completed, Florence Wright, died at age twenty-four of a massive stroke. The artist finished the painting and added the partially opened rose to signify that his subject died an untimely death before the rendering was done. Cary and Gibson also found out that the artist was later killed when he fell down an open elevator shaft in New York City.

Gibson adds that many say they can see the young woman blush when they stare at her portrait. But now that Florence Wright's picture has regained its original hues and hangs proudly in a fine old home, it seems unlikely that she will ever again extinguish her colors.

# The Dollhouse Ghost

Cherie and Steve Edwards of Bermuda Hundred, outside of Richmond, have an interesting hobby. They like to build, from unassembled kits, complex dollhouses. These are on a one-twelfth scale, one inch to one foot. They take these kits and improvise or redesign them to their own individual tastes.

In 1996, they bought such a kit from Jean and Leonard Bell, who run a miniatures store near Richmond, and assembled it. The house was fully furnished, but there were no dolls in it. This particular house was a granite block house similar to the old New Orleans-style architecture. It had a large sweeping veranda. About a year later, Cherie was making a videotape of some of their houses. Steve wanted to take it to his office to show it to co-workers. Nothing out of the ordinary transpired during the taping.

Sometime later, Cherie and Steve sat down to view the tape. As the camera panned across the veranda of this one particular doll-less house, the Edwardses suddenly sat up, stunned. "Did you see what I saw?" Cherie exclaimed. "I think I did," Steve replied. "Run the tape back and let's see it again." Cherie did. It was there again!

What they both saw, clearly, was a figure seated at a table on the porch—the miniature figure of a woman! Here is how Cherie describes it: "As the camera panned down the veranda, there was a woman sitting at a table. She is wearing a flowered dress and is tiny sized, fitting perfectly with the scale of the house. She is looking down and her hands are on the table. She has gray, curly hair and a rather large nose for her face. She is just sitting there. Then, in a few seconds, she gets up from the table—and walks out of camera range! We couldn't believe what we had just seen."

The Edwardses ran the tape over and over, and each time the vision appeared. They invited the Bells over. They confirmed the sighting. Leonard said you could see through the woman! "I didn't see her at all when I was doing the filming," Cherie adds. "It's all so weird."

Cherie Edwards graciously invited me to view the video. I did. I saw the ghost lady. I cannot explain it.

## Dining out with Ghosts

Should you wish to dine on gourmet cuisine in an historic old house, and possibly experience a ghostly encounter, you might well make reservations at one or both of two fine restaurants, within a few miles of each other in Chesterfield County, south of Richmond. One is an upscale steakhouse where servers are dressed in tuxedos, and the other is a more informal seafood emporium.

Ruth's Chris Steak House is located in Bellgrade Plantation, a historic manor home built in 1732. A Dr. Friend who once lived here assisted Dr. Hunter McGuire in the amputation of General Stonewall Jackson's arm during the Civil War. Confederate general A. P. Hill used Bellgrade as his headquarters when the fighting broke out in the vicinity. When Union soldiers marched past Southern trench lines outside of Petersburg, Hill was shot and killed by a Northern soldier. In his will, Hill requested that he be buried standing up at Bellgrade. And so he was. After the war ended, however, his body was re-interred at Hollywood Cemetery in Richmond, again buried in a vertical position.

It was some time before the Civil War that Bellgrade gained notoriety. In the 1840s a French bachelor named Anthony Robiou bought the house. He met a fourteen-year-old girl who lived nearby—the daughter of John S. Wormley, a prominent lawyer and wealthy landowner. Despite the difference in their ages, Robiou asked for, and was granted, her hand in marriage. The wedding took place in 1851, and the couple moved into the groom's mansion.

After only a few weeks of marital bliss, Robiou arrived home unexpectedly one afternoon and found his new bride in a "compromising position" with her former boyfriend, nineteen-year-old James Reid. Incensed, Robiou threw the girl out of the house and demanded a divorce. Angered and humiliated, her father, Wormley, talked Reid into retaliation. Late one evening, the two hid in front of Bellgrade and when Robiou reached his porch, Wormley shot and killed him. Both Wormley and Reid were arrested for murder and jailed in the county courthouse.

Clay Thomasson, current owner of the steakhouse, says Reid was later released because it was deemed he had been duped into the plot. Wormley subsequently was tried for murder, but as he had made many friends during his long years in the area's judicial system, he cunningly concocted a plot to get a mistrial. He arranged for a deputy sheriff to "liquor up" two of the jurors. It worked. However, a second trial was ordered. This time, since the case had become so well-known locally, jurors had to be summoned from neighboring towns. Wormley was found guilty and sentenced to hang.

On the day of the execution a crowd of about five thousand people came to witness what became a bizarre spectacle. Three ministers preached for nearly two and a half hours. Wormley, dressed in a new black frock coat, a black silk shirt, new boots, and a silk hat, was then placed in a wagon and driven to the gallows in an open field near the woods. This was done to accommodate the huge throng. He then spoke for fifteen minutes before he was swung into eternity.

But the saga was not over. The young widow soon after married Reid. Within two weeks, however, she fell down the front stairs of the plantation home and died. Thomasson says there are two varying accounts. One is she fell on a sewing basket and scissors punctured her heart. The other is she broke her neck.

Both she and her murdered first husband, Robiou, apparently occasionally return to the site of their tragedies. "A number of people have said they have seen their apparitions in the boxwood gardens in back of the house," Thomasson says. One who saw them was a former employee at the steakhouse, a woman named Willamena, who died a few years ago. Several others have witnessed the spectral couple.

The sightings raise some pertinent questions. If one is Robiou, is he back to scold his bride, or to seek vengeance for his murder? Does the girl appear in remorse for what she did, or is she looking for her lover, James Reid? And why does the ghost of John Wormley not join them? Whether or not a present-day patron will see such images is, of course, up to chance. But the dining experience alone is worthwhile here, and the ghost legend is printed on the menu.

### The Glass-Throwing Little Girl

Crab Louie's Seafood Tavern is located just a few miles from Bellgrade in a house formerly known as Midlothian, built around 1745. The name was also given to the coal mines nearby, and Midlothian later became the name of the town. In 1875, John Jewett purchased the property and he and his wife raised six children here. They ran a popular boardinghouse. In the mid-1900s a descendent operated a nursery school in the building. In 1975, a restaurant was opened, but a year later a fire partially destroyed the east wing of the house. This was rebuilt and in 1981, Crab Louie took over.

"Actually, I think we may have several different ghosts here," says owner Floyd Sinkler. One, the figure of a man, has been sighted by him and others. "In the summer of 1985," he says, "I was sitting at the bar one night after we had closed, and I suddenly got the feeling that someone was behind me. I turned and saw him. Well, maybe not all of him. I saw the upper half of a man wearing clothes that seemed to be from the nineteenth century. He had on a black suit with a white collar and his face was all powdery. He turned and disappeared, heading toward the attic. It scared the bejabbers out of me."

Several other inexplicable incidents have occurred over the years. Once, a truck jumped a curb outside and knocked out the power. Floyd started doing some bookwork by hand when he heard a loud crash. A load of ice had dropped in the ice machine. How? The power was still out. Then, as he watched in astonishment, a roll of paper began pouring out of an electric adding machine—by itself. Floyd assumed the power had been turned back on, but it hadn't.

There may be a haunted table at Crab Louie—table ten. One night a group of a dozen people lingered late. Every staffer except Floyd and a waiter had gone home. After the party finally left, he and the waiter went over to table ten to reset it. Floyd told the waiter, Scott, to go to the kitchen and bring out the bread plates. Scott looked dumb-founded. "Floyd," he said, "we already brought those plates out." The plates had somehow vanished before their eyes.

On another occasion, again late at night just before closing, Floyd and a server were stacking paper napkins on table ten. Incredibly, the napkins, in sequence, fluttered off the table and landed neatly in a single pile on the floor! The window was closed and there was not even a hint of a breeze. "If I hadn't been there and seen it for myself, I never would have believed it," Floyd says.

One night Floyd clearly heard some small children singing "Happy Birthday" at table ten. A waitress passed by, and he asked her where the children were. She turned pale and said, "that's not even funny." He asked her what she meant, and she told him she had heard the singing, too, but there was no one there. Two new employees, on their first day on the job, asked about the ghost stories. They soon became believers. Right in front of them, three drawers on a bread warmer cabinet opened and slammed shut.

But of all the paranormal manifestations at Crab Louie, perhaps none can match the "shenanigans" of the spirit employees have come to know as "Rachel." They occurred in the mid-1990s. Glasses began sailing off the bar racks. "They didn't drop out of the racks onto the floor," Floyd says, "They moved. They would land several feet away." One night a glass flew right over a man's shoulder and hit another man in the foot. They were both sitting about ten feet away from the bar. Both diners and employees experienced this phenomenon.

One evening a busboy and two servers decided to do some research on this mischievous poltergeist. They went into the attic and, on an Ouija board, asked for the ghost to tell who it was. The name "Rachel" was spelled out. She "told" them, through the board, that she was a little girl of about six or seven, and that they couldn't see her because she was afraid and wouldn't come out in the open. When Floyd told his own six-year-old daughter, Kelsey, about the incidents, she said Rachel "was lonely." So she gave Floyd one of her dolls and told him to put it in the restaurant. He did. Rachel's glass-throwing tantrums ceased, and have not recurred since.

A short time later, a airline pilot came into the tavern and told Floyd he was a direct descendent of the Wooldridge family that had initially owned the house. Floyd told him about Rachel. "When I mentioned the name, he turned white as a ghost," Floyd says. "He then told me that one of the first Wooldridge daughters who lived in the house died when she was about six or seven years old."

Her name was Rachel!

## A Premonition of Disaster

"Premonition" is defined as "a forewarning; anticipation of an event without conscious reason."

Over the past four centuries Richmond has had more than its share of tragic events. In the 1600s Indians killed many of the early settlers. In 1811, more than seventy city residents, including the governor, perished in a fire that destroyed a crowded theater. During the closing days of the Civil War, in April 1865, much of Richmond was burned to the ground by Union forces. Five years later, an upper floor in the state's capitol building gave way during a celebrated trial, sending sixty-two men plunging to their deaths and seriously injuring 250 more. Several times floods have inundated downtown streets, causing major businesses to close for months.

And then there was the calamitous railroad tunnel collapse.

A few years after the Civil War ended, as the city was being rebuilt from charred ruins, Richmond became a major rail center. Traffic grew so fast, and became so overloaded with strain, that it was decided to build a new tunnel under the Church Hill residential section to help alleviate the problem. It was to run nearly four thousand feet underneath houses from Nineteenth Street to Twenty-ninth Street.

Digging began on February 1, 1872, and there were ominous signs from the beginning. The earth here, blue marl and clay, was unstable, especially following rainstorms that caused the clay to slip. Four months after the work began, two men were partially buried in a soil collapse, an inspection engineer was knocked unconscious by a falling chunk of clay, and another engineer was crushed by falling clay and died five days later. Less than a year later, telltale fissures and cracks began appearing in the yards of those living overhead. Gas lines broke and fires flared up in the sky. On January 14, 1873, a 120-foot section of the tunnel caved in, destroying several houses.

Despite these repeated warnings, officials declared the tunnel safe to continue, and the first train successfully passed through it in December 1873. It was used for the next twenty-eight years without incident, and then was retired from active service in 1901, when a new James River viaduct was opened. By 1925, however, rail traffic had again become so congested that officials decided to reopen the aging Church Hill Tunnel, despite the fact that earlier that year a water main broke overhead, which should have indicated future problems.

What happened next is perhaps best described in a *Richmond Times-Dispatch* article printed some time later and written by Louis D. Rubin Jr. "It is shortly after 3 o'clock on the rainy Friday afternoon of Oct. 2, 1925. A Negro laborer, Lemy Campbell, is working near the entrance to the tunnel at 19th Street and Marshall. He is one of a force of several hundred men engaged in rehabilitating the old tunnel for further use. Campbell works in silence and listens to the wheeze of the little passenger locomotive being used to switch flat cars inside. It is resting some 100 feet inside the tunnel.

"Suddenly, he hears the sound of a brick falling from the roof of the tunnel. He looks upward. Several more bricks fall. Then there is a crackling sound from along the roof. Campbell drops his tools and bolts from the entrance. Behind him the roof comes crashing down. The screams of frightened, trapped men, the roar of earth, bricks and timber smashing to the tunnel floor, and the hiss of escaping steam from the locomotive tear the air.

"There is a frenzied dash for safety on the part of the gangs of laborers and the train crews. A few bolt for the western exit a few hundred yards away, and make it. Most of the others flee in the other and safer direction, toward the eastern opening to the tunnel nearly a mile away at 31st Street and Grace."

Rubin went on to write that the lights suddenly went out, causing further chaos. Groping for safety, a number of workmen at or near the stalled and buried train crawled under the cars. Others fled as best they could for the tunnel entrances, slipping and sliding as they went. Inside the cab of the locomotive, engineer Tom Mason was pinned to his seat by the reverse lever and was quickly scalded to death by the escaping steam. Fireman B. F. Mosby managed to slip out of the cab, crawl underneath the ten flatcars, and miraculously reach an entrance. He too was badly scalded, but in a poignant gesture, he told rescuers to let his wife know he was okay. He died that night in a hospital.

Other crew members were more fortunate. Some were knocked senseless by the avalanche of clay, but somehow worked their way to safety. Throughout the afternoon and evening, as thousands gathered at the site, more sections of the tunnel fell in, until the train was entombed under countless tons of earth. Rescue efforts started almost immediately. A huge steam shovel began digging down from above the tunnel, and men began trying to dig at both entrances. The effort went on for days. Finally, nine days later, a shaft was driven down to the site of the trapped rail cars. A workman wedged his way to the locomotive and saw a ghastly sight. There, sitting bolt upright in the locomotive cab, was Mason's body.

For some time afterward there was confusion over just how many men were buried in the tunnel. From employee lists, it was determined that one and possibly two laborers were missing and presumed dead. But there were strong rumors that several other men had been hired that day and hadn't been included on the work sheets. The exact number of how many perished will probably never be known, for after the frantic efforts to recover the bodies were deemed too dangerous to continue, the tunnel was filled in completely and sealed off forever. Over the next three-quarters of a century there were at least three more crumblings of the earth over the tunnel. In 1962, part of the park above disappeared; in 1988, two houses and part of a tennis court sank, as did a pharmacy building in 1998.

## Ghostly Echoes

It is at such sites of great disaster that parapsychologists and others believe the victims are often likely to return. This theory seems to be borne out at the tunnel, for over the years there have been a number of reports of unexplained activity here. Several residents, basking in the park overhead, claim to have heard muffled cries for help that seemed to come straight up out of the ground. One night several Richmond college students went to the site and a challenge was issued to some young men to go up and touch the concrete wall that seals one of the entrances. As they walked forward, they suddenly stopped dead in their tracks. They later said they heard the distinctive sound of metal train wheels rolling—inside the tunnel! They abruptly left.

For years, the Richmond Cold Storage warehouse was located next to the western entrance to the tunnel. The facility is vacant now, but some time ago a man was working there on the graveyard shift. He told of hearing the sounds of pickaxes clanking on brick and rock—again, inside the tunnel. He and others, who reported similar accounts, believed it was the ghosts of the missing laborers still trying to claw their way out.

The tunnel collapse has reached the status of a folklore legend, only this one is founded in truth. Even to this day, curiosity seekers still tramp through the bramble overgrowth to catch a glimpse of the tunnel entrances. A song has even been dedicated to the disaster. The lead stanza goes:

> Remember the Church Hill Tunnel
> Near a mile under Richmond
> There's a story I want to tell you
> Of a train that'll never be found

The chorus:

> Brothers keep shovelin'
> Pickin' in the ground
> Brothers keep listening
> For the train that's never been found

And, finally, there is this chilling premonition that was revealed forty-three years after the tragedy. It was in 1968 that one Mrs. Mason, the widow of engineer Tom Mason, told the *Richmond Times-Dispatch* that her husband "knew something was going to happen" on that fateful day. She said he came back after leaving home that morning, and kissed her goodbye—again!

## The Lady Who Talks With Animals— Both Dead and Alive!

Patty Summers has a gift, a very special gift. She talks with animals, or, to be more specific, she communicates with them. It works both ways: Patty receives "messages" from her feathered and furry friends, and she gets her ideas across to them. This often results in a mutual understanding, basically, through telepathic communication.

"You know how thoughts sometimes pop into your head an instant before you say something?" Patty explains. "That's kind of like how it happens. Sometimes I get a mental picture, like a movie going on in my head, flashing montages or images"

Patty, who has worked with animals all her life, has fine-tuned her gift to the point where today she is a full-time animal communicator. Pet lovers and others from all over the United States consult with her when problems arise with their dogs, cats, horses, or whatever. How did it all start? Patty's first recollection of her unusual ability came at the age of five. Her younger sister had Down's Syndrome, and Patty was too young to understand why, because of the illness, her parents devoted so much time and energy to her sister. She felt left out.

Then one day while she was sitting in her bedroom, Cuddles, her cat, jumped up in her lap. A telepathic link developed between the two. Patty received a thought wave from the feline, explaining the situation. Cuddles told, in effect, why so much attention had to be paid to the sister, but that didn't mean that her parents' love for Patty had diminished at all. They loved her, too. From then on, Patty seemed to know her calling. She became a petsitter. Later, she worked as an animal control officer and in shelters and clinics. And she began applying her singular gift, which transcends earthly bounds. She communicates both with live animals and those in the spirit world.

One day, while working at a shelter, someone brought in an abandoned young kitten, found by a dumpster. Its eyes were matted almost shut, and it was so weak and emaciated it couldn't stand. Patty knew at first look that it was dying. Tears streamed down her eyes. "It was so sad," she recalls. "I talked to the kitten about euthanizing her, and the kitten agreed. It went peacefully. Still, I was devastated. Someone needed to mourn for her. Then, suddenly, I had a vision. I saw a group of female beings in human-like form. They appeared to be angelic girls between the ages of six and twelve. They seemed to sparkle and exude light. Then I heard giggling. They were reaching out to something at their feet. It was the kitten! Only now it was healthy and radiant. One of the angelic beings picked her up, and they all began to stroke her. I heard the most pleasant sound of loud purring. And then a message came through—'No need to mourn. She is with us now.'"

In another case, Patty was asked to find out why a cat was so stressed out. The cat communicated to her that there was a disturbed woman in the house where it lived. Patty then learned that the woman was not mortal. She was the ghost of a person who had been murdered in the house. The cat could see the ghost, but its owners couldn't, thus the energy in the house was affected, causing unrest. The spirit later "moved on," and the cat fully recovered. "Animals can pick up on seeing such things as ghosts whereas humans sometimes cannot," Patty says.

Several years ago, Patty told of a most compelling incident in an article she wrote for a publication called *Echo*. "I have always believed in angels, or spirits that come to help those of us still in physical form. I had a friend, Dorothy, who named her poodle, 'Angel.' She never realized how appropriate that name would be. Dorothy had contacted me concerning another poodle named Nicole who recently had passed into the spirit world. It was an unexpected death, so she wanted me to contact Nicole in hopes of making some peace with her passing. She wanted to know if Nicole was okay.

"'Yes,' I responded, 'she is peaceful, relaxed, and says she can now breathe freely. There is no more struggling.' Nicole had difficulty with her trachea, and the morning she died it was due to her trachea's collapse. Dorothy asked if there were any other dogs with Nicole. 'Yes,' I answered. 'I see a small white poodle licking Nicole in the face.'

"'That's Angel,' Dorothy exclaimed. 'Angel was a toy poodle I had twenty years ago. How wonderful, but Nicole did not know Angel. Why was Angel there to meet her?' 'Because,' I said, 'she was aware of Nicole's transition and it was her job to be there for Nicole. She knew Nicole was your dog.' Dorothy then said 'Oh, this brings so much joy to my heart.'"

Another time, a man came to Patty for help. Hi faithful and beloved Labrador mix, Sheba, had disappeared. She was seventeen years old. The man was distraught. He asked Patty if she could find his dog. She tuned in, and Sheba communicated from the spirit world. She had gone into the woods near her home to die. Patty received a most touching and eloquent message Sheba wanted to convey to her owner. Part of it went, "I could not bear to bring you more pain by allowing you to see me die. My decision to go was not an easy one because I knew the pain it would cause you, however, I knew it was my time. I had grown accustomed to my physical pain, but my body was just worn out. I had done what I had come to do in this lifetime—remember the joys and lessons of our friendship. Mostly, I enjoyed just being with you, at your feet or by your side. When you think of me, I am there; when you need me, I am there; when the time is right I will return in physical form to live with you again."

Unlike humans, Patty says, animals have absolutely no fear of death. They sense that it is part of life, and that while they have outlived their bodies, their spirit moves on.

"When my dad died some years ago," she notes, "he came to me in a dream. It was a lot like what happened in the movie *Ghost*. I saw his image and there were people behind him. He appeared young, smiling, and radiant. He told me my sister would die well before me, and that he would be there for her. He said not to worry. After my sister died, she appeared to me in a dream, too."

Patty has had other psychic experiences involving mortals, or rather mortal spirits. When she was an animal control officer in Lynchburg in the late 1980s, she was walking down a city street one day looking for an injured dog. "I came to a house with a wrought iron fence around it. I stopped cold. There, in the yard, I saw people all dressed in colonial costumes. They were having a tea party. I could hear talk and laughter. I clearly remember seeing a woman carrying a tray, serving drinks. Somehow I knew it was not a reenactment." Patty said the vision lasted a few seconds and then it vanished. On another occasion, she saw the spirits of native American Indians on her land. "I guess I really am psychic," she says, "but I don't consider myself a professional. I am an animal communicator."

Today, Patty lives on her farm south of Lynchburg with her husband, Joseph, two dogs, five cats, four goats, a red-colored Amazonian bird, and an iguana. They all thrive in harmony. "I value my role as a bridge between humans and our animal brothers and sisters," she says. "The bridge leads to a table that exists for all of Mother Earth's children to sit at: the two-legged, the many-legged, those that burrow, those that fly, those that swim, those that crawl, the stone people and the plant people. While at this table, all walk in balance and harmony. Even though some humans have forgotten the table exists, the invitation to return is always open." Patty believes anyone can learn, at least to some extent, to talk with animals.

Here are some of her suggestions. "Clear your mind of emotions. Animals complain because human minds are cluttered with many thoughts and emotions, and this is sometimes confusing to your pet. Anger, fear, or excitement will cloud your communication. Give your animal your full attention, no TV, no distractions. Speak from your heart. Be positive. Tell them what you want. If you are having a problem with a particular behavior or exercise in training, do not talk about what they did wrong, tell them how you want it done. Openly accept whatever communication you receive. The animal may send you a mental picture, a feeling, a thought. Acknowledge to your friend that you have received the message. Thank them."

Patty's most poignant case involved her "partner dog," Mauvree. "She was twelve years old when I learned she was dying of cancer in the year 2000," Patty recalls. "I said to her, if you want to reincarnate as a cattle dog, it's okay with me. Two or three days later, after she passed on, I was driving down a dirt road, when a song came on the radio. Mauvree had always chided me about playing the radio too loud. It was a Phil Collins song, 'You'll be in My Heart.' The lyrics had always had a special meaning for me: 'When destiny calls you, you must be strong. I may not be with you, but you've got to hold on. They'll see in time, I know. We'll show them together. Look over your shoulder and I'll be with you always.'

"As these words came over the radio, I looked around in the back seat, where Mauvree had always loved to ride, and her spirit was there! It was a good thing I was on a dirt road and not in town, because I would have wrecked the car. Tears started streaming down my face. I heard that song again the day I got Mauvree's ashes. She let me know that she was all right and she would always be with me.

"A few months later, she came to me again, and said I had to let her go. She said I was going to get a cattle dog. Some time afterwards, I found a seven-month-old puppy, 'Indigo.' He was a cattle dog. He belonged to someone else at the time, but I was told he was supposed to be with me. I later adopted him. Is he the reincarnation of Mauvree? I can tell you that this was, without question, the most beautiful and profound experience I could ever describe!"

# The "Pocahaunted" Parkway

In June 2002, the eastbound lanes of the new 8.8-mile, $314 million Pocahontas Parkway were opened, connecting southern Chesterfield and eastern Henrico counties, south of Richmond. The cutting-edge stretch of road includes a towering bridge over the James River high enough to give oceangoing ships access to the Port of Richmond's deepwater terminal. The parkway features the region's first high-speed, open toll design. Participating motorists are able to travel designated lanes and pass through toll facilities at highway speeds. Drivers who have a fear of ghosts welcome the fact that they don't have to slow down or stop—because this superhighway is purported to be haunted!

Strange sounds and sightings began a month after the parkway opened, and it didn't take long for the word to spread. One of the first encounters was witnessed by two of the engineers who were involved in the construction. One said, "We were heading home late one night and as we approached the Mill Run Overpass, an Indian ran right dead smack in front of us. We almost hit him. Then he just vaporized. We got out of the car and confirmed to each other what we had seen. It really shook us up."

From then on, reports of such strange sightings began to pour in almost nightly. Toll plaza attendants on the graveyard shift started hearing the sounds of howls and drumbeats. A truck driver said he saw "three flickering points of light" on a high bluff as he approached the toll area. He told an attendant he had seen three Indians in the middle of the highway, each holding a torch. He said he had let loose a blast from the truck's air horn to warn off two more phantom Indians standing in front of him. State police were called to the scene, but found nothing.

It was the first of scores of calls to law officials. Once, they were summoned when employees saw a mysterious figure running around a loading dock. It was described as having "cloudy but fully formed legs, arms and torso, with only the vaguest outline of a head. When state troopers arrived, it had vanished, but officers said they heard "howls and drums" they couldn't explain. The police also investigated a report that someone was "banging" on a shed located behind the office near the toll booths. A responding officer confirmed the sounds. Then the blinds in the office began to open and shut by themselves and lights flickered on and off. When the building was searched, nothing was found.

A few nights later, this same officer was called again when someone was spotted running back and forth across the roadway. While one trooper went out to the area where the sighting occurred, the officer went into the office, which is equipped with sophisticated surveillance videos. The trooper on the road said he saw nothing, but the one in the office replied, "That's weird. We're looking at you on camera and someone is standing beside you right now!" Others in the office verified the incident.

The *Richmond Times-Dispatch* sent staff writer Chris Dovi to the scene. She interviewed several people and said both troopers and workers told of hearing Indian drums. "Equally hard to handle are the mingled whoops, shouts and cries of seemingly dozens of voices that on occasion emerge over the din of passing tractor-trailers," she wrote. "The frenzied chants and howls usually come long after midnight. Rare is the night that the voices hold their peace." State police spokeswoman Corinne Geller confirmed that the "noises are real." She added that three separate times during one night watch, she and fellow officers reported hearing high-pitched howls and screams—not the screams of a person in trouble, but whooping. "There were at least a dozen to fifteen voices," she noted. "Every hair on my body was standing up when we heard those noises."

When the first newspaper article was published, two months after the road opened, hundreds of curious onlookers descended on the parkway. One woman said, "As soon as I arrived, I noticed huge puffs of smoke coming from the woods up a steep hill." Everyone saw it. Some thought it was from a train, but trains hadn't been in the area for years. Others thought it was factory smoke, but there are no factories nearby. Besides, this was not a steady stream of smoke, but rather short puffs that appeared to be in a sequence, such as what Indian smoke signals would make.

As the sightings and sounds continued to be reported by motorists, transportation department workers, and state troopers, things got pretty wacky. Police were called to respond almost nightly, and hundreds of people came to rubberneck. They parked on the road shoulders, causing safety problems. Many were drinking. The parkway took on a carnival atmosphere. One night a woman ignited a piece of shrubbery as "a peace offering to the spirits." Serious ghost hunters came but could not conduct a meaningful investigation because of the uproar. Finally, police had to threaten to ticket anyone who stopped in the area.

A female tollbooth operator said she heard chants, whoops, and hollering nightly. One night she and her supervisor both saw a horse with an Indian standing near it on the side of the road. They then faded away. The woman became obsessed with the phenomena to the point where she lost her job. She started a Web site called "The Pocahaunted Parkway" and declared, "There will be no more articles printed on this subject in any newspaper. The corporate office at the parkway has ordered everyone to keep their mouths shut about the spirits."

It later was discovered that the new road had been built at a site where Powhatan and Arrohateck Indian tribes once lived, hunted, fished, and died. Ben Keys, a shaman and local spirit guide, said the area was "a very spiritual place, a holy place for the Indians." Ron Hadad, owner of picnic grounds less than a mile from the parkway, said he and his mother had lived there forty years and that they had always heard "a lot of hooting and hollering." He added that the daughter of a local Indian chief once told him there "were a lot of spirits here."

Archeologists said there was evidence of Indian habitation in the region of the parkway dating from the 1600s to as far back as 3500 BC. A dig was done before the bridge was constructed and Indian artifacts were found scattered all over. Many came to believe that the parkway, named for a famous Indian princess in Virginia, had, in fact, been built directly over burial mounds and sacred grounds.

"What is needed here," said Keys, "is quiet and reverence."

## A Spirit Message from Iraq

Donald May Jr. always wanted to be a Marine. His interest began at an early age. His parents, Donald May Sr. and Brenda May, were both Marines; in fact they had met at Quantico, Virginia. At age twelve, Donald became a naval sea cadet, and, later, a police scout. When he decided to join the service in 1991, shortly after graduating from Meadowbrook High School in Richmond, Brenda said she was proud of him—scared, but proud. He served in the first Gulf War, guarding Iraqi prisoners, and then left the military for two years, but rejoined as a tank commander. "Just like his father," Brenda says.

When the second Iraq war broke out, Donald was there. "I always had a feeling of dread," Brenda recalls, "so every time I talked to him I made sure I said I loved him." She worried that he was not getting enough rest, but he would say, "I'll get enough sleep when I'm dead."

On May 25, 2003, Donald and his fellow Marines were in a tank on a convoy mission. They had not slept for more than four days. On their way back to home base they ran into a blinding sandstorm. As the tank crossed the Euphrates River, it ran off the bridge and plunged into the water, landing upside-down on the bottom. Everyone strapped inside drowned.

At that exact time, Donald's grandmother, who had nodded off while watching television in Richmond, suddenly awoke and saw his apparition. It quickly dissolved before her eyes. She was so shaken by the incident she didn't tell Brenda until months later.

That evening Brenda, who had an inexplicable "gut-wrenching" feeling that day, went into the laundry room to do some wash and said she "smelled" her son. "He used to come home on weekends to do his laundry at our home, and I could recognize his smell anywhere," she says. "I knew then that he had died in Iraq. I said out loud, 'I know you're gone. You need to be with your wife.'" She was later told by a service representative that Donald was "missing in action."

Two days later, after his death had been confirmed, the representative came back to inform her that Donald had indeed drowned. She told him, "I already know!"

Donald May Jr. was the first Virginian killed in the second Iraq War. Brenda was inundated with media coverage. The *Richmond Times-Dispatch*, the *Washington Post*, the Associated Press, and numerous other newspapers and radio and television stations carried reports. As a result, Brenda received sympathy cards and letters from people all across the United States. She keeps them in a trunk.

Paranormal experts call what Brenda and her mother experienced a case of "crisis apparition." That is, when a loved one is at the moment of serious injury or death, somehow they are able to communicate from beyond the bounds of the explainable.

There is an ironic footnote to Donald Jr.'s story. In 1991, his father was out on a body of water, fishing. A sudden squall came up. Strong winds lifted the boat up and it came crashing down on his head. He drowned.

# South
## *and*
# Southwest
# Virginia

# A Treasure Trove of Ghost Lore

During the years of the Great Depression, the U.S. government created the Works Progress Administration to help provide employment for the jobless. One section hired writers to collect oral histories, including folklore. In Virginia, the most prolific of these authors was James Taylor Adams, a native of Wise County. From the mid-1930s to the early 1940s, Adams interviewed thousands of native residents in southwestern Virginia. Among his papers is a rich collection of more than two hundred authentic ghost stories, part of the commonwealth's storied heritage. A representative sampling is recounted here with the permission of the Blue Ridge Institute at Ferrum College, near Rocky Mount.

## The Stuttering Spirit

This story was told to James Taylor Adams on October 14, 1940, by Dicy Adams.

"You wouldn't think a schoolteacher would believe in ghosts, but I am pretty sure my father, Shade Roberts, who was a teacher, did believe in them and that dead people could come back and haunt the living. I've heard him tell about an old man who lived in his neighborhood when he was a boy growing up. This old man stuttered awful bad, and when he tried to talk he made a funny noise. Pap said he got to mocking the old man and that one day the old fellow got mad and swore that he would get even with him if he had to come back after he was dead and haunt him. Pap said that it sort of bothered him and he thought a whole lot about it.

"After Pap was grown and the old man was still living, he forgot all about it. He went and joined the army and served all through the Mexican War. When he got his discharge, somewhere in Ohio, he struck out for home. In those days people had to walk wherever they went, or ride horseback, and Pap didn't have a horse, so he walked all the way home to the head of the Guesses River in Wise County.

"He said he got near home one night along about midnight, and being so tired and not wanting to go in and disturb the folks at that time of night, he just crawled over in a field and laid down and tried to go to sleep. But he couldn't, because something wouldn't let him sleep. Something just kept making a noise right around him all night. He knew it reminded him of something, but it was a long time before it come to him what it was. It was plimeblank (exactly) like the old man a-stuttering. So he laid there till daylight and the noise never let up. Right round and round where he laid.

"When day light started, it hushed and he got up and headed on home. He stumbled over something, and he seen it was a rough tombstone. He struck a match and looked at it, and found it was the grave of the old man that had said he would come back and haunt him for laughing at his stuttering! He had died while Pap was away in the army. Pap believed the longest day that he lived, that that old man had really come back from the dead to haunt him."

### Chased by a Dead Horse

This story was told to James Taylor Adams by Mary Carter on October 9, 1940.

"I've heard a lot of strange things in my life and seed 'em, too. A lot of things I didn't know what was. Maybe it was sumpin' and maybe not. But the quarest thing I ever know'd a happin' like that, was to my brother, Frank Adams. Best I can remember it was thisy way. Pa had an old bay horse and the old horse got down with the bot or something. They worked on him. Give him everything they could think of, and Pa is a good doctor that way, too. But he got worse and worse. At last, he got plum on the lift, and Pa always said when a horse got on the lift you'd just as well to knock him in the head. You could swing a cow and get up and again, Pa said, but you couldn't a horse.

"So Pa told us children that the old bay horse was sure going to die. Frank was a great big young man then and the old horse was about a mile down the creek from where we lived. So one evening Frank, he slipped off down that way and when he come back he looked kind of sheepish and guilty of something. Pa asked him what was the matter and what he'd been doing, but Frank wouldn't tell. Pa went down to see how the old horse was getting along, and come back and told us he was dead. Frank had killed him; had knocked him in the head with a pole axe. Frank owned up and said he was just getting the old critter out'n his misery.

"That was in the spring of the year and it went on till fall. One night we was all sitting round the fire when in jumped Frank. And I honestly believe he was the worst scared feller I ever seed! He said that he was coming long up the branch and just after he passed where the old horse's bones was, he heard something like a horse coming behind him. He looked back and seed the old bay horse just as plain as he ever seed him in his life, a running after him. Every now and then he would let out a snort. Frank said he started to run and the faster he run, the faster the horse run. He liked to run hisself to death before he got home.

"He had nearly a mile to come. Just before he got to the house there was a big flat rock in the road, and he said that he looked back and the fire was just a-flying out of that rock when the horse's feet struck it. And just as he got to the fence in front of the house, the horse turned and went back down the road with his tail over his back, just a rarin' and pitchin' and snortin.'

"We couldn't never get Frank to pass that place again after dark. He'd stay all night over at Grandpap's or Aunt Peggy's before he come home after dusk. Course, I never seed this myself, but I know the way Frank acted that he shore seed something. He'd killed that old horse, you know."

## The Flames of Hell!

James Taylor Adams recorded this story in an interview with Mrs. Lenore Kilgore of Big Laurel, Virginia, on February 26, 1941.

"I've heard Uncle Sam tell the awfulest tale about old Ran Hubbard. He said old Ran lived on Critical Fork of Guesses River when he died. That's been 50 or more years ago. He had been a very wicked man, but on his death bed he was converted, and requested that the Bible be buried with him. Now most of the neighbors objected to putting the Bible in the coffin with him, saying it was a sin to bury the word of God. But old Ran had said to bury it with him, and here, in this part of the country, when a dying person makes a request it is carried out. So they finally placed the book in his hands on his breast and buried him that way.

"Well, it went on for a few weeks, and Aunt Pop, that was old Ran's wife, had a log rolling one day. Old Ran had cleared up a new ground before he died, but hadn't rolled the logs off it. So all gathered in to roll the logs off of the new ground. They had made one log heap right close to the house and that night, after most of the people had gone, someone stepped out and come running back in the house, pale as death and trembling all over.

"Said he'd seen something out there in the log heap that was burning in the yard. Uncle Sam said that him and Grandpa Roberts, who was Aunt Pop's brother, went out with some others who had stayed for supper and to talk a while, and sure enough, as plain as they ever seen anything in their life, there was old Ran Hubbard right there in the rolling flames, with the Bible in his hands!

"They watched it for a long time and it was still there till they went to bed or went home. Everybody believed that it was a sign that old Ran had went to hell and was reading his Bible in the flames of torment!"

## The Tell-Tale Teethmarks

This account was told by James Taylor Adams himself in 1940. He said he had heard it as a child from his mother.

"Years ago the old log cabins didn't have any locks on their doors like they have today. They had a hole honed through the door facing, and they ran a chain through there and put a padlock on it, and they also had a hole in the door where the cat could go in and out at night. This one woman kept having this dream. She would dream of a night that she would hear the chains a-rattling on the door there, and every time they rattled, there would be a big black cat jump up on her head and get on her chest and it would just almost smother her to death. She said she couldn't hardly breathe with the cat on there; was like a dead weight. And this happened just night after night.

"She finally told someone about it, some of the neighbors, and one of them said, 'You know this old lady that lives down the road here by herself? She is a witch, and says she got mad at you about something, and this is her. She turned herself into a cat! The next time she does that, you get her by the foot and bite her and that will stop her.'

"So the next night this woman went to bed and said just before she went to sleep, she heard the chains rattle on the door, and here come the cat. It jumped right up on her in the bed. It was so heavy, she felt like it was going to mash her plumb through the bed, and said she couldn't hardly breathe. Said she grabbed the cat by its front paw and stuck it in her mouth and bit it real hard. Said the cat squalled and jerked its foot back and took off through the door. She heard the chains rattle as it went out the door.

"And the next day, some of the folks walked by the house where the old witch lady lived down there, and she had her hand all bandaged up. She died a short time after that, but she wore the bandage on her hand as long as she lived. After she died, some of them took the bandage off.

"There were teeth marks on her hand!"

## The Ghost Children's Revenge

This account, reminiscent of that of the Bell Witch of Tennessee, was told to James Taylor Adams on August 4, 1940, by Clinton Sexton Jr., who learned it from his grandparents.

"There was a man who lived at the forks of a creek. His wife had died and he had two little girls. He married again, and his second wife didn't like the children and wanted to get rid of them. So she killed them one day and took them up the left-hand fork of the creek and buried them in a sinkhole and covered them up with some logs. After that, every night they would hear something just screaming and crying and coming right down the left fork of the branch. His wife told the man the children had gone over to their granny's to spend some time. When she heard the screaming, she would pull the covers up over her head and scrooch down in the bed and say, 'Oo-oo-oo! I'm afraid!'

"This kept on for a week or more. The neighbors come in to hear it and see if they could find out what it was. They could all hear it, but they didn't know what it was. The sounds would come right down the left-hand hollow, up to the house, and then inside around the bed where the woman slept. But nobody could see anything. One night, they decided they would keep whatever it was out. So all the men and women in the area came to stay all night. They cut a whole heap of back sticks and fore sticks, and some big old logs. They had the door covered up with sticks of wood.

"When they heard it coming, the crying and screaming, down the left fork of the hollow, the men all got against the door, too. They said they knowed they would not let it in that night. On it come, just screaming and crying, and it come right up to the door. Then it began to scratch at the door. The woman, she scrooched down in the bed and started crying, too. In spite of all they could do, it tore the door down, but they still couldn't see a sign of anything.

"The next thing they knowed, the woman began screaming that it had her, and there, before their eyes, she was drug out of the bed, and right across the floor she went, screaming as loud as she could for them to take it off her, but they couldn't see anything. And then, right out the door she went, kicking and screaming, saying, 'It's got me! It's got me! I'm gone!' And the last they saw of her, she was hollering for them to take it off, as she went out of hearing up the left-hand fork of the branch. They hunted everywhere, but they never found a sign of her!"

## The Squeaking Door

Mrs. Celia Ann Maggard, of Norton, Virginia, told this story to James Taylor Adams on October 15, 1940.

"When I was a little girl, been about 40 years ago, Pap bought Preacher Wes Collins' house over on Collins' branch and we moved there. Preacher Wes had had a little boy to die there about a year or two before that. They told us they'd heard things there, but we didn't pay any attention to it. The neighbors said the little boy had rid [rode] the door, which was an old-fashioned door hung on the outside on pegs. They said that Preacher Wes had whupped his son for it. The boy then took down sick and died, and after that they said they couldn't keep the door shut.

"Well, sir, the first night after we moved in, we was all settin' thar and the door was fastened with a string on the inside, when all of a sudden that string broke and the door flew open and begin to swing backwards and forwards, going 'squeak, squeak.' Pap got up and shut it. Nothing more happened till we'd gone to bed and it waked us all up, squeaking again. So it just kep' on that way and after while Pap said he'd fix it. So he shut it one night, tied it with a rope, made a wooden peg and pegged it shut, and then leant a big back stick again it. He said now he'd like to see anything get it open. Well, sir, we hadn't been in the bed but a little while till we heard a kerlatermen [loud banging], and the door flew open and started squeaking. It went plimeblank [exactly] like a child snubbin' and cryin'. The rope was broke slapdash in two; the peg was out; and the back stick was a-layin' out in the yard!

So Pap said he'd take the door down and hang it to the stable over across from the house. He did, and all night long we could hear it goin' 'squeak, squeak.' Never stopped. We couldn't sleep for it. Then Pap took it down and put it up in the stable; left it on some fodder. Even that didn't do any good. For from about ten o'clock every night, it would go 'squeak, squeak,' just like it had when it was hung. And we'd listen to it and we could hear just as plain as could be, a child snubbin' and cryin'.' Made a-body feel awful quare, I can tell you. Pap talked of selling the place, but he decided to try one more way to get it to hush. Him and brother Jimmie took it and carried it away up in a cove about half a mile from the house, and laid it on a big poplar stump. And we never heard anything more.

"I believe as much as I'm settin' here right now, that it was that little boy hainting his Pap 'cause he whupped him for riding on the door. I'll never believe anything else."

## The Ghost Dog that Broke a Man's Toe

Finley Adams told this story to James Taylor Adams on May 7, 1941.

"Talking about ghost dogs, I guess you've heard about the dog ole Si Collins seed. One night, Si was out in the yard between the house and kitchen and he noticed the kitchen door was a-standing open, and he looked in and seed a big black, shaggy-haired dog standin' in there by the table. Strange dog to him. He scolded it, but it never let on, never moved. He ventured in, spoke to the dog, and tried to march him out, but it wouldn't move.

"Si got mad. He drawed back and kicked at it. His foot went right on through the dog and struck the table leg and broke his big toe. I seed it. He couldn't wear a shoe for a month or two and hobbled around on a cane with his big toe all swelled up and turned blue. After he broke his toe, he run out of the kitchen and hollered for Aunt Peggy to fetch a light. She brought a light and they searched all over the place and couldn't fine hair nor hide of any dog. He believed as long as he lived that it was the Devil he seed as a dog."

## Big "Fraid" and Little "Fraid"

This classic anecdote, still told and retold throughout southwestern Virginia, was related to James Taylor Adams at an unspecified date in 1940, by Mrs. Dicy Adams of Big Laurel.

"One time there was a man, and he had a little boy. And he'd send the boy after the cows in the evening. And the boy would stay and stay. Wouldn't get the cows home till way after dark. The man would whoop the boy, but that didn't do any good. He would be late just the same. One day he told the little boy that something would catch him some night if he didn't quit staying out that way. He asked him if he was afraid. The boy laughed and said he'd never seed a 'fraid.' That gave the old man the idea of how he would scare the boy. So he told him there was 'fraids,' and he bet him that he'd keep on laying out till one would get him some night.

"So the next evening, they sent the little boy after the cows. Had to go a long ways, maybe a mile. After he'd been gone a long time, and it was getting dark, the man told his wife he was going to cure the boy of staying out that way, and he pulled a bed sheet off the bed and took off up the road.

"Well, they had a pet monkey, and it had been taught to do everything it seed anybody else do. So it pulled a white tablecloth off of the table and took right after the man. He never looked back and didn't see the monkey following him. So he went on till he come to a briar patch, and he wrapped the sheet around him and hid in the briar patch. The monkey then wrapped the tablecloth around it, and slipped in right behind the man. He never noticed the monkey.

"It wasn't long till he heard the cowbells coming, and the boy whistling along behind them. He let the cows get by and just as the boy was right ference where he set, he raised up and stepped out. 'Hoomph!' said the boy, 'a fraid!' About this time, the monkey stepped out, too. The boy laughed. 'Another fraid,' he said. 'Two fraids. A big fraid and a little fraid.'

"The old man looked around and seed the monkey standing there wrapped in the tablecloth, and thought it was a real ghost. He took right down the road just as hard as he could go, and the monkey took right after him, right at his heels. The man looked back and seed it was following, and he ran faster than ever. The boy clapped his hands and hollered, 'Run, big fraid, or little fraid will catch you.'

"And the man never tried to scare the boy with hants again!"

## The Highwayman Who Saw the Light

You likely won't find the name of Joseph Thompson Hare in any of Virginia's history books. In fact, he wasn't even a native of the commonwealth. He was born in Chester County, Pennsylvania, in 1780. In a way it's somewhat of a shame that there are so few references to Hare, because he was one of the most colorful, charismatic, and swashbuckling rogues of the early part of the nineteenth century. His exploits, covering travels from New Orleans to Canada, are truly legendary.

He was, above all else, a highwayman—a robber who laid in wait for unsuspecting travelers in the frontier wilderness. He was also much more. Hare was as well-known for his superior courage and generosity as he was for his daring and bold criminal escapades. Some likened him to an American Robin Hood. During his relatively short lifetime he successfully fought off attacks by Indians, a host of most unsavory characters, scores of pursuing lawmen, and a giant panther.

He had a lifelong struggle, which he lost in the end, of trying to convert his considerable talents to lawful practices. He is included in this collection of ghosts because it was in Virginia that he encountered a singular powerful apparition that, for a time at least, changed the direction of his ways.

Joseph Hare came from a respected, well-to-do family. The oldest of six children, he apparently was wayward and self-willed from a very early age; when his mother died when he was only sixteen, he plunged more deeply into wild and vicious courses.

He began his twisted career by stealing $500 from a neighboring farmer, a caper so easy and exhilarating to him that he plummeted openly into excesses of a most disreputable nature. Soon after, he left home for good and set out for New Orleans. There he was initiated into the mysteries and low trickeries of gaming, and became familiar with all the practices and arts of professional thieves. After a while he tired of this, possibly influenced by the tightening security in the streets of New Orleans, and he struck out on the road.

It was during this early period that Hare began gaining a reputation for having compassion for his victims, a highly unusual trait for a man in his profession. When, for example, he robbed a man of $250, the victim protested that it was all the money he had in the world. Hare gave him back $40 and told him to "thank his lucky stars that he had not fallen into the hands of men who were entirely devoid of principle."

His mode of operation was simple. He usually worked with two or three confederates. They would lay in hiding at some remote but well-traveled spot. Then, when an unsuspecting party would come along, he would bound out in the center of the road and demand of them to "deliver or die." "I want your money," he would declare, "and if you show the least disposition to resist, we will blow you to hell in the twinkling of an eye." The threat was enough. Rarely did he have to resort to violence. Over the next few years, Hare and his merry band roamed the southern countryside waylaying whoever was unfortunate enough to cross their path. He escaped death a number of times, once after fighting off the attack of a large panther with his bare hands, and once by dodging a bullet fired by an assailant at point-blank range. He spent much of his time keeping one step ahead of persistent posses and pursuers, often holing up in desolate caves.

In 1807, it appeared that Hare had wearied of this type of life. With a stake of $4,000, he said, "I thought that perhaps no better time would offer for me to carry out my old intentions to reform." He then received a letter from a friend in Richmond, inviting him to come and take part in a legitimate business. It was at this juncture, as Hare traveled to Virginia, that he entered upon an extraordinary adventure, which included a shocking encounter with a vivid apparition. The following is the account in his own words.

"At Abingdon [Virginia], I fell in with a drover from Franklin County, who was on his way home from Kentucky, where he had been on a trading excursion, and a pretty profitable one, too, as I thought from the display which he made of his money. The devilish infatuation of my previous course of life seized possession of me, and in spite of all my previous resolutions, and of the important prospects which I had in Richmond, I determined to rob him. I followed the drover to within 15 miles of the Franklin County courthouse, and, dashing up to his side, half mad with my own irresolution, I fiercely demanded of him his money or his life.

"He hesitated for a moment, and then paid me over, with trembling hands, the sum of $450. I seized the money with eager haste, and turning my horse, struck in my spurs and galloped away as if flying from the most sharp and inveterate pursuit. I cannot account for the unusual feelings which seized possession of me, unless it was a warning from some mysterious and supernatural power, or a forerunner of what was about to happen. I felt like a man under the influence of some hideous nightmare, and every time I urged my beast to speed, it seemed to me as if a crowd of fiends was whistling in my course, and on the point of laying their avenging grasp upon my shoulder, I rode and rode, without one moment's disposition to hold up, and when the powers of my tired animal began to flag, I kept moving forward in my saddle, like a steersman in a boat, in the hope that this would aid my motion.

"Suddenly, I merged into an open rise, and there, in the moon's silvery light, stood, right across the road a pure white horse immovable as marble, and so white that it almost seemed to be radiating light. I was a little startled by the first glance at the apparition, but expecting it to give way, I pressed towards it. But it did not stir, but stood with its small graceful head stretched out, its tail slightly raised, as if in a listening attitude, and its ears cocked sharply forward and strained toward the moon, on which its gaze seemed to be unwaveringly fixed. When within almost six feet of it, my horse suddenly recoiled upon its haunches, and, opening his nostrils with affright, gave a short cry of terror, and attempted to turn around.

"I trembled in my saddle as if struck with a sudden ague, but not daring to return into the gloom behind, I closed my eyes, bent my head, and driving my sharp heels deep into my horse's side, pressed onward at the fearful object. My steed took but one plunge, and then landed on its fore-feet, firmly resolved not to budge another inch. I opened my eyes and the apparition had disappeared. But an instant had elapsed and no trace of it was left. My most superstitious terrors were then confirmed, and I feared to go forward over the charmed space where the strange figure had stood. I recollected a roadside inn which I had passed a mile behind, and touching my rein, my horse turned swiftly around and obeyed the summons with a fleeter heel than he had shown previously.

"I have been told that I was laboring under a state of mental hallucination that night; an illusion super-induced by a peculiar state of nervous agitation, and that these things were mere chimeras of a feverish brain—but I know better!

"The vision was the cause of my arrest, for during the night, a party of 15 men, consisting of the drover's friends, surrounded the house and bore me off to Franklin County prison." Hare's biographer wrote: "The specter was present to his sense, and having terrified him from a sure escape and delivered him up into the hands of his pursuers, may be recognized as the supernatural decider of his fate." Hare later said, "I think the white horse came to warn me of my sins and to make me fear and repent." He was found guilty of highway robbery and sentenced to eight years in the state penitentiary.

For the rest of his life, Hare was in and out of jails, and eventually was caught holding up a stagecoach carrying U.S. mail. For this he was hanged on the morning of September 10, 1818. It is likely he never forgot the moment when the spirit white horse confronted him in the backwoods of Virginia, delivering a terse paranormal warning for him to quit his wicked ways; a warning he wished ever after that he had heeded.

# The Corpse That Demanded to be Reburied

The following narrative is a time-honored legend that has been passed down through generations in Virginia for more than 150 years. There are several variations. This one was said to have occurred in Lee County, in the tip of the southwestern "toe" of the Old Dominion. It was recorded by Works Progress Administration writer Richard Chase in an interview with an unnamed mountaineer in the late 1930s. Chase called it "The Ha'nted House Tale." It is paraphrased here.

One night, in a driving, freezing rainstorm near Blackwater, a preacher stopped at a farmhouse and asked if he could spend the night there, a common custom in those days, especially in the mountainous regions of rural Virginia. The farmer said he didn't have any room in his house, but there was an old empty house in a field against a mountain, and the preacher could stay there—if he wasn't afraid of ghosts! The house was suspected of being haunted. After supper, the farmer took the preacher over to the isolated house and helped him gather some wood to make a fire for the night.

The preacher, who later related his experience to the grandfather of the man Chase interviewed, built up a good fire, sat down in an old chair, and read his Bible for a couple hours before falling off to sleep. He woke up some time later as the fire was about to go out. He struck a match to see what time it was. Almost midnight. Suddenly, he heard a terrifying noise. He said it sounded "like a wheelbarrow load of rocks" falling against the roof of the house. He went out to see what caused it, but there wasn't a sound of anybody or anything except the rain falling. So he went back in the house and put some wood on the fire. He then heard what he said sounded something like "a rooster starting to crow right at the door, but it cut off quickly like somebody hit it with a rock and knocked the crow out of it."

A little unnerved, the preacher nevertheless sat back down and started reading his Bible again. All at once, he heard somebody moan. He couldn't tell where this came from. He put his book down and stoked up the fire. Then he heard "the awfullest moanin' and groanin' all through the house. Sounded like a woman going through the rooms sobbing like she was lost. Then it sounded like it was coming from the cellar, just like somebody strugglin' and dyin'."

The woman, or whatever it was, next screamed "somethin' awful three or four times and stopped all at once." The sound that then followed was even more frightening. The preacher heard footsteps coming up toward a door at the back of the house. Shaken to the core by this time, he grabbed a stick and stood with his back to the fire. Ever so slowly, the door opened, and the apparition of what appeared to be a woman formed. He could only make out a "sort of dim shape." The preacher gripped his stick tightly. The figure seemed to be sobbing; then it disappeared and the door closed.

He tried to resume his reading, but the groaning and sobbing continued. Then the door opened again and the vision reappeared. "In the name of the Father, the Son, and the Holy Ghost," the preacher exclaimed, "what do you want?" The spirit "sobbed sort of quick, like it was catching its breath, and come on up to him like it was half floating and half falling, and grabbed him by his coat lapels!"

This close, he could see it was the apparition of a young woman, probably in her early twenties. She had on a faded dress, and "her hair was hanging all tangled up around her head. She smelled earthy, she didn't have any eyes, just black holes where her eye sockets was, and she didn't have any nose to her face!" At this point, the preacher was having great difficulty breathing, and his fear was so paralyzing, he couldn't even raise his stick an inch.

"I want to be properly buried," the vision spoke. "You'll find my bones under the hearth rock there. My sweetheart killed me for my money, and if you do what I tell you, you can come back here tomorrow night and I'll tell you where it's hid." The preacher, frozen, listened intently as the voice continued. "You take all my bones but the end of my left hand, little finger, and give me a churchyard burial. Then you invite all the folks in this neighborhood to a supper, and put my finger bone on a plate and pass it around, and it'll stick to the hand of the one who murdered me."

With this, the apparition sobbed, sank down on the hearth, and evaporated before the preacher's eyes. Sighing heavily, the preacher finally managed to move. He couldn't sleep and he couldn't read. He just sat there trying to make some rational sense out of what had just happened. There were no more strange noises or visions the rest of the night. The next morning he got up, went to the main house, and told the farmer about his experience with the haunt. Together, they uncovered the bones, reburied them in a cemetery, and the preacher gave a good funeral service.

That night, a big supper was held with several men attending. A plate with the finger bone was passed around, and when it got to a certain man, it stuck in his hand. "He started hollering and trying to get it off, but it stuck just like it had growed on him. He was then a pretty old man, and nobody had ever suspected him of the killing." It was speculated that the murder must have occurred forty or fifty years ago. The man was so horrified by the bone sticking to his finger that he confessed to the crime and was subsequently hanged.

The preacher went back to the deserted house the next evening and the apparition reappeared and told him where to find the money. After that, it was said that the house wasn't haunted anymore. "But the ha'nts' handprints were seared on the preacher's coat lapels where she took hold of him, and it looked just like they were burnt in."

# The "Red Fox" of the Cumberlands

It is said that in the nineteenth century, when railroads first began winding their way through the narrow valleys, that the mountain folk of Wise County, Virginia, were governed by a "code of the hills." They were rugged individualists who settled their difficulties without recourse to the law, made and sold their moonshine liquor, and viewed all "furriners" with suspicion. Perhaps that is why it took a native son, John Fox of nearby Big Stone Gap, to capture the color-ful lifestyles of these hardy backwoods people who battled bears, Indians, and the harsh elements to carve out a living from this "toe" of land in the extreme southwestern part of the state. Fox immortal-ized some of these legendary characters in his classic book *On the Trail of the Lonesome Pine*.

And what wonderful characters! One, for example, was "Devil" John Wright, who was married three times and fathered thirty-seven children. Another was a wizened old moonshiner named Ira Mullins. But perhaps the most notorious of all was the fabled "Red Fox" of the Cumberland Mountains—Dr. Marshall B. Taylor. He was a medical doctor, a preacher, and a sanctioned law officer all rolled into one. He also was charismatic, enigmatic, eccentric to the borderline of madness, and widely feared. He was once described as having a dual character, showing in his face kindness and benevolence on one side, a wolfish snarl on the other, and both plain to any eye that looked.

How much time has embellished the mystique that surrounds Taylor is not certain. It is believed that he was born in Scott County and that his parents and brother and sisters were all honorable and respectful. He too reared a proper family. As a young man, Taylor went to Lee County to study medicine, and later moved to Wise to practice. It was during this period of time that his extraordinary feats, mostly taking place in the surrounding mountains, began to take root.

He was, for instance, noted for having a "ghostly presence" in the woods. One tale involved a man named Riley Mullins. He was walking down an old trail one day when all was quiet and he felt no one was within a mile or two. Suddenly, out of nowhere, Doc Taylor appeared, and began walking beside Riley, never saying a word. Riley, who himself had a local reputation as being "mean as the Devil," got so spooked when Taylor just as mysteriously disappeared that he could barely speak. Then, down the road a ways, he found a little piece of candy poke, and written on the wrapper were the words, "Watch out Uncle Riley or the Devil will get you when you mess with the Fox." Scared stiff, Riley ran as fast as he could till he got to a house at the foot of the mountain. He was so sure he had left Taylor far behind, that when the doctor stepped out in front of him, Riley, as his nephew later described it, "like to a-tore the whole woods down getting away from there." Doc Taylor then took his ever-present Winchester rifle and cut down the bushes all around him as he ran.

Taylor showed as much zeal in his part-time job as a law officer as he did as a doctor, and he gained many enemies among the mountain folks by bringing in a number of moonshiners. There were so many threats on his life that he began taking evasive measures in the woods, which eventually earned him the nickname, "Red Fox." In a 1941 interview, Jeff Mullins told a Works Progress Administration writer about some of these exploits: "They was always trying to get a pot shot at him [Taylor], but they'd follow him for days some times and then find out he'd been in the other end of the county all the time. He fooled them by his tracks being made backwards." One of his pursuers claimed he was so sly and smart that he "was as slick as a red fox." Mullins said Taylor would wear his moccasins backwards, so that those tracking him would always be going in the opposite direction. Mullins added that after awhile outlaws quit trying to ambush Taylor, "as it was too dangerous to try. A fellow wasn't apt to get back from such a trip!"

By 1892, Taylor, now in his sixties, had been involved in a running feud with an illegal whiskeymaker named Ira Mullins for years. Ira had allegedly offered $300 to anyone who would kill the doctor. It was because of this, it is believed, that on the morning of May 14, 1892, Taylor and two brothers, Calvin and Henon Fleming, hid behind covering rocks at a point in the mountain pass near Pound Gap, since called the "Killing Rock." They had learned that Ira Mullins and his family were headed that way. Sometime between 9 and 10 A.M., Taylor and the Flemings opened fire on the unsuspecting Mullins, and within minutes had killed Ira, his wife, and three others, plus two horses. Said one historian, "the trail was soon running red with mixed human and animal blood."

Two members of the party, a woman and Ira's fourteen-year-old son, John, somehow escaped the blazing fusillade, though John's suspenders were shot in two. Although they wore masks, Doc Taylor and the Fleming brothers were identified by the survivors, and went into hiding. Taylor had himself crated in a box and shipped on a freight train to Bluefield, West Virginia. But word of his innovative escape attempt had leaked out and he was apprehended and brought to trial in Wise County. Even his trial was bizarre. Taylor said he had a witness who would speak for him, and when the judge asked who it was, the defendant answered, "Jesus Christ. Will you hear him?" Taylor then pulled a small Bible from his coat pocket and began reading passages dealing with false witnesses and oppression. Nevertheless, he was found guilty and sentenced to hang.

In his 1938 book *A Narrative History of Wise County*, Charles A. Johnson vividly described the scene: "The little courthouse town of Gladeville [Wise] was packed full of people in spite of the drizzling rain that fell all the afternoon. The farmer, the businessman, the crossroads merchant, the water-wheel miller, the 'seng digger,' the fur gatherer, the herb doctor, the spiritualist, the witch and the witch doctor, the backtown sightseer, the old and the young men, women and children, the halt and the blind, the fool and the smart alec, had all come to see and hear, and if not to see and hear, to be told by others of the scene and the agonies of another dying man, at the end of a hangman's rope. House-tops were groaning with the weight of the curious, tree tops were swaying with the bodies of the curious, fence tops were lined in black with the curious, and hill slopes were crowded with the excited curious—all striving to get one glimpse of the condemned man over the open top of the enclosed scaffold. Such is human nature."

At his specific request, Taylor was attired, from neck to foot, in snow-white linen, topped with a brown derby hat. After a reading from the Bible, his hands were tied with a white handkerchief. A white cape, instead of a black one, was pulled over his face. As the props were being removed under the trapdoor, jostling Taylor, he fell in a heap on the platform, and had to be helped up. Johnson wrote, "The trapdoor swung from under him and the body of Doc Taylor, the Red Fox, hung between heaven and earth, and his spirit went to another world than ours."

But did it? Even in apparent death, the strange nature of this extraordinary man asserted itself. He had asked that his body be kept unburied for three days. At the end of that time, he had told all who would listen to him that he would "arise from the dead and go about preaching the gospel." After the three days, he was buried in the town cemetery on a hill overlooking his home in an unmarked grave.

While there are no eyewitness accounts of the Red Fox's resurrection, there are some old-timers who contend Doc Taylor's spirit does appear on occasion in the darkened woods of the Cumberland Mountains he so loved to roam in life. Only these times, they say, he leaves no tracks at all!

## The Light Among the Tombstones

One might believe that Gen. Jubal Early has just cause to return to his native state in spirit form and continue to lead phantom charges against the hated Yankees. He did, after all, spend the last thirty years of his life seeking justification for Southern secession and an explanation for the ultimate defeat of the Confederate forces in the Civil War. However, it is not the general's ghostly figure that has been sighted roaming across an isolated, long-deserted graveyard in the Burnt Chimney region of Franklin County. It is, rather, the specter of his brother, William Early, who continues a ghostly search for his life's savings, which disappeared from his grave in a bizarre manner nearly a century and a half ago.

William Early's nocturnal ventures manifest themselves as a strong light in the mountain foothills, a light that has been seen but never explained by hundreds of area witnesses over several generations. "Many people have seen it," says local historian Gertrude Mann, "but nobody knows what it is." It is said to be the gentle golden light of Early's lantern as his spirit wanders restlessly from tombstone to tombstone, eternally looking for his lost money.

Early is believed to have died in the mid-1860s, and was buried with his money. Just why his wife and children allowed this has never been explained. Maybe he thought you really could take it with you. In time, his widow fell in love with the farm overseer and they decided to get married. This appalled her children, who felt their mother was lowering herself socially. They planned to do something about it. They hoped to stop the wedding with the help of an "uninvited guest." It was deemed that drastic measures were necessary, and their actions were shocking to say the least.

William Early's sons went to their father's gravesite, dug up his coffin, and carried it back to the farmhouse. There, they stood the glass-covered coffin straight up at the base of the stairs to greet their mother when she descended the steps in her wedding gown. Alas, the macabre plot did not work. Mrs. Early defiantly strode past the decomposing corpse and walked into the parlor, where she was married. Chagrined, the sons reburied the remains of their father in another grave, the exact location of which is unknown today.

Somehow and somewhere in the process, William's money was either lost or stolen. Ever since then, Early's light has been sighted dancing across the remote graves in the Burnt Chimney region of

Franklin County. Many have seen the light move about in the eerie darkness. Many have chased it, seeking a sane and sensible explanation for its appearances, but no one has succeeded.

Some residents dismiss the light as being caused by swarms of fireflies, but others say there are no such fireflies in the dead of winter. Some have said it is the light of hunters' lanterns, but no woodsmen have ever stepped forward to justify this possibility. It is, contend old-timers, the ghostly light of William Early, who cannot rest in peace until he finds his money.

# A Bevy of Bristol "Hants"

The following section on Bristol, Virginia, area ghosts is recounted here with the gracious permission of V. N. (Bud) Phillips, who has lived in that city for the past half-century. He spent much of that time interviewing old-timers and researching archives, family histories, and diaries while gathering folklore. In his 2002 book *Partners in Paradise*, Bud included a hundred-page section on Bristol haunts.

## The Dead Husband Who Broke Up a Wedding

On a bright spring morning in 1867, June Ann Strother, a young Bristol widow, starched and dressed in her best dress, baked a cake and put fresh flowers in her house on Fourth Street. This was to be her wedding day. Actually, it was to be her second wedding. Her first husband had been killed in the Civil War. Promptly at noon, she was to take her vows with Jason Bland, a young widower from the nearby town of Blountville. The Rev. Asa Routh was to preside. As the hour approached, friends had gathered, and the bride and groom stood near the fireplace. The reverend stood before them. "Are you ready?" he asked. Then he suddenly gasped aloud and fainted! Women screamed. Two or three swooned, men yelled, and a number in the audience took off running for the nearest exit. June Ann, at first puzzled at what was happening, looked to her right, shrieked, and fainted dead away. One man shouted, "Great gawd a'mighty, it's shore him!"

The cause of all the pandemonium? Just as the reverend was about to begin the service, the ghost of June Ann's former husband had materialized next to her. And it wasn't just a wispy, whitish wraith. He appeared in full body, just as he had died. There was a visible bullet hole in his throat and blood seemed to be flowing down his gray Confederate uniform. It was, to say the least, a most shocking sight to behold.

Poor Jason Bland, the expectant bridegroom, didn't see the startling vision at first, and stammered, "What happened?" An ethereal voice, heard by several witnesses, responded, "It's what didn't happen that pleases me." The figure then vanished as suddenly as it had appeared. Jason raced out of the house in huge leaps, jumped on his horse, and dashed off to Blountville. He never called on June Ann again.

## The Ghosts of Roosters Past

Phillips says that in Bristol's earliest days the high knob on which the oldest portion of East Hill Cemetery is located was known as "Rooster's Hill." It was here that some pioneering citizens attended cruel cockfights, which often left the grounds littered with dead and bloodied roosters. The fights were promoted by an ex-convict named Webb Sykes. When he died in 1874, he was buried in the East Hill Cemetery, at a site where the cockfights, long since outlawed, had once been held. One of those in attendance at Sykes's funeral was a colorful town character named Old Daddy Thomas, then seventeen years old. Phillips quoted Thomas on what happened at the burial.

"Old Zack Burson had just preached his piece and they was a ropin' old Webb's coffin down [lowering the casket using ropes], when all of a sudden, roosters begin crowing right loud like all around us. Ye couldn't see nary a one. Land, they seemed to be everywhere, under us, over us, and all out in the bushes around us. And, lawsy, they wuz a gettin' louder and more uv 'em. We all knowed it wuz hants, and thought them old slaughtered roosters wuz rejoicin' that old Webb was a getting' his due.

"And blessed Becky, them ropin' men dropped that coffin. They said that they wuz crowin' all down in that grave jist like it was full of roosters. And I don't rightly know what happened after that, fer I wuzn't there no more! I tore outta that graveyard and run down the hill towards town, and they wuz plenty of folks a runnin' with me. Land, ye could hear them roosters a crowin' up there on the hill plumb down past the depot. They wuz extra loud, fer they weren' real. They wuz hant roosters. Folks up that way said that some of them wuz still crowin' at dark. You know, sir, it was one of the quarest kinds of hants that ever wuz in this town."

## The Documented Ghost

Bud Phillips says that the appearance of a ghost is recorded in official chancery court records in Washington County. In the early 1880s, a man, his wife, and their four children lived in a little cottage on Railroad Street in Bristol. In the spring of 1882, an epidemic of diphtheria hit the town. The couple's youngest child, Rachel, was the first to die from the dreaded disease. Her father contracted typhoid fever about a month later and lingered for several weeks before he too passed away.

Times were hard, and the young widow soon fell deep in debt. She was eventually sued by a local merchant, and the chancery court of Washington County ruled that the woman's home must be sold to satisfy her creditors. Col. David Bailey, an early Bristol lawyer, was appointed a commissioner to conduct the sale. The property was advertised in the local newspaper. The poor widow pleaded with several neighbors to buy the house and rent it back to her, but none offered to do it. One of the attendees of the sale, Tom Findley, told Phillips what happened on the day of the sale.

"I tell you, sir, I saw it. I was right there and I'll never forget it if I live to be a hundred years old. I couldn't believe my eyes, but I had to. That's been around sixty-five years ago, but there's never been a day but what I thought of that strange happening, and I've had several bad dreams about the thing. Just as Colonel Bailey opened for bids, that dead man suddenly appeared at his left side, and he was holding little Rachel in his arms! I knew them well. I was there when both of them died. I helped to lay them out. He [the deceased husband] said not a word but just looked that crowd right in the eye. The little baby smiled just like she used to do so much when she was living.

"I'll never forget what effect it had on that crowd. Nearly all the folks there knew well who they were. Instead of wildly scattering like a bunch of chickens that a hawk's landed among, as usually happens when a hant's around, those people just froze in awe. Now that broke up the sale. Colonel Bailey, not knowing at first that the hant was standing by him, begged for bids. Then he realized that no one was looking at him, but was looking at something near him. When he finally saw the ghosts of that man and child, he went dumb and just couldn't seem to say another word. Then the man and child just slowly faded away. I never saw the beat of it."

In a few days Colonel Bailey submitted a paper to Judge Kelly, explaining why his duties had not been completed. Along with that paper, he offered his resignation as commissioner. He stated that he supposed his Honor had heard of the strange matter, in that much notoriety had been given to it. He called it "a mystical happening," which he could hardly believe, but certainly could not deny. He further said that in light of such curious developments, he doubted that a successful sale could ever be made, "for everyone believes that if it is ever tried, the ghost will appear again."

There is no further mention of the case in the chancery court records of Washington County.

## The Ghost that Craved Onion Soup

About a hundred years ago, a young woman named Holly Tidwell worked in a notorious Bristol brothel. One day she quit on the spot, and married a much older man named Henry Kimes. Some townspeople thought she had reformed, but Holly had a sinister motive. She believed, mistakenly, that old man Kimes was rich. He wasn't. He lived in a little cottage on Virginia Street, and spent his days whittling and chatting with some cronies on a long bench in front of a store.

During his absences, Holly rummaged through his personal effects in a vain attempt to find money that wasn't there. She did, however, discover a life insurance policy for $500 in a small trunk Kimes kept under the head of his bed. She quickly hatched a diabolical plot. Her husband loved onion soup, so one evening she made up a heaping pot of it—laced with carbolic acid! She told him she was not feeling well and excused herself from the dinner table. Kimes ate a big helping. Not long afterwards, he staggered up from his featherbed and cried, "Help me, Holly. I'm so sick." He didn't live through the night.

It was thought that he had died from old age and heart failure, and he was buried in the East Hill Cemetery. The next night, Holly's Aunt Bess came to spend the night and console the lonely and disconsolate young widow. After dinner, they sat in the parlor. Then they heard a rustling sound come from the adjoining bedroom—and the apparition of Henry Kimes appeared in the shadowy doorway, holding his stomach, and wearing the suit in which he had been buried! To the two women's horror, the figure said, in a soft, wavering voice, "Help me, Holly. I'm so sick."

The terrified women ran out of the house and spent the night at Aunt Bess's place. The next evening, however, the ghost of Kimes appeared again, and repeated his mournful wail. Holly and Aunt Bess again fled. Over the next several nights, no matter where Holly went, the wraith-like vision followed her, even when she checked into the Virginia House Hotel, hoping that "he" would not show up in such a public place. But when he materialized at the hotel, Holly went into a "kicking, flailing, screaming fit." She had to be forcefully dragged from the room, and was then taken to the Western State Hospital at Staunton. On the way there, the guilt-ridden woman, persistently taunted by the ghost, confessed to having killed her husband.

But apparently even this was not enough to satisfy the elderly victim. When he made yet another appearance at the hospital, Holly again went into a prolonged, physically and emotionally wrenching fit that lasted until midnight and ended only when she died on the spot, frightened to death by the relentless spirit.

Perhaps it was just as well that she never found out that the insurance policy—the reason she had poisoned Kimes—had long ago lapsed for failure to pay the premiums!

## The Ghost that Saved a Train

On a cold snowy night in late February 1876, a passenger train was heading toward Bristol from Lynchburg. With snow blanketing the ground and a full moon overhead, it was almost as light as day. As the train approached Bristol, engineer Brooks Menifee looked ahead and clearly saw a man in a bright red shirt frantically waving his arms over his head in a danger signal. Menifee slammed on the brakes and the train came to a screeching halt. As it did, the phantom waver disappeared. Though Menifee could see a great distance ahead in the reflected light, there was no sign of the man.

A brakeman examined the tracks where the man had stood and found that someone had loosened the rails. Had the train not stopped at that exact moment, it would have derailed and careened over a high embankment that dropped sharply down to Beaver Creek. The result would have been disastrous. It was believed that a disgruntled railroad employee had tampered with the track.

Who was the man who had saved the train? Old-timers recalled that twenty years earlier a railroad employee had been murdered at the precise site where the figure had appeared on the tracks. It was remembered that the man had been wearing a red shirt!

## The Ghost that Cried for Christmas Cake

In November 1868, a destitute Civil War widow named Betsy Clanton and her two small children appeared at the door of Dr. R. M. Coleman's house in Bristol. She begged for food and shelter. The Colemans took the family in and gave the mother the job of housekeeper and cook. On December 23 that year, Mrs. Clanton baked a huge cake for a Christmas celebration. The pungent aroma caused her five-year-old daughter, Betts, to come into the kitchen, and, as her mother lifted the cake from the oven, she asked for a piece.

Mrs. Clanton said she would have to wait until Christmas Day. The little girl began to cry and made a most strange comment: "But," she said, "I won't be here at Christmas time." Her mother, busy, paid little attention. At supper that evening, when Betts didn't appear, Mrs. Clanton went to look and found her unconscious with a high fever. Despite the efforts of Dr. Coleman and other physicians, little Betts died at 3 A.M. on Christmas Eve.

Mrs. Clanton never recovered from the remembrance of what her daughter had told her: that she would not be here at Christmas time.

It drove her insane, and she had to be admitted to the Western State Hospital in Staunton.

A year later, on December 23, 1869, Mrs. Coleman was alone in her home when she became aware of the strong aroma of baking cake. She went into the kitchen to investigate. The stove was stone cold, but then she heard the distinct sound of a little girl crying. It so unnerved her that she ran out of the house. This haunting sensation was repeated through the years; the odor of baking cake was experienced, accompanied by the sobbing of a little girl no one ever saw. Long after Dr. Coleman died and his wife moved, the phenomena continued.

Later, the house was enlarged and became the Grigsby Maternity Hospital. On December 23, 1947, patients became excited when they smelled cake baking and asked a nurse when the dessert was going to be served. Puzzled, the nurse said the dessert that evening was peaches and ice cream.

As the legend spread, many curiosity seekers came to the site on that date each year, and they were never disappointed. The scene was repeated annually until the building was torn down in the 1960s.

## The Ghost Quilt

In 1882, a young Bristol couple died in an epidemic of typhoid fever, leaving three small boys, all less than six years old. They were taken in by the young wife's mother. They were beautiful children, each with light blond hair and bright blue eyes.

With winter coming on, the boys' grandmother purchased wool suits for them, but the following spring, disaster struck the ill-fated family again when a diphtheria epidemic swept through Bristol and took the lives of all three boys. Grief-stricken, the grandmother made a patchwork quilt out of the wool suits, but could not bear to use it herself. She gave it to her younger sister, who ran a boardinghouse downtown. Here, Bud Phillips picks up the story:

"The sister used the quilt for two or three nights, and then took it off her bed. She never explained why. She then put it on a bed in one of the rented rooms. That night she lost her first roomer. He told her he'd had the most vivid dream of three little blond-headed, blue-eyed boys. He then awoke to find the same youngsters in his room, slowly pulling the covers from his bed! In a moment they just vanished into thin air. He said 'he knowed they were hants,' and he just would not stay another night in a room where hants had been. He had no prior knowledge of the three deceased boys.

"The quilt was then moved to another room, where the same thing happened—the vivid dream followed by an ethereal appearance of the boys. Another roomer was lost. The quilt was moved to a third room where there was a repeat of the ghostly performance. Finally, it was given to a poor family that badly needed bedcovers. But the quilt only was used two nights, with that many visitations by the boys' spirits. Without telling what had happened, the family sold the quilt to a middle-aged spinster. She thought it was a unique bit of handiwork and was pleased with it, but her pleasure was not for long. At first, she put it in a blanket chest that was kept in a small room behind her bedroom.

"One night she retired early and was drifting into peaceful sleep, when she was suddenly jolted back to wakefulness by what sounded like children's voices coming from the back room. She quickly sprang up and, with lighted lamp in hand, went to the open doorway of that room. There, around the chest, trying to lift the lid, were three little blond-headed boys! After a moment, they faded away. It was a disturbing experience, and she hardly slept through the long night. There was no recurrence of the manifestations over the next several months, so she lost her nervousness about the matter. At the time, she did not connect the three boys with the quilt.

"When fall came, she put the woolen quilt on her bed. During the wee hours of the next morning she had a vivid dream in which she saw the same boys who had so strangely appeared around the blanket chest in her back room. Awaking in great fright, she was horrified to find the youngsters—pulling the quilt from her bed!

"She didn't wait for them to vanish. It was she who vanished from the room. She spent the rest of the night with the family that lived adjacent to her. The next morning, acting on the advice of a local psychic, Pocahontas Hale, she ventured back to her house, gingerly picked up the 'hanted' quilt, and carried it to the backside of her garden. There, she poured a gallon of kerosene over it and set it afire. For fear that the ghosts might appear again, she did not stay to watch it burn."

Perhaps the advice of the local psychic was well given; after the burning of the ghost quilt, the three little blond-headed, blue-eyed boys never materialized again.

# A Classic Collection of Coal Mine Ghosts

Many of Virginia's ghost legends are associated with coal mines. From the late 1800s to the mid-twentieth century, mining was one of the commonwealth's leading industries. Tens of thousands of miners dug the "black gold" from beneath the earth in a huge stretch of land where southeastern West Virginia, northeastern Kentucky, and southwestern Virginia converged. It was a hard and dangerous job and many paid the supreme price for their labors—their lives. In the days before stringent safety laws were enacted, hundreds of men were killed in horrific mine explosions and cave-ins. This, along with the fact that a great number of miners were highly superstitious to begin with, led to the general belief that tunnels where accidents occurred were haunted by the ghosts of those who never made it out. Here is a small selection of some of these time-honored traditions.

## The Ghost that Found Its Own Body

According to an account that has been published in newspapers, magazines and books over the past ninety years or so, in the early 1920s there was a terrible explosion in Section Five of a coal mine located near the Virginia-West Virginia border. Several men were killed and a few miraculously survived. All were accounted for except one, a man named Frank Cooper. At the time, the policy was that if a body was not found, the coal company had no obligation to compensate his wife, and in this instance, his six children. In fact, to avoid payment in this case, the company even suggested that Cooper had not been in the mine, but had instead abandoned his family. The miners knew otherwise, but it seemed there was nothing they could do.

Volunteers were sought to reenter the damaged area of the mine to shore up new beams and clean the section so new track could be laid. Just one man stepped up to do the dangerous job. He was known only as Louie. He began his work, alone, deep in the bowels of the dark mine. He heard a strange sound and turned around. He saw the shadowy figure of what appeared to be a fellow miner. Louie was pleased that he had some help, even if this chap looked "different." He was extremely gaunt, his skin had a milky blue pallor, and his eyes were so far sunken into his skull that they were not even visible. Still, Louie thought, any aid was welcome.

As Louie was scraping away loose debris, the bony figure suddenly snatched the shovel from his hands, and commanded, "No, not there. Over here!" Puzzled, Louie nevertheless obeyed, and began digging at the spot designated. There, under more than a foot of slag, he found a man's body. He whirled around to tell of his discovery, but the mysterious figure had vanished!

The next night, Louie, who swore to the truth of the encounter to his dying day, said he was awakened late at night by a knock at his door. He opened it, and there stood the emaciated figure of the man who had helped him in the mine. The man spoke in a faint voice, "Thank you. Now I can rest and my family will be cared for." The figure then faded away before Louie's eyes.

The next day it was learned, from the tags of the dead man found in the mine, that the body was none other than that of Frank Cooper.

### A Tragedy Avenged

Another intriguing case, which also occurred in the 1920s in the same general area, has been handed down generation to generation ever since. It involved a love triangle gone sour, a murder that went unsolved for years, and a final vengeance by the ghost of the slain man.

Two young coal miners, Fox Carter and Aaron Conoway, were both in love with a young lady named Terry Hite. Carter was said to be a strapping, handsome young man, while Conoway was just the opposite. His only distinction was that he owned a pair of boots, pointed, fancy-stitched, and laced in blue. Yet for some unaccountable reason, the maiden seemed to favor Conoway, a fact that deeply disturbed Carter.

There was an accidental explosion in the mine one day, in an area being worked by Carter, Conoway, and a man named Leo Pasinsky and his thirteen-year-old son. By chance, the boy had gone for a drink of water, only to see the mine ceiling come crashing down. He also saw Carter shove Conoway into the collapsing shaft, a fact so horrifying to him that he didn't tell about it until years later. The cave-in killed Conoway and the boy's father. Both bodies were recovered, but one of Conoway's legs had been severed and wasn't found.

Curiously, long after the funeral, Carter could be observed taking flowers to his former rival's grave. In time, Carter and Terry Hite were married. It wasn't long after, however, that she and others, including miners, noticed that Carter had become a changed man and that he acted very strangely. For one thing, he steadfastly refused to go near the site where the accident had occurred, even though it had long ago been repaired. He appeared to be petrified whenever he was near the area. Once, when the mantrip doors were being opened to the accident scene, he was reported to have inexplicably screamed, "Shut the doors. Don't let it in!"

Carter acted peculiarly at home as well. He was forever glancing suspiciously about the house as if looking for something or someone. He had trouble sleeping. He began going to bed with his boots on. His troubled wife tried everything to comfort him, but he seemed inconsolable. One day a blackbird flew into the couple's cabin. This struck stark fear into Terry's heart, for superstition stated that such an incident was the precursor of an impending death.

That very evening, men brought Fox Carter's body home. They told Terry that when they went to work that morning and entered the section where the accident had occurred, Carter had run away, screaming, "It's coming, it's com . . .," and had tripped and fallen across the tracks in front of an oncoming buggy. He had been killed instantly.

In the wet slag, just behind where his crushed body lay, the miners found the imprint of a single pointed boot.

### Another Vengeful Miner's Ghost

There is yet another legend about a coal miner, near Bluefield, who came back from the dead a century ago, this time to take revenge on his unfaithful wife. The miner left work early one day, ill, and went home to find his wife with another man. Enraged, he gave the man a good thrashing, then confronted his wife. She laughed at him and said she wanted a divorce. Shaken and upset, he returned to the mine and went back to work.

But his mind was not on the job, and he carelessly fell in front of a moving, loaded coal car. It killed him. At his funeral, his miner friends told his widow that he had vowed if something happened to him, he would return to gain vengeance. Again, she laughed and said she and her lover were going to get married and move far away. But her boyfriend took the threat more seriously and left town, abandoning her. Lonely and heartbroken, she was thereafter rarely seen out of her house.

Exactly one year after her husband had died, neighbors heard a terrible scream from the widow's house just after midnight. Some men went to the house and knocked sharply on the door, but there was no response. They broke the door down, but found the bedroom door also locked. When there still was no answer, they smashed through the door and entered the bedroom.

There, they found the woman lying dead across the bed. Her face had been scratched beyond recognition, and there were signs that a terrific struggle had taken place. The window was locked from the inside, as the doors had been, and there was no evidence anyone, at least anyone mortal, had ever entered the house.

## The Headless Miner

The following account is attributed to a Mrs. Kerns, who was a grade school teacher in a mining town near the Virginia-West Virginia border in the 1930s. She said there was a bad accident in the mine one day and her neighbor's husband had been killed; his head had been blown off by the powerful gas blast. Mrs. Kerns invited the neighbor woman to stay with her for a few days. Everything went as well as it could until the night after the funeral. The two women were sitting by the fire when they heard a knock at the door.

When Mrs. Kerns opened the door, the woman's dead husband walked in—with his head in his arms! The women screamed in horror. Without saying a word, he walked through the house and out the back door. When he got to the porch, he dropped something, and the women heard a metallic clink. After he had disappeared into the night, Mrs. Kerns locked the doors and windows.

When Mr. Kerns came home from work the next morning, he found a gold wedding band on the back porch. The neighbor-widow identified it as the ring of her deceased husband—which had been buried with him!

## The Ghost Dog that Saved Its Master's Life

In the 1920s, when the coal mining industry was booming, one of the satellite characters of the era was the itinerant peddler: the gypsy-like salesman who traveled the treacherous mountainous roads between mines to sell everything from household cleaning items to snake oil ointments guaranteed to cure all ills. In this instance, still recounted in the part of rural southwestern Virginia where it happened, a peddler was driving to a company town one night when he rounded a curve and suddenly slammed on his brakes. A large black dog, with red eyes glaring in the reflection of his headlights, materialized directly in front of him. There was something eerily strange about the dog. It refused to move from the middle of the road. Frustrated, the peddler got out of his vehicle. The dog then proceeded to walk to a grassy spot by a small stream and lay down.

The peddler decided this would be a good place to spend the night, so he set up camp at the site and kept his eye on the dog. Later, the dog got up and seemed to beckon the man to follow it. He did. The dog led him to a site by the hillside, turned and looked at the peddler, and then vanished. The next day, the man plied his trade in a nearby town and that evening retraced his route. When he got to the place where he had camped the night before, the same black dog again appeared out of nowhere. As before, the peddler followed the animal before it jumped into the bushes and disappeared once more.

The next morning, as the salesman drove into a neighboring town, he immediately sensed something was wrong. In front of the long line of coal company row houses, he saw men dressed in their Sunday-best clothes, talking in small groups. Women and children were clustered on front porches. This wasn't Sunday. The men should have been at work in the mines. Curious, the peddler stopped and walked up to a woman on a porch. She told him there had been a tunnel collapse in the mine and several men had been killed. One miner was still unaccounted for and presumed dead.

One of the women who had gathered showed him a picture. It was of the missing miner, her husband. The peddler recoiled in shock. Next to the miner in the photo was a large black dog—the same dog he had seen the past two nights in the middle of the road. He told some men and women about his sightings. The woman told him that her husband always took the dog into the mine with him, and if he had seen the dog, maybe her man was still alive. The peddler told them exactly where the dog had appeared, and then evaporated. The men became excited. It was where the tunnel collapse had occurred. Could it be that the lost miner was still there, and his dog was trying to lead rescuers to the site?

Dozens of miners followed the peddler to the spot. They stripped away brush at the back entrance to the old mine and began digging. They worked in shifts into the night, and finally broke through. Miraculously, they found the missing miner still alive.

They told him his dog had led them to where he was. He said that was impossible. His dog had been killed when the tunnel caved in.

### The Psychic Rat that Saved a Miner

There have been, in the recorded annals of parapsychology, legions of stories about psychically sensitive animals, principally dogs, cats, and horses. Some involve incredible exploits: cases where pets have traveled hundreds of miles across country to rejoin lost families, where animals have saved human lives by warning of impending dangers, and where ghosts unseen by mortal beings have been sensed by furry and feathered creatures.

But a psychic rat? Apparently there was such a case, reported by a University of Toronto researcher named Ian Currie. He told of an extraordinary event that happened in a coal mine in southwestern Virginia early in the twentieth century. It concerned an elderly man who owned a small mine that he worked alone, gathering just enough coal to heat his own house.

According to Currie, the man noticed that a rat would stay near him as he worked in a darkened tunnel. Over a period of several months, they became accustomed to each other in a strange sort of bonding. The miner would feed the rat scraps from his lunch box, and whenever he used explosives to loosen coal deposits, he would chase the rat away so it wouldn't be injured.

One day, as the miner was working, the rat seemed to be unduly agitated and kept scurrying up to the man and then running off. Curious, the miner put down his drill and followed the rat around a corner to see what was bothering the creature. Just as he moved away, the tunnel roof collapsed, in the exact spot where he had been working. The miner would have been hopelessly buried under an avalanche of debris and likely killed.

How did the rat know? Currie concluded that it must have employed an animal's intuition for danger, and somehow it was able to communicate with the human who had befriended it.

## The Curse of the Trapped Miners

The following extraordinary adventure was told a few years ago by a young man named Jon Henry McClinton, who lived in the tiny community of Pacerville in the rolling hills of southwestern Virginia. Through research, he had become intrigued with a legend that involved an old coal mine tragedy that occurred there in the 1920s. Three men had dug their way into a mine near Fiddler's Hill. It was only fifty yards deep and about five feet high. It was a sodden, smelly, dangerous shaft, but times were tough and the men had to keep their families warm in the winter somehow. One day, as they burrowed deeper into the mountainside, the tunnel roof collapsed.

An effort was made to rescue the men; had they survived another day or two, it might have been successful. Once the rescuers got to the men, they found an oath scrawled on a wall inside the death chamber, cursing the town for not reaching the men in time. Ever since, rumors have flourished that the three dead men became vengeful ghosts that would haul any visitors back into the murky shaft and smother them. Such rumors were reinforced years later when two teenage boys were found suffocated in the mine.

McClinton, intrigued with the legend, decided to see for himself, so one day a few years ago he and some friends camped out at the site. They planned to sleep outside the entrance to the old mine, but when a thunderstorm struck suddenly, they sought shelter in the tunnel. "We were cold and miserable," McClinton recalls. "Along about 2 A.M., we finally dozed off. I was the first to hear the muffled voices talking just outside the entrance. I froze in my covers, thinking some drunken hillbillies had come by to kick up some trouble. But I couldn't see anybody at the entrance. I could hear the conversation continuing, but I couldn't make out what was being said. It was like they were talking into their sleeves or something. As I neared the opening, the chattering stopped."

At this point, McClinton says all hell broke loose. "It sounded first like a freight train in the distance rumbling down the tracks. Then came the sound of boulders and rocks crashing down in the tunnel. The noise was deafening, and I was afraid my friends would be crushed. But when I looked up, there was no debris, or even any dust. Then, one of the girls screamed, 'somebody's in here with us!' My blood curdled as I looked toward the back of the shaft. There, in the pitch dark, stood three faintly glowing figures, each leering at us with incandescent eyes. All three were filmy and transparent, but I could still see their soiled, rumpled clothes, their hat lamps, and their picks. One of them raised his tool and seemed to float toward us.

"That's all it took. My friends let out a whoop and a holler and bolted straight out of the tunnel and down the gravel embankment. I sucked in a deep breath and dove for the entrance, too, but the ghost, or whatever it was, grabbed my suspenders and pulled me back. I screamed for mercy and flailed at the phantom, hoping to break away. My skin turned to ice and I was struggling for air, as a filmy substance plugged my mouth and nostrils. Then I blacked out."

McClinton concluded his scary saga by saying, "They found me outside the mine hours later. I was cold and blue, but alive. I've never returned to the mine and I never will, nor will my friends. To this day, we don't really know if we saw the three ghosts, or if it was just some illuminated mine gas. The only real unaccountable thing was the battered miner's hat that was found lying by me at the tunnel entrance. It dated to the 1920s!"

# The Screaming Chimney

More than half a century ago, southwest Virginia historian and folklore expert D. C. Pratt collected true ghost stories via interviews with old-timers in the Elk Garden section of Russell County, in the middle of the "foot" of the Old Dominion. One of the most compelling accounts, dating to the late nineteenth century, concerned a tenant house located on a large farm.

No one would stay in the house more than a few days. Families would move in, then abruptly leave, some after staying only one night. The prevalent rumor was that the place was haunted; a baby could be heard screaming, but no source for the dreadful sounds was ever found, although extensive searches were launched.

The crying came only at night, lasted for about twenty minutes or so, and was loudest in one of the front rooms near the chimney. A number of possible causes were suggested: it could be the wind, someone playing a trick, or an animal trapped behind the walls. But all of these possibilities were eventually ruled out. The farm owner, a skeptic, thought those who had left were ignorant and superstitious. He refused to believe the sounds were supernatural in nature.

One day, a new family moved into the house: a man, his wife, and four sons and two daughters. When the screams were heard by the boys the first evening, they were afraid to tell anyone. But on the second night, the parents were also aroused, and when they went to the boys' room they found them shaking with fright, the bed covers pulled up over their heads. Everyone got up and began looking around the walls. Then they went out with a lamp and searched under the house, thinking that maybe a cat was squalling. The father saw "a black thing" move around one of the wood pillars and crawled toward it, only to find himself face-to-face with a frightened skunk. The resulting stench caused his wife to order him to sleep downstairs on the couch.

After three more sleepless nights, the family gave serious thought to moving, but decided to stay one more evening and try to solve the absorbing mystery. When the screaming started, they were ready. They knocked a hole in one wall, but found only scraps of old, mouse-eaten newspapers. They followed the sounds to a flue in one of the bedrooms. The screams seemed to be echoing through the chimney.

They discovered that there was no hole for a stovepipe to be used. Strange, they thought. Then they found a spot where the hole had been sealed up. They removed some bricks and the father reached up and pulled out an old wooden box.

Inside the box were the skeletal remains of an infant! They took the box out behind the garden and buried it. The screams were never heard again.

## Arisen from the Frozen River

The following account is excerpted from Brita Elizabeth Johnson's 1923 book *Rural Life in Old Virginia*. The setting is a farm in south-central Virginia in 1886. Mrs. Johnson says one of the favorite pastimes of that era was to sit around the fireplace in the evening and tell true ghost stories. Here is one she remembered, told by a Mr. Krantz.

"When I was seven or eight years old, in the years before the Civil War, a man named Gerald Pearson was crossing the iced-over river a few miles from my home, and was never seen again. No one had seen him since he started to cross the river. Ice covered the river in the winter and was a great highway to market. Pearson was a friend of my father, and he grieved because the family was left poor. The neighbors provided them with what was needed, but it was whispered around that it was a case of desertion; that they had not lived well together. Such suspicious talk went from almost every mouth, and at last it reached the mourning wife. The poor woman became troubled and came near losing her reason, because she knew there was some truth to it. Gerald had not been the man of her choice.

"One morning about the last of February, my father slept late and when he awoke he said he dreamed that he had a long talk with Gerald Pearson. 'He says he lives; he stands at the bottom of the river only 150 yards from the boat landing. He says he hears the church bells ring and many other sounds, and it hurts when people drive over him on the ice. He says you will not believe me when I say I am not dead, but it is true. I had drunk brandy with my friends; they went with me to the landing and bid me farewell, and then went home. I felt giddy, lost my balance on the ice, and here I stand. Go tell my friends.'

"Father then gasped for breath and fell back on the pillow. He then went to tell some friends about his dream. Several men in the village seemed very interested, and they decided to form an investigating party. They measured and cut holes in the ice and used hooks on poles. At last, they used nets with weights and hooks, and the body came up and was as natural as though it had not lain a day in the water.

"It was taken to the house and many people went there to see it. The day before the funeral, the wife's relatives went to stay until the last rites were over; her brother and two sisters. When the chores were done, they locked the doors, set a lighted candle in the front room where the corpse lay, and went into the family room by the fire and sat talking about him. The brother reclined on the sofa, one sister lay down on the bed by the mourning wife, the other in a reclining chair.

"The logs in the fireplace were red with jets of yellow flame, when, hark! The door knob turns, hinges creak, and in steps—Gerald Pearson, just as he used to! He walked to the fire, held out his hands to the heat, and then turned his back to the fire, standing there looking at the visitors one at a time. He then stooped over the cradle, kissed the baby, and went to the trundle bed and kissed the children, and next reached his hand over the sister's face and patted his wife's cheek with a cold hand. He went back to the fire and poked the logs so they fell apart, and dropped the tongs as though they had burned him. He went to the door, opened it, and went out, shutting the door behind him.

"The family was overwhelmed with superstitious fear. The brother raised up, held his breath, and stared; the sisters went into hysteria, but the wife sat up and said, 'Thank God. He forgives all.' They never forgot it, for they all saw, heard, and felt that there was action even after human life ends. Truth is stranger than fiction."

### The Dead Soldier's Reunion

A strikingly similar paranormal event—that is, of a dead man's visual return that was witnessed by more than one person—occurred a generation later at a site near the North Carolina-Virginia border a few miles south of Galax. The year was 1918, the first world war was nearing its end, and American troops were preparing to come home from Europe. What should have been a joyful time for one couple living in a farmhouse here quickly turned to grief and mourning, however. They received a telegram announcing that their son, John, had been killed in France when his unit charged a German trench.

Oddly, his body was not recovered. John's mother suffered a breakdown, and his younger brother, Jacob, could not accept the fact that John would never come home. In time, the mother slowly recovered, but she never forgot her son's last words to her as he left for boot camp. "Don't worry, mother," he said. "No matter what, I'll always be with you."

A short time later, after the war had ended, Jacob's friend Everett came to the farmhouse to visit. At the evening meal, Jacob said a blessing, which included a prayer that his brother would somehow return home safely. He had never given up hope. It was raining heavily outside and as the men folk sat down to eat, the mother was in the kitchen stirring a pot of stew. She looked out the window, and by the light of a lightning flash, saw what appeared to be a horse and its rider coming toward the house.

She looked again and gasped. "Dearest God," she suddenly exclaimed. Her husband asked her what was the matter. With tears streaming down her eyes, she pointed. Jacob, Everett, and the father peered out the window. "It's Johnny," Jacob cried. "See, I told you he'd come home!" "Is it possible?" the father asked. As they all stared fixedly, the rider dismounted, opened the barn door, and led his horse inside. The father said he would go outside, put up the horse, and send John inside. As they all waited, they saw the father come out of the barn, alone, shaking his head. When young Jacob asked him where his brother was, the old man stammered, "I don't know." Pointing to the barn, he added, "He ain't in there, and there ain't no horse either." Unbelieving, Jacob ran to the barn, only to find it empty.

All four of them had seen the phantom figure approach. There was no doubt of that. Everett wondered if their minds hadn't played tricks on them. They had wanted to see something so badly, could they collectively have imagined it? As the temperature dropped, the rain turned to sleet and then snow. Everett decided to spend the night there, rather than trying to reach his home. When the mother and father went to bed, he and Jacob stayed up late, talking about the bizarre sighting. Finally, Everett slipped off to sleep in the main room before the fireplace, while Jacob went to his room.

Some time later, Everett awoke, and in the darkness, as he got up to put some fresh logs on the fire, he realized that he was not alone. There seemed to be a presence in the room. When the flames licked up, Everett froze. There, standing before the fire, was John! His face was clear in the firelight. He was wearing his army uniform. It was tattered and riddled with bullet holes.

And then, poof! John was gone. He had vanished before the startled man's eyes. Everett then searched the entire house but found no trace of the ethereal soldier. When Jacob woke up the next morning, he found Everett sitting in a rocking chair, staring at the wall, stone silent. Jacob asked him what was wrong, but got no reply. Everett gathered his things and left mysteriously without saying a word. It was many years later before he told anyone about what he had seen that dark, stormy night.

## The Snow-White Dove Spirit

This account is excerpted and recounted, with permission, from a December 1940 interview of an African American servant woman named Melviny Brown, by Works Progress Administration writer Bessie Scales in Danville. Brown talked about what she perceived to be supernatural events that occurred at an unnamed area plantation in the early years of the twentieth century.

Brown called it "the big house" and said she and the other servants and field hands adored their "master and mistress." She described her mistress as being pretty and real smart, and added that the lady loved her flower garden and would spend endless hours in it when the flowers were in bloom. The plantation's young master loved his bride "more'n anything," and everyone talked about how happy the two of them were.

And then suddenly, tragedy struck. One night, Brown said, when the brightest moon she'd ever seen was shining and all the servants were sitting outside in front of their cabins, a huge screech owl, perched in a big tree over the main house, began making terrible screeching sounds. This went on for some time, greatly unnerving the more elderly men and women, including Brown's mother, who flatly exclaimed that someone in the big house would soon die. It was, she said, a true harbinger of doom.

Within a week the owner's wife collapsed in the flower garden. Deathly ill, she made a startling revelation and a mysterious prophecy. She knew, she said, that she was about to die. Then she declared that she would come back to earth in the form of a snow-white dove, and she would sit on the snowball bush in her garden. Soon after, she died. The master nearly grieved himself to death, and later closed up the house and went off on a journey that would last many years. Brown and others continued their work in the gardens and fields and looked for the spectral return of the white dove, but it never came. Eventually, a letter came from the master. He said he was returning to Danville with a new mistress who he had recently married.

On the day they arrived, as they stepped onto the front porch, a strange low wail was heard coming from the garden. Melviny Brown gasped as she saw, on a limb of the snowball bush then in full bloom, a snow-white dove! From that day on, the bird returned to the bush every evening and moaned. The servants all were scared and convinced that this was their original mistress, back as she said she would be. The phenomenon so disturbed the new bride that she wouldn't even enter the haunted garden.

So, according to Brown, the master came out one evening with a shotgun and stalked down toward the garden. As he neared the snowball bush, the dove took flight heading directly to him. Just at twilight, he raised his sights and fired. A woman's screams pierced the air above the garden, and the dove flew away with a large red stain over its breast.

That very night, the master died in his bed of unknown causes. The new mistress soon left and the house was abandoned. In time, white doves flew in and out of its broken windows.

"It sho' was the old hanted house," Brown said.

## The Haunted Tavern on the Hill

The Tavern today is a rustic restaurant serving fine cuisine, including a variety of German dishes such as Wienerschnitzel and Kassler

Rippchen. On the back of the house menu is a short history of the establishment. It is said to be the oldest of Abingdon's historic buildings, built in 1779. It was originally used as a tavern and overnight inn for stagecoach travelers. Guests included Henry Clay, King Louis-Philippe, and President Andrew Jackson. During the past two centuries, it has served as a tavern, bank, bakery, general store, cabinet shop, barbershop, private residence, post office, antique shop, restaurant, and temporary hospital for wounded Civil War soldiers. Over the past thirty years it has been carefully and skillfully restored. It has been owned by Mary Dudley Porterfield, wife of the founder of the Barter Theatre in town, and has been operated as a restaurant since 1994 by Max Hermann.

There are, according to Max, bartenders, waiters and waitresses, tourists, and others, several ghosts active here. And why not? If one digs into the unwritten history of the place, there is just cause. There have been, dating to the early 1800s, at least two murders here, both of which went unsolved. One need only to visit the former hospital ward on an upper floor in the building, where the numbers for the beds during the Civil War are still visible, to almost feel the presence of young, bloodied bodies moaning in agony.

The manifestations are multiple, and have been witnessed by a number of people over the years. Dinner tables have been cleared and reset by unseen hands when no one was nearby. Glasses mysteriously sail off the bar racks, land several feet away, and don't break. Loud footsteps are heard upstairs when no one is there. Heavy doors swing open and slam shut on their own. Visions and shadowy figures appear: young Confederate soldiers swathed in bandages, a woman who was a prostitute during the War Between the States, a cattle drover who was killed over a card game, and a man who was shot by his lover's jealous husband.

The drover is perhaps the oldest ghost in the tavern. He may date as far back as the 1820s. It is said that he came one night and got involved in a big-money card game. He won. His companions, not the sort one would invite over for dinner, accused him of cheating. He was killed in an alley outside the tavern, but his murderers were never brought to trial. It was rumored that their identities were known, but Abingdon was virtually lawless in those days, and witnesses were too afraid to step forward. The drover's ghost still hangs around, throwing a shadow here, casting an unexplained light in a window there, seeking redress for his untimely demise.

A light has been seen in an upstairs window by townspeople, tourists, and staff members, always when no one is upstairs; when investigated, there is never a rational source to explain it. Some believe it may be a light said to have been used by a "lady of the evening" in the mid-1800s. The legend is that a drunken roughneck went berserk in one of the upstairs rooms and assaulted her. Her screams were heard throughout the tavern, but when men reached her, she had been beaten to death. Her assailant escaped and was never seen in town again. But the woman's apparition has been sighted, and her screams sometimes still echo on occasion. And there is the light. It is generally seen from the street and usually in the wee hours of the morning when the tavern is closed. At other times, a faint silhouette is sighted behind drawn curtains.

There is one other theory as to who one of the spirits might be. When one walks into the tavern, there is a picture of a man on the back wall, a man from another era, with a handlebar mustache. The caption beneath the photo reads: "Capt. Gordon William Riffe, 1843–1880. Buried near Whites Mill, Riffe's death allegedly involved an argument over a woman. Oral historical accounts state Riffe was murdered when leaving the building. As he mounted his horse, Stephen Alonzo Jackson shot and killed him. Riffe dragged himself to the nearby courthouse steps and died there, May 20, 1880." He was thirty-seven years old. Jackson was acquitted at his trial. Riffe was said to be a womanizer and Jackson was a jealous husband. Maybe that was justification for such a crime in those days. And maybe the slaying was justification for Riffe's ghost to return.

Max Hermann says when he took over the restaurant, a maintenance man told him that he had put in new air conditioning and heating equipment in 1978. He said that during the installation, all hell broke loose. For no explainable reason, the power went out, and when the man went upstairs to check things out, the Civil War hospital numbers, which are black, had burned "blood red."

"I must admit when I first came here, I was pretty much a skeptic about these sorts of things," Max says, smiling. "But now, I don't know.

Strange things happen here. I was closing up one night around 1 A.M. I was finishing some paperwork when the door behind me suddenly opened. Now, you don't just open that door. It is very heavy and it takes a whole lot of muscle and effort. Cassie, the bartender, was there. When that happened she had absolutely no color in her face. Who opened the door? We looked. There was no one there. We both left the building together. I tell you, I don't like to close the restaurant by myself anymore. Actually, no one here likes to close alone."

In 1998, Max invited several friends and customers to have a Halloween party at the tavern. "I told them to bring their sleeping bags, if they dared, and spend the night here. Several of them did. I didn't stay. Something happened in the middle of the night because they all got up and left rather abruptly. They told me later they hadn't actually seen anything, but they all felt a presence. They said they didn't know exactly what it was, but they felt they had to leave."

Max says he can't promise the appearance of one or more apparitions, the sound of mysterious footsteps, or the eerie sight of bar glasses flying across the room. "All I can promise is good food and a good atmosphere," he adds. "But I think all that has happened here makes the place interesting and unique."

## Apparitional Actors at the Barter Theatre

When it comes to haunted showplaces in Virginia, undoubtedly the most famous is the Barter Theatre in Abingdon, in the deep southwestern corner of the commonwealth. The building dates to the 1830s and originally was built as the Sinking Springs Presbyterian Church. Later it was run by the Sons of Temperance and was known as Temperance Hall. In the Virginia guide authored by Works Progress Administration writers during the Great Depression, a paragraph says: "The Barter Colony occupies the three brick buildings formerly used by the Stonewall Jackson Institute, a Presbyterian girls' school founded in 1869 and closed in 1932. Around an inn, theatre, workshop, and dormitory revolves the life of the Barter Theatre, established in 1933 by Robert and Helen Porterfield."

Robert Porterfield was born in 1905 near Austinville in Wythe County. He was destined for the stage. His father had wanted him to be a preacher, but as a young man, Robert answered his call by going to New York City to attend the Academy of Dramatic Arts. He appeared in a number of bit roles on Broadway in the late 1920s and early 1930s. Whether or not he would have made it as a star will never be known, for when the Depression hit, the lights in hundreds of theatres across the country went dark and thousands of performers were thrown out of work.

But Robert was more than a budding actor. He had a flair for the overall business of show business, and he had an idea. Why not take a troop of actors to his native southwest Virginia and establish a repertory theatre there? If they accepted produce, meat, and other edibles as the price for tickets, at least they wouldn't starve. An so, in 1933, he brought a group of unemployed actors and actresses to Abingdon, bought the building, and opened the Barter Theatre. Edible commodities, from calves to huckleberries, were accepted as payment for admission.

The first play produced, John Golden's *After Tomorrow*, was held on June 10, 1933, and the audience arrived lugging country hams, baskets of eggs, homemade pickles and jams, a rooster, a squealing pig, and a devil's food cake. Robert once remarked, "Nine out of ten theatergoers paid in anything from beans to cottage cheese. We ate well, and the culture-hungry Virginians thrived on the entertainment." The late comedian Fred Allen said the only way Porterfield could tell if he had had a successful season was to weigh his actors. In addition, the resourceful producer paid off the writers whose plays he staged with country hams. These were well received, it was noted, by all but George Bernard Shaw, who protested that he was a vegetarian. Robert shipped him a crate of Virginia-grown spinach.

The theater's survival through the Depression years and success afterwards exceeded Robert's fondest dreams. Over the next forty years some of the biggest names of stage, screen, and television cut their thespian teeth on small-town stages. Among those who trod the boards in Abingdon were Gregory Peck, Hume Cronyn, Ernest Borgnine, Patricia Neal, Ned Beatty, and Claude Akins.

Robert Porterfield died in 1971, but he was so profoundly devoted to his beloved theater that, it is said by many, he has never left it. There are scores of actors, stagehands, viewers, and others who swear they have seen the amiable founder still roaming around backstage or in the aisles, dressed in his omnipresent gray sweater. During plays, some performers have claimed to have spotted him in the audience. Actress Cleo Holladay told Mark Dawidziak, author of *The Barter Theatre Story*, that she looked up from the stage one night and saw a man in the last row in a white dinner jacket. She was convinced it was Porterfield, and said that was the same night the pipes rattled and "we took it as a sign that he approved of the show."

Others have seen a mysterious figure flitting about inside the building in the late hours of the night when everyone has gone home. However, when the theater is searched, no one is found. Once a Barter employee was walking by when he saw a man in a gray sweater sitting on a stoop. He recognized the figure as that of Porterfield, and, without thinking, he spoke to him. Then he suddenly realized that the man had been dead for several years. He looked back and the apparition had disappeared.

There also is said to be another roving specter in the theatre, and this one is the antithesis of Porterfield's friendly spirit. It has been described as malevolent and vindictive. Folklore author Charles Edwin Price said "its presence filled the living with dread and deadly dangers, and no one knows its identity." According to one popular legend, noted actor Ned Beatty was once so frightened in his dressing room by this unnerving haunt that he ran out of the room and into the street in his underwear to get away from it.

Equally chilling was the experience had by Barter publicity director Lou Flanigan a few years ago. He said he "felt a presence," one that somehow seemed to be so evil that he had to get out of the building at once. "I had this horrible feeling that something was going to get me," he recalled. He raced across the stage, went down the stairs, and ran to a door that leads to an alley. All the while he had an overpowering compulsion of fear. "If I had turned around and seen it," he said, "it probably would have been fatal. It was like it was following me." To add to his terror, he couldn't get the door open. He tore it down and darted outside. "One second more and I'm sure it would have grabbed me!"

At the venerable Barter, regular theatergoers have become accustomed to the possibility that some of the actors and others may be invisible to mortal eyes.

# Clocks That Strike Death

Old Virginia superstition says that if there is a death in the house, all the clocks there must be stopped at once. If one strikes while a corpse still lies in the house, it is striking another member out of the family. Also, the "time cycle," which culminated in the death of a person, must be broken so that further deaths do not occur. If clocks are stopped, then time must wait; it cannot continue its destruction.

There is, too, a line in the old German folk song, "My Grandfather's Clock," that goes, "it stopped short, never to go again when the old man died." It is prophetic because there have been countless cases where the sudden stopping of a clock or watch has, in fact, signaled the death of its owner or someone close to the owner. Here are some representative cases in Virginia with unusual twists.

## Death Times Five

Eunice Anderson of Vinton, near Roanoke, tells of an electrifying experience her mother, Helen, once had when she was thirteen years old. She was babysitting for her sister one night when all of a sudden an old clock, which hadn't worked in years, began to chime. It struck five times. Helen had never heard it strike before. She was petrified. She grabbed the child she was sitting for and ran out of the house.

Shortly afterwards, when she went back in, the telephone rang. Helen was told that there had been a bad accident. Her brother and five others had been struck in their car by a train. Her brother had survived, but the five other people had all been killed. It was later learned that the accident had occurred at the precise time the old clock had struck! It had tolled five times—one for each fatality.

## The Day Time Ran Out

This experience was related to Works Progress Administration interviewer James Hylton on September 25, 1941, by Elmer Morgan. It had been passed down to him by his father.

"We had an old 'regulator' clock made by a firm in Kaintuckey in our home in Wise County when Ma [his grandmother] was still with us in life. She always saw to it that it was running and keeping the best of time. She thought a lot of that old clock, and it seemed as if it was part of her life. I've gone in the room when she'd be settin' in the old rocker that she always set in, and she'd rock herself to sleep, and that old clock would be tickin' along, making a sound you could hear all over the place. Well, she'd look after that clock no matter what else they was to do about the house. The clock come first thing in the morning.

"Well, we never thought so much about it at the time, but late one evening, about two months after Ma'd not been feelin' so well, she laid down on the bed to rest. I went to the door of the room where the clock was, and I seed that it had stopped. Then I looked over at Ma and noticed she was mighty quiet-like. I went over to the bed and I saw that she was dead! Then we all remembered that Ma once said she had bewitched the clock and when it would die and stop tickin' for good, she would die, too. We figured the clock must have stopped about the exact same time Ma died.

"After we all was talkin' about this, we then realized how close to Ma that old clock had been, and we hadn't thought to wind it since she died. We went and took it down, and it was wound tight and the big drum wouldn't budge an inch after we turned wheels and things for a half hour or more. We got a feller down in Wise to fix it, but I went back in a day or so to get it and he told me there wasn't anything he could do for it. It had just wore itself out and died."

## The Cursed Watch of the Mines

The following legend has been recorded in anthologies of southern folklore and been passed down from generation to generation for more than a century and a quarter. It occurred somewhere in the coal mining region of southwestern Virginia near Grundy. It began one winter night when a miner slipped into a mine to steal some coal to heat his house. He was buried under a sudden avalanche of coal. It was known that this particular man, whenever he was working, had a habit of always taking off his watch and hanging it on a nearby timber. But rescue workers never found the watch, and it was assumed that it had been lost under tons of rubble.

Over the next few months, strange things seemed to happen. Men would hear what they said was the sound of a watch ticking in various areas of the mine. And whenever this was experienced, a terrible accident would befall the person working in that area. It was noted that the ticking was louder than that of an ordinary watch, but no one was able to find the source. In one written account of the phenomenon, it was reported that the watch eluded all measures of force and merely mocked men's curses. It was as inevitable as death itself. There were stretches of weeks or months when it kept silent. Then, with the suddenness of a fall of top rock, there would come the fateful "tick-tick."

In the already superstitious minds of the miners, the threat of hearing the ticking created stark fear throughout the community, especially after several accidents, some fatal, closely followed the discovery of the sound.

Then one night, the fire boss, on his usual inspection rounds, heard the watch himself. He said it sounded weird and awesome in the empty mine. He immediately left the site. The next morning, he was waiting at the entrance of the mine when one of his workers, Jim Kelly, approached. The fire boss told him he had heard the dreaded ticking in Kelly's work area, and warned him to take the day off. "Otherwise, you'll be killed," he said.

The miner turned pale. He needed the work because he had a large family to feed, but the curse of the ticking watch was so strong he heeded the advice and headed home. As it was early on a Sunday morning, Kelly thought that if he went straight home and changed his clothes he still might make the 8 o'clock mass at his church. He hurried to his house, changed, and started down the road. When the got to a railroad crossing, the guard gates were down, but he was in such a hurry he ran onto the tracks.

At 7:55 A.M., the speeding flyer train killed him on the spot.

## The House Where Time Stood Still

About forty years ago, Russell Simons moved into a boardinghouse in Williamsburg. He was sound asleep one night when something suddenly woke him. When he opened his eyes he saw what he described as a smallish apparitional woman with dark hair and a "kindly face," about ten feet from his bed. He said she was staring at him and appeared to be "floating" a few inches above the floor. The figure seemed to be transparent, because he could see the window frame and curtains through the woman!

Simons said he inexplicably felt completely at peace, and had the strong impression that the woman meant no harm to him. She then evaporated. The next morning when he got up, he noticed that his electric alarm clock had stopped during the night, and he could not get it running again. He mentioned to his landlord that the clock had stopped and he needed to buy another one. The man told him not to waste his money. The landlord then said that when his wife had died, every clock in the house except one had stopped at the precise moment of her death. He said he had gone out and bought some new clocks, but none of them would work in the house. He then opened a desk drawer and showed Simons several clocks. They had all stopped at the same time Simons's had. The landlord then pointed to a very old clock hanging over the mantel. He said it was more than a hundred years old and had been with his wife's family for genera-tions. For some unknown reason, this was the only clock that would keep time in the house.

Also in the room was an old photograph of a woman. The land-lord said it was a picture of his deceased wife. Simons was astounded. It was the same woman he had seen in apparitional form in his room. He had been sleeping in her room.

Shortly afterwards, Simons moved into new quarters. He plugged in his alarm clock—and it worked perfectly!

## Roanoke's Phantom Woman in Black

She appeared out of nowhere. One witness described the unnerving experience like this: "It was as if she had arisen out of the earth!" Her voice sounded real. Her touch felt real. She appeared to be real, although quite a few of the gentlemen involved had great difficulty looking her in the eye. A peripheral glance was the best some of them could manage in their fright. She never caused any physical harm, or at least none was reported. It seemed obvious at the time that for every man who summoned up enough courage to speak of her presence, there were probably three or four others who kept the mysterious meetings secret.

Those who did look at her were unanimous in at least one phase of her description: she was breathtakingly beautiful. One man said she was tall and handsome, with "dancing eyes." Another said she was about five foot nine or ten and dressed entirely in black, with something like a black turban on her head. It was, he added, fixed in such a manner so that it was drawn around her face just below her eyes, forming a perfect mask. She also wore a long black Ragian cloak. She would suddenly appear, seemingly out of nowhere, and then in a flash she would be gone. She would vanish, leaving the men she escorted stunned and speechless.

This was the legendary "Woman in Black," who, for a brief period in March 1902, struck terror into the hearts of the men of Roanoke. The local newspaper reported: "Her name was on every lip; strong men trembled when her name was spoken; children cried and clung to their mothers' dresses; terror reigned supreme!" Who was this woman of dark intrigue? What was her mission? Why was she so feared? As the newspaper pointed out: "Just why the Woman in Black should be so terrible has never been known. She made no attack on anyone. It was probably due to the unexpected appearance in places unthought of, and at hours when the last person of the city is expected about should be a woman."

She apparently had come north from the town of Bristol, which the *Roanoke Times* reported: "Is just recovering from the effects of the scare produced among the citizens of the town by what was known as the Woman in Black. Hardly a day passed for weeks that the press failed to have a long account of the antics and performances of her on the night before." On March 18, 1902, the *Times* said: "For the last ten days she has been unheard of; has completely disappeared from the city of Bristol, and expectation has been rife as to where she would make her next manifestation.

"More or less anxiety has been felt by a few people of Roanoke, who, through necessity or otherwise, are kept up until a late hour at night, lest she make her appearance before them; and true to the pre-sentiment, to Roanoke she has come and in a quiet way is beginning to stir up some uneasiness and not a little excitement. Just what her mission here can be, what her object is in waylaying certain parties, has not exactly been figured out; but of one thing there seems to be a unanimity of opinion, and that is, she has a proclivity for attacking the married men, if 'attack' is the proper word."

The *Times* said there had been several recent encounters with the mystery woman. Here was one: "The most current instance is that of a prominent merchant of the city, who on the night after payday, hav-ing been detained at his store until after midnight, was making his way home, buried in mental abstractions, when at his side the woman in black suddenly appeared, calling him by his name. The woman was only a couple of feet behind him, and he naturally increased his pace; faster and faster he walked, but in spite of his efforts, the woman gained on him until, with the greatest of ease and without any appar-ent effort, she kept along side of him. 'Where do you turn off?' she asked of him. He replied, in a hoarse voice, 'Twelfth Avenue.' Ere he was aware, she had her hand upon his shoulder. He tried to shake it off, but without success. 'You are not the first married man I have seen to his home this night,' she spoke in a low and musical voice.

"Reaching the front gate, he made certain she would then leave him, but into the yard she went. This was a little more than he bar-gained for. It was bad enough to be brought home by a tall and hand-some woman with dancing eyes; but to march up to the front door with her—well, he knew his wife was accustomed to wait for him when he was detained, and he did not dare to go to the trouble of making an explanation to her; besides, such explanations are not always satisfac-tory. The merchant admits that he was a nervy man, but in spite of his efforts, he could not help being at least a little frightened.

"'Twas the suddenness of the thing,' is the way he expressed it. But as he reached the door, he looked around. She was gone. Where had she gone, and how, he didn't know. But he didn't tarry on the doorstep either."

Two others who experienced these strange visitations were a black porter and a young telegraph operator. Both were married, and in each case she appeared to them late at night on deserted streets. Each said she moved over the sidewalk with an "almost noiseless tread." The porter was terrified by the apparition. He ran two squares as fast as his legs could carry him, and fell into the door almost in a fit. The telegraph operator said she called out to him to "wait a minute," but like the porter, he ran hard all the way home. Both men later said the woman had called them by name.

Whoever she was, she stayed in Roanoke only a short time. Within a few days the reports of her appearances ceased altogether. But soon there were accounts of her nightly sojourns in the town of Bluefield, also in March 1902. Then, the *Roanoke Times* carried a short article from Alma, Nebraska. It was headlined, "Prominent Men See Ghost." The story said, "The spirit form of a young woman is walking the streets of Alma. She exudes from the depths of some dark alley and rushes past lone pedestrians." One man said he saw it vanish in the moonlight, and another was chased by "it" after he scoffed at it. The dispatch added: "The Alma ghost is remarkable in that instead of being garbed in proverbial white, it walks about clothed in deep black!"

Who was she? Why did she appear only to prominent married men, always late at night while they were on their way home? It has been speculated that perhaps she was a wife herself once who had found her husband unfaithful. And thereafter, she returned to make sure potentially wayward mates did not succumb to temptations of the night.

# A Pair of Deathly Premonitions

There are, in the recorded annals of psychic phenomena, countless cases of what are commonly called premonitions of death. Many of these incidents involve dreams or nightmares, in which the dreamer envisions a close relative, often a mother, father, son, daughter, brother, sister, husband, or wife. The vision may be calling for help, or it may just appear, as if to say a final goodbye. In many more cases than can be dismissed by coincidence, the dreamer later learns that the person they visualized either died or suffered a terrible accident at the precise time the dream occurred. Such phenomena have never been fully understood or explained.

What is much more rare in psychic realms is when someone has such a premonition, in dream form or otherwise, of their own death. Yet this apparently is exactly what happened to not one, but two persons involved in the same chilling event early in the twentieth century at the Carroll County Courthouse in tiny Hillsville, near Galax, in the southwestern part of Virginia. It was here on March 14, 1912, that one of the most tragic episodes in the history of the commonwealth occurred. It has forever been known as the Hillsville Shootout.

This was hill country, and if the mountain folks who lived there could be summed up in one word, it would be "independent;" in two words, "fiercely independent." From the latter part of the eighteenth century, well into the twentieth, these pioneering people battled savage Indians, wild beasts, and the harsh environment of the land to build their cabins and farm the rough hillsides to scratch out a meager living. They mostly kept to themselves and resented any intrusion on their privacy. They lived by their own code of ethics, which often included self-administered justice. In this backwoods region, this generally meant an eye for an eye.

This was the overall atmosphere that prevailed in Carroll County in 1912. One of the most feared clans in that day was made up of members of the Allen and Edwards families. Unlike the common stereotype of the backwoodsman, however, the Allens in particular were said to be respected businessmen and farmers and of average education. Still, the Allen men and their kinsmen, the Edwardses, were described as possessing personalities characteristic of many inhabitants of the Virginia highlands. They were rugged individuals, independent, fiercely proud, and hot-tempered.

The incident that directly led to the ensuing calamity is still somewhat clouded in confusion. There are at least three versions. One says that two of the young Edwards boys had been arrested for moonshining and were being brought to jail in Hillsville. Another says simply that the two had been arrested on a minor misdemeanor charge, while the third states the boys had been captured for disturbing a church meeting.

Whatever, they were manacled on their horses and being escorted by deputies. Onto this scene came Floyd Allen, the fifty-something-year-old uncle of the boys. In one version of what followed, he asked the deputies to unshackle the Edwards boys. The officers drew their guns. Floyd then went berserk, wrested the gun from one of them, and smashed it on a rock. The officers fled. In another report, Floyd met the deputies and beat one of them senseless, leaving him for dead on the ground and scurrying off with the boys.

In either case, the result was a warrant for Floyd's arrest. He was indicted and released on bond. In the days leading to the trial, Floyd consistently vowed that he would never go to jail; that he would die before being confined. Those who knew him had no doubts of his sincerity. In the days before the trial, both Judge Thornton L. Massie and commonwealth attorney William M. Foster received death-threatening letters from the Allen clan, saying revenge would be inflicted for any punishment rendered to Floyd.

The jury heard the evidence in the case for several days and then the verdict and sentence were to be handed down on the morning of March 14. The entire Allen clan, dressed in long coats, rode up to the courthouse that day and wedged their way into the packed courtroom. The night before, Foster, expecting trouble, pleaded with Judge Massie to deputize some men to protect the court, but the judge refused. Nevertheless, Foster had court officials appear the next day carrying concealed weapons.

The jury filed in sometime after 8:30 A.M., and read a verdict of "guilty as charged" with the penalty of one year in prison. The judge denied the continuance of Allen's bond and directed the sheriff to take charge of the prisoner. At that moment, all hell broke loose.

Floyd Allen arose from his seat, threw back his coat to reveal two revolvers, and loudly proclaimed, "Gentlemen, I ain't going!" Bedlam ensued. Sheriff Lewis F. Webb immediately rushed toward Allen, and at the same instant shots rang out from the courtroom. Judge Massie was hit five or six times and died immediately. The sheriff and Floyd fired away at each other in such close quarters that shots carried powder burns as well as bullets. The sheriff was killed and Floyd was hit by half a dozen or more shots.

The entire courtroom exploded in a furious eruption of gunfire that, one witness said, "sounded like the crackle of mountain laurel." Several members of the Allen-Edwards clan, with pistols and rifles, began firing, and their charges were answered from the guns of the court officers. The smoke from such a fusillade was so thick it was difficult to see anyone or anything. According to one contemporary written account of the scene, "A second after Judge Massie had fallen over his desk, an outlaw blazed away with his Winchester, and commonwealth attorney William Foster threw up his hands and tottered backwards, a corpse. Sheriff Louis Webb saw the shot and the man who fired it.

"Raising his revolver, he drew a bead on the outlaw, but before he could pull the trigger, a shot from across the room struck him in the head. The revolver, still undischarged, flew out of his hand as he sank dying to the floor. The wounded lay about the floor with the dead, and the place resembled a shambles. Blood was everywhere. While the shooting was in progress, the spectators were making panic-stricken efforts to escape. A number of them had been hit by stray bullets and lay gasping on the floor. Those who escaped the leaden hail had scattered in all directions and were fleeing for their lives.

"Within less than a minute, seventy-five shots were fired!"

In the pandemonium, the Allens and Edwardses, including Floyd, who was riddled with bullet wounds, left the courtroom, mounted their horses, and fled. The judge, the commonwealth attorney, the sheriff, one member of the jury, and one witness were dead. Several others were wounded. Floyd was so badly hurt that he couldn't make it to the mountains, which the others headed for. Such was the fear that the attack created in town that no deputies tried to subdue them. They were arrested the next day after an army of law officers from all over southwest Virginia arrived.

Over the next few weeks, a relentless succession of posses rounded up most of the clan. Only Sidna Allen, Floyd's brother, and Wesley Edwards, a nephew, eluded the manhunt by hiding in the mountains. They, too, were captured about six months later. A trial was held in Wytheville and Floyd and his son, Claude, were sentenced to death. A number of other members of the clan were sent to prison. On March 28, 1913, a little over a year after the shootout, Floyd and Claude were electrocuted in Richmond. Each man, it was said, walked unflinchingly to the chair, calmly resigned to his destiny.

Was Floyd Allen's fate preconceived? Did he envision how he was going to die even before the shootout? There is some suggestion that he did have a premonition of his doom. He is said to have told this to his brothers as he awaited the results of his trial.

And what about the commonwealth attorney? Did William Foster foresee his future, too? Maggie Mae McManaway, then secretary to Foster, was an eyewitness to the tragedy that auspicious day in 1912. In 1940, she was interviewed for a newspaper article on the shootout. The night before, she was with Foster when he had asked Judge Massie to arm the courthouse with extra deputies.

"The next morning," she said, "Mr. Foster and I were in the office, and he appeared worried. As he left to go to the courtroom, he told me goodbye, and said I'd likely not see him anymore!"

## The Haunting Disaster at Rye Cove School

One of the worst natural disasters in the history of Virginia occurred in Scott County, in the far southwestern section of the commonwealth, on May 2, 1929. It was a tragedy with supernatural overtones. A psychic premonition of what was to come happened about a month earlier. It was at that time that a seventh-grade teacher, Effie Flanery of the Rye Cove Consolidated School, had a prophetic dream. The school then was a two-frame building of seven rooms, serving 250 students from the surrounding area. She dreamed of teaching in a "new and entirely different place, and all about were evidences of a newly constructed complex."

A month later, on the morning of May 2, a second omen of imminent impending danger occurred to Miss Flanery. She said in a letter to a friend, "About ten o'clock in the morning I was teaching a review class in sixth grade mathematics, and was solving a problem on the chalk board for their observation. Suddenly, something like a nicely finished mahogany table appeared at my right side, and a flash of something like lightning came down the wall and across the table and split it in two along an irregular line. I can't say if it were a voice or thought which came to me in these words, 'Rye Cove is not a safe place to be.'"

Miss Flanery was so stunned and frightened by this phenomenon that she thought seriously about going to the principal and asking him to dismiss all the students immediately. But for some inexplicable reason, perhaps because she felt the principal would think her crazy, she did not act. Thus, the eerie premonition went unheeded.

Three and a half hours later, at about 1:30 P.M., an unbelievably powerful tornado struck about half a mile down the valley from the school. It destroyed several buildings in a path that led straight to the schoolhouse. It hit with such sudden and fearful force that there was no time to seek shelter. In seconds, the unearthly vacuum created by the huge funnel blew out windows and snapped timbers like matchsticks. The entire school was ripped asunder, strewing the wreckage over a distance of several hundred yards. The building was torn from its foundation, lifted into the air as if by a giant hand, and then slammed back down to earth.

The air was filled with large shards of glass, spears of shattered wood, and the bodies of terrified children. It was a horrific scene. A six-foot wooden plank was driven through one girl's body, and another student was nearly decapitated by the hurtling glass. Scores of others were buried under heaps of fallen debris, their pitiful cries muffled under the cacophony of the roaring storm.

It was all over in seconds. When rescuers arrived, it looked like a Civil War battlefield. Twelve children and one teacher were dead. More than fifty others had to be hospitalized, and many more pulled themselves from the wreckage battered, bruised, and bloodied. Everywhere, there were mournful cries, moans, and screams.

A memorial plaque was erected at the site, honoring those who perished in that terrible moment of tragedy. The date was forever frozen in the memories of everyone in the county. And those memories seem to be perpetuated on each anniversary of the debacle. For it is said, and it has been passed down ever since, that every May 2, no matter what the weather is, calm or stormy, an ethereal wind of mighty proportions is heard gushing through the valley where the school once stood, and the anguished cries of the petrified children are again heard.

Miss Flanery's prophetic dream came true. A new school was built.

# Vindication from the Beyond

Dan Starrett, a part-time police officer in Martinsville, will never forget April 17, 1973, as long as he lives. It was on that date that, shortly after three in the morning, he was suddenly awakened from a sound sleep by a violent shaking of his bed. He rose up on his elbows, rubbed the cobwebs out of his eyes, and saw a man standing at the end of the hall. He was stout and broad-shouldered, wore a black vest with a shiny badge attached to it, and had on a felt "bobby" hat, much like the ones British police officers wear. To Starrett, the figure looked like an old-time railroad policeman

This sent an immediate chill down Starrett's spine. His grandfather had been such an officer. He had been killed in the line of duty on Christmas Eve 1917. "I shook my head," Starrett recalls, "and when I looked up again, he was gone." Fearing ridicule, he told no one of the ethereal visit. Exactly one year later, just after 3 A.M. on April 17, 1974, the same spirit manifested again, only this time by way of sound, not sight. It spoke, asking the startled Starrett, "Why are you here?" Starrett didn't have a clue as to the meaning. Then, precisely one year later, on the same date, he "felt a presence," but did not see or hear anything. That day—April 17, 1975—he got word his father had died.

Starrett's father had for years tried to find out the true story of what happened to his father, Walter J. Starrett, the railroad officer who had been killed in 1917, but he was never fully successful. Starrett's grandfather had died in Mitchell, Indiana, and there always had been a veil of mystery surrounding his death. All that anyone knew was that the grandfather apparently had killed a man who had been popular in Mitchell, and had been jailed while awaiting a trial. He was later released, still pending the trial, and had been killed during the interim.

Eventually, it dawned on Starrett that the vision he had seen and later heard was his grandfather. But why had he appeared? What did he want? The mystery gnawed at him. He wrote to the Baltimore and Ohio Railroad headquarters seeking any information they could provide. His grandfather had worked for them at the time he died. This resulted in a newspaper article about Walter Starrett, but it left many questions still unanswered.

Then, out of the blue, Starrett received a small package from the police chief in Sparrow's Point, Maryland. In it was the original police badge his grandfather had worn when he had worked in that town early in the twentieth century. "All of this ran through my mind for a long time," Starrett says. "I was always curious. It was something that had always bugged me. I needed to find out what had really happened to my grandfather."

As if his curiosity wasn't enough, Starrett began waking up at exactly 3:06 A.M. He had set no alarm or radio. It just seemed to happen that whenever he first opened his eyes, the clock would read six minutes after three. What did this mean? Finally, he had had enough; first the apparition, then the voice, then the presence; his father's death; and the constant awakenings at 3:06 A.M. There were just too many coincidences. There had to be some meaning. So, on April 17, 1997, another coincidence, Starrett and his wife traveled to Mitchell, Indiana, looking for answers.

They found that his grandfather had, in the summer of 1917, shot and killed a man described as the town's friendly drunk, a man well liked. The man had pulled a knife on Walter Starrett, and the shooting was in self-defense. Still, he was jailed for two months and then released before a trial began. On Christmas Eve 1917, Walter, then working on the Baltimore and Ohio's Mitchell-to-Cincinnati run as a railroad detective, was called out to the yard to investigate a report that some boxcars had been broken into. As he rounded a rail car, he saw a man running off in the dark. He shouted for him to halt, but the man kept running. Walter chased him for six blocks, repeatedly calling for him to stop. Finally, he fired his pistol and hit the man in the buttocks, and he fell. Walter walked up to him and bent over to see how badly he was hurt.

As he did, the man pulled a revolver hidden in his coat and fired twice at point-blank range. One bullet went through Walter's heart. He slumped over dead.

It was 3:06 in the morning!

Armed with this information, which vindicated his grandfather, Dan Starrett used it to convince officials to add Walter's name to the National Law Enforcement Officers Memorial in Washington, D. C.

Since then, Starrett has been able to sleep through each night without waking up at 3:06 in the morning.

Of his grandfather, he says, "He's kind of left us alone after that. But he's welcome to return any time he wants. Looking back on things, I think he wanted his name cleared and that's why he appeared to me, and maybe that's why I kept waking up at the exact time of his death. How else do you explain it?"

When Starrett's incredible story became public, he became the subject of several newspaper and magazine articles, and appeared on national television. He even wrote a book about his experiences. It is titled *The Father, the Son & the Railroad Ghost.*

## The Ghost Light on Holston Mountain

At 8:32 P.M. on the night of January 8, 1959, the pilot of a Southeast Airlines DC-3 radioed the Tri-Cities Airport, serving Bristol, Virginia, and Kingsport and Johnson City, Tennessee, that he was circling to make a normal approach for landing after a flight from Memphis. It was a stormy night. Two hours earlier, a heavy snowfall had blanketed the area, leaving a four-inch mantle on the ground. It was now hazy, with limited visibility. However, the runways had been cleared.

When the plane didn't arrive on schedule, airport employees began to worry. Nothing further had been heard from the pilot. A quick check was made to other airports, but no report of the missing DC-3 had been logged. By 2 A.M., when fuel would have been exhausted, it was feared the plane had crashed or had made an emergency landing. A search party was organized. Southeast Airlines released to the media the names of the three crewmembers and the seven passengers aboard.

The search teams included volunteer rescue team members, state highway patrolmen, sheriff's officers from neighboring counties, and Civil Air Patrol (CAP) personnel. Sometime before daylight, one of the teams reported to CAP operations officer Virgil Peck that it "had a light under observation" in the Holston Mountain region, a rugged and isolated range about twenty miles east of the airport. The team said the light "answered the signals" of the searchers. Highway patrolmen were dispatched to the site and confirmed the report.

The point of observation was on U.S. Route 421, about two miles east of South Holston Lake, a few miles due south of Abingdon, Virginia. Capt. Ed Allen of the Civil Air Patrol said it "was a bright, steady light" that "shone continuously" a considerable distance away. Allen then took a powerful emergency searchlight and waved it from side to side. The distant light then waved back side to side, as if to signal the message had been received. Allen moved the light up and down, and the faraway light did the same. What could it mean? Were there survivors? Was someone signaling the location of the crash site? An old-timer, familiar with the region, said there were no cabins or campsites in that area. What else could it be?

Captain Peck radioed the airport operations center and had a C-45 National Guard plane fly over the area. Because of the haze and low-hanging clouds, the pilot didn't see anything below. But as he passed directly over the area, the men on Route 421 said the mysterious light "went crazy" waving furiously in all directions. Peck said there was no question in his mind that this was someone at the scene of the crash trying to direct the rescuers. The signals continued until daylight, then the light disappeared.

After noon that day, January 9, ground parties arrived at the crash site. It was apparent that the DC-3 had slammed directly into the face of the mountain. Only the tail section survived intact; everything else had been smashed to bits and was scattered over a wide area. Bodies were strewn over several hundred feet. All ten of those who had been on the plane were confirmed dead. It was also obvious that they all had died instantly. Who, then, had been signaling with the light?

One of the first to arrive at the scene was newspaper reporter David McBride. He carefully examined each body and the area around it. He said the fresh snow was "undisturbed," and there was no light of any kind, not even a flashlight, to be found. McBride wrote, "I was intrigued by the light, but none of the victims could have been responsible for it." Trees and underbrush had been charred by the flash fire that followed the crash, but not even a spark or whiff of smoke was evident to the rescuers.

The possibility of an open flame was ruled out since it was highly doubtful that any hunters would have been out in the freezing cold and heavy snow. Also, no footprints were found by rescue members. It was later recalled that a twin-engine Navy aircraft had crashed in the same region a year earlier, and because of the rough, almost impenetrable terrain, it had taken twelve days for teams to reach the crash site.

No rational explanation has ever been found for the mysterious light. What is known is that whatever it was, it focused the search on a specific isolated, uninhabited mountain site and led to an early discovery of the wreck scene that otherwise would have taken days or weeks longer.

## The Pearisburg Poltergeist

A week-long series of heavy-handed poltergeist activity, similar to that which happened in Buchanan, occurred more than a century later at a remote mountain farmhouse near the small town of Pearisburg in Giles County. The bizarre events, which took place here between the nineteenth and the twenty-fourth of December 1977, remain an unexplained mystery to this day and townspeople still talk of the "supernatural spectacle."

The action revolved around a nine-year-old boy whose identity was kept secret. He was a foster child, living with a sixty-five-year-old woman named Beulah Wilson, and was described as being a fine kid, very polite and mannerly. Although many felt that it was he who was causing the frightening disturbances, neither he nor anyone seemed to know why things happened as they did.

It began simply enough at about 9:30 on the evening of the nineteenth when apples and oranges started falling from a table for no apparent reason. At first, Mrs. Wilson thought her cat might have been responsible, but it was nowhere near the table. Then a cake pan and some silverware fell to the floor. She placed them back on a cabinet, and the pan fell again. When dishes started shattering and large pieces of furniture toppled over, Mrs. Wilson became scared and called a neighbor and then phoned the police. Both later said they heard objects crashing in the background. Mrs. Wilson asked the neighbor if he felt like an earthquake was taking place. She told him something was tearing her house to pieces.

The neighbor, Martin Caldwell, went in her house and said, "I saw this old sewing machine rise about three inches off the floor and fall over. Everything in the kitchen was turned over except the Frigidaire, stove, and washing machine." Caldwell was deeply shaken. The first investigator to arrive on the scene was deputy sheriff Jimmy Niece. He said, as he drove up, he saw "a carton of soda bottles on the back porch fall to the ground." He noted that the bottles were in a rack and would have had to be lifted out of the rack in order to fall to the ground. He didn't see anyone touch the bottles. Other deputies added that large cabinets and pieces of furniture were toppled or moved toward the center of three rooms in the house. None of them believed that the boy or Mrs. Wilson had the physical strength to move such pieces. One said, "It's unbelievable. I went up there, checked for strings, trick mirrors, went under the house, checked the foundation, and still couldn't find anything wrong."

The next evening, Donald Wilson (Mrs. Wilson's son), his brother, and the boy were in the house straightening things up, when the activity started again. A cabinet that had fallen over the night before, but had since been placed upright, fell over again. Wilson said he could see the boy and that he did not knock it over. The three of them quickly left the house. Mrs. Wilson and the boy moved in with Donald and his family, partly to escape the strange happenings, and partly to elude the army of curious onlookers and television crews that had descended on the tiny community in efforts to see the "evil spirits" at work. The sheriff eventually had to seal off the house.

Three nights later, on December 23, the disturbances began again, this time at Donald's house. The boy said he went to shut the TV off and the table moved. Then an eighteen-inch trophy fell to the floor without being touched. "I called the local church people in and we prayed," Donald said. On Christmas Eve, the boy went upstairs and things began falling once more. Books from an upstairs bookcase in the hallway started flying down the stairs like someone was throwing them. "I shouted 'in the name of Jesus, stop it!'" Donald said; then he took the boy outside. Only then did the manifestations stop.

At this point Donald Wilson said he had had enough. Although he didn't understand what was going on, he felt the events were somehow tied to the boy, and he was afraid for the safety of his family. Wilson's young daughter was in hysterics. He called the county authorities and asked them to take the boy back. He was later placed with another family and no further activity was reported.

Dr. J. G. Pratt, then a University of Virginia parapsychologist, came to Pearisburg and investigated the case. He suggested that the cause might be rooted in "a peculiar manifestation of psychic energy, along the lines of a poltergeist. There is a release of such energy. It starts suddenly for no real reason and seems to stop just as quickly." Pratt added that he had never encountered a case in which so much happened in such a short period of time.

Martin Caldwell, the neighbor, summed it up when he said, "I've gone over the thing time and again in my mind and I just don't have any explanation for it. All we can do is accept that it happened and hope that time will end it."

## The Lady Who Talks with Dead People

If Virginia is shaped like a foot, then the small community of Hurley is a corn on the big toe. It is in Buchanan County, a few miles north of Grundy, in the heart of what was once a booming coal industry. It is the home of Evelyn Clevinger, a natural psychic. She has a gift. She communicates with those who have passed on to the "other side." Some people might call it a curse, but Evelyn likes to think of it as a blessing, although there are times when things get so intense and depressing that she'd like to "turn it off."

"I'm just a country girl," she says, "and I can't explain it. I don't understand it. It just happens." She has had this ability since childhood, but had always been reluctant to talk about it for fear of being thought "tetched" in the head. It all began one night when she was about ten. Born and raised in Hurley, she was spending the night with a girlfriend who lived in an old house in Slate Creek. "We slept in the same bed," she recalls. "You know in those days it was all right to do that. Well, in the middle of the night, I felt something heavy get on my feet. I thought it was my friend, but she was way over on the other side of the bed, fast asleep. I sat up and saw what looked like a white clump. I could see through it! I don't know why, but I just said something like 'go away,' and as I did, it floated off."

It was about the same time that Evelyn had her first conversation with a ghost. One of her uncles appeared to her one night. He sat on the edge of the bed and told her he had just shot and killed himself, and he asked her not to tell anyone about it until after her grandmother (his mother) had passed on. Evelyn was raised by her grandmother. Her father, grandfather, and one brother were all killed in coal mine accidents. Half an hour after her uncle's spirit had appeared to her, Evelyn's aunts came to the house to inform everyone that their brother (the uncle) had been found dead. Evelyn never said anything about how he had died until years later, when it was confirmed that he had taken his own life.

As the years passed, Evelyn realized she had an unusual, if unexplainable, ability. Not only did she receive messages from the dead, but she also had sharp, distinct premonitions of events that would occur in the future. And, almost without exception, the events would take place just as she had envisioned them. Once, for example, she told a young man he would marry a woman with blond, curly hair. He did. "One time," she says, "I saw a woman I didn't know in a grocery store, and immediately I had a vision that she had lost a son who had been killed in a motorcycle accident." She mentioned this to the woman, who verified the fact. "I never know when such things will flare up," Evelyn says. "They just do."

One of the most convincing such incidents occurred a few years ago when Evelyn was working for an ambulance company. She foresaw one of the firm's ambulances turned over, upside down. Within days, an ambulance was indeed involved in a terrible accident. It rolled over five times and landed upside down.

Sometimes, the premonitions and spiritual encounters involve sadness and depression. At other times they can cause peacefulness. Evelyn bears this range of emotional highs and lows as if she were the victim. "You take on the pain they have," she explains. She empathizes with those departed who communicate through her. A classic example was her sister's unexpected death a few years ago. She had taken her own life, and for a long time afterward, Evelyn felt guilt. "I kept asking myself, was there something I could have done to prevent it? It was eerie. I could feel her touch me when I went to her grave. Then one day she appeared to me. She told me to stop blaming myself for her death. There was an overwhelming feeling of calmness and serenity. It put me at peace."

Many of Evelyn's otherworldly experiences concern her boss, Mickey Caudill. He owns the ambulance company. His mother died in 1999. Evelyn barely knew her. However, since her death, Mrs. Caudill has materialized to Evelyn several times. "It began one day when I went to Mickey's house," she says. "He lives alone, and the minute I walked in, I felt a presence. It got very cold. Mickey's mother began talking to me. She told me all about her death, and that she was worried about her son. He smoked, and she wanted him to stop. Over the next few months, she came to me a number of times. She said she wanted Mickey to forgive her, that she felt she hadn't been the best mother to him. She wanted me to look after him, to be sort of a surrogate mother to him."

After the first "visit" from Mickey's mother, Evelyn began to write down some of the things she was being told by the spirit. The first messages contained only disjointed words. As the sessions progressed, however, Evelyn began receiving more coherent instructions for Mickey. One included: "I failed you in life. I was jealous, lazy, noncaring. I have found someone to care for you [Evelyn]. Help her. Stop fighting her love and caring. I must go. She must stay. I am sorry. She is what I could never be. Don't fail me or yourself."

Later, the deceased mother spoke directly to Evelyn, as follows: "I'm leaving you now. My baby is in your care. He needs extra love, mother's love, like yours. Keep him strong. Be stern." "I didn't know what to do," Evelyn says. "I was afraid to tell Mickey about it. I mean how would it sound if I went to him and said I've been talking to your mother. It would sound crazy. You can't just walk up to someone and tell them you talk with dead people. So I didn't say anything about it for some time, but Mickey knew something was wrong. He finally pressed me to tell him and I did. I even wrote down the things she told me and gave him a copy." Mickey, naturally, was stunned at first, but Evelyn revealed some things that only he and his mother could have known. Evelyn feels that once Mickey forgives his mother, she will move on.

Mickey's dead father also communicated with Evelyn. He told her, "It's okay with the move." She didn't understand what he meant, but when she told Mickey about it, he said he had been planning to rebury his father into a family gravesite and had been worried about the move. "I think his father was letting him know he was okay with it," Evelyn says.

Only once has Evelyn been frightened by her encounters. That occurred a few years ago when her son, Heath, called and told her he believed that an evil spirit was in his apartment in Richlands. Evelyn said she felt a "dark presence" the minute she entered the apartment. "It was an overpowering feeling of hate," she remembers. "I knew in my heart that there was the spirit of an old woman there. Why, I don't know, but she wanted my son out of that place. It was a mean spirit. I sat down on the couch, and she choked me. I could feel her icy hands around my neck." Her son moved.

Evelyn says most of the time she just hears voices of the dead, speaking to her. But occasionally, she will see images as well. "I don't know how to describe it. Sometimes it appears as an iridescent color, kind of white with a blue tint. It's something like when you take a roll of Saran wrap and you move it, you see different colors. And it's not like the objects walk. They seem to float!" Sometimes the entities touch Evelyn on the cheek, and the sensation is always freezing cold.

Evelyn says there is no rhyme or reason to what she experiences. "It's not like I have a button you can push on and off. Sometimes I wish I could turn it off. I can't call up the spirits. They just come whenever. Still, it happens. I'm just a country girl and I don't know why it happens to me, but it does. I accept it, and except for that one instance with the mean old lady, it doesn't frighten me. Like I said, I consider it a gift."

## Haunting Humor from the Hollows

Following are some anecdotes about incidents in southwest Virginia, which were thought to be ghostly but turned out not to be. They are, however, told as being true, and are quite humorous.

## Never Shoot a Ghost!

The details of this account are somewhat sketchy. It was said to occur shortly after the end of the Civil War at a site southwest of Roanoke, and involved a man called "Grandpappy Sparks." He was known throughout his community as a fervent raccoon hunter. One night around midnight he woke up from a sound sleep feeling kind of peculiar. A beam of moonlight shone down through a hole in the roof, and illuminated the room.

Grandpappy looked down at the end of his bed and then rubbed his eyes in disbelief. There, he saw something "white and square, fluttering back and forth." He always kept his trusty shotgun by his side, even when he slept. He grabbed it, aimed it at the object, and yelled out, "Speak if you're human!" There was only silence. He repeated the warning, adding that he was going to shoot if there was no answer. More silence. Grandpappy then blasted away—and blew off all five toes on his right foot!

## The Corpse that Ate a Potato

There is an old African-American folk tale still told in Floyd County concerning the death of one of the elder members of a family that lived in a log cabin in a rural farm area. The deceased was in a coffin in the main room and relatives and friends were performing the age-old ritual of sitting up with the dead. They had put some potatoes on the fire to roast, but, as it was late at night, they had all fallen asleep.

By chance, two coon hunters came upon the little cabin, perhaps drawn by the smoke from the chimney. They peered through one of the windows, sized up the situation, and concocted a plan. They slipped inside and stole the potatoes. Before they left, however, they set the head and shoulders of the dead man up in the coffin, pried his mouth open, and stuffed one of the potatoes in it.

Then they went outside and looked again through the window, waiting to see what would happen when the others woke up. The first one who arose stretched and then looked back toward the body. He let out a screaming yell, saying, "He done come to and eat up all the potatoes! Now he sits with one in his mouth." He lit out of the house as fast as his legs would carry him, and the others followed in close pursuit.

The last one, however, caught his overall suspenders on the door latch, which had a hook on it, and, fearing he had been grabbed by the corpse, fainted dead away. It was daylight before any of the mourners came back to check on him.

## The "Corpse" that Talked Back

The following is recounted from Samuel Hurst's 1929 book *The Mountains Redeemed*, a personal history of the hills and valleys of southwest Virginia. Hurst told of a young doctor he knew in the 1890s, who in his zeal to learn more about human anatomy, robbed a grave one night to have a cadaver to practice on. The doctor hired a horse and buggy, and then went out to an isolated graveyard and resurrected the body. He sat the dead man upright in the buggy, tying him to the back of the seat, so as to not arouse curiosity.

As he headed home, the doctor passed a saloon. A little shaken by his ordeal, he stopped to get a pint of whiskey. While he was in the tavern, someone who knew what had been going on decided to play a joke. He cut the straps and laid the corpse aside in some bushes. Then he got up into the seat himself. The doctor, unknowing, came out and grabbed the reins.

After going a short distance, he took a swig from his bottle; in a playful mood, he stuck the whiskey under the nose of his "rider," and said "have a snort." When the jokester instantly replied, "Don't mind if I do," the doctor instantaneously dropped the reins and unceremoniously leaped from the buggy and hit the ground running. The man said he rode on for a mile or more and never caught a glimpse of the fleeing medical man. Author Hurst said that after that the doctor stopped his practice, and it was thought he went into the ministry.

## How to Get Rid of a Mother-in-Law

In his entertaining book *Pioneers in Paradise*, V. N. "Bud" Phillips tells hundreds of marvelous true anecdotes about the city of Bristol, Virginia, including one hundred pages of ghost lore. The following hilarious account is excerpted, with permission, from that collection. Phillips wrote about a house that bordered East Hill Cemetery back in the days when "outdoor plumbing" was still used. The backside of this particular house's outhouse was only a few inches from a monument marking a grave.

A young couple from Abingdon moved into the house, and everything went well for the husband, except when his mother-in-law came to visit. She was described as a "rather obese and lazy woman, was querulous and nitpicking, and daily gave an abundance of unsolicited and unappreciated advice." Though she constantly complained about the house—it was too close to what she called "that scary old graveyard"—she came often to visit her daughter, and stayed long. Her bedroom faced the cemetery, then largely overgrown with weeds and bushes, and she was terrified of what she called "hants."

It was her habit to retire each evening promptly at nine o'clock, and just before going to bed, she would visit the outhouse. She knew about the sunken grave just in the back of it, and each night as she walked across the yard, she would sing an old ballad in an apparent attempt to drown out any ghostly sounds that might arise from the cemetery. He son-in-law even thought she made the trip with her eyes closed, since she seemed to stagger on the way.

It eventually dawned on the young man that perhaps he could use the old woman's fear to his advantage in getting her to shorten her stays. He conceived a devious plan. He got a neighbor's boy to sneak out behind the outhouse one night. Precisely at nine, he heard the woman singing; then she closed the door and sat down. Suddenly, there was a sharp rapping on the back wall of the outhouse, then a loud moan that turned into a wail. The woman stopped singing and shrieked, "Lordy, what was that?" The boy, in a quivering ghostly voice, replied, "I'm coming in to get you!"

In stark terror, the woman shot up from her seat and didn't even bother to unlatch the door. She crashed into it, knocking it off its hinges onto the ground outside. Because she hadn't even stopped to pull up her underbritches, she leaped over the fallen door like a frog trying to escape from a snake, then hip-hopped smack into the middle of a thorny rosebush. Undaunted by the scratches, she pogo-jumped all the way up onto the porch and through the back door of the house. She then slammed it shut and locked it.

Inside, she ran to her room, packed her bags, and announced she was going to take the late train home to Abingdon. Her quickly obliging son-in-law, biting the tip of his tongue not to laugh out loud, escorted her to the depot on time. There, she dramatically exclaimed that she would not return to that dreadful place until they moved. They did, years later, after the mother-in-law had passed on.

## One More Mother-in-Law Story

Folklore collector Elmer Smith of Harrisonburg relates a last wish that ended on a note of wry humor. A dying woman asked her husband for one last favor before she passed away: for him to let her mother ride with him to her funeral. Without hesitation, he replied, "Why can't she leave earlier? Then she could ride with you!"

## Risen From The Dead!

Carl DeHart, a Martinsville, Virginia, historian associated with the Blue Ridge Library, tells of a humorous yet frightening event that occurred sometime in 1938 on a dairy farm in Henry County. An African American named "Doc" Smith and his aged grandmother lived on the farm. She was described as wraith-like, with long white hair strung down her back. Youngsters in the area referred to her as "the ghost woman."

One morning, in the winter of 1938, when there were five inches of snow on the ground, Doc found his grandmother apparently dead. He could discern no pulse or heartbeat. As was the custom in those days, a "sitting up with the dead" session was held. The grandmother was laid out on a table in the main room of a two-room log cabin with a sheet over her. Close friends and relatives gathered to pay their respects.

As it was freezing cold outside, a fire was going full blast in the fireplace, and everyone was huddled around it with their backs to the table. Suddenly, the sheet began to flutter, and the old woman sat up! She had not died; she had lapsed into a deep coma, and the heat from the fire had somehow revived her. Unnoticed by the others, she slid off the end of the table, walked over to the group, slapped a man on the back, and said, "Sure is cold out tonight, ain't it?"

There was an immediate stampede for the exit. The terrified friends and relatives banged into each other heading for the front door in a crazed dash. Hysterical screams filled the tiny cabin and there was a frantic pile-up at the door as the men and women clawed at each other in a panic trying to get through the narrow opening. One gentleman was so rattled by the old woman's sudden resurrection that he desperately tried to squeeze his overweight body up the chimney, even though the fire was still going.

It was said that it took several days to reassemble the group of would-be mourners to explain what had happened.

## The Tree that Revived a Dead Woman

There is a strikingly similar case to that of the reawakened grandmother. It occurred more than a century ago and was told by Dr. Jim Miller, a folklore historian, as follows: "There's this feller over in Pulaski County whose wife allegedly died. Had the undertaker come for her. They carried the body out the front door on a big board, across the porch, down the steps, and as they went across the yard, headed for the horse-drawn hearse, one of the men slipped and the board banged into a maple tree.

"There was a discernable moan, and the woman's eyes fluttered. They begun to work on her, and she revived up. That woman lived another ten years!

"Then she died for real. When the undertaker come for her this time and started across the yard with her, her husband hollered, 'Uh, boys, watch out for that tree there!'"

## Another "Corpse" that Sat Up

Sometimes, however, the dead really are dead, but the appearance is otherwise. Such a case is related by Mary Daughdrill of Norfolk. She says her grandfather ran a sizable farming operation in the early 1900s at a plantation in southwest Virginia, despite suffering from a very severe physical handicap. He was a hunchback, and his impediment was so great that he was nearly doubled over when he walked. He died in 1915, and morticians had a difficult time fitting him into a casket. Mary says they had to strap him in to get the lid shut. They placed his casket on the back of a wagon and headed to the church for services. The road, however, was deeply rutted and it was a jarring ride.

The church was packed, not only with friends, relatives, and loved ones, but also with a large number of plantation servants who filled the back rows. At one point in the service, a gentleman went over to raise the lid of the coffin so everyone could get a final view of the dearly departed.

But unbeknownst to the brethren, the jolting ride to the church apparently had loosened or broken the straps holding the man down. So when the lid was raised, the body popped bolt upright, which caused instantaneous panic in the church. The building, in fact, was emptied within seconds!

# The Wedding Dress

Was it a premonition or just plain coincidence? Whatever the case, it was highly unusual, and surely qualifies to fall within the shadowy realm of the unknown.

The experience, told anonymously by a woman on the Internet and reported in a southwest Virginia newspaper, is this: Thirty years earlier, the woman was moving from her house to an apartment as she was leaving her second husband. Her first marriage, to her high school sweetheart, had ended tragically after five years when he was killed in an auto accident.

Some of her items were left by mistake in her second husband's house, including her first wedding dress, which she prized. She went back to retrieve them several times but was unsuccessful in that no one would ever answer the door.

Fast forward thirty years: "One Friday," she says, "I was dusting and I happened to look up at a picture of me in that wedding dress, and I was thinking about the dress and how wonderful it would be to have it for my granddaughters. The following Monday I decided to paint some chairs, but had to go to the hardware store to get some paint."

She got in the car and instead of turning left to the store, she for some unexplained reason turned right. She then thought at long as she was headed that way, she would go to a fabric store in that direction for some material to cover the chairs.

But instead of parking in front of the fabric store—again without conscious reason—she pulled in at the other end of a mall. She asked herself why she had done that.

So she began the long walk to the other end of the mall. "As I did," she says, "I passed an antique consignment shop that I had never been in. I decided to go in there. I went in and turned to the right and was looking at some things when I heard a voice say, 'Go in the back!' I turned and went in the back. I looked up and someone had a little booth with a louvered door, and on that door was a dress—my wedding dress!

"I was so stunned, I started shaking. I ran and got the clerk. I asked her to get the dress down because I wanted to buy it. She said, 'Don't you want to know how much it costs?' I said, 'No, I don't care.' The lady asked how I knew it was mine. I told her to look inside and she would see a label. It came from Lazerus, an old dress shop in downtown Roanoke, Virginia. I knew it was mine because when we bought it, it was one of a kind. Isn't that wild? It's the wildest thing that ever happened to me."

The woman concluded by saying, "There is no such thing as coincidence. I was being led there! Even though he [her first husband] has been dead all these years, you just never forget."

When the woman posted her experience on the Internet, another woman responded: "You are right. It was no coincidence. We are guided every day of our lives, although at times we may not realize it, and at other times, like your case, we know we had help. With all the rush in the world today, most of us do not stop to listen."

# Tidewater Virginia

# The Wicked "Witch" of Pungo

She was a devoted wife and mother who loved her family. She was also the most maligned woman in Virginia history, abused and ridiculed for decades, unjustly incarcerated in dank prison cells, and humiliated by the superstitious beliefs and laws of her time. She was reputed to be the Old Dominion's most infamous witch.

Her name was Grace Sherwood.

It was the last decade of the seventeeth century, a time of rampant superstition. Much of this was brought over from Europe, where it was estimated that more than a hundred thousand people had been executed for allegedly practicing witchcraft. The madness spread across the Atlantic Ocean. In the early 1690s, nineteen women, supposed witches, had been hanged, and one man, a suspected warlock, had been pressed to death in Salem, Massachusetts.

The general belief, even among some of the better educated, was that a witch was most often a woman who had sold her body and soul to the devil. For this, she was given special powers that ranged from the incredible to the ridiculous. For example, witches were thought to be able to cast spells that could blight gardens, ruin crops, and cause the injury and sometimes death of farm animals, or even humans. At least they were blamed for such disasters. If a cow suddenly went dry or gave bloody milk, it was a witch's doing. If someone became deathly sick overnight, a witch had "spelled" them. Even marital infidelity was blamed on unsuspecting crones. There are actual cases where ships were disabled in storms at sea off the Virginia coast, and some poor woman on board was labeled as a witch and hanged or drowned. Almost every misfortune that occurred was believed to be caused by the "devil's apprentices."

There was virtually no limit to the extraordinary myths associated with such women. They were thought to have signed a contract with Satan in their own blood. Some contended they took an oath by putting one hand on the top of their heads and the other on the soles of their feet. Each witch could be identified by having certain physical oddities on her body—an unusual abrasion, wart, or mole, generally well hidden. Even more astonishing was the notion that witches could turn themselves into cats, typically black ones, and they supposedly had the power to ride through the air on a broomstick.

Who were these women? Unfortunately, most of them were harmless, but ugly, old, disliked and misunderstood. If an old woman lived alone and kept to herself, she was suspected, especially if a neighbor had recently lost a cow or sheep or if their crops failed. Others believed to be witches were those who might possess strange powers or sensitivities. Such was the case with Grace Sherwood, a simple farmer's wife in Princess Anne County, on land that is now part of Virginia Beach. It is likely Grace had some psychic abilities that confused and frightened others.

The insanity began officially in 1697, when Grace was in her thirties. It is on record that she and her husband, James, filed a suit in court against John and Jane Gisburne, for defamation of character, saying the couple had slandered her, declaring her to be a witch and that she had cast a spell that blighted their crop of cotton. The case was quickly dismissed. Within months, the Sherwoods were back in court, this time seeking a hundred pounds in damages from Anthony and Elizabeth Barnes. As bizarre as it sounds, Elizabeth said Grace had come to their home one night in the form of a black cat, had jumped upon her in bed, driven and whipped her, and had gone out of the room by the keyhole or a crack in the door! Although these charges were also dismissed, Grace and her husband inexplicably were assessed "the cost of attendance and entertainment of nine witnesses for four days."

James Sherwood died in 1701. Four years later, the widowed Grace brought suit against Luke Hill, who she claimed had "assaulted, bruised, maimed and barbarously beaten her to her great damage." Luke's wife, Elizabeth, said that Grace had "bewitched her." Grace asked for fifty pounds in damages, but she was awarded just twenty shillings. Still, it was a technical victory, clearing her name. But it didn't last long.

Soon after, the Hills formally charged Grace with practicing witchcraft. Now, for the first time, she was the defendant. The sheriff was ordered to provide a jury of "discreet and knowing women" to examine Grace. The foreperson of the jury was none other than Elizabeth Barnes, who had earlier maligned Grace. The twelve women strip-searched Grace and found "several spots" on her body, like warts and "undoubtedly very suspicious"

Actual court papers record this incident: "Whereas a Complaint have been to this Dug Court by Luke Hill & his wife yt. one Grace Sherwood of ye. County was and have been a long time suspected of witch-craft & have been as such represented wherefore ye. Sherr. At ye. last court was ordr: som a Jury of women to ye. Court to serch her on ye sd. Suspicion she assenting to ye. Same—and after ye. Jury was impannelled and sworn & sent out to make due inquirery & inspection into all cercurstances after a mature consideration they bring in yr Verditt: were of ye. Jury have sercath; Grace Sherwood & found two things like titts with several other spots. . . ."

In those unenlightened days, it was thought that the special mark of a witch was commonly a third pap or "teat" in an abnormal position on a woman's body. This was said to be withered and senseless except when sucked by the devil. The reverend John Bell of Gladsmuir explained: "This mark is sometimes like a little Teate, sometimes like a bluish spot; and I myself have seen it on the body of a confessing witch, like a little power mark of a bleak color, somewhat hard, and withal insensible, so as it did not bleed when I pricked it."

Now, the Princess Anne court didn't know what to do. It was a precedent-setting case. Wisely, they referred it to the Governor's Council in Williamsburg. This august body then passed it back to the original court in Princess Anne. It seemed like no one wanted to rule on such a controversial matter. Court records reveal what happened next: "Being of opinion yt. there is great cause of suspicion doe therefore ordr. Yt. ye. Sherr. Take ye. said Grace Sherwood into his safe custody until she shall give bond & security for her appearance to ye. next court." The sheriff was ordered to search Grace's house and "all suspicious places, carefully for all Images & such things as may any way strengthen the suspicion."

It was then determined that Grace should be subjected to a quaint, time-honored trial to determine if she was a witch or not. It was called "witch ducking." The theory was this: If you tied up a suspected witch with a rope secured around her right thumb and left big toe, and left thumb and right big toe, and threw her into a body of water and she swam or floated, she was indeed a witch! If she sank, she was not, and if she was lucky, she would be pulled from the water before drowning. How ludicrous was such a practice? One historian pointed out that when the suspected witch drowned, she would have the satisfaction, in the next world, of knowing that she had been vindicated in this world.

Remarkably, this trial by water was delayed once because, of all things, it was too rainy! Some said it was the devil that caused this postponement. Finally, on Wednesday, July 10, 1706, at 10 A.M., Grace was brought to a spot on Lynnhaven Bay. The sheriff, with "boats and men took ye sd Grace forth with & put her into the water above man's depth." As crowds of curious spectators looked on, Grace was unceremoniously dunked into the water.

She surfaced, somehow freed of her rope restraints, and swam to the shore. She was thus deemed a witch! Five women then again searched the poor woman and declared under oath that "she is not like ym nor noe other woman yt they know of." Grace was then jailed in irons to await sentencing.

But this is where the recorded documents end. Grace Sherwood's name does not appear in court again until 1733, when she filed her will. She died in 1740. Most historians theorize that Grace languished in jail for a relatively short time; then, since officials did not know what to do with her, she was released. Apparently, she was never again accused of being a witch, or at least not officially.

## The Fantasies

Grace's death did not stop the legends that her ill-fated life spawned, supernatural traditions that were once believed by some and have been faithfully told and retold in articles and books over the past three hundred years. Here are examples: Grace was cooking one evening and needed some rosemary. She went to Lynnhaven Bay, commandeered a ship, and sailed to England and back in a day with the needed spice. Old-timers say rosemary never grew in Princess Anne County until that time. There also is a site at Lynnhaven Bay, where Grace was taken for the dunking, on which allegedly no grass has ever grown since.

Perhaps the best-known, most often repeated, and most outlandish tale is about a time when Grace was in Currituck County, North Carolina. A group of men were headed to a frolic by boat and she asked them to take her with them. When they refused, she warned them she would get there before they did. While crossing Currituck Sound, the men spotted a giant egg bobbing on top of the waves. As they arrived on shore, the egg washed up, cracked open, and Grace, in her Sunday-best clothes, stepped out and laughed at the shocked men.

There have been many other preposterous legends associated with Grace Sherwood over the past three-plus centuries. But none are really needed. The true story of her real-life ordeal is strange enough in itself. It is also why a popular street in Virginia Beach is today known as Witch Duck Road!

## A Tragic Toast at Brandon

In a book on the historic homes and gardens of Virginia, it is written about Brandon Plantation that "It does not seem possible that so much loveliness can belong to one old house." Boxwood hedges, more than a century old, flank this manor home on a 4,500-acre farm located in Prince George County, on the south side of the James River between Surry and Hopewell. Here, a dazzling array of flowers in every hue of the rainbow gracefully coexists with giant elms, ancient yews, hollies, tulip poplars, dogwoods, redbuds and varieties of magnolias, pecans, oaks, horse chestnuts, hickories, persimmons, hawthorns, and locusts to form magnificent gardens.

The estate dates to 1616, when a vast grant of land was made to Capt. John Martin, who accompanied John Smith on his first voyage to Virginia. In 1720, the property was acquired by Nathaniel Harrison. The main part of the house was built in 1765 by Nathaniel Harrison II as a wedding present for his son, Benjamin, who was a friend of Thomas Jefferson.

During the latter part of the eighteenth century, and for most of the nineteenth, Brandon was a prime site for the gala social life enjoyed by the landed gentry. Lavish parties, dances and weddings were held here for the rich. Well-known gentlemen and ladies arrived in ornate coaches, or by boat from the north side of the river, from such great mansions as Shirley, Berkeley, and Westover. It was from such an aura of refined gaiety that the main character in what evolved into a haunting tragedy emerged.

Her name was Jane Evelyn Harrison, the eighteen-year-old daughter of William Byrd Harrison of Williamsburg. She has been described as a charming heiress endowed with position and beauty, with capricious blue eyes and a winning smile, and she used every feminine wile she could summon to entrap and smash the hearts of young men. She was a real-life Scarlett O'Hara.

It was at a typically jubilant spring dance at Brandon that Jane met and immediately entranced a young Frenchman named Pierre Bondurant. He fell hopelessly in love with the fickle belle, and repeatedly proposed marriage to her. By applying feminine mystique beyond her years, she left Pierre more or less dangling. She told him, as he was leaving for a lengthy trip to Paris, that such a union would be possible only with the expressed approval of her father, knowing full well that this would be all but impossible. Pierre was persistent, suggesting that they elope to France, but Jane demurred, saying that she planned to spend the summer at Brandon partying with her friends.

Saddened, but ever hopeful, Pierre departed for Paris. He had hardly been there a month when he received a letter from a friend, the news of which devastatingly tore at his very fiber. William Byrd Harrison had announced the engagement of Jane. She was to wed Ralph Fitzhugh Cocke of Bacon's Castle in late November. The wedding was to be one of the grandest events of the year. It was to be held at Brandon so as to accommodate more than a hundred guests, including, surprisingly, Pierre Bondurant. And so, on the last day of November, a sumptuous feast was held, featuring the finest foods and the best wines and liquors in the commonwealth.

Curiously, Pierre asked the groom if he could propose the first toast at the wedding dinner and his request was granted. "Whatever fate may be," he said, "and this day alone will tell, may both of you be happy and free from sorrow, malice and ill." No one could imagine at the time what fate Pierre had in mind. The wedding took place at 4 P.M., and was followed by an extravagant reception.

At one point during the festivities, Pierre pulled Jane aside, handed her a glass of champagne, and asked her to exchange toasts with him. Delighted that he seemed to show no lingering bitterness from their past fling, she agreed, and they each drank to the other's happiness. Just then Ralph walked up, unnoticed by the couple, and overheard Pierre offer a strange poem to Jane: "Twas you I loved when we first met. I loved you then and I love you yet; 'tis vain for me to forget, Lo! Both of us could die before sunset."

Obviously embarrassed when he realized Ralph had heard him, Pierre gulped down his champagne, made excuses, and nervously left the house. By the time all but the houseguests had left, Jane had become deathly ill and collapsed on the drawing room floor, gasping for breath. She was whisked to an upstairs bedroom and died that evening. Although it wasn't known then, she had been poisoned. A veil of silence and sadness descended on everyone.

Oddly, as Jane's body was being prepared for burial, it was discovered that her wedding ring was missing. No one could shed any light on this mystery, and she was laid to rest. A few days later, a messenger arrived from Williamsburg with the shocking news that Pierre Bondurant had been found dead in his carriage when it arrived in Williamsburg on the night of the wedding. Even more discomforting was the fact that Jane's wedding ring had been found—in Pierre's pocket! The mistress of Brandon, Elizabeth Richardson Harrison, Jane's aunt, declared in an extraordinarily peculiar gesture that the ring now bore a curse, and she had it embedded in the plaster on the ceiling above the spot where Jane had fallen.

During the years following, there were periodic reports from residents, guests, and servants of seeing a wispy apparition of a young woman in a flowing white gown who seemed to appear only in late November. Brandon slowly began gaining a reputation as being haunted. In fact, when Helen Lynne Thomas became mistress of the plantation a full two generations after the tragedy, the real estate agent had casually referred to a "resident ghost."

That fall, Helen met the spectral being firsthand. It was on a stormy, dark night as she was walking past the family cemetery. Amidst the weathered old tombstones, she got a glimpse of a wraith-like figure drifting toward the main house. She trembled with fear, nearly fainted, then regained her composure and hurried into the great hall. There, she heard a thud that sounded like something heavy had fallen in the adjacent drawing room. She walked across the hall, opened the door, and saw that some plaster had crashed down from the ceiling.

Then, as her eyes adjusted to the darkness, she saw something else—the same ethereal, white-robed phantom she had seen outside. It appeared to hover about the room for a few seconds and then settled over the pile of plaster as if it were searching for something. Helen could hardly breathe. When either the door or a loose floorboard creaked, the figure straightened up, slid toward the door, and vanished.

As it did, Helen screamed, and then fainted dead away. When she was aroused more than an hour later, she told members of her family and the servants who had rushed to her what had happened. It was then that one of the servants, Hattie McCoy, told her about Jane Harrison and Pierre Bondurant. Hattie's grandmother had been at Brandon on that fateful wedding day.

After she recovered, Helen sorted through the fallen plaster and found a blackened, tarnished wedding ring! She had it suspended from the ceiling by a small wire several inches long. It can still be seen there today.

## The Heartbroken Wraith of Westover

Two large metallic eagles adorn the gateposts leading into Westover Plantation in Charles City County. The estate is halfway between Williamsburg and Richmond, set majestically along a beautiful stretch of the James River. Built early in the eighteenth century, the house is considered an outstanding example of Georgian architecture. Westover was, for generations, the ancestral home of the William Byrd family, one of the most powerful and influential clans in the colonies.

The plantation was the scene of lavish social entertainment among the more affluent colonists during the eighteenth century. Great parties, some lasting for days, were held here with the rich and famous as frequent guests. But the house is also filled with sadness and tragedy, and for centuries has been said to be haunted.

If there is such a thing as a benevolent spirit, or at least one who is determined not to frighten those who experience it, then there is no better example than the gentle, almost fragile ghost of Evelyn Byrd. Though she has been dead for more than 250 years, her apparition still occasionally reappears here, a wraith-like figure most often dressed in white, sad and haunting, as if seeking the happiness that eluded her in life so long ago.

Born in 1707, Evelyn was a bright child, a bit spoiled, precocious, and high-spirited. She was the daughter of William Byrd II, master of Westover and one of the most prominent statesmen of his time—secretary of the Virginia colony for years, adviser to the governor, founder of the city of Richmond, wealthy landowner, and country squire.

When she was ten, Evelyn's father took her to England for proper schooling. There she flowered into a beautiful young woman, with porcelain-white skin, shining chestnut hair, slanting, almost Oriental blue-green eyes, and an enigmatic, Mona Lisa-like smile. It was in London that Evelyn fell deeply in love with a handsome Englishman, Charles Morduant, the grandson of Lord Peterborough. Her father violently objected to the romance, telling her that if she proceeded with it, "as to any expectation you may fondly entertain of a fortune from me, you are not to look for one brass farthing. Nay, besides all that, I will avoid the sight of you as a creature detested!"

And so, against the desires of her heart, Evelyn returned to Westover in 1726, a different young woman. The spark of her personality was diminished, and she spent long hours by herself, withdrawn, reclusive. A number of potential suitors from nearby plantations paid her visits over the next few years, but she spurned them all, much to the chagrin of her father, who referred to her as "the antique virgin."

She confided only in her close friend, Anne Carter Harrison, of the adjacent Berkeley Plantation. They would walk in the formal gardens and talk among the giant boxwoods, passing the afternoons away. It was amid a poplar grove one day that the two young ladies made a secret pact. Whichever one died first would try to return to visit "in such a fashion not to frighten anyone." Did Evelyn have a premonition? Perhaps, for soon after she passed away, some said of a broken heart.

On her lone tombstone was inscribed the following: "Here in the sleep of peace reposes the body of Evelyn Byrd. The various and excellent endowments of nature, improved and perfected by an accomplished education, formed here, for the happiness of her friends, for the ornament of her country. Alas, Reader! We can detain nothing, however valued, from unrelenting death. Beauty, fortune, or valued honour! So here is proof! And be reminded by this awful tomb that every worldly comfort fleets away. Excepting only, what arises from imitating the virtues of our friends and the contemplation of their happiness. To which, God was pleased to call this Lady on the 13th day of November, 1737, in the 29th year of her age."

For months, the saddened Anne Harrison did not venture among the trails and trees she and Evelyn had so often walked together. But one day she finally did go out to the poplar grove and felt a presence. She turned and saw a figure approaching. It was Evelyn. She was dressed in white, "dazzling in ethereal loveliness. She drifted forward a few steps, kissed her hand to the beholder, smiling happily—and vanished!"

In the following generations, many others, among them Westover owners and guests, have captured fleeting glimpses of Evelyn's apparition. In 1856, for example, one woman told John Seldens, who then lived in the manor house, that she had awakened in the night and found a young lady standing in the room who quickly went through a closed door. The woman described the lady and her dress. "Oh, yes," Mr. Seldens remarked, "that was Evelyn Byrd."

In the early 1900s, a workman was dispatched to do some repair work in an upstairs bedroom. Minutes later, he came running down the stairs, saying to the owner, "You didn't tell me there was a young lady up there!" He had seen her combing her hair before a mirror. When he and the owner went back upstairs, there was no one there. In December 1929, a guest of Richard Crane, who owned the plantation then, reported seeing the "filmy, nebulous and cloudy figure of a woman, so transparent no features could be distinguished, only the gauzy texture of a woman's form." It seemed, the guest said, "to be floating a little above the lawn."

In fact, when the Cranes bought Westover in 1920, Mrs. Crane said, "Oh dear, we'll never get any help because of the ghost." But they had no trouble, because even though the legend of Evelyn's reappearances was well known throughout the county, servants believed her to be a friendly spirit. And indeed, the servants too experienced the phenomenon. One old butler was coming through a narrow passageway in the hall when he saw a lady. Presuming it to be Mrs. Crane, he stepped aside to let her pass. She dissolved before his eyes.

More recently, a Mr. Bagby, who lives in a small house between the mansion and the graveyard where Evelyn is buried, was in his kitchen one evening when he saw a woman at eye level outside on the lawn. Thinking it was Mrs. Bruce Fisher, then mistress of Westover, he went outside to say hello. There was no one there. Then he realized that if he had seen the woman at eye level, since his kitchen is raised, she would have had to be at least ten feet tall!

But of all who have claimed sightings of Evelyn, no one yet has offered a reasonable explanation as to why her restless spirit would want to periodically return to a place that apparently caused her so much unhappiness in life. Some have speculated that ghosts come back to the world of the living to carry out some unfinished business. Could it possibly be that Evelyn reappears to announce that she has found in death the bliss she had been denied in life?

# The True Story of "Taps"

It is, without question, one of the most haunting melodies ever written. No matter where or when its mournful refrain is played, tears stream down the cheeks of those who hear it.

This is "Taps"—the emotion-wringing, twenty-four-note dirge, always performed by a single bugler, at military funerals, wreath layings, and memorials. Its colorful history involves intrigue and conflicting theories of its origin and its composer, including a heart-rending legend, the true story, and even a ghostly encounter.

There is no dispute, however, that the first sounding of "Taps" took place here in Virginia, at the site of Berkeley Plantation (then known as Harrison's Landing) in Charles City County during the Peninsula Campaign of the Civil War in July 1862. The fierce fighting of the Seven Days' Battles had just been concluded and the Union Army of the

Potomac, under the command of Gen. George McClellan, encamped on the grounds of Berkeley, one hundred thousand strong.

This is the point where fact and legend part ways. According to a long-standing tradition, Capt. Robert Ellicombe one night heard the moans of a wounded soldier lying in the field nearby. Risking his own life, he crawled on his stomach through some still-occasional gunfire to reach the distressed man. He pulled him back to the Union lines, only then discovering that it was a Confederate soldier—and he was dead!

The captain then lit a lantern and went numb with shock. In the dim light he saw the boy's face. It was his son! Unbeknownst to Ellicombe, his son had enlisted in the Southern army after previously studying music. The next morning, heartbroken, the captain asked permission of his superiors to give his son a full military burial service, with a group of bandmembers to play. Because it involved an enemy soldier, his request was partially denied. He was told he could have only one musician.

He chose a bugler, then asked him to play a series of musical notes he had found on a piece of paper in the pocket of his dead son's uniform. This wish was granted, and "Taps" was played.

That's the sad legend that has endured for nearly 150 years. The only problem is that there is no authentic evidence to support it. Army historians who have done thorough research on the subject say no such Capt. Robert Ellicombe can be found on the roster rolls of the Army of the Potomac.

What, then, is the true story? The historians say it is this: At that same time and place, July 1862 at Harrison's Landing, there was a short melodic piece used to signal "lights out" to the troops at the end of the day. Union general Daniel A. Butterfield, who was later awarded the Medal of Honor for his courage in the Civil War, apparently didn't like the notes being used for this, and began scribbling down some of his own, written in pencil on the back of an envelope. He then summoned a bugler. Several variations were then played until Butterfield finally approved. "Taps" resulted. What was most strange about all this was the fact that the general could not write a single note of music! He made the arrangement solely by ear. Butterfield later explained: "The call of 'Taps' did not seem to be as smooth, melodious and musical as it should be, and I called in someone who could write music, and practiced changes in the call until it suited my ear."

Thus, while Butterfield is not recognized by historians as the true composer of "Taps," since the notes were revised from existing ones, he is recognized as the "father" of the song.

The first known use of "Taps" at a funeral occurred during the Peninsula Campaign in 1862, when a captain of the Union 2nd Artillery ordered it played for the burial of a cannoneer killed in action. At the time, the tradition was to fire three volleys of shots, but in this instance, since the enemy was so close, it was thought this might trigger further fighting, so "Taps" was played instead. It has since become the standard for military funerals.

That first sounding of "Taps" at a funeral is commemorated in a stained glass window at the Chapel of the Centurion (the Old Post Chapel) at Fort Monroe, Virginia. It is based on a painting by Sidney King that shows a lone bugler and a flag at half-staff. Interestingly, in that picture, a drummer boy stands beside the bugler. The grandson of that drummer boy, Malcolm Jamieson, later purchased Berkeley Plantation and had a monument dedicated to "Taps" erected at the site.

## The Ghost Bugler

There is a paranormal footnote to the "Taps" story. It occurred at a pre-Civil War house in Fauquier County known as "Roland," and was first documented by Marguerite DuPont Lee in her 1930 book *Ghosts of Virginia*. Apparently, the Civil War-era owner was a Southern sympathizer, and was said to have successfully hidden wounded Confederate soldiers in a secret room in the house.

Some twenty years later, according to Mrs. Lee's informant, four women were in the house one night and the subject of the hiding place came up. They decided to look for it.

In a bedroom closet they found a trapdoor, opened it, and discovered the secret space, easily large enough for a man to stand or lie down. One of the ladies then said, "As we four stood silent and awestruck, suddenly just out of the air close at hand a bugle blew clear and sweet. It sounded 'Taps'! Four of us heard it, and none ever forgot the wonderful experience. We knew there was no man within miles of Roland that night!"

# Baffling Revelations at Bacon's Castle

It was, to the Virginia colonists, an ominous sign of impending disaster. It occurred sometime during the latter months of 1675. A great comet appeared in the sky, sweeping across the heavens and trailing a bright orange tail of fire. Soon after this eerie phenomenon came the flight of tens of thousands of passenger pigeons. For days, they blanketed the sky, blotting out the sun. Then, in the spring of 1676, a plague of locusts ravaged the colony, devouring every plant in sight and stripping the trees of their budding leaves.

To the colonists, the comet was the worst sign. Many remembered that another comet had streaked across the horizon just before the terrible Indian massacre of 1644. Because they believed in such spectral omens, it was no real surprise to them when the following year, 1676, featured one of the bloodiest and most notorious chapters in Virginia history.

It began on a quiet summer Sunday. Some colonists passing by the Stafford County plantation of Thomas Mathew while on their way to church discovered the overseer, Robert Hen, lying in a pool of blood. He was mortally wounded, but before he expired he managed to gasp, "Doegs! Doegs!" The words struck fear in the ears of the passersby, for that was the name of a tribe of Indians known for their fierce attacks on white men and women.

And so, the seeds were sown for what was to lead to the largest and most violent insurrection of the colonial era up to that time—Bacon's Rebellion. Dashing young Nathaniel Bacon had arrived in Virginia only three years earlier. Well-educated, he has been described by biographers as "a slender, attractive, dark haired man with an impetuous, sometimes fiery temper, and a persuasive tongue." Above all else, he was a natural leader.

While Gov. William Berkeley remained inactive and inattentive in Jamestown, planters sought out Bacon to lead retaliatory strikes against the marauding Indians. When his own plantation was attacked and his overseer killed, Bacon agreed. He proved to be a skilled and capable military commander. On one march his forces drove the Pamunkey tribe deep into Dragon's Swamp. Later, Bacon overpowered the Susquehannocks, killing one hundred Indians and capturing others.

Berkeley, furious at the unauthorized raids launched by this rebellious group, dispatched his own troops to capture Bacon and his men. For the next several weeks, the two men waged a cat-and-mouse game that involved daring, intrigue, and bloodshed. At one point, Bacon surrendered, was brought before Berkeley, and was forgiven when he repented. But then he escaped, returned with a force of six hundred men, and captured Jamestown, demanding a commission to fight the Indians. With no other choice under the show of arms, Berkeley granted the wishes, but when Bacon set out again chasing the Indians, the governor repudiated all agreements and sent his troops after the rebels.

After several skirmishes, Bacon recaptured Jamestown and had it sacked and burned to the ground. Berkeley, who had retreated to the Eastern Shore of Virginia, meanwhile was regrouping his forces for a final and decisive confrontation. It never came to pass. Bacon had suffered an attack of malaria and fell critically ill in Gloucester. He died of dysentery there on October 16, 1676, at the age of twenty-nine. With the leader lost, the rebellion fell apart and Berkeley's forces captured many of Bacon's men. A large number of them were hanged, continuing for several more months the tragedy foreboded by the appearance of the comet.

For a short time in 1676, about seventy of Bacon's followers occupied a large brick mansion in Surry County, just across the James River from Jamestown. It was then called "Allen's Brick House," but has since been known as "Bacon's Castle." Now operated by the Association for the Preservation of Virginia Antiquities, this imposing brick structure was built some time after 1655. It stands amidst a large grove of oaks. There are two expansive, paneled first-floor rooms; two more rooms on the second floor; and what has been described as a "dungeon-like" attic on the third.

Accounts of hauntings at the castle have been passed along for more than 350 years. Many of those who have experienced strange sightings, sounds, and presences believe they are manifestations of the devil. Others have felt it may be the spectral return of Bacon's men, still seeking redress of the grievances they held against Governor Berkeley and the colony so many years ago. Whoever or whatever is causing them, the happenings that have occurred here through the centuries have taken many forms.

Consider the revelations of Mrs. Charles Walker Warren, whose family once owned the castle. When she was a young woman, early in the twentieth century, a visiting Baptist preacher who was spending the night stayed up late reading his Bible. Sometime in the wee hours of the morning he heard footsteps descending the stairs from the second floor. Someone or something, he said later, opened the parlor door and walked past him. He saw no one, but felt the strong sensation that he was not alone. Then, mysteriously, a red velvet-covered rocking chair began moving back and forth as if someone were sitting in it, though the preacher could see no one. He shouted, "Get thee behind me Satan," and the rocking stopped immediately.

Mrs. Warren and a number of guests reported hearing footsteps on the stairs late at night many times. One guest distinctly heard "horrible moaning" in the attic directly above her bedroom, though she was assured the next morning that no one could have been in the attic. Once, Mrs. Warren came into the downstairs parlor and found the glass globe from a favorite nickel-plated lamp had been shattered into tiny fragments. Yet, strangely, not a drop of kerosene from it had spilled onto the carpet. Also, a leather-bound dictionary had been "flung" across the room onto a sofa, and the iron stand upon which it rested had been hurled to a distant corner.

Richard Reynolds, curator of the castle from 1973 to 1981, used to tell of the time one morning at 3:30 when he was awakened by the sound of his two-year-old son laughing in his crib in an upstairs bedroom. "Daddy, where's the lady?" the child asked Reynolds when he reached him. "What lady?" Reynolds said. "The lady with the white hands. She was tickling me," his son replied.

On another occasion, a tour guide was standing in the great hall one morning before the castle opened to the public when "something" ran by her from the outside passageway, went through the hall, and dashed into another chamber on the other side. She heard feet running on the hardwood floor but did not see anyone. As the sound of the steps was passing by, something brushed her arm and gave her a chill.

These and other such incidents, however, merely serve as a preamble to the most shocking supernatural appearance at Bacon's Castle, one that reappears regularly at varying intervals and which has been seen and documented by a number of credible witnesses from several different generations. It takes the form, say those who have seen it and been terrified, of a "pulsating red ball of fire." It apparently rises from the graveyard of Old Lawne's Creek Church, a few hundred yards south of the castle, soars about thirty or forty feet in the air, always on dark nights, and then moves slowly northward. It seems to float or hover above the castle grounds before slowly moving back toward the ivy-covered walls of the ruins of the church, where it disappears.

One eyewitness, G. I. Price, a former caretaker at the castle, described the phenomenon to a local newspaper reporter: "I was standing," he said, "waiting in the evening for my wife to shut up the chickens, when a light about the size of a jack-me-lantern came out of the old loft door and went up a little. It traveled by just floating along about 40 feet in the air toward the direction of the old graveyard." Skeptics, of course, contend that the fireball is merely some form of physical manifestation that can be explained scientifically. But those who have seen it, including members of the Warren family and others, could never be convinced that it was not of a mystical, spiritual nature. Some even called it an appearance of the "Prince of Darkness."

One guest reportedly had the wits frightened out of him one night when the fiery red ball sailed into his bedroom at the castle, circled over his bed several times, and then disappeared out the open window. A former owner of the building told of seeing the fireball blaze overhead and enter the barn. Fearful of it igniting his stored hay, he ran toward the barn. Then the bright, glowing light turned and went back toward the graveyard. In the 1930s, members of a local Baptist church, meeting at an evening revival session, collectively saw the strange sphere. It is said the praying that night was more intense than ever before in the congregation's memory.

One legend says that a servant a century or so ago was late with his chores; as he was walking home in the darkness, the red object overcame him, burst, and covered him with a hellish mass of flames, burning him to death.

What is the origin of this eerie fireball, and why does it reappear every so often? One theory is that the light was somehow tied to hidden money in the castle. Some money was found years ago when two men were removing some bricks from the fireplace hearth in the second floor's west room. Apparently, only a few people ever saw or knew about the money, and since it was discovered, no one has seen the light.

Many old-timers, however, prefer to believe that the fireball is a periodic reminder of the brilliant comet that flashed across the same skies more than three hundred years ago, forewarning that tragedy and bloodshed would soon follow. There are, in fact, those who are convinced that spirits frequent Bacon's Castle to this day, sad spirits from long ago, still seeking relief from their troubled and grief-stricken past.

## The Puzzling Riddle of the Refusal Room

It has been described by some architectural historians as the most beautiful house in America. Indeed, the stately Georgian mansion, shaded by a row of enormous old tulip poplar trees overlooking the James River, is a magnificent building even though it is more than 250 years old. Carter's Grove, in James City County west of Newport News, is rich in history. Construction of the house began in 1750 on a 1,400-acre tract of land bought by legendary Virginia colonist Robert "King" Carter, one of the wealthiest and most influential men of his time. He chose the site for his daughter, Elizabeth Carter.

It was a showpiece residence and many lavish and memorable parties and dinners were held here for the wealthy and famous of eighteenth-century Virginia. Like other plantation homes along the river, Carter's Grove has its share of colorful legends and anecdotes. There are, for example, deep scars in the handsome handcrafted stair railing leading up from the front hall on the first floor. They were made by a British cavalryman, Banastre Tarleton, during the Revolutionary War. He rode his horse up the stairway, hacking the balustrade with his saber as he ascended!

If ever there was a site ripe for spiritual hauntings by restless souls, it well could be Carter's Grove. That's because a great tragedy occurred here more than 350 years ago. Archeologists, searching for eighteenth-century artifacts, uncovered the remnants of a colony of early settlers dating back to 1619. The settlement was known as Martin's Hundred, and all residents were massacred by Indians in 1622.

Through the years there have been a number of strange, unexplained occurrences. Phantom footsteps often were noticed. An old gardener said he occasionally heard a woman playing a harp in an upstairs room. No known source for the musical interludes was ever found.

But it is in a downstairs drawing room that the "real" ghost of Carter's Grove resides. Longtime servants at the mansion are convinced that the room is haunted. It was here that a pretty young woman, Mary Cary, allegedly turned down a proposal for marriage in the mid-eighteenth century from an ardent suitor—George Washington! Some years later, in the same room, Thomas Jefferson offered his hand to the fair Rebecca Burwell. He, too, was rejected. This parlor subsequently became known as the "Refusal Room."

In the years since, peculiar things have kept happening in the room. Most notably, whenever white carnations are placed in it, they are mysteriously ripped to shreds overnight and scattered about. No one knows who does this, or why only white carnations are chosen, and only the ones in this particular parlor. Other flowers in the house remain untouched.

In 1939, the Associated Press carried a nationwide article on the phenomenon, quoting Mrs. Archibald McCrea, then owner of Carter's Grove. She said at the time that it was true that something was coming in at night to "blight her blooms." Traps were set for mice but they were never sprung. John Coleman, an elderly butler, said it was "ghosts!" No one at the site, past or present, has offered any semblance of an explanation for such curious activity. It also is highly doubtful that the torn petals were the work of a prankster, because when the house is open, tour guides are always in or near the room, and when the house is closed at night, security guards keep a close watch. There are alarm systems throughout that would be triggered by anyone prowling about.

Could it be the spirit of one of the two famous spurned lovers, unable to contain his rage at rejection? Some believe it more likely may be the return of one of the women who refused. It is said that when Mary Cary watched the triumphant Continental Army enter the area after the Yorktown surrender in 1781, commanded by General Washington, she was so overcome by chagrin that she fainted dead away in her husband's arms. So it is speculated that it may be her spirit that sometimes slips into the house late at night to tear the carnations in a fit of anger at what might have been.

## Good Samaritan Spirits

The following incident is excerpted from Herenood Carrington's 1920 book *Phantasms of the Dead*.

"In 1664, Captain Thomas Rogers, commander of a ship called *The Society*, was bound on a voyage from London to Virginia. The vessel being sent light to Virginia, for a loading of tobacco, carried little freight in her outward hold. One day they made an observation. The mates and officers brought their books and cast up their reckonings with the captain, to see how near they were to the coast of America. They all agreed that they were a hundred leagues from the capes of Virginia. Upon these customary reckonings, and heaving the lead and finding no ground at a hundred fathoms, they set the watch and the captain turned in. The weather was fine; a moderate gale of wind blew from the coast; so that the ship might have run about 12 or 13 leagues in the night after the captain was in his cabin.

"He fell asleep, and slept very soundly for about three hours, when he woke, and lay still till he heard the second mate turn out and relieve the watch. He then called to his first mate, as he was going off watch, and asked him how all things fared. The mate answered that all was well, though the gale had freshened, and they were running at a great rate; but it was a fair wind and a fair, clear night.

"The captain then went to sleep again. About an hour after, he dreamed that someone was pulling him, and bade him turn out and look around. He, however, lay still and went to sleep once more; but was suddenly reawakened. This occurred several times; and, though he knew not what was the reason, yet he found it impossible to go to sleep anymore. Still, he heard the vision say, 'Turn out and look around!'

"The captain lay in this state of uneasiness nearly two hours, until finally he felt compelled to don his great coat and go on deck. All was well; it was a fine, clear night. The men saluted him; and the captain called out, 'How's she heading?' 'Southwest by south, sir,' answered the mate; 'fair for the coast, and the wind east by north.'

"'Very good,' said the captain, and as he was about to return to his cabin, something stood by him and said, 'Heave the lead!' Upon hearing this, the captain said to the second mate, 'When did you heave the lead? What water have you?' 'About an hour ago, sir,' replied the mate; '60 fathoms.'

"'Heave again,' the captain commanded. When the lead was cast, they had ground at 11 fathoms! This surprised them all; but much more when, at the next cast, it came up seven fathoms. Upon this, the captain, in a fright, bid them to put the helm alee, and about ship, all hands were ordered to back the sails, as usual in such cases.

"The proper orders being observed, the ship 'stayed,' and came about, but before the sails filled, she had but four fathoms and a half water under her stern. As soon as she filled and stood off, they had seven fathoms again, and at the next cast, 11 fathoms, and so on to 20 fathoms. They then stood off to seaward; all the rest of the watch, to get into deep water, till daybreak, when, being a clear morning, the capes of Virginia were in fair view under their stern, and but a few leagues distant.

"Had they stood on, but one cable-length further, as they were going, they would have been ashore, and certainly lost their ship, if not their lives—all through the erroneous reckonings of the previous day. Who or what was it that waked the captain and bade him save the ship?

"That, he has never been able to tell."

## A Spectral Helping Hand

The following is recounted with the permission of Lillie Gilbert, Belinda Nash, and Deni Norred-Williams, co-authors of *Ghost Witches and Weird Tales of Virginia Beach*.

For decades, one of the scariest stretches of highway in eastern Virginia has been a two-way corridor that cuts through the wetlands linking the cities of Virginia Beach and Chesapeake. It is called Elbow Road, and is part of the 1,500-acre Stumpy Lake Natural Area. According to the authors, the region "has seen more than its share of tragic accidents, and, indeed, has been the depository for several murder victims through the years." This chilling background, combined with the dark remoteness of Elbow Road, has made it an ideal spot for teenagers to scare their unaware dates. It also has spawned a number of spooky legends.

Among them is the ghost of a woman who once lived on the road and was thought to have been murdered, although her body was never found. Witnesses have told of lights turning on and off in the vicinity of her house, even though the house was long ago torn down.

Also, supposedly, if one sits still at a certain curve at midnight, child-size footprints unexplainably materialize, as if someone were walking forward. It is believed to be the spirit of a little girl who drowned in the lake while fishing with her father.

But of all the incidents, perhaps the most curious occurred a few years ago and is vividly remembered by Brenda Scolamiero, who grew up on Elbow Road. Late one night, there was a frantic knock on the family's front door. It was a young woman. She was wet and bleeding and her clothes were muddy and torn. Brenda's parents wrapped the girl in a sheet and comforted her.

She then told them her story. She worked at a nearby convenience store, and after her shift was over that evening, she had accepted a ride home from a male customer. As they drove down the darkened Elbow Road, the man pulled his car off the road next to the lake at an isolated spot, and then attempted to assault her. Terrified, she ran from the car and plunged into the lake, cutting her feet on debris on the water's bottom. She began screaming. The man, fearing exposure, drove off, leaving her struggling in the swampy morass.

Suddenly, a hand reached out from nowhere, and helped the girl climb out of the lake. Without thinking where the aid had come from, she ran, cut and bleeding, to the nearest house. Only later did she stop to consider what had happened in the lake. Who had helped her?

Where did he or she come from? And what happened to the person, or whatever it was?

The good Samaritan was never found. Strangest of all was the fact that when the site of the incident was examined, only the footprints of the escaping woman were found. There were no other tracks leading out of the muddy lake!

# A Death Prophecy

The following, excerpted here, was found in an unpublished manuscript in the archives of the Library of Virginia in Richmond. It was written sometime in the late 1800s by Louisa Emmerson, and tells of the singular, inexplicable fate of a young clergyman in Portsmouth.

"It was many years ago that in a portion of the county called Port Norfolk, there was what was known as the Glebe. The earliest point of interest that I know is that it was bought in 1761. Now, at this old Glebe farm, there lived, at the time of which I write, the second rector of Trinity Church—Parson Braidfoot. He had been a chaplain in the Continental Army. The Glebe house was in attractive style, situated about 200 feet from the waterfront. Back of the house was a beautiful set of woodlands.

"One lovely morning, as the Parson was taking his usual stroll through the wooded part of his farm, he is said to have encountered a Ghost, who told him that on a certain date, he would pass to the world beyond. The day named happened to be the birthday of the Parson."

A more definitive and slightly different description of this meeting with the specter was written in 1930, by Marguerite DuPont Lee in *Virginia Ghosts*. "Driving home one evening," she wrote, "his horse stopped suddenly and Mr. Braidfoot perceived an apparition standing in the road. Astonished, but not unduly alarmed, he awaited in silence some further demonstration from this spirit from another sphere. The Rev. Braidfoot's great-granddaughter said her grandmother stated the apparition spoke to her grandfather, telling him that upon the following February 6, he would die at home. The prophecy was also imparted to his wife. Upon three or four occasions, in the same manner, while driving along some country road, the phantom appeared and repeated the dire prophesy."

Mrs. Emmerson's narrative continues: "This troubled him, and he brooded over the warning, until his wife became greatly disturbed. After thinking the matter over, she decided to have a big dinner on the date, believing that the preparations and the pleasure of having a group of friends for entertainment, would so divert her husband, that the day might pass without a thought being given to the doleful warning.

"Everything went as planned, until, in the midst of the dinner, the Parson arose and asked his guests to excuse him for a few minutes. He remained away from the table long enough to cause his wife anxiety, and she followed him to find the reason for such an unusual performance.

"On reaching his room, she found, to her horror, that the old parson had quietly gone on his last journey!"

## The Mystery of the Bloody Millstone

"Oh, she's still around. We still hear from her every once in a while. We find things out of place, you know, where they shouldn't be. And the stain still appears on the stone every time it rains. She's still part of her family."

Sam Nock is talking about the resident ghost at Warwick, the ancestral home of the Upshur family in the small town of Quinby in Accomack County on the Eastern Shore of Virginia. Sam is a high school teacher there. The ghost is that of Rachel Upshur, who died a terrible and tragic death on Christmas Day more than 250 years ago.

Sam says Rachel married Abel Upshur sometime around 1725, and they had five children. Abel was the grandson of Arthur Upshur, who had arrived on the Eastern Shore as a cabin boy sometime during the first half of the seventeenth century and became one of the leading citizens of the area. Abel and Rachel moved to Warwick, one of the earliest brick houses still standing in the county, in 1738.

Eleven years later, on a bitter, blustery, and rainy winter night, the couple was awakened by a loud commotion in their chicken house. Although he was ill at the time, Abel got up to check on the noise, although Rachel begged him not to go. She told him she had a terrifying nightmare in which a "white shrouded, grinning skeleton with upraised arms had solemnly warned her not to venture out of the house that evening." If she did, she would "meet death in some horrible manner!" Abel assured her that everything would be all right, and for her to stay in bed.

But when he didn't return within a reasonable time, she became worried, hastily threw a coat over her nightgown, and went out barefoot to see what was going on. She found Abel standing in the cold wetness. The chickens were still making a racket, but he had not discovered why. She implored him to go back into the house. As they walked toward the door, Rachel stepped up on an old millstone that was embedded in the ground at the foot of the steps. As she did, a fox darted out from under the steps and sank its teeth into one of her heels. Blood spurted out on the millstone as she limped inside.

The fox was rabid, and a few days later, Rachel contracted hydrophobia. There was no known cure at the time for this horrid ailment that viciously attacks the nervous system and causes a victim great pain, suffering, and madness. Family members, with no choice but to put her out of her misery, smothered her to death between two feather mattresses on Christmas Day, 1749. She was buried in the family cemetery at Warwick.

The old millstone is still there today. It is a solid gray, well-worn stone. Curiously, Nock says, whenever it rains and the stone gets wet, a large dark-red stain appears on the precise spot where Rachel bled when the fox bit her so many years ago.

## The Celebrity Spirits of Fort Monroe

There are so many ghosts, famous or otherwise, at historic Fort Monroe in Hampton, Virginia, that it's hard to know where to begin. The star-studded list of apparitions who have allegedly been sighted here at one time or another includes Abraham Lincoln, Jefferson Davis and his wife Varina, Marquis de Lafayette, General Ulysses S. Grant, Indian chief Black Hawk, and budding young author Edgar Allan Poe. The roster of haunts is not, however, limited to the well known. There are numerous nameless ones also, such as illicit lovers, a bevy of perky poltergeists, and even occasional reports of a reptilian monster who has been seen stirring in the ancient moat that surrounds the fort.

Dennis Mroczkowski, former director of the Casemate Museum here, offers a thought about why so many spirits seem to linger at the site. "With the hundreds of thousands of people who have been assigned to the fort," he says, "there's a large population to draw from for ghosts. There have been many sightings of strange apparitions and many repeat themselves and become identified in people's minds with the famous figures that have been here." He also believes that the dank and dreary corridors and the thick-walled casemates possibly could have provided some inspiration to the later macabre writings of one-time resident Poe.

The history of the area dates to the time of the initial English settlement in America, when the first colonists landed in 1607. Old Point Comfort, where the fort is located, was the land the settlers saw before they arrived at Jamestown. A year later, Capt. John Smith deemed it an excellent site for a fort. Various military installations have occupied the area since 1611. Construction of the present fort took fifteen years, from 1819 to 1834, and it was named for James Monroe, a Virginian and the fifth president of the United States. One of the chief engineers during this period was a young officer named Robert E. Lee.

So impregnable was this bastion, and so ideally located, it was one of the few Union fortifications in the South that was not captured by the Confederates during the Civil War. In fact, President Lincoln had no qualms about visiting the fort in May 1862, to help plan an attack on Norfolk. It was here, too, in April 1864 that General Grant outlined the campaigns that led to the end of the war.

It was at Fort Monroe a year later that the imprisonment of Confederate president Jefferson Davis led to one of the first and best-known ghost legends associated with the site. On May 23, 1865, Davis was placed in solitary confinement in casement number two. His wife, Varina, got permission from President Andrew Johnson to join her husband at the fort, and she brought along their young daughter, Winnie. It is, say some, the apparition of the iron-willed Varina who has been seen on occasion, appearing late at night through the second-floor window of quarters directly across from the casemate where Davis was held. Several later residents reported seeing her. One awoke early one morning and glimpsed the figures of "a plumpish woman and a young girl peering through the window." The witness got out of bed and walked toward them, but when she reached out to touch the entity's billowing skirt, the figures vanished.

A wide range of psychic phenomena has been experienced in a plantation-style house known as Old Quarters Number One. Manifestations have included the clumping of unseen boots, the rustling of silken skirts, strange sounds, and the mysterious shredding of fresh flower petals in midwinter. It was here, appropriately enough in the Lincoln Room, that the image of the slain president has been seen, clad in a dressing gown and standing by the fireplace. The spirits of Lafayette, Grant, and Chief Black Hawk have also made spectral appearances here to those who later lived in the house.

"Ghost Alley," a lane that runs behind a set of quarters known as "The Tuileries," is the setting for one of the oldest and saddest supernatural traditions at Fort Monroe. It is here, always under the cloak of darkness, that the fabled "Lady in White" has been seen searching for her long-lost lover. She was a beautiful young woman who once lived in a Tuileries unit with a much older husband, a captain. Being of a flirtatious nature, she attracted the attentions of a dashing younger officer, and their obvious longings for each other soon became apparent to all but the unimaginative captain. One evening, however, he returned home unexpectedly and caught the lovers. In a fit of rage, he shot his wife.

Ever since, she has been sighted fleetingly in a luminescent form, roaming the dark alley looking for her lost companion.

Undoubtedly, the most famous enlisted man ever to serve at Fort Monroe was a nineteen-year-old lad named Edgar Allan Poe. He arrived on December 15, 1828, and almost immediately sought help to get out of the army. He was discharged after serving only four months. He returned to the area twenty years later, when he recited his poetry at the adjacent Hygeia Hotel on September 9, 1849, just four weeks before his death in Baltimore. It is his spectral image, many have speculated, that was seen in the late 1960s at a house that backs onto Ghost Alley. A lady tenant heard an unexplained tapping coming from a downstairs room one night. She then saw the figure of a man dressed in a white shirt with puffed sleeves, a red vest, and dark pants. In an instant, he evaporated in a gray mist. The shadowy figure was sighted again in 1969, moving down a hallway, where he was said to have gone through a closet door without opening it.

In other parts of the fort, playful and noisy ghosts—suspected poltergeists—have both bewildered and frightened residents. At a house next to the chapel, occupants once found that a heavy chest had been moved during the night and fireplace andirons had been rearranged. Phantom footsteps have been heard, dresser drawers opened and closed on their own, doors slammed, and loud bangings occurred. Some items, such as a cake stand and a Dresden figurine, were discovered broken overnight with no apparent cause.

The curious thing about these multiple happenings, aside from the sheer number of them, is the consistency with which they have been told and retold over the years—in most cases by more than one person, and in some cases by many. Another thing is the durability of the incidents. Some are alleged to have taken place as much as a century or more ago; others are far more recent. They continue to this day.

Workers at the Casemate Museum, for example, tell of a relatively recent visit by an obviously shaken wife of an officer. She had heard of the ghostly tales at the fort and wanted to share her own unnerving experience. She had been in a bedroom with her two teenagers watching television one night while her husband was in the basement. Before their startled eyes, a bedside table lifted up and flew across the room, smashing into the fireplace, shattering the marble top. She and the children screamed, and their dog went wild, scratching at the floor.

And finally, there was the officer and his wife who were living in the quarters where Robert E. Lee was once housed. The husband was in the kitchen one night when a wet dish cloth sailed across the room and smacked him soundly in the face. He yelled at his wife, asking her why she had done that. She didn't answer. He discovered later that she was outside the house at the time.

The sometimes playful ghosts at Fort Monroe apparently were at it again.

# Interludes of Divine Intervention

Sprinkled intermittently through Virginia's history, and involving some of the commonwealth's most famous and infamous names, are some curious vignettes that have to do with communicating with spirit matter of the highest order. In rare instances, it has been claimed that certain messages, in the form of signs, direct callings, or otherwise have descended to mere mortals straight from the Holy Ghost or a close disciple. These messages have, in turn, been interpreted by those who say they have received them, or by others who were witnesses, as expressions of Divine Providence.Whether or not such examples involved some higher form of supernatural activity obviously is arguable, but to those to whom these things happened, there is no way to convince them that they were not genuine. Take, for instance, the charismatic aura that surrounded legendary Confederate general Thomas "Stonewall" Jackson. He was a deeply religious man, to the point of fanaticism, and prayed incessantly. He was unanimously acknowledged to be a military genius, but many of his followers felt part of the reason for his at-times incredible successes went beyond mere human capabilities. During the Shenandoah Valley campaigns it was said that his men came to believe that Jackson was in "direct communications with the Almighty."

And what of the fate of John Wilkes Booth? After hiding out for roughly two weeks following his assassination of President Abraham Lincoln in April 1865, Booth was cornered in a barn in Caroline County. Union soldiers were under strict orders not to shoot, but to capture him alive. Nevertheless, a single shot rang out, striking Booth in the back of his skull, oddly at virtually the same spot his bullet had entered Lincoln's head. It proved fatal. A sergeant named Boston Corbett, known to his friends as the "Mad Hatter," admitted that he had pulled the trigger. When he was asked why, Corbett said, "God Almighty directed me."

Possibly the most bizarre "calling" of all, leading to one of the most notorious episodes in Virginia history, occurred in 1831 in Southampton County in the southeastern section of the commonwealth. It was here, near the present town of Courtland, that the greatest slave uprising in the history of the United States took place.

It was led by an intense, Bible-reading, thirty-one-year-old slave named Nat Turner. He seemed to have a hypnotic, mesmerizing power over his fellow workers, and convinced them they should free themselves and "go to Jerusalem."

The rebellion began at a Sunday camp meeting in August 1831. Exhorted to frenzy by Turner, who they believed was guided by the spirits, this ill-fated group of slaves armed themselves with corn knives, axes, and scythes, and followed their leader in what was termed an orgy of butchery. They struck first at the Travis Plantation, where Turner worked, wiping out the entire family. Then they marched across the county, plundering and gathering recruits as they went. Eventually, their force swelled to more than fifty, and they proceeded from house to house, murdering all the white men, women, and children they could find.

Once word of the insurrection got out, many houses were quickly evacuated, leading Turner to comment, "We found no more victims to gratify our thirst for blood." In all, fifty-five people, including twelve students at a girls' school, were slaughtered before troops summoned from Richmond and Norfolk arrived. Many of the rioting slaves were slain by the soldiers, and nineteen others were hanged.

Turner escaped, for a time, as hundreds of men searched for him. Here is how he described his escape: "After having supplied myself with provisions from Mr. Travis, I scratched a hole under a pile of fence posts in a field, where I concealed myself for six weeks, never leaving my hiding place but for a few minutes in the dead of night to get water." Turner was finally betrayed by a dog that had discovered the food in his sanctuary. Within days, he was captured and later tried and hanged.

Historians have recorded their belief that Nat Turner appeared to have been a victim of superstition and fanaticism. He was able to arouse his fellow slaves to his cause when he told them he was acting under "inspired direction." In a confession he made while awaiting execution, Turner said that in his childhood a circumstance happened that made an indelible impression on his mind and laid the groundwork for the wild enthusiasm that terminated so fatally to so many.

"Being at play with other children," he wrote, "when I was three of four years old, I told them something which my mother, overhearing, said occurred before I was born. I stuck to my story, however, and related some things which went, in her opinion, to confirm it; others being called on were greatly astonished, knowing these things had happened, and caused them to say in my hearing, I surely would be a prophet, as the Lord had showed me things which happened before my birth." His parents strengthened him in this belief, and said in his presence that he was intended for "some great purpose," which they had always thought from "certain marks on his head and breast."

After a "variety of revelations from the spiritual world," Turner stated in his confession that "On the 12th of May, 1828, I heard a loud noise in the heavens and the Spirit instantly appeared to me, and said the serpent was loosed—and that I should take it on and fight against the serpent, for the time was fast approaching when the first should be the last and the last should be the first, and by signs in the heavens that it would make known to me that I should commence the great work."

The sign that appeared to Turner in 1831 was the eclipse of the sun. He said it was the event "which determined me not to wait longer."

Curiously, Nat Turner ended up in Jerusalem, as he had prophesied. He was hanged there. The name of the town of Jerusalem, Virginia, was later changed to Courtland.

## A Spirit-Raising Séance

The following singular account of an impromptu séance that foretold of events of the future during the American Civil War was recorded in an article published in the *Religio-Philosophical Journal* on October 3, 1885. It was titled "A War Episode," and was written by a Union officer identified only as "J. L.," who apparently was psychic.

"The occurrence I am about to relate took place during the siege of Yorktown, in the early part of May 1862. The cavalry regiment in which I had enlisted was then encamped in dense pine woods. Our position was hidden from the Confederates. I was detailed as officer of the guard.

"After making a tour of the camp to see that sentries were properly posted, vigilant, and on the alert, all lights were extinguished. I wended my way towards one of the tents. I heard voices raised in debate, and there saw several officers seated around the mess chest. On my entrance I was hailed by having my attention called to the subjects of table tapping and spiritualism, and to the improbability of the return of the dead, and the power of spirits to manifest intelligently. I had previously argued with a number of the gentlemen present on the subject. I was then appealed to for proofs.

"I was instantly stirred up and suddenly felt the power from on high descending upon me. I replied, 'Gentlemen, if you will keep silence and obey my instructions, I think I can show you things little dreamt of in all of your heathen philosophy.' They assented, and silence reigned for some five or six minutes. After I had arranged the circle around the mess chest, I directed each one to place their hands thereon, and taking a position myself, the dim flickering light of a single candle shed its rays upon the solemn faces.

"In a few minutes, the large chest began to sway to and fro, and raised itself halfway to our knees, slowly returning to the ground. It then began to tip from one of its corners to the others, shake itself, and then settle. Taps were heard growing louder and louder around the sides and on top; there followed a blow underneath, resembling a musket report. Nearly all involuntarily jumped to their feet exclaiming, 'Why! It is alive! What, the devil!' The manifestations thus far were extraordinary to them but not to me. Directly, the taps were resumed, sounding inside and outside of the mess chest. Its contents of tin plates, knives, forks, bottles of table sauce, hams, etc., began a medley and chorus of noises.

"The expressions and glances of those present, presented a scene not easily forgotten after a long lapse of years. My pen cannot do justice to the occurrence. Again, the noises ceased, and the raps began in a steady, business-like way, and I commenced to question the spirit intelligence. Its reply was to this effect: 'About midnight, your camp will be shelled by the enemy.' (The enemy had not, as yet, got range of us, not knowing our whereabouts.) 'The general alarm will sound, and the whole army will be under arms. Your regiment will take the advance on Yorktown and find it evacuated!'

"This was inexplicable; the very idea of the rebel's famous stronghold being evacuated seemed nonsense. At this juncture of the affair, a loud musket rap was sounded, nearly overturning the chest. This concluded the séance, as I could no longer control the comments.

"In conclusion, I will add that just about midnight, as we were leaving the tent to retire to our different quarters, the rebel shells began pouring into our camp, bursting with considerable destruction among men and horses. The bugles began their calls: 'To arms! To arms!' The general alarm among the infantry, cavalry and artillery of the whole Grand Army of the Potomac followed, but all was darkness amid the rain of shell in our camp. In the morning before daylight, our regiment did take the advances of the army. We did find Yorktown evacuated and the enemy gone!

But few of the witnesses to this incident are now living; the others have joined the army of the disembodied, and no doubt now believe in the truth of an existence after earth-life. Philosophizing on these manifestations, I could say, can such possibly be accounted for on any other hypothesis—than the work or manifestations of intelligent beings?"

# The Cat in the Coffin

The following interview with an unnamed African-American woman, at Point Comfort, Virginia, was conducted in the late 1930s by Harry Middleton Hyatt, and later published in a five-volume set titled *Hoodoo-Conjuraton-Witchcraft-Rootwork*. It is reprinted here courtesy of the Blue Ridge Institute at Ferrum College.

"I did hear one time that there was two girls which were partners; used to go to and fro together. So one Sunday they decided to go to church. They went to Sunday School in the morning, also to eleven o'clock service, and that night one of the girls decided she wanted to go to the night service. So when the one girl got to the other girl's house, the other girl was combing her hair.

"She told the other girl, 'Leave us go to church.' The other girl said to her in reply, 'Before I go to church I'd rather go to hell with both eyes open without my hair being combed.' After then, they went. The next day, which was Monday, this girl was taken sick. Tuesday, she died. On Thursday, they were getting ready for her funeral. They had taken the corpse to the church.

"They went to pick up the coffin to get it to the hearse and they couldn't nobody move it. At last, a gang of men put the coffin in the hearse. They had four horses pulling the coffin. All four of the horses couldn't move it. It was an awful thing to see the great excitement. Then they decided to take this coffin out of the hearse and open it to see what was the trouble.

"So when they open the coffin, there was a black cat in there, combing the girl's hair with its paw!"

# The Legend of the Norwegian Lady

Tens of thousands of tourists in Virginia Beach pass by the bronze statue of "The Norwegian Lady" at 25th Street and Oceanfront each summer without knowing the gripping, tragically sad story of why the figure is there. The following account of this absorbing saga has been compiled from newspaper articles and interviews with descendants of actual witnesses to the events. The story has also been published in several books, including *Haunted Virginia Beach*, by Alpheus Chewning.

It began on the morning of March 3, 1891, when Captain J. M. Jorgensen sailed out of Pensacola, Florida, on a small Norwegian three-masted bark, the *Dictator*, bound for England with a cargo of yellow pine lumber. The ship carried a crew of fifteen, along with Jorgenson's wife, Johanne Pauline, and their four-year-old son, Karl. Three weeks later, just north of the Bahamas, the *Dictator* ran into a violent nor'easter and was unmercifully buffeted both by almost hurricane-force winds and mountainous seas. Two of the five lifeboats were swept overboard and lost in the surging ocean, and the ship sprung a leak. The captain wanted to attempt to ride out the storm, but the disgruntled crew virtually forced Jorgensen to alter his course and head towards Hampton Roads to make repairs.

On the morning of March 27 the ship, suffering greatly from the pounding waves, was sighted off Virginia Beach. How it got there is not clear. Some believed that during the previous night the captain saw what he thought were the lights of the Cape Charles lighthouse, when in reality they were the lit windows of a beachfront hotel. The crew of the Dam Neck Mills Lifesaving Station was alerted, but the vessel was too far off shore to attempt a rescue. The Seatack Lifesaving Station, then located where 24th Street is today, was also informed.

By 9:30 A.M., crowds had gathered as the *Dictator* passed by the old Princess Anne Hotel on 16th Street. According to eyewitness accounts, the spectators watched in horror as the ship struggled helplessly north. A little over an hour later, it foundered on a sandbar about three hundred yards offshore, a half mile north of the lifesaving station. The situation was now desperate. The lifesaving crew first attempted to cannon shoot a breeches buoy line to the ship, but this failed due to the excessively high winds. By now two of the remaining lifeboats also had been lost. Captain Jorgensen then decided to send four of his men in the last boat, and, somehow, they miraculously made it through the crashing surf to safety. Finally, after many unsuccessful attempts, a line from the beach to the ship was secured to the top of the main mast, and a breeches buoy was sent out in hopes of rescuing the remaining thirteen people.

But the ship was rolling so much in the high seas, the line would tighten and then slacken with each wave, either dunking the crewmember into the ocean, or throwing him high into the air. Despite this, however, the first man made it to the beach unharmed. Jorgensen then told his wife and his son to try it, but paralyzed with fear, she steadfastly refused. So another sailor was dispatched and reached the beach. Jorgensen again pleaded with his wife to go, but she still refused. Two more sailors did make it to safety before darkness halted the buoy operation.

There were now six crewmembers and the captain and his wife and son left. Having been pounded by the relentless surf all day on the sandbar, the *Dictator* began breaking up. As a last resort, the captain had his son strapped to his back, and left his wife with a French seaman. They then lowered themselves into the swirling waters, littered with loose boards of pine lumber. The surging surf quickly tore little Karl from his father's back, and he drowned. So, too, did the sailor and Mrs. Jorgensen. The captain was washed ashore and found unconscious but alive. One other sailor survived.

The next day, the figurehead of the *Dictator*, a carved wooden robust woman, was found and was placed on the boardwalk as a memorial to those who had lost their lives. The bodies of the crewmen and Mrs. Jorgensen were then buried at Elmwood Cemetery in Norfolk. Little Karl's body was not found for several days, until a beachcomber saw it washed up near 17th Street. The man who discovered it didn't realize it was Jorgensen's son; he didn't know who it was, so he took Karl to his minister at a church south of Rudee's Inlet, and the remains were buried there.

Within days, the eerie sounds of a child crying for its mother were heard at this cemetery by a number of witnesses, but no one saw anything, nor could they explain how or why the cries were heard. After this phenomenon repeated itself for several days, it was learned that the captain's son's body had not been found with the others, and the connection was made. Karl's body was exhumed and reburied next to his mother at Elmwood Cemetery. When this happened, the ghostly cries of the child were no longer heard in Virginia Beach.

The figurehead of the Norwegian Lady decayed over the years and was replaced in 1962 by a bronze memorial created by Norway's famed sculptor, Oernulf Bast. It was presented to Virginia Beach as a gesture of friendship by the citizens of the *Dictator*'s home port, Moss, Norway. And so she stands today, gazing out at the ocean, the scene so many years ago of a stark tragedy that took some lives, but, by the heroic efforts of Virginia Beach citizens, saved several others.

## Jack the Ripper—in Virginia?

At 4:50 on the steamy hot, foggy morning of April 6, 1888, in the seedy Whitechapel section of London, England, waterside laborer John Reeves left his flat in the George Yard Building and headed for work. He noticed a large, dark, lumpish figure lying on the floor near the entrance. When he stooped to look, he saw that it was a woman. She was dead and covered in blood.

Police later identified her as Martha Tabran, a forty-year-old prostitute who was known to have walked the slum streets of the area at night seeking enough money to buy a bottle and find lodging before dawn. Tragic incidents involving such unfortunate women were not all that uncommon in this district at the time. What set this murder apart from others, however, was the furious rage obviously exhibited in the killing. Tabran had been stabbed with deep thrusts—thirty-nine times!

Despite a spirited, widespread investigation, no one was arrested. Over the next few months four other "women of the night" were found on the back streets and in the darkened hallways of Whitechapel. Each of their bodies had been horribly mutilated, some almost beyond recognition. In at least two instances, it appeared that an enraged madman had tried to sever the head with his knife. One woman's heart had been ripped from her chest.

Although the brutal slayings obviously appeared to have been committed by the same person, the murderer was never found—despite the fact that the largest manhunt in history was launched, involving teams of the finest detectives and investigators in England. A number of suspects were rounded up, temporarily jailed, and interrogated, but eventually each one was released for lack of evidence. This triggered a prolonged reign of abject terror and sheer panic throughout London. For years afterward, women were afraid to venture out onto the streets at night. In time, the brutal slasher came to be known as "Jack the Ripper."

More than 120 years later, his identity is still unknown. Hundreds of articles and books have been written, and great numbers of theories have been offered, in what most criminal experts call the greatest murder mystery of all time. In recent years, a novel new hypothesis of who the Ripper was, and why he did what he did, has surfaced. It has a strong Virginia tie-in, and a series of bizarre twists and turns.

## The Norfolk Connection

James Chandler Maybrick was born in Liverpool, England, on October 24, 1838. His family was wealthy and accepted in the highest circles of local society. As a young man, Maybrick became a successful cotton merchant, and in 1874 he sailed to Norfolk to open a branch office of his company in this important emerging port city. Barely nine years after the end of the American Civil War, Norfolk had become a hotbed for the exportation of U.S. cotton.

The details of Maybrick's life in Virginia are sketchy, but this much is known: he first lived in a house on York Street with another gentleman and a Negro servant. Although there is some evidence that he was married to a woman in Liverpool, which he never publicly acknowledged, he gave the appearance of being an affluent bachelor in Norfolk. According to biographers, his constant companion in the city was a woman named Mary Howard. She was the madam of a popular brothel. Years later, she was to recall that he visited her establishment at least two to three times a week.

At some point during his tenure in Norfolk, Maybrick contracted malaria. He was prescribed quinine, but this didn't improve his condition. He then learned that the poison arsenic, when administered in extremely moderate doses, could give him relief. So he began taking it. He also thought the drug increased his virility. The dispenser was Santo's, the chemist on Main Street. There were two problems with arsenic. An overdose, of course, could be fatal. Secondly, the drug was addictive, which proved to be the case with Maybrick. He was to take it for the rest of his life, and it eventually led to his premature death.

## A Fateful Voyage

Over the next few years, Maybrick frequently traveled between Norfolk and Liverpool to conduct his business. In March 1880, he boarded the sailing ship *Baltic* in New York, bound for England. During the six-day cruise he met a young Alabama socialite named Florence (Florie) Chandler. Despite the fact that he was then forty-one and she was but eighteen, and the implied fact that if he was already married, he had never attained a divorce, they fell in love and were married a year later in London. When they arrived back in Norfolk, the couple moved into a house on Freemason Street.

In 1884, they moved back to Liverpool for good. They wound up in a large manor house, Battlecrease, the family home. They had two children, a boy and a girl.

As the years passed, the marriage began to deteriorate. Maybrick was still taking small doses of arsenic to relieve his suffering, and he became subject to severe mood swings. He also was having a barely hidden affair with another woman, who some historians believe may well have been his first wife. Florie was deeply hurt by this, and began to have her own extramarital liaison. When Maybrick discovered this he became violent, and sometimes brutally beat Florie.

In April 1889, Maybrick became seriously ill and took to his bed. Within two weeks he was dead. The cause was ruled as an overdose of arsenic, and although he had been taking the substance for more than a dozen years, suspicion fell on his wife. A maid said Florie had recently purchased some flypaper that contained the poison. And when police searched Florie's trunk in the house, they found three bottles of arsenic, and a rag and handkerchief impregnated with the poison—enough in all, doctors said, to kill fifty people! Further, it was learned that Florie's mother had been a suspect in the poisoning death of her first husband, and that her mother's second husband had also died under suspicious circumstances.

Despite her fervent protestations of innocence, and the known fact that Maybrick was an arsenic addict himself, Florie was charged with her husband's murder. She was the first American woman charged with such a crime in English courts. The trial was a sensation, drawing international attention. Press coverage clearly indicated that Florie's defense attorney was patently incompetent, and the judge was highly prejudiced. He frequently made damaging remarks to the jury, saying flatly that he thought the woman guilty. Consequently, she was convicted and sentenced to hang.

This created a monumental controversy and a national barrage of outrage. Yielding to the overwhelming public demand, Florie's sentence was converted to life imprisonment. She served fifteen years, although there was a continuing outcry for her release. Finally, in 1904, following a reexamination of her trial, she was pardoned by Queen Victoria. Florie died in Connecticut in 1941. Her body was found in her cottage, surrounded by several cats.

## The Diary

In 1991, a Liverpool scrap metal dealer named Mike Barrett went to the house of his friend and drinking buddy, Tony Devereux, and was given a parcel wrapped in brown paper. "Take it," Tony said. "I want you to have it. Do something with it." No explanation as to what the package contained or where it came from was given.

When Mike got home and unwrapped the parcel with his wife, Anne, they found a very old Victorian-era scrapbook, quarter-bound in black calf. The first forty-eight pages had been cut out with a

knife, leaving sixty-three pages of an unidentified handwritten manuscript in ink. When they began reading it, they were dumbfounded
and shocked beyond belief. It appeared to be a diary, written by Jack
the Ripper!

In it were startling passages describing, in minute and horrifying
detail, the murders that had been committed in London more than a
hundred years before. It appeared to be the author's blatant confession to those unsolved crimes. The words were bone-chilling. Here
are some excerpts:

"I have walked the streets and have become more than familiar
with them. I said Whitechapel it will be and Whitechapel it shall. No
one could possibly place it together. The next time I am in London I
shall begin. I have no doubts, my confidence is most high. I am thrilled
writing this. No one will ever suspect. Tomorrow I will purchase the
finest knife money can buy. Nothing will be too good for my whores."

"I am convinced God placed me here to kill all whores, for he must
have done so, am I still not here? Nothing will stop me now. The more
I take the stronger I become."

In the writer's description of his killing of a woman named Mary
Jane Kelly, he tells of the emotional rush he got out of it. "I left nothing of the bitch, nothing. Like the other whore, I cut off the bitches
nose, all of it this time. The taste of blood was sweet, the pleasure was
overwhelming. Will have to do it again. It thrilled me so. They wanted
a slaughterman so I stripped what I could, laughed while I was doing
so. Like the other bitches, she ripped like a ripe peach."

There were even references to cannibalism. Of one victim whose
body had been torn to shreds, he wrote: "I took some of it [body parts]
away with me. It is in front of me. I intend to fry it and eat it later, ha
ha. The very thought works up my appetite." On another occasion he
wrote: "One of these days I will take the head away with me. I will boil
it and serve it up for my supper."

On the night of a double murder, he notes: "To my astonishment
I cannot believe I have not been caught." And after the first victim
had died, he tells of the second: "Within the quarter of the hour I
found another dirty bitch willing to sell her wares. The whore, like all
the rest, was only too willing. The thrill she gave me was unlike the
others. I cut deep, deep, deep. Her nose annoyed me, so I cut it off.

Could not get the bitches head off. The whore never screamed. I took it all away with me. I am saving it for a rainy day. Ha ha."

As Michael Barrett and his wife continued to read the gruesome script, they found a number of references that they were to learn later covered facts that only Jack the Ripper could have known. For example, after the death of Mary Jane Kelly, the diary writer said: "I will pray for the women I have slaughtered. May God forgive me for the deeds I committed on Kelly. No heart, no heart." When Kelly's mutilated body was found, her heart had been ripped out and was missing. This was never disclosed by the police. Only the killer would have known about it. There were other such telling clues distributed throughout the diary.

While there was no mention of the author's name anywhere in the diary, there were a number of items that pointed to one man who had never before been even considered as a suspect—James Maybrick! There were references to the author returning to his house in Liverpool—Battlecrease, the home of the Maybricks. There were several references to Florie, who Maybrick had discovered was having an affair with another man. "The bitch and her whoring master will rue the day I first saw them together," the diarist wrote. In another passage referring to Florie, he added: "My desire for revenge is overwhelming. The whore has destroyed my life."

There were other clues as well. In one killing, the initials F. M. (Florie Maybrick) were scrawled on a wall behind the victim. In another instance the letter M was carved into the cheeks of a body's face. There were enough such hints regarding Maybrick's wife for analysts later to deduct that her affair was the event that set the killer off on his violent rampage. No other motive for the murders has ever surfaced. It appeared to have been, solely, Maybrick's jealous rage.

Additionally, there are several references to the fact that the diary author was taking arsenic for his medical condition. And, toward the end of the text, there are clear indications that the author was dying. "May God help me," he wrote. "I pray each night he will take me. The disappointment when I awake is difficult to describe. I do not have the courage to take my life. I pray each night I will find the strength to do so, but the courage alludes me. I pray constantly all will forgive. I believe I will tell her [Florie] all and ask her to forgive me as I have forgiven her. I pray to God she will understand what she has done to me. Tonight I will pray for the women I have slaughtered."

And, later, in indicating that he possibly told his wife of his dark deeds, he wrote: "The pain is unbearable. My dear Bunny [Florie] knows all. I do not know if she has the strength to kill me. It would be simple. She knows my medicine, and for an extra dose or two it would all be over. I have begged Bunny to act soon." These words lead to an interesting question. Did, in fact, Maybrick's wife really kill him with an overdose of arsenic, or did he do it himself?

The last entry in the diary, dated May 3, 1889, reads: "Soon, I trust I shall be laid beside my dear mother and father. I shall seek their forgiveness when we are reunited. God I pray will allow me that privilege, although I know too well I do not deserve it. My thoughts will remain in tact, for a reminder to all how love does destroy. I place this [the diary] now in a place where it shall be found. I pray whoever should read this will find it in their heart to forgive me. Remind all, whoever you may be, that I was once a gentleman. May the good Lord have mercy on my soul, and forgive me for what I have done. I give my name that all know of me, so history do tell, what love can do to a gentle man born. Yours truly, Jack the Ripper."

## A Storm of Controversy

After reading the diary, and after getting over his total shock, Michael Barrett tried desperately to learn more about the manuscript and where it came from, but he never did. His only source of information, his friend Tony Devereux, died unexpectedly before he could tell where he had gotten the diary.

Barrett then spent the better part of a year researching everything he could find on Jack the Ripper—and there was plenty. It is arguable that more has been written on the Whitechapel murders than on any other crimes in history. There are, even to this day, countless thousands of "Ripperologists"—fervent fans who devour any and everything written on the subject. As best as Barrett could ascertain, the dates, facts, and clues studded throughout the diary seemed to click with the known accounts that were in the public domain. But Barrett finally came to the conclusion that he was in over his head. So he sought counsel.

After a couple of misfires, he contacted a reputable London literary agent who agreed to review the manuscript. In 1992 he met with the agent and author Shirley Harrison. They pored over the pages and came to the conclusion that there were three possibilities. One, the diary was a hoax. Two, James Maybrick may have suffered under the delusion that he was the Ripper. And three, the diary was genuine and Maybrick was, in fact, the man whose identity had been cloaked in mystery for more than one hundred years.

Then, with the job of verifying authenticity, and in so doing composing a published book, Harrison set out on what was to become a perilous mission.

She tracked down authorities on two continents, Europe and North America. Experts were consulted on the scrapbook and the paper—was it late nineteenth-century? Did the ink used correspond to that era? Did the handwriting match with Maybrick's? Were the details of the murders in sync? Were there forensic clues available? Psychiatrists were sought out to see if the profile of the diary author was consistent with known serial killers—and if the habits of an arsenic addict coincided with Maybrick's comments.

After months of such exhaustive research the publisher and Harrison decided to go ahead with the project, and in 1993 the book *The Diary of Jack the Ripper: the Discovery, the Investigation, the Debate* was released. It includes a complete transcript of the diary, both in handwritten form and in type. What followed, almost immediately, was a hurricane of controversy.

Few Ripper experts gave it any credence from the outset and most dismissed it entirely as a hoax. Still, some were open to the possibility that it was true. One writer summed up what many thought when he said, "the saga of the Maybrick diary is confusing, complicated, and inescapably tortuous." While the authenticity of the journal was hotly debated, said another, it nonetheless has yet to be proven a forgery. There was some belief that whether it was fake or real, the diary maintains a remarkable consistency with the known facts. There is even a section on the pros and cons of it in the book.

Summing up on the situation, publisher Robert Smith wrote: "But for this diary, James Maybrick would never have been suspected of committing the Whitechapel murders. The style of the book is to present Maybrick as Jack the Ripper. However, the author gives you the facts and the evidence as objectively as possible, so that you can decide for yourself whether Maybrick was indeed guilty of murdering five prostitutes during the summer of 1888."

Still, there are many questions unanswered. Where was the diary all those years? What was meant by the cryptic line in the manuscript, allegedly written by Maybrick—"I place this [the diary] now in a place where it shall be found"? Was Maybrick murdered, did he kill himself, or was it an accidental death? And, of course, the ultimate question— was James Maybrick really Jack the Ripper? We may never know.

His story is retold each year on the Freemason neighborhood ghost tour hosted by Nauticus in downtown Norfolk. Were the seeds of his sinister and evil behavior sown during his years in Virginia? It is another question lost in time.

Here is yet another curious Virginia tie-in. It surfaced in a statement given by C. B. Fleet, a noted druggist in Lynchburg at the time. He once was visited by Fred H. Mael, who had a drugstore near the corner of Main and Church streets in Norfolk. He told Fleet that James Maybrick often stopped at his place to buy arsenic. He said Maybrick "frequently went on sprees, resulting in a complete breakdown, and used the poison as a pick-me-up and was habituated to its use." He added that he had been summoned to England as a witness in Florie Maybrick's trial and that his evidence would do "much towards clearing her." In an ironic twist, however, Mael became ill and died just before he was due to sail to England!

## The Incredible Feats of "Old Crump"

It is one of the most baffling cases of poltergeist activity on record, one that even intrigued master psychic Edgar Cayce and his sons. And to add to the singular nature of the phenomena, it lasted for more than forty years, and was investigated by dozens of experts, none of whom ever came up with a plausible explanation for the bizarre events. The following narrative is based on interviews with witnesses, old newspaper and magazine clips, and excerpts from a personal family history.

The saga began one night in 1898. Young Henry Stone, who had recently been blinded in a hunting accident, came to spend the night with his friend, Eugene Burroughs, at an old farmhouse in the Sigma area of Virginia Beach. They were each eight years old at the time, and because the house was crowded with guests, the boys slept on a pallet on the parlor floor. Burroughs was roused when his pillow "slid away from under his head." He blamed Stone, who claimed innocence. Then Stone's pillow sailed across the floor. The boys got into a fight, which Burroughs's father broke up.

When the boys told him what had happened, he laughed and said it was just the spirit of "Old Crump." He explained that a man named Crump Bonney, a cussed old codger, had died in the house a century before. For the next forty-plus years, whenever Stone and Burroughs got together, some sort of "invisible force" inexplicably moved objects about, and not just small objects. Pot-bellied stoves, bunk beds and chests of drawers slid across rooms they were in, and men and women were sometimes "jostled about."

"I cannon explain it," Burroughs said years later, "but that's the way it has been ever since Henry and I were boys." Such incidents were witnessed, documented, and written about by a number of investigators, including lawyers, doctors, scientists, and newspaper reporters. In fact, as time passed and the story of the awesome manifestations got around, hundreds of people from all over the country came to see special séances Stone and Burroughs held. They were rarely disappointed. Two of the most expert witnesses were Edgar Cayce, the famous psychic, and his son, Hugh Lynn.

As the boys grew older, the happenings grew stronger and more varied. Burroughs, for example, recorded the following in a privately published family chronicle: "We went to bed early. Hardly had we put the light out and gotten into bed before our pillows left the bed and the covering followed. We decided to let the invisible force take everything it wanted and not try to get anything back, but the force threw everything back on the bed. Just then, a big old-fashioned rocking chair hopped on the bed. It only felt as heavy as an ordinary chair when it first landed, but the longer it stayed the heavier it got. We thought it best to put it on the floor, and that is when the wrestle started. It took about thirty minutes to get out from under the chair. We then decided to put the chair, pillows, and covering out of the room. We put the pillows in a big wood chest in the hall and the chair near the chest. We came back and fastened the door with an old night latch. We got back in bed, and the pillows from the hall were already there! Again, before we had time to do anything, the chair was back on the bed."

Burroughs said Crump, or whatever force it was, "made objects, heavy or light, even people, go sailing about, irrespective of gravity, thick walls, or the personal wishes of those present." Particularly disturbing events occurred during the winter of 1906. Burroughs's parents were away from home for a few days, so Henry and another boy, Joe Walters, came over to stay with him. The first night, they couldn't keep the pillows and covers on the beds. The next night it happened again, so the boys hatched a plan to "catch" the invisible force.

Burroughs continued, "After locking all the windows and doors, we knew there was only one place where Crump could enter—through the stove pipe hole in the chimney. Henry agreed to sit by the chimney. When we were sure the spirit was in the room, Henry was to put heavy cardboard over the hole. Then it would be up to Joe and me to catch Old Crump. Joe and I went to bed, and it wasn't long before Henry yelled, 'He's got my hand!' Joe and I rushed to him, but he had been dragged under the bed. The cardboard had been torn in two. We were very frightened, so we decided to keep the lamp burning and sit up the rest of the night. That was enough for Joe, however. He went home."

Two nights later, with Stone and Boyd Beecham there to spend the evening, the activity continued. "After a half hour," Burroughs said, "our shoes fell heavily onto the bed, and the covers crept away. We lit a lamp. I'd scarcely gotten into bed when the lamp flew over from the dresser, about 15 feet away, and nudged me. It was still burning. I returned it to the dresser and crawled back into bed. The lamp sailed right back and was on us again. We got a lantern and a piece of rope from the barn. I tied the lantern to the bedpost with the rope, whereupon the lantern began to rattle. 'You can jump as much as you please,' I told the lantern, 'but you can't get on the bed this time.' With that, the bed turned upside down!"

Stone and Burroughs did not get together again for two years. In April 1908, they both were working for a fish company in Virginia Beach. Dog tired after a hard day's work, they decided to spend the night in the company's bunkhouse. After all, Crump had only shown up in Burroughs's home. Burroughs recalled what happened next: "During the night a terrible crash shattered the quiet. The pipes of the kitchen cookstove at the far end of the house had fallen. The stove came sailing 25 feet in mid-air and stopped by our beds. The next night, several fellows saw shoes, clothing, fishing gear, everything, thrown onto the bunks. We went to bed with the lantern lit. It landed on us, still lighted. Henry Flanagan, the plant engineer, came by and suggested we tie the lantern. With us, he saw the lantern rattle and jerk from its lashing. It sat on us; then, after five minutes, flew back to the floor. When it came back to us again, we grabbed it. The upper frame stayed in our hands, but the bottom section and chimney fell to the floor."

As the years passed, curiosity-seekers came from all over, beseeching the two men to make the mystery force appear. On one such occasion, Burroughs's sister-in-law brought a group of women to the farmhouse in Virginia Beach. Burroughs wrote about it in the family publication. "The force seemed to take pleasure in entertaining everybody," he said. "It began by throwing pictures around the room, very much to the amusement of our guests. It then began throwing pillows. Everybody began to relax. Just then, we heard a noise in the next room. In came an automatic shotgun loaded with five shells. We all came near fainting. We moved very carefully and took our time extracting the shells from the gun."

Then, Stone, Burroughs, and several others were thrown to the middle of the floor and their chairs were piled on top of them. Fear took over. Finally, everyone settled down, but not for long. Burroughs added, "There came a crash and in came our coats. They had been put in the adjoining room on a bed. We decided it was time for everyone to go home. Soon, a little noise was heard in the bedroom, then, in came a quilt and a mattress. Another loud crash! This one sounded as if the door between the living room and the bedroom was coming down. We investigated and found the bedstead jammed in the door leading to the bedroom. Everyone went home after that."

Through all the "visitations," Burroughs maintained that neither he nor Stone had any control over what might happen when they were together. He recalled one special incident that seemed to bear him out. "Once," he said, "Stone and I met by accident on a street in

Norfolk. Immediately, stones, bottles and other things began rolling toward us. We had to get off the street before we alarmed passersby." There was one extraordinary happening, however, that suggested they could possibly, on occasion, "will" the spirit. Stone once owed some money to a country grocer in the Pungo section of Virginia Beach, and they got into an argument over it. One day the grocer's stock "moved" from the shelves to outside the store!

One person who had firsthand knowledge of "the Stone and Burroughs show" was Thelma LaBarrier, who in 1990 still lived in Virginia Beach. She remembered a time when her late husband and a friend stayed with the two men one night, sitting on their bed to hold the covers on. The covers kept coming down anyway. She said things would come off the wall and fly around the room whenever Stone and Burroughs got together.

In 1925, Dr. J. Malcolm Byrd, from *Scientific American* magazine, came to the area to investigate the force. He told Burroughs that they should try to communicate with the spirit by means of tapping. "The first time we tried to talk to Crump," Burroughs noted, "I said, 'Invisible Force, I have been informed that you will talk to us. If so, speak.' No response. 'How about talking to you in code?' I said. 'One knock for yes, two knocks for no, three knocks for I don't know. If this is satisfactory, knock once.' We heard one loud knock! My stomach contracted with fear. I had a thousand questions to ask him and all of them left me. I did manage to ask, 'Who are you?' He replied, 'Uncle Billy.' He was my mother's uncle and had died a few years before the beginning of all the poltergeist activity. We still called him Old Crump."

Dr. Byrd warned the men to never make the force mad. "You don't know what you're dealing with, nor how much harm it may do you," he said. "We've never made the force mad as far as we know," Burroughs said. "No one was ever hurt by it, except a few who have hurt themselves in the haste to get away when things happened."

Burroughs said Old Crump could create all kinds of physical noises including, for example, the "rip" of stitches being torn apart, or the grinding of a hole being bored through a wall, or even music from a piano. Once, when Burroughs's uncle came for a visit, a lot of toilet articles sailed into the room. He told his nephew that he bet nothing else would move in the room when he propped himself against the door. "At that moment, we heard a boring sound as of an auger boring a hole through the wall," Burroughs said. "Then a Coca-Cola bottle appeared in Uncle Jerome's hand. He marked it to identify it, and put it in another part of the room. It returned to him as mysteriously as before."

Burroughs said some persons experienced a cold rush of air on their cheek, or the feeling of being tapped on their legs, or having ice put down their backs. "Once, a pillow in my hands began to breathe like it was a living thing! I beat on the pillow to make it stop, but it jumped out of my hands and slid across the room," he added.

One of the most terrifying of all "force" experiences took place when Stone and Burroughs were talked into giving a special séance during a vaudeville-type show. They had stopped giving séances because they felt they could not control the spirit, but on this one occasion they relented. The event drew headlines in the local newspaper, and so many people tried to wedge their way into Girkins Hall in Norfolk that Stone and Burroughs had to have a police escort to get there.

The force apparently had temporary stage fright that night, because the men sat on the stage for nearly an hour and nothing happened. With the audience getting restless, Burroughs appealed to some of his spiritualist friends to see if they knew something that would "hurry things up." About twenty-five people joined hands and said a prayer. "In a few minutes," Burroughs said, "a young lady opposite me rose to her feet. She put her hands out, and, in a moment, sailed over to me. She traveled a distance of 12 feet after swaying a minute there in her place. Fortunately, I was able to catch her. I gave her a hard push and let go. She stretched out in a horizontal position—about two feet above the floor! She was lowered slowly to the floor in about five minutes.

"I then tried to stand her up straight, but she was completely rigid. We called a doctor. He checked her and whispered in my ear, 'Burroughs, she's dead! She has no heartbeat or pulse.' I asked him how she could become so rigid in so short a time. I was alarmed. A friend of mine, Captain Ford, helped the doctor and me to stand her back on her feet. She was so stiff you could have broken her fingers like matchsticks. I kept telling her she was all right, and after about ten minutes, she drew a long breath. She relaxed and we were able to sit her on a chair. I asked her to explain to the audience that she was not a part of the show and to tell us what had happened to her. She said she didn't remember anything."

Burroughs said he, too, had been suspended in mid-air "many times." Other persons were transported about the room during such sittings. "I never attributed this power to myself," Burroughs said, "but always to the invisible force. Certainly, I was not conscious of any will to transport myself or anyone else."

Another time, Stone and Burroughs and two friends were approaching a barn when a corn planter with no one driving it headed directly toward them. They stopped it and tried to take it back to the barn, but it rolled out in the yard for some distance and fell over. Inside the barn, a grass scythe hanging on a wall came down from its hook and fell across one of the men's laps. Burroughs also said that many times people tried to "trick" the force, or to catch it, never with any success, and often with unnerving results. One photographer who had brought his camera to take pictures one night was, according to Burroughs, "heaved, camera and all, out the door."

Throughout their lives, Henry Stone and Eugene Burroughs never really found out what caused the psychic invisible force. "I keep hoping I'll understand some day about the strange powers Henry and I possess," Burroughs once said. "We have discovered that our sons also engender the force when they meet sometimes. Is it inherited?" Indeed, the younger Burroughs said in 1968 that he "had witnessed the events brought about by his father's association with Stone," and that he himself also had been the victim of similar happenings when in the presence of Stone's son. "It has been many years since anything has happened," he added. "We were teenagers the last time the force manifested itself."

"Is the force part of our subconscious minds?" the senior Burroughs once asked. "Is it mischievous spirits that enjoy our amazement at their pranks? Or is it really Uncle Billy Cox? Or is it Old Crump?"

Whatever it was, it was very real. Said Hugh Lynn Cayce, son of Edgar Cayce: "I have talked to many honest, intelligent people who certainly believe they heard and saw all manner of poltergeist activity. I cannot explain it."

# The Multiple Mysteries of Old House Woods

Of all the ghost legends of Tidewater Virginia, none is more widely known, or has been told, retold, written about, and rewritten more often that of Old House Woods, also called Old Haunted Woods, near the tiny crossroads town of Diggs in Mathews County northeast of Gloucester. And for good reason. The colorful stories that have been passed down for more than two hundred years about this fifty-acre patch of pine woods and marshlands near the Chesapeake Bay contain some of the most bizarre and unusual psychic phenomena ever recorded.

They include, for example, swashbuckling pirates burying stolen gold, retreating British soldiers hiding colonial treasure during the Revolutionary War, a full-rigged Spanish galleon that vanishes into thin air, skeletons in knights' armor wielding threatening swords, phantom groups of shovelers digging furiously late at night, and ghost horses and cows that appear and disappear before one's eyes.

"Yes, it's true. All those tales and more have come out of Old House Woods" says Olivia Davis, a lifelong resident of the area. She should know. Her great-great-grandfather bought the land in 1838, and it was kept in the family and farmed for more than a century. Old House Woods got its name from a large frame house that stood in the midst of the forest in the late 1700s. Later, after being abandoned for decades, it fell into disrepair and thereafter was called "the Old House."

Does Davis believe the accounts are true? "I consider them just exactly what they are, stories," she says. But there are scores of others, residents and visitors, who swear by them. And then there are those who have personally experienced the manifestations in one form or another. There is no way these people will ever be shaken in their beliefs. They were there. They saw for themselves, and they never forgot, carrying their terrified memories to the grave in some cases.

There are allegedly three reasons why Old House Woods is haunted. According to one tradition, the crew of a pirate ship came ashore here in the seventeenth century, buried their treasure somewhere deep in the woods, and then returned to sea where they perished when their ship sank in a furious hurricane. That explains, say proponents of this theory, why mysterious figures have been seen digging feverishly in the woods on dark nights by the lights of tin lanterns. They are the pirate ghosts returning to claim their lost loot.

Another version of this was recorded by *Richmond Times Dispatch* staff writer Bill McKelway in 1973. "Some say," he wrote, "that Blackbeard, the infamous Edward Teach, intercepted the treasure and then murdered the men who were hiding it. At any rate, legend has it that those murdered men still haunt the woods today, preying on those who dare to trespass the blood-stained earth in search of the lost treasure."

A second possible reason for the hauntings may also have occurred in the second half of the seventeenth century. After being defeated at the Battle of Worcester during the English Civil War in 1651, the deposed Charles II of England was said to have considered coming to Virginia. In preparation for his trip, a group of his followers dispatched several chests of money, silver plate, and jewels to the colony by ship. However, the riches never reached Jamestown. Instead, the ship sailed up the Chesapeake Bay and anchored in waters at the mouth of White's Creek, near Old House Woods. There, the treasure was offloaded, but before it could be safely hidden, the Royalists were attacked and murdered by a band of renegade indentured servants. In their rush to escape, these bondsmen took only part of the loot, planning to come back later. But they, too, ran afoul of the elements. A sudden storm struck the bay and all hands on board drowned when their ship capsized.

It may well be that the storms which took the lives of the pirates and the renegades account for one of the many area ghost stories— that of the "Storm Woman." She has been described by those who claim to have seen her as "a wraith of a woman in a long nightgown, her long hair flying back from her shoulders." Reportedly, whenever black clouds gather over this section of the bay, foretelling a coming gale, her wispy figure rises above the tops of towering pine trees, and she wails loudly to warn watermen and fishermen to take cover.

The third theory about the cause of the hauntings originated in late 1781, just before British general Charles Cornwallis's army was defeated at Yorktown. The legend is that two British officers and four soldiers were entrusted by their superiors with a huge military payroll. They slipped through enemy lines and headed north, hoping to find a British ship on the Chesapeake Bay. They buried the money in

Old House Woods before they were found and killed by a unit of American cavalry. Thus, it may be their spirits that still hover over the site in eternal guard.

Paranormal sightings over the years have been prolific and explicit, however far-fetched they may sound today. One of the most talked about witnesses was Jesse Hudgins, described as a respectable merchant of unquestioned integrity, who ran a store in the town of Mathews in the 1920s. Hudgins told of his experiences to a *Baltimore Sun* reporter in 1926, and to anyone else who would listen, and he swore to their authenticity.

"I do not care whether I am believed or not," he often said. "I am not apologetic or ashamed to say I have seen ghosts in Old House Woods. I have seen them not once, but a dozen times. I was 17 when I first actually saw a ghost. One October night I sat by the lamp reading. A neighbor whose child was very ill came asking me to ride to Mathews for the doctor. We had no telephone in those days. I hitched up and started for town. The night was gusty, clouds drifted now and then over the moon, but I could see perfectly, and whistled as I rode along.

"Nearing Old House Woods, I saw a light about 50 yards ahead, moving along the road in the direction I was going. My horse, usually afraid of nothing, cowered and trembled violently. I felt rather uneasy myself. I have seen lights on the road at night, shining lanterns carried by men, but this light was different. There was something unearthly about it." Hudgins continued: "I gained on the traveler, and as I stand here before you, what I saw was a big man wearing a suit of armor! Over his shoulder was a gun, the muzzle end of which looked like a fish horn. As he strode, or floated along, he made no noise. My horse stopped still. I was weak with terror. I wasn't 20 feet from the thing, whatever it was, when it, too, stopped and faced me.

"At the same time, the woods, about 100 feet from the wayfarer, became alive with lights and moving forms. Some carried guns like the one borne by the man or thing in the road, others had shovels of an outlandish type, while still others dug furiously near a dead pine tree. As my gaze returned to the first shadowy figure, what I saw was not a man in armor, but a skeleton, and every bone of it was visible through the armor, as though it was made of glass! The skull, which seemed to be illuminated from within, grinned at me horribly. Then, raising aloft a sword, which I had not hitherto noticed, the awful specter started toward me menacingly.

"I could stand no more. Reason left me. When I came to, it was broad daylight and I lay upon my bed at home. Members of my family said the horse had run away. They found me at the turn of the road beyond Old House Woods. They thought I had fallen asleep. The best proof that this was not so, was that we could not even lead my horse, 'Old Tom,' by those woods for months afterwards, and to the day he died, whenever we approached the area, he would tremble violently. It was pitiful to see that fine animal become such a victim of terror."

Hudgins' story, strange as it may seem, was corroborated some years later, according to newspaper reports. One account said, "A Richmond youth had tire trouble at a lonely spot on the road near the haunted woods one night very late. As he knelt in the road, a voice behind him asked 'Is this the King's highway? I've lost my ship.' When the youth turned to look, he beheld a skeleton in armor within a few paces of him. Yelling like a maniac, the frightened motorist ran from the spot in terror and did not return for his car until the next day."

Arguably the most unusual phenomenon sighted in Old House Woods is the legendary ghost ship. It allegedly has been seen by men, some from a far distance, some from frighteningly close range. One of the most descriptive accounts was given more than eighty years ago by Ben Ferbee, a fisherman who lived along the Chesapeake Bay early in the twentieth century. His vivid recollection, told in 1926, is as follows: "One starry night I was fishing off the mouth of White's Creek, well out in the bay. As the flood tide would not set in for some time, I decided to get the good fishing and come home with the early moon. It must have been just after midnight when, as I turned to bait up a line in the stern of my boat, I saw a full-rigged ship in the bay. I was quite surprised, I tell you. Full-rigged ships were mighty scarce then, besides that, I knew I was it for it if she kept the course she was on. On the ship came, with lights at every masthead and spar, and I was plumb scared.

"They'll run me down and sink me, I thought. I shouted to sailors leaning over the rails forward, but they paid no heed to me. Just as I thought she would strike me, the helmsman put her hard a-port and she passed so close that I was almost swamped by the wash. She was a beautiful ship, but different from any I had ever seen. There are no ships like her on any ocean. She made no noise at all, and when she had gone by, the most beautiful harp and organ music I ever heard came back to me.

"The ship sailed right up to the beach and never stopped, but kept right on. Over the sandy beach she swept, floating through the air and up to the Bay Shore road, her keel about 20 feet from the ground. I could still hear the music, but I was scared out of my wits. I knew it was not a real ship. It was a ghost ship! Well, sir, I pulled up my anchor and started for home, up White's Creek. I could see that ship hanging over Old House Woods, just as though she was anchored in the sea. And running down to the woods was a rope ladder, lined with the forms of men carrying tools and other contraptions.

"When I got home," Ferbee continued, "my wife was up, but had no supper for me. Instead, she and the children were praying. I knew what was the matter. Without speaking a word, she pointed to Old House Woods, a scared look on her face. She and the children had seen the ship standing over the woods. I didn't need to ask her. I started praying, too!" Soon after, Ferbee and his family moved from the area.

Many others claimed to have sighted the fabled ghost ship. One was a fourteen-year-old Mathews County boy who related his experience this way: "A friend of mine and I were taking a boat from Mathews Yacht Club over to the Moon post office. You go up Stutts Creek and then over to Billups Creek. It was just after sunset and everything was sort of misty. Then, about half a mile from the mouth of the creek, we saw it. We both saw it, but couldn't believe it. I'd never seen anything like it before.

"There was a big sailing ship floating in the marsh. It had two or three masts and was made of wood. There's only about a foot of water there, but it looked like it was floating. It was the kind of ship pirates used. We watched for awhile and then it just disappeared! I went home and told my mother, but she just laughed. She said everyone knew of the stories about the ghosts in Old House Woods."

Another who saw the phantom galleon, and many other things, was Harry Forrest, a farmer-fisherman who lived only a few hundred yards from the edge of the woods. "I've seen more strange things in there than I could relate in a whole day," he once said before his death in the

1950s. "I've seen armies of marching British redcoats. I've seen the 'Storm Woman,' and heard her dismal wailings, and my mother and I have sat here all hours of the night and seen lights in the woods. We have sat on our porch overlooking the Chesapeake Bay and seen ships anchor off the beach and boats put into shore, and forms of men go in the woods. I would see lights over there and hear the sound of digging."

Forrest told of his ship sighting this way: "I was out fishing right off the beach one day in broad daylight when I saw a full-rigged ship headed straight for me, just 100 yards away. I rowed to shore as fast as I could, and just as I got on the beach, she started drifting, and she lifted and sailed straight to Old House Woods, and you heard the anchor chain clank." On another occasion, Forrest remembered, "Tom and Jack Diggs and I were going through the woods one night when one of those ships must have been just about to land. There was a terrible racket right close to the Old Cow Hole as she dropped anchor, and then she drifted off with that blaze of light running right along through the hawsepipe. I've seen many a one, and they all go off that way. It's the chain running out too fast through the hawsepipe that starts the blaze. And such bumping you never heard. Most of 'em are square riggers."

The Old Cow Hole is where Forrest believed treasure was buried. It is somewhere near the center of the woods. He once took a newsman to the site. The reporter described it as being a "small, circular pool of gray water, which seemed to swirl, and yet it was dead still." "This is where the money is buried," Forrest told him. "I think they must have killed a pirate and put him with it. There's everything in there. You hear chains rattle sometimes. I've seen everything on earth a man could see in these woods, not so much in the day time, but it's bad enough then."

While Forrest claimed he was not afraid of the dead, even though he believed the dead could come back, one experience he told of shook even him to the bone. "Once, I went out one brilliant November night to shoot black ducks," he said. "I found a flock asleep on a little inlet where the pine trees come down to the edge of the water. As I raised my gun to fire, instead of them being ducks, I saw they were soldiers of the olden times. Headed by an officer, company after company of them formed and marched out of the water.

"Recovering from my astonishment and bewilderment, I ran to my skiff, and tied up on the other side of the point. Arriving there, I found a man in uniform, his red coat showing brilliantly in the bright moonlight, sitting upright and very rigid in the stern. I was scared, but mad, too. So I yelled at him, 'Get out of that skiff or I'll shoot!' 'Shoot, and the devil's curse to you and your traitor's breed,' he answered, and made as if to strike me with the sword he carried. Then I threw my gun on him and pulled. It didn't go off. I pulled the trigger again. No better result. I dropped the gun and ran for home, and I'm not ashamed to say I swam the creek in doing it, too."

Forrest also used to tell of seeing a white ox lying in his cornfield one night. "I went out to drive him away," he said. "When I reached the spot where the animal was lying, I saw it was a coffin covered with a sheet, and borne along by invisible hands, just at the height pallbearers would carry a corpse. I followed until it entered the woods. Well, sir, the following Wednesday they brought the body of Harry Daniels ashore from Wolf Trap lightship. Harry was killed when the boiler blew up aboard the ship. As the men carried him up the beach to the waiting hearse, I recognized instantly the coffin I had seen borne into Old House Woods. The men were carrying it in the self-same manner in every particular, a somewhat clumsy swaying motion I had observed in my cornfield."

Still another incident that has been printed in both books and newspapers involved a farmer's wife who lived adjacent to the haunted woods. One evening at dusk she went into a pasture to bring home the work horses. She drove them down a lane towards the barn. Arriving at the gate, she called to her husband to open it. He did not respond at once, and she opened it herself. As she did so, her husband came out of the barn and laughed at her, saying he had put the team in the stable two hours before.

"Don't be foolish," she said. When she turned to let the team pass through the gate, instead of two horses standing there, she saw two headless black dogs scampering off towards Old House Woods! "That woman," says Olivia Davis, "was my great-grandmother." Over the years, there also have been numerous reported sightings of headless cattle wandering aimlessly in the woods.

Through the decades, there have been many mysterious disappearances in the area, involving both animals and humans. In 1950, Harry Forrest told of one. "It was near about 100 years ago that Lock Owens and Pidge Morgan came through these woods with their steer, on the way back from a cattle auction, and nothing's been seen of them since. Steer, carts, and everything disappeared in there. Lock had a little black dog and the only thing that ever was found of it was a little bunch of hair off of that dog's tail.

"There used to be a lot of cattle down on these points, but they got to wandering in here and never came out," Forrest said. "Everything that comes in here heads for the Old Cow Hole, and disappears! It's very strange. One night that old hole will be covered with water, and the next day it's dry. Some nights it'll be light enough to pick up a pin in these woods, and black and storming outside. And sometimes you'll come in here and it'll be pouring down. You get wringing, soaking wet. And then you come out and you'll be perfectly dry."

Finally, there is the tragic story of Tom Pipkin, a local fisherman who lived in the area around 1880. Fired up by the age-old legends of buried or sunken gold, he took his small boat into the woods, following an old channel some say was originally cut by pirates two centuries earlier, and headed for Old Cow Hole. Several days later, his boat was found in the bay. Inside the boat were two gold coins of unknown age, and a battered silver cup covered with slime and mud. One coin bore a Roman head, and the letters "IVVS" were distinguishable. No one would take Pipkin's boat, and it rotted away on nearby Gwynn's Island. He was never heard from again.

"A thousand people have been in here after that money, but they'll never get it," Harry Forrest once said of Old House Woods. "The trees start bending double and howling. It storms, and they get scared and take off. The woods is haunted—that's what it is!"

## Coffins, Wanted and Unwanted

There are two remarkable incidents involving storms and coffins on the Eastern Shore near the border between Maryland and Virginia. The first, told by area historian Thomas Flowers, occurred during the devastating hurricane of 1933. In addition to the enormous destruction wreaked by this powerful storm, a number of coffins, buried in small, low-lying family cemeteries, were unearthed and washed out to sea.

Some of these were recovered, but the strangest recovery story was that of a widower sea captain named Elleck Travers. He lived on the second floor of a boat-building shop, which was in imminent dangers of collapsing in the raging waters of the tidal flooding.

As the surge reached the second floor, Travers saw a coffin float up to the door. It was his wife's! He straddled it and paddled away to safety. In death, she saved his life.

### "I Didn't Mean It!"

There is a popular legend on the Eastern Shore, off Deal Island, about a woman who got her wish—and then didn't want it. When her husband died nearly a century ago, she had him buried in the island cemetery, but it was hard for her to let him go. It was said you could hear her crying late at night, "Oh Lord, send him back to me."

Several weeks later a strong hurricane swept across the Chesapeake Bay, flooding the island at high tide. The storm unearthed the coffin of the woman's husband and washed it up to her doorstep! When she saw it out the window, she allegedly screamed, "Oh Lord, I really don't want him. I didn't mean it! Take him back!"

# Caught in a Colonial Time Warp

It was on historic Jamestown Island, a spit of heavily wooded land jutting into the mighty James River, that America's first band of English settlers chose to begin a new life. It was here that they anchored and came ashore for good in May 1607. And it was here, 364 years later, that a small group of the early adventurers apparently "returned" for a brief period in an extraordinary occurrence witnessed by Gerry McDowell of Virginia Beach and her late husband, Gus.

The McDowells liked to travel, and often visited regional sites in the off season. It was on such an excursion to Jamestown Island in 1971 that the "event" happened. They were there very early on a chilly autumn morning because, as Gerry says, "we liked to be out when no one was around so we could enjoy the solitude and Gus liked to feed the animals."

The story is best told in Gerry's own words: "I can remember it as clearly as if it happened yesterday," she recalls. "It was real early on a Sunday morning, about 6 A.M. It was damp and misty. You could see the fog rolling off the river. I was listening to one of those audio recordings which told all about the first settlement, when I had the strangest sensation. There was a deathly stillness in the air.

"I turned around and there, coming down a path toward us, was a group of about 20 people, men, women, and children. They were all dressed in colonial costumes. The men wore knickers with white stockings and shoes with buckles. They had on jacket blouses with wide, white collars and very broad-brimmed hats. The ladies were wearing long gray or black dresses, with shawls over their shoulders, and bonnets.

"They were very animated. The men and women were talking and laughing, and waving their arms as they walked. The children were running in and out of the group. I thought at first that it might be some reenactors or a troop of actors who were coming to participate in a play or something. I looked at Gus, and he saw them, too. We stood together and watched as they approached us.

"It was then that we realized there was something very different taking place. While they seemed to be talking, there was no sound whatsoever. Instead, there was only a stony silence. They didn't appear to be ghosts, because I think most ghosts are wispy and trans-parent, and they weren't. You couldn't see through them. And then we noticed. They were ghosts, because they were not walking on the ground! They were elevated above it by a few inches.

"Gus and I froze. We stood still and didn't say a thing. We felt together that any movement or sound on our part would dissolve them. On they came. They marched right by without noticing us. It was as if we weren't there. We could have reached out and touched them, but we didn't. They moved past us and walked straight up the path to the old church. When we turned to follow them, we could barely believe our eyes. The church had suddenly transformed from its present state to how it must have looked like in the early 1600s, complete with steeple and all! Gus and I both gasped.

"They opened the door and, one by one, went inside. When the last gentleman entered, he turned and appeared to stare at us. Gus said he had a wry smile on his face. He then slammed the door forcefully, but, again, there was no sound. We stood there for a few seconds in silence, transfixed. And then the church appeared in its present state again.

"Neither of us is afraid of ghosts, so we were not really scared. Still, it was a few minutes before either of us could speak. Then Gus finally said, 'Nobody is going to believe this!' I don't know much about such things, but I think now that we had somehow gotten into a time warp for that brief instant. I have heard about such things, although I don't really understand them. But how else can you explain what happened? All I know is that it was a once in a lifetime experience that I will never forget."

## The Man Who Missed His Own Funeral

The following is recounted, with permission, from the book *Terrifying Tales 2 of the Beaches and Bays*, by Ed Okonowicz. Ed was told the true account by a woman named Polly, postmistress at a small post office on the Eastern Shore south of Salisbury, Maryland.

Polly was working one afternoon a few years ago when a young woman marched in and asked her for a package. She handed Polly a slip of paper with the name and address. Polly excused herself and went into the back room to look for it. After a few minutes, the bell on the counter began ringing loudly. When Polly came back to the front, the woman demanded that the package be given to her, that she was going to be late for a memorial service. She was shouting.

Polly explained that she couldn't locate the package. This sent the woman into a tizzy. She started pacing back and forth, waving her hands in the air. Finally, Polly managed to calm her enough to find out what the problem was. The woman said she had been sent here to pick up the remains of "Uncle Wilbur." He had died in Michigan two weeks earlier, was cremated, and the urn that held his ashes was to be sent

to this post office. The burial service was to be held in the town's cemetery in less than an hour, so she needed the package immediately.

Polly said maybe the package had mistakenly been sent to a
neighboring post office on the Eastern Shore. She could make some
phone calls to see if anyone else had received it, but the woman was
frantic. She declared even if that was so, there wouldn't be enough
time to get the ashes to the cemetery. The woman next told Polly to
get her a large official postal box. To Polly's amazement, the woman
ran out the front door, picked up a large stone off the walkway leading to the post office, came back in, and slammed it on the counter.

She told Polly to put the stone in the postal box, seal it with prior-
ity tape, slap a lot of stamps on it, and cancel the stamps so it would
look official. She said she would take this to the graveyard and tell the
mortician it was Uncle Wilbur's remains for burial. Polly asked her
what would happen if the mourners wanted to see the urn that was
supposed to be inside the box. The woman said she would take care
of that; she would say she couldn't bear to look inside, and besides,
that was her problem, not Polly's. She then said she would be back in
a week to get the package that hadn't arrived. With that, she snatched
up the "fake" box, stormed out the door, and drove off in a car.

Polly never saw the woman again. She never came back to claim
the package. A few days later, Uncle Wilbur's remains arrived. The
postmistress put the package on a shelf in the back room. After a
month, Polly got annoyed that neither the woman nor anyone else
came to get it. Polly had a part-time assistant named Justine, who
worked whenever extra help was needed. Justine was into tarot,
astrology, and other things psychic.

After several more weeks had elapsed, Justine one day told Polly
that she was hearing strange noises in the storage room—a steady tapping sound. She said whenever she went into the room to investigate,
the tapping stopped abruptly. Polly at first dismissed it and tried to
convince Justine that it was just the wind, or tree limbs hitting against
the building. But then one Saturday, a female customer came in and
asked Justine why she was playing her radio so loud. Justine told her
it was to drown out the tapping sounds from the back room, which
were scaring her. The woman said when she had been in the previous

week, she too heard the mysterious sounds. Justine was delighted that she had confirmation of the sounds from someone else.

At that moment, both women heard a loud crash in the back room. Startled, they raced to the doorway to see what happened. There, in the middle of the floor, lay Uncle Wilbur's package! It was not at the base of the shelf where it had rested; it was fifteen feet across the floor. There is no way it could have fallen and traveled that far. It was as if it had been flung through the air. The customer, shaken, looked at Justine and ran out of the building, leaving her stamps and change on the counter.

Justine called Polly at her home. She was terribly frightened by the experience. She told Polly she was going to bring in blessed candles and incense and wear a special charm to ward off evil spirits. Polly sent her home, then resealed the box and took it to an outside storage shed. But that didn't work. The incessant and unexplained tapping not only continued, but grew louder! It could be heard all the way inside the post office. Now Polly was getting rattled.

She was afraid to tell her regional manager. He would think she was crazy. So she went to Henry, a friend of hers. Henry was a well-educated, worldly man who seemed well-versed in the paranormal. She told him everything. Then the two of them concocted a plan. They decided Uncle Wilbur needed to be put to final rest. Perhaps he had been unhappy that his remains had not been properly buried, and he used the tapping sounds to voice his displeasure. So one night they opened the package and took the urn to the cemetery. There, they spread the ashes among the tombstones. Once this was done, the tappings were never heard again.

But there was more. Henry came into the post office three weeks later and showed Polly a photocopy of a newspaper obituary. Uncle Wilbur, it turned out, had been a Baptist preacher in Michigan, and when he died his family had wanted him buried back in the Eastern Shore town where he had been born.

Henry then theorized that perhaps Uncle Wilbur had been disturbed so much, and made his noisy protests at being held in the post office, because a century earlier the building had been a saloon and house of ill repute frequented by gamblers, drunken sailors, wild women, and others. Perhaps Uncle Wilbur had been trying to get away from evil temptation. Polly, however, had another interpretation. Maybe, she said, after a lifetime of chaste and stern discipline, he wanted to get out of the box, kick up his heels, and have a good time with those rowdy spirits of the past!

## The Ghost That Saved His Grandson

Sam Watkins, a retired fireman from Newport News, is psychic. So many strange things have happened to him, he wants to write a book about his paranormal experiences. For one thing, he steadily gets premonitions of incidents that are going to take place in the future. "Most of the time when the phone rings, I know who is calling, and I don't have any service that tells you that," he says. "I just know." Once, he and his brother were about to enter a tavern at night, when Sam suddenly got the strong feeling that they shouldn't go in. Danger was inside. He couldn't talk his brother out of it, however, and that night they both narrowly escaped death in a barroom brawl.

"I know when someone is sick, when they are going in a hospital, and when they are going to die," he says, matter-of-factly. On one such occasion, in the early 1970s, Sam took a photograph of his dog. When the print was developed, there was an image of his brother in it, although his brother had been in another town when he took the picture. His brother was holding his elbow and his side. At first, Sam didn't understand. Then he got word that his brother had just been in an auto accident and had been injured—on his elbow and his side!

In the following interview, Sam tells of a life-saving supernatural experience he had in 1996: "I was always very close with my grandfather, very close. He died in 1991, and I miss him. However, I still feel, on occasion, that he is still with me. He used to love egg sandwiches. Now, every once in a while, I find myself making egg sandwiches, and sometimes when I am eating them while sitting on my bed, I can see my grandfather's image there.

"What I am about to tell you, you won't believe, but it really happened to me. I think my grandfather is my guardian angel. I have no other way of explaining it. It was in the winter and it had been snowing. I had been in a bar having a couple of beers one night. When I left to go home, I was in good shape. I wasn't drunk or anything like that. Well, I was driving down a road a little too fast. There was a turn up ahead and I had to brake pretty hard, and when I did, the car hit a patch of black ice or snow and began to skid.

"The car turned sideways. I was out of control and I was heading straight toward a telephone pole. And I didn't have my seatbelt on. I was scared. Just as I was about to collide with the pole, something physically lifted me out of the driver's side of the front seat and pulled me into the back seat! The impact of the collision was tremendous. The telephone pole snapped in two places. The car was totaled. The steering wheel broke off and the steering column was jammed into the back of the front seat. It would have killed me instantly had I not been lifted into the back seat!

"But I know what happened. My grandfather saved me. He was the one who yanked me out of the front seat just before the car hit the pole. I felt his presence. I know he was there. He was watching out for me. You can say what you want—luck, a miracle, or anything else. But I know it was my grandfather. If I live to be a hundred, you'll never convince me otherwise!"

## The Girl Who Was "Born to See"

"She was," says Gabrielle Bielenstein, "'born to see.' Isn't that a marvelous expression? It means, of course, that a person is psychic. Some people are born with perfect pitch, and some can play the piano by ear. She was born to see." Gabrielle is talking, in the dark, high-ceilinged parlor of her Art Nouveau home in Old Towne Portsmouth, about the teenage African American girl who worked for Gabrielle's mother more than a half century ago.

The house was built in 1885, has twenty-odd rooms (including six bathrooms), a beautiful spiral staircase, and exquisite wood paneling throughout. Behind it was a splendid walled garden that was a showpiece of the area. Gabrielle says the young girl came to work there in the early 1940s. Almost immediately, she began to "see" things that others didn't. "There had been some strange occurrences in the house before,"

Gabrielle notes, "but we never paid much attention to them. One would hear tales. Some of the other servants would talk occasionally about a rocking chair that rocked by itself on the front porch. We would hear someone descending the staircase, but wouldn't see anyone. Things like that."

But the servant girl saw, felt, and sensed presences in and around the house almost from the day she began work. And with uncanny accuracy, they perfectly fit descriptions of past residents, both animal and human, alive and dead. Consider, for example, the buried pit bulls. "My mother, Florence, had about given up on having any children before my sister and I came along," Gabrielle says, "so she had a number of pit bull dogs. At the time, these dogs were fairly rare. Few people knew what they looked like. But my mother didn't have much luck with them. Most of them died very young, and they were all buried in little pine coffins in a corner of the yard.

"When the young girl came to work for us, there hadn't been any pit bulls around for years, and I don't believe she had any way of knowing what they looked like. Yet, she told us she saw the dogs playing in the yard. When she was asked to describe what they looked like, she said they were just like Miss Julia's dog. Miss Julia was a neighbor who had a Boston Terrier, which closely resembles the pit bull. How did she know what those dogs looked like unless she saw them?"

The girl also saw the apparition of Miles Portlock. Born a slave before the Civil War, he had been a servant to Gabrielle's great-grandmother. "We considered him a part of the family," she says. He died in 1939, at the age of ninety, well before the girl came to the house to work. Yet she said she saw him in the garden with his cane, and she described him precisely, too.

And then there were the sightings of Miss Edmonia, Gabrielle's grandmother. The girl said she saw an "old woman" on the staircase at times. "We had a lot of photos in the house in those days," Gabrielle says, "but there were no recent photos of Edmonia before her death, because she refused to have any taken after she reached middle age. She had been a beautiful woman.

"We took the girl around to view all the pictures, and she immediately picked out an earlier portrait of Edmonia, and declared that was who she saw. She said it was the same person, only she was much older now. How did she know? How did she pick out that one photo out of all the ones in the house? She had no way of knowing what Edmonia looked like.

"I can't explain it, other than she was born to see!"

## A Mother's Last Visit

When it comes to eccentric and charismatic characters in Virginia, Roger Rageot surely ranks at or near the top of the list. A Frenchman by birth, he spent most of his life (he died in 2006 at age seventy-five) in the Norfolk area.

What were some of his idiosyncrasies? Roger was first and foremost a naturalist, but he was also an explorer, author, photographer, artist, and museum curator. He had a propensity for eating roadkill, snapping turtles, and snakes. He kept a variety of animals, including a full-grown gila monster, in his small apartment in Ghent. To supplement his income, he collected and sold specimens of insects, snails, millipedes, birds, bats, fish, amphibians, and reptiles.

As an artist, he created watercolor paintings that ultimately sold for hundreds of dollars, and his pen-and-ink sketches of wildlife appeared on several magazine covers.

From 1951 until its closing in 1967, Roger was the curator of the Norfolk Museum of Natural History, and he was a co-founder of the Virginia Herpetological Society. Later, he traveled to remote areas in South and Central America, collecting rare specimens of everything from insects to animals. In 1973, for example, he ventured to Chile to help find a way to control vampire bats that attacked cattle.

Roger's first love, however, was the Great Dismal Swamp that borders the North Carolina state line. For years, he spent scores of nights here, alone. The snakes and others specimens he gathered here wound up in exhibits and museums from Norfolk to the Smithsonian Institution in Washington, D. C.

He once startled a campfire group of two hundred Boy Scouts on an outing by the James River when a large yellow-billed cuckoo flew down and landed on his shoulder. What the scouts didn't know was

Roger had nursed and fed the bird from youth after it had fallen from a tree, thus developing a strong bond.

In his old age, with his snow-white hair flowing down over his ears, Roger looked exactly like Albert Einstein.

Aside from being a lifelong dedicated naturalist, Roger had a second love—the supernatural. He wrote a number of articles on the subject for magazines, and also authored a collection of the unexplained, which he called *Rageot's Horrors*. Unfortunately, these papers could not be found after his death. One such intriguing account of the paranormal has survived, however. Roger wrote about an incident that occurred when he was still with the Norfolk Museum.

Roger and a friend, a fellow biologist, were talking late one winter night in his office. The doorbell rang. Here is how he described the incident: "I got up to answer the door. There stood my mother! A four-inch snowfall lay on the ground, and she stood so small and frail, with snowflakes blowing around her. There is nothing really unusual about one's mother ringing your doorbell at 11 o'clock at night. But I happened to know my mother was a continent away—in a hospital in Paris, France—dying of bone cancer! And I was in Norfolk, Virginia!

"I stood in stupefaction! I'll never know what made me say what I said to her. Maybe it was that strange look on her face—a very peculiar smile, one common to a contented person. Her eyes were vacant, possessing an indescribable light; they appeared almost phosphorescent. I could see that her mind was transported into another, more distant world. She didn't speak.

"'When did you die?' I blurted out. She chuckled shyly and replied, 'How do you know I'm dead? Didn't I tell you I'd come over to America someday? Well, here I am.'"

At this point, Roger's friend, Roland Young, interrupted and said, "I don't know what you two are trying to put over on me, but I simply refuse to believe any of it!"

"But this is my mother, Roland," Roger said. "How could you not believe it?"

Roland then replied, "Your mother's sick. How could she have traveled over here?"

"She's dead!" said Roger.

"My mother and I then started reminiscing; soon we both were so lost in the past that Roland's presence in the room was completely forgotten. In the museum itself all was quiet. Later, mother said, 'It's getting late, son, and I must see your sister in Kentucky. I'd better leave now if I want to get there by tomorrow morning.'

"She arose and handed me something. I accompanied her to the front door and was about to bid her goodbye—but she suddenly vanished! I turned to Roland, who stood transfixed. He stared at the spot where, only a few seconds ago, my mother had stood. 'What did she give you?' he asked.

"Until then I hadn't noticed. I opened my closed fist. It was a tiny locket, one that I had given her when I was a little child. There was an inscription on it which read, 'To mommy, with love, Roger.' I showed it to Roland, who said this was all too much for him. 'Well,' I replied, 'you and I have often discussed the realm of the supernatural. It is everywhere. It surrounds us; it even penetrates us. Science tries constantly to peruse it, but cannot even get near it.'

"The day after my mother's apparition appeared, I received the following letter from my father, from Paris. "'My dear son; Because the news that I'm about to bring you will cause you much pain, you must have great courage. I'm sorry to relate that your devoted mother passed away yesterday.

"'It was with the deepest personal anguish that I saw her close her eyes for the final time. Believe me, it was all for the best. Before she passed on, she suffered horribly. Although her death brought to me a great emptiness of soul, I was actually happy to see her go that way, for her disease was totally incurable. At least I now know that, in death, her suffering will be alleviated. May her soul rest in peace. I sincerely hope that you will try to bear her departure with true dignity, and I shall also try my level best to do likewise.

"Your devoted father."

Roger concluded his description of the incident by saying: "I have often participated in intellectual discussions of the supernatural. I used to participate theoretically. But my experience with my mother's apparition has changed things. Now I discuss the supernatural with confidence and some authority."

# Dead Man (Still) Walking

"Dead Man Walking" is an expression used by prison guards and others to describe when an inmate awaiting execution is outside of his cell.

It was one of the most notorious and most widely covered murder cases in Virginia history. At 9:06 P.M., on the evening of May 25, 1995, prisoner Willie Lloyd Turner was injected with lethal chemicals and died at the Greenville prison ten miles north of Emporia. He had been convicted and sentenced to death for the 1978 murder of a jewelry store owner in Franklin, Virginia. He was on death row longer than any other condemned person in the state's recent history.

Willie Turner was an extraordinary man. Slight in stature, he was five foot nine inches tall and weighed 150 pounds. He was above all, until that fateful night in May 1995, a survivor. Despite practically no formal education, Turner was considered a genius, with an IQ estimated to be in the 160 to 180 range. Although he spent two-thirds of his forty-nine years incarcerated, Turner gained the grudging respect and admiration of virtually everyone who knew him.

He is said to have had a mesmerizing effect upon inmates and prison guards and officials alike. He seemed to have a spellbinding power that was immediately apparent to anyone who met him. He had an uncanny skill in the art of the locksmith, one that enabled him to flee from several Virginia prisons, and in 1984, to engineer perhaps the greatest escape ever accomplished in the commonwealth.

He was also a man of violence, determined to survive in the harsh prison environment at all costs. Inmates who outweighed him by a hundred pounds or more feared him. Some believed he was possessed by an "evil spirit." Others were convinced he had supernatural powers. Yet, curiously, when the time came for his execution, he chose to go quietly, even though he had a loaded pistol cleverly concealed in a typewriter in his cell. He could have attempted a dramatic last-minute escape with such a weapon, but he didn't. To this day, state authorities still don't know how he got the gun or where it came from.

To understand Willie Turner, one must go back to his squalid past. He grew up in rural Southampton County, in the town of Franklin. His mother and father both were alcoholics. At an early age, Willie was sent out into farming fields to gather crops. What little money he earned was confiscated by his father, who was a brutal abuser of his children. Willie drifted in and out of trouble with the law as a teenager, and was sent from one correctional facility to another. Early on, he became incorrigible, often getting into vicious fights with other inmates. In one bloody brawl, in which he claimed self-defense, he killed a man. He also displayed an uncanny knowledge of jailhouse mechanisms by continually escaping, only to be recaptured a short time later.

Eventually, he was paroled and went home to Franklin, where he became a popular barber, using skills he learned in prison. It was then that he committed a capital crime for which he later was to pay for with his life. The details of this haunting episode are clouded by differing versions of what actually happened. According to Willie, he walked into a Franklin jewelry store carrying an unloaded sawed-off shotgun. He said he only went in because he had seen a police car outside and he knew if he was caught with a weapon it would violate his parole conditions and he would be sent back to jail.

The jeweler set off a silent alarm and a policeman came into the store. Willie disarmed him, and in the confusion that followed, he shot the jeweler, killing him. Willie maintained to his dying day that it all was a colossal misunderstanding. Witnesses in the store, however, told a different story. They said Willie, mad that the alarm had been set off, shot the jeweler in cold blood. Whatever the truth of the matter was, he was convicted and sentenced to death.

Because of his charismatic personality and his brilliant capacity to learn quickly, Willie became somewhat of a *cause célèbre*. High-profile lawyers worked on his case pro bono, and scores of appeals were filed. This resulted in delay after delay of his execution. Once, he came within five hours of being strapped into the electric chair, only to be spared by a last-minute appeal to the U.S. Supreme Court.

In 1984, while on death row at the state's Mecklenburg facility, Willie masterminded one of the greatest and most daring escapes in penal history. Six killers successfully made it out of the prison, though at the last minute, quixotically, Willie chose not to go. He thought the breakout would end in bloodshed. Instead, he remained behind, and saved and later freed guards who had been taken hostage during the escape. Within weeks, all six men were captured and returned to custody.

Eleven years later, the appeals finally ran out, and Willie was put to death. Even this event had a bizarre twist. Willie left behind a cryptic, single-word note: "Smile." He also left word to one of his lawyers to examine his typewriter case. He had used the typewriter not only to draft legal documents, but also to write his autobiography. He left behind a six-hundred-page manuscript. When the lawyer opened the case, he found a blue-steel .32-caliber Smith & Wesson revolver, tucked into a cut-out hiding place. It was loaded. Also found was a plastic bag filled with bullets. This discovery created a sensational ruckus, which Willie would have thoroughly enjoyed. Despite an exhaustive investigation, how and where the gun had come from was never found out. It caused a massive shakeup in the prison administration.

And, too, there was the puzzling question of why Willie had chosen not to use the gun in a desperate last-minute attempt to avert his execution. He easily could have taken someone hostage, or even killed some of the prison guards. One of Willie's uncles later said that he had talked to his nephew shortly before the execution and Willie told him he had put his family and friends through enough. He was, it seemed, resigned to his fate.

Don Gamache of Norfolk is a psychological counselor at the Greenville prison. He had gotten to know Willie intimately during the last year of the prisoner's life. "I got very tight with him," Don recalls. "Believe me, if there is any way to figure out how to come back from death, Willie would be the one to do it. He believed in the hereafter." Whether Willie believed in ghosts is not known, although he did discuss the subject in his manuscript. In 1980, he was transferred to the Virginia State Penitentiary in Richmond, and had this to say: "The guards that worked down there (the basement of the building on death row, near the electric chair, which was then used for executions) spent most of the time telling each other about the ghost tales they had been told, associated with previously executed prisoners.

"They especially talked about how the place was haunted by some weird old man who said he had been framed, and that he was coming back to damn the place forever if they killed him. He was executed anyway, and the place has been spooked with the smell of his burned flesh, sightings of his shadow, and sounds of his voice. They also told of how ghosts of other prisoners who died there were sometimes seen and heard. Lights would sometimes dim on their own in a ghostly fashion, just like when a prisoner was actually being electrocuted. There were all kinds of weird stuff, like objects floating around in mid-air by themselves."

In April 1985, ten years before he died, Willie had what some experts would probably consider an ethereal experience of his own. It took the form of a prophetic dream, much like the one Abraham Lincoln once had before his assassination. Lincoln envisioned the explicit details of his death, including seeing himself lying in state in the White House. In Willie's case, he foresaw his own demise in what may have been an out-of-body experience. He dreamed he had entered another world in which he saw all the people he knew who had died before him, including his parents, grandparents, other relatives, and friends. Had Willie been given an advance glimpse into the eternal beyond? Did he believe in the possibility of a spiritual return to earth?

Consider what Don Gamache had to say. "About a month and a half after Willie's death, one of the prisoners on death row told me he had seen Willie! Over the next several months, four or five of the other inmates there each told me the same thing. They told me independently. They hadn't known that others had told me about their encounters. The consensus was in each case, they would hear footsteps in the cell block late at night. Someone would be approaching. They would look up and see Willie. They said he appeared not in the form of a wispy apparition or anything like that, but just as Willie had looked in life! They said he would walk up to their cell and peer in at them. Sometimes the vision would last a few seconds, sometimes longer. He never said anything. Then he would just fade away before their eyes.

"Now let me say," Don continued, "that there was no reason for these men to say this if they didn't believe it. These were relatively stable men as prisoners go. I am convinced they were not making it up. One even said the first time it happened to him, he was scared to death. No one on death row would admit to such a thing unless he believed it really happened."

The sightings have continued periodically. The case that Willie's ghost reappears is strengthened by personal incidents that have happened to Don himself. "I feel him sometimes," he has said. "There have been times when I was sitting at my desk in my office, alone, when I felt someone or something tapping on my shoulder. When I looked around, there was no one there. I think it's Willie. Maybe he's letting me know that everything is okay with him. Maybe he's doing that to his former inmates as well. I don't know."

Another incident involving Don is even more compelling. On the night of the execution, May 25, 1995, Don was at home with his girlfriend. They purposely didn't watch television that evening. At precisely 9:06 P.M., Don's girlfriend felt a sharp jab in her ribs. Neither she nor Don could explain the phenomenon. Later, they turned on the 11 P.M. news and learned, to their astonishment, that Willie had been executed exactly at 9:06 P.M.!

Finally, there is a chilling set of coincidences involving history. It concerns a stunning relationship between Willie Turner and Nat Turner, who in 1831 incited a massive slave rebellion that resulted in the killing of fifty-five white men, women, and children, and the reprisal massacre of a large number of slaves, perhaps one hundred or more, plus the trial and hanging of about twenty of the insurrectionists, including Nat. The parallels between Nat and Willie Turner shockingly border on the supernatural.

- Both men were from Southampton County, born only a few miles apart.
- Both were charismatic, enigmatic, and possessed powerfully magnetic personalities.
- Nat Turner was about five feet eight inches tall and weighed 150 to 160 pounds. Willie Turner was five feet nine inches and weighed 150 pounds. Both were light-complexioned.
- Both were mesmerizing leaders. Both believed in unalterable fate.
- It was said that a streak of wildness ran through Nat Turner's family. Willie Turner once said he experienced "mysterious spells during which it seemed like I get evil."
- Both men displayed uncanny talent for successfully eluding the law, for a time. Nat was not found for two months after his revolt. Willie escaped from prison several times.
- Both were named Turner, although it is not known if they were related.

- Both were sentenced to die and were calm and composed as they faced death.
- Both possessed an inner integrity, and both declined to give a last statement.
- And both men were executed for their crimes: Nat Turner at Courtland (formerly Jerusalem); and Willie Turner at Greensville (Jarrett)—sites only a few miles apart!

# Bibliography

## Books

Alphin, Elaine Marie. *Ghost Cadet*. New York: Apple Paperbacks, 1991.

Biggs, Elizabeth. *Beyond the Limits of Our Sight*. Flint Hill, VA: Lelil Books, 1978.

Bruce, Louise. *Historical Gardens of Virginia*. Richmond: James River Garden Club, 1923.

Bryce, C. A. *Up and Downs of a Country Doctor*. Ashland, VA: Ashland Company, 1904.

Carrington, Hereward. *Phantasms of the Dead*. New York: Dodd Mead, 1920.

Carter, Robert. *Four Brothers in Blue*. s.p., 1913.

Catton, Bruce. *Bruce Catton's Civil War*. New York: Fairfax Press, 1984.

Chewning, Alpheus. *Haunted Virginia Beach*. Charleston, SC: The History Press, 2006.

Cooke, John Esten. *The Surreys of Eagle's Nest*. New York: G. W. Dillingham, 1868.

Dawidziak, Mark. *The Barter Theatre Story*. Abingdon, VA: Appalachia Consortium, 1982.

Devens, R. M. *Our First Century*. Springfield, MA: C. A. Nichols & Co., 1878.

Dougherty, Shirley. *A Ghostly Tour of Harpers Ferry*. n.p.: Eigmid Publishing, 1982.

Gilbert, Lillie, Belinda Nash, and Deni Norred-Williams. *Ghosts, Witches & Weird Tales of Virginia Beach*. Virginia Beach, VA: Eco Images, 2004.

Harrison, M. Clifford. *Home to the Cockade City*. Richmond: Dietz Press, 1942.

Holzer, Hans. *The Phantoms of Dixie*. New York: Bobbs-Merrill, 1972.

Hurst, Samuel. *The Mountains Redeemed*. Appalachia, VA: Hurst & Co., 1929

Hyatt, Harry. *Hoodoo-Conjuration-Witchcraft-Rootwork*. Racine, WI: Western Publishing Co., 1971.

Johnson, Brita. *Rural Life in Old Virginia*. n.p.: Sigfrid Olson, 1923.

Johnson, Charles. *A Narrative History of Wise County*. Wise, VA: Norton Press, 1938.

Johnson, Clifton. *Battlefield Adventures*. Boston: Houghton-Mifflin, 1915.

Kaye, Ruth. *Legends & Folk Tales of Old Alexandria, Virginia.* s.p., 1975.

Kinney, Pamela. *Haunted Richmond.* Atglen, PA: Schiffer Publishing, 2007.

Knox, Anne. *The Gentle Ghosts.* Lexington, VA: Brandon Publishing, 1981.

Lee, Marguerite DuPont. *Virginia Ghosts.* Richmond: William Byrd Press, 1930.

McElhaney, Judy. *Ghost Stories of Woodlawn Plantation.* McLean, VA: EPM Publications, 1992.

Moses, Grandma. *The Autobiography of Grandma Moses.* New York: Harper, 1952.

Nagel, Paul. *The Lees of Virginia.* New York: Oxford University Press, 1992.

Okonowicz, Ed. *Terrifying Tales 2 of the Beaches & Bays.* Elkton, MD: Myst & Lace Publishing, 2001.

Phillips, V. N. *Partners in Paradise.* Johnson City, TN: Overmountain Press, 2002.

Polonsky, Jane, and Joan Drum. *The Ghosts of Fort Monroe.* Hampton, VA: Polydrum Publications, 1972.

Price, Charles Edwin. *The Mystery of Ghostly Vera.* Johnson City, TN: Overmountain Press, 1993.

Russell, Randy, and Janet Barnett. *Ghost Dogs of the South.* Winston-Salem, NC: John F. Blair, 2003.

Rutherford, Mac. *Historic Haunts of Winchester.* Winchester, VA: Lucky Books, 2003.

Smith, James L. *The Autobiography of James L. Smith.* 1881.

Smith, Suzy. *Prominent American Ghosts.* New York: World Publishing, 1967.

Starrett, Dan. *The Father, the Son, & the Railroad Ghost.*

Summers, Patty. *Talking with the Animals.* Charlottesville, VA: Hampton Roads Publishing, 1998.

Taylor, L. B. *The Ghosts of Virginia.* 8 vols. s.p., 1993–2009.

———. *Civil War Ghosts of Virginia.* s.p., 1995.

———. *A Treasury of True Ghostly Humor.* s.p., 2003.

Thorne, Jack, Newspaper Correspondent and Story Teller [D. B. Fulton]. *Eagle Clippings: A Collection of His Writings to Various Newspapers.* Brooklyn, NY: circa 1907.

Viemeister, Peter. *The Beale Treasure.* Bedford, VA: Hamilton Books, 1995.

Weems, Mason. *A Biography of George Washington.* 1806. Reprint, New York: J. P. Lippincott, 1918.

Wise, John S. *An End of an Era.* New York: Houghton, Mifflin, 1899.

Works Progress Administration Writers. *The Virginia Guide.* Richmond: Virginia State Library and Archives, 1992.

## Magazine Articles

"A Convention of Ghosts." *Southern Literary Messenger,* May 1851.

"German Mystics in Virginia." *Virginia Magazine of History & Biography,* January 1964.

"I'm in Hell!" *Galaxy Magazine,* Feb. 1867.

"Locket from the Dead." *Fate Magazine*, November 1963.
"A Mother's Last Visit." *Banisteria* 29, 2007.
"A Night in a Haunted House." *Southern Literary Messenger*, June 1855.
"A War Episode." *Religio-Philosophical Journal*, October 3, 1885.

## Newspaper Articles

"A Ghost Carpenter." *Richmond Examiner*, September 27, 1874.
"Ghosts of the Crater." *Petersburg Progress Index*, October 31, 2008.
"Mysteries of Green Castle." *Page (CO) News & Courier*, November 20, 1997.
"The Pitt Street Ghost." *Alexandria Gazette*, July 20, 1885.
"The Ship Captain's Ghost." *Alexandria Gazette*, October 13, 1897.
"Skeleton of J. E. Carwell Found on Mountain." *Highland (CO) Reserve*, December 9, 1921.
"Spirits of the Pocahontas Parkway." *Richmond Times-Dispatch*, July (various dates) 2002.
"A Talking Ghost in Virginia." *Lexington (Va.) Gazette*, January 24, 1871.
"Virginia Justice." *New York Times*, January 21, 1872.
"The Woman in Black." *Roanoke Times*, March 18, 1902.

## Unpublished Manuscripts

Adams, James Taylor. Archival files of the Blue Ridge Institute. 1940–41.
Beeler, Elizabeth. "Incidents of the Beeler Family." 1761.
Burgess, Jim. Ghost sightings files, Manassas National Battlefield Park, 1995.
Burroughs, Eugene. "Autobiographical Notes." 1936.
Chase, Richard. "The Ha'nted House Tale." 1939.
Emerson, Louise. "A Death Prophesy." 1893.
Kruson, Jessie. "A Brief History of Tuckahoe Plantation." 1975.
McConnaughey, Cary. "Ghosts of Haw Branch Plantation." 1975.
Smith, Elmer L. Personal papers. James Madison University Historical Collections. 1965.
Turner, Nat. "Confessions." 1831.
Yount, III, J. B. "Ghosts and Frights of Stonewall Cottage." 1979.

## Web sites

http://www.arlingtoncemetery.net/taps.htm
http://www.brandystationfoundation.com.
http://www.civilwar.org./historyclassroom.
http://www.insidenova.com.haunted.
http://www.mail-archive.com./mythfolk.
http://www.psychicexperiences.com.
http://www.yourghoststories.com.

# About the Author

L. B. Taylor Jr. is a native Virginian. He was born in Lynchburg, received a B.S. in journalism from Florida State University, and resides in Williamsburg, Virginia.

For ten years, he served as a public information officer for NASA and aerospace contractors at the Kennedy Space Center in Florida. He retired in 1993 after nineteen years as public affairs director for BASF Corporation. As a freelance writer, he has published more than three hundred national magazine articles and forty-five non-fiction books, twenty-one of which are about Old Dominion ghosts. In 2007, he received the Virginia Writers Club's Lifetime Achievement Award.